GW00758711

Dead Before Dawn

*A Heavy Bomber Tail-gunner
in World War II*

Dead Before Dawn

A Heavy Bomber Tail-gunner in World War II

Frank Broome

Pen & Sword
AVIATION

First published in Great Britain in 2008 by
Pen & Sword Aviation
an imprint of
Pen & Sword Books Ltd
47 Church Street
Barnsley
South Yorkshire
S70 2AS

ISBN 978-1-84415-738-9

A CIP catalogue record for this book is available from the British
Library

Typeset in 10.5/13pt Palatino by
Mac Style, Nafferton, E. Yorkshire

Printed and bound in the UK by
CPI

Pen & Sword Books Ltd incorporates the Imprints of Pen & Sword
Aviation, Pen & Sword Maritime, Pen & Sword Military,
Wharncliffe Local History, Pen and Sword Select, Pen and Sword
Military Classics and Leo Cooper.

For a complete list of Pen & Sword titles please contact
PEN & SWORD BOOKS LIMITED
47 Church Street, Barnsley, South Yorkshire, S70 2AS, England
E-mail: enquiries@pen-and-sword.co.uk
Website: www.pen-and-sword.co.uk

Contents

Dedication

To the memories of

Clifford A Wheeler
Warrant Officer Navigator, 150 Squadron
RAF Hemswell, Lincolnshire 1944/5
(Lancaster & Lincoln Bomber Aircraft)
My colleague in war, my friend in peace until his untimely
death at fifty-eight years of age in 1974.

Duncan McLean, DFM
Warrant Officer Navigator, 626 Squadron, and later
Navigation Instructor at RAF Finningley.
My colleague in war, my friend in peace until his tragic
and untimely death in 1962, at thirty-eight years of age.

Acknowledgements

I would like to thank the following very kind friends for their really special help in the preparation of the original manuscript and also for the special work done in preparing the computer disks:

Sue Perry and Nina Stone – all original manuscript typing and computer disks.

Peter Jones – record documents.

Bernard Wheat – for really valued support.

Former Squadron Leader Richard Lane DFC

Edna Cartwright O'Donnell – who came back into my life after 63 years.

PART I

Twin Engine Pilot

Introduction

Many people have asked why I am writing a World War II story in the twenty-first century. Firstly, it was a request by my close family. Secondly, I kept a wartime diary with a book in mind. Finally, the appreciation of the RAF bomber effort in World War II now seems extremely tarnished and misleading.

The first two reasons need no further explanation. The third is the result of many current distorted viewpoints from various sources. Often people who have strong views on the subject have little or no connection with the World War II 'Bombers' War'. It is understandable that after some sixty years, bomber warfare waged upon any nation for any reason must seem almost unbelievable, quite horrendous.

Few people realise that in the 1930s and 1940s air navigation, especially at night, was in its infancy. Apart from super navigation specialists like Don Bennett (who flew the Mercury component of the 'Mayo Composite Aircraft' in the 1930s, later to become the RAF Pathfinder C in C), there were few who could cope by day and fewer by night.

However, because today the majority of people have been flown quite expertly in some form or other (usually by jet airliner), it is easily forgotten that up to and including World War II less than 1 per cent of the civil population had flown at all.

One has only to consider the historical and heroic record-breaking flights that took place between the two world wars, without the modern electronic navigation aids of today. As a junior schoolboy I, along with many school friends, was overawed with the exploits of such people as Amy Johnson, Jim Mollison, Amelia Earheart, Charles Kingsford-Smith and Jean Batten to mention just a few.

The media then had a very different reaction to these historical and courageous aviators of yester-year. Today, the crews of RAF Bomber Command face the sternest criticism from an apparently mindless load of nincompoops. These critics take apart yesterday's necessities with today's modern, often useless, analysis. We all know that everyone is wiser with hindsight. Yet the thoughtful and careful will look at the situation as it was in the terrible years of 1940–41 when the UK, alone, faced the most ferocious and cruel opponent that Europe had known for at least 100 years. The 'Bully of Europe' also had at that time the most efficient fighting forces that the world had ever known.

Apart from the offensive efforts of the Royal Navy (then the largest navy in the world), the small and relatively ineffective RAF Bomber Command was the only other offensive weapon the British possessed that could strike at Nazi Europe. Bomber Command's future possibilities in this respect were not fully recognised at that time but were highly welcomed by the British public.

When 'Bomber Harris' ('Butch' to his adoring crews) was promoted to C in C Bomber Command in 1942, he had an almost impossible task to complete successfully, or face an uncompromising and degrading dismissal. Harris boldly set about his task with great foresight and fortitude. If he won by bombing, he would get no recognition and be pilloried for it being a nasty way (no matter how essential) to win a war. If he failed, the enemy would hang him from the nearest lamp-post. There are people in the UK (the mindless, nameless nincompoops already mentioned) who, given the chance, would hang him now, if he were still alive.

As schoolboys, my friends and I were thrilled with the exploits of Fighter Command in the Battle of Britain. All we wanted then was to fly Spitfires as soon as we were old enough. We would not be put off by older, wiser people who told us we were too young to fly aged seventeen. What we weren't told was that most of us would end up flying four-engined bombers, death-dealing machines both for us as bomber crewmen and for the enemy.

Boys from all walks of life took the newly formed Air Training Corps or ATC (February 1941) very seriously – it was the answer to our boyhood prayers. 'Please God may I fly in the Royal Air Force over enemy-held Europe.' 'Please God let me pass all the tests, get my wings and become a Sergeant.' 'Please God I will do anything to fly.' 'Please, please help me.'

What our dear Lord didn't tell me was that when the day dawned and I finally flew over Europe in the Lancaster, a flimsy Pepsi Cola can-type structure, loaded with a 4000-pound cookie (a blockbuster, high-capacity bomb) plus over 1000 4-lb incendiary bombs with anything from 1200 to 2154 gallons of high octane fuel, I would be absolutely scared witless.

'Well, that's what you get your three stripes for. You're a sergeant, aren't you? Then for Christ's sake, act like one.'

The high-ranking officer who made this remark (not to me) was unable to foresee that sixty years later because we flew for Britain and did what the UK government and the British people wanted us to do, some of our good British people (including a Coventry canon) and the odd German from Dresden, think that we committed a war crime. They think we committed a war crime because RAF Bomber Command paid Germany back with interest for the damage done to Britain and occupied Europe (Poland, Norway, France, Holland, Belgium, Luxembourg, Channel Islands, Denmark, Czechoslovakia, Austria, Greece, Yugoslavia, Bulgaria, Hungary, Albania and a large part of the Soviet Union).

No one in Germany, it appeared, thought the RAF bomber offensive did anything to break the enemy's will to continue. Yet no one in that country loved the *Terrorflieger*. When Germany began World War II no German believed that the Fatherland would take such a pasting from the air. No one, the world over, likes to be proved wrong. Also, it was a 'piece of cake' to bomb most European countries, which at the time were seriously lacking a defence system that could effectively deal with the *Luftwaffe*. Not only were the German bombers heavily escorted during their daylight operations, but the night-time *Blitzkrieg* attacks were opened by *Luftwaffe* fire-raisers (Pathfinder Group KG 100 – Coventry 1940/41). So much for the German terror bombing! It was the Germans that coined both of the words *Blitzkrieg* and *Terrorflieger*. They cheered the Fatherland and the *Führer*. Later in the war, they heard the sound of the RAF four-engined bombers, sometimes 600 to 1000 Lancaster and Halifax heavies supported by Pathfinder Mosquitoes laying target indicators by Oboe radar (with 50 yards' accuracy). They used the term *Terrorflieger* and no German cheered.

No one wants to bomb women and children but can anyone tell me why in 1944/5 these people were not evacuated? It wasn't as if the war had just started. Most major cities in almost any European country had an immense capacity for producing war materials. It was of no surprise to a sixteen-year-old in 1940 that the City of Coventry received almost a knock-out blow during the three major Blitzes. Many Coventrians believed that those raids were indiscriminate – on a city that was possibly geared for up to 80–90 per cent war production. The two factories that I worked for prior to the Volunteer Reserve (VR) produced very little else.

The bombing of any city or town where civilians are killed is a great tragedy (as is war anyway, anywhere). Yet, is he who makes or loads the gun any worse than he who fires it? We would all be quite mad if we permitted this sort of industrial hari kari to go on unchecked.

Several people have asked me, in a semi-derogatory tone, if I went to Dresden. These comments usually come from people with little or no air/war experience and often too young or unborn at the time of the tragic raid. Their comments are a product of media hysteria, an all-too common modern-day symptom. I attended the briefing for the raid on that city in an official capacity. The reason given for the Dresden raid was that it was a Russian support target since the Soviet Army was approximately 70 miles away. In the absence of actual German intelligence at the time, RAF intelligence officers informed the crews that it would be a valuable supply point for the hard-pressed German *Wehrmacht*, as were Breslau and Chemnitz, which had received earlier raids. Also, in addition to helping the Russians (who were regularly clamouring for Allied support *in any form*) it would also give a demonstration of the power of RAF Bomber Command to any Russian foolish enough to drive too far west.

The risk to civilians in any city at war is always great. Britain and Germany had been at war for nearly six years. It was not known to the bomber crews that Dresden was packed with refugees. In any case, had I flown on that sortie I don't think at the time it would have bothered me. They were mostly German people who perhaps gave little thought for the populations of the cities of Poland, Holland, Belgium and Norway who had been subject to massive attacks by *Luftwaffe* bombers without any warning whatsoever. Nazi news media at the time portrayed most Germans as being in favour of and highly delighted about their military successes by whatever means. There was also immense approval by most Germans of their forcible military occupation of Europe. There is no wonder that the Fatherland was christened 'The Bully of Europe'.

The UK and Commonwealth effort in World War II was without comparison with the efforts of most countries in the last 100 years. Britain was the only country that came into the war purely voluntarily (to implement guarantees given to lesser military European powers in the advent of aggression by Nazi Germany) and remain undefeated until victory almost six years later.

During those years the cream of British and Commonwealth manhood was lost in a bomber offensive that almost everyone in the UK at that time considered to be absolutely essential. We received approval from all walks of life. At no time, while on leave in Coventry or on railway trains or stations, was anyone ever uncomplimentary about Bomber Command. On numerous occasions I received encouragement. 'Drop one for me Sergeant, next time you go', was the sort of comment that came from the occasional passer-by as well as friends and close relatives.

I leave the reader to enjoy my story and hopefully to reach a more sincere picture than that given by some would-be historians. You will note the training detail of the days I spent with the ATC and later RAF Training Command. Many readers will be unaware of the amount of time, money and enthusiasm given to young men who were absolutely mad keen to get into the air to fight. We didn't take any pushing and had no thought of waiting for the call-up for National Service. Such are the ways of the young. Most volunteer wartime aircrew were never to regret it.

CHAPTER 1

Gott Straffe England

Venture Adventure

'The Bombers' War' was my war – I was a schoolboy of fifteen years and three months when it all began, on Sunday 3 September 1939. I wondered how long it would be before the fireworks started. I never gave a thought about participating. Most people thought it would be over quickly, including myself, although I thought it would certainly not be over by Christmas. I left school in November 1939 because, owing to the risk of air attacks, we were only attending two days a week. My first job in engineering was at Humber Ltd, Coventry. They were making military staff cars at the time, including the Super Snipe, as well as armoured cars.

This was the time of the so-called phoney war, which continued until the breakthrough on the Western Front and the Dunkirk evacuation. It was about this time, the end of May 1940, that an RAF Hampden bomber hit one or more of Coventry's balloon cables. The first cable was almost certainly from the balloon site at London Road in the fields opposite the cemetery. The balloon was missing the next morning.

We could see the glow of the fire and the effect of exploding ammunition from our bedroom windows in Gulson Road. The sirens had not gone, so my father assumed it was 'one of ours' and he was correct.

The next day, on the way to work at the Humber factory, I rode on in the direction of the crash. I found that the aircraft had narrowly missed houses and had crashed into the Coventry & North Warwickshire cricket ground next to the 'Bull's Head' on Binley Road. The crew were all killed, one member having baled out just before the impact, his parachute still trailing outside the hole he had made in the tiled roof of an outbuilding of the pub. The police and ambulances were still busy sorting it all as I continued on to work, arriving at 8 am. The crash was the main topic of conversation in the office that day. I never forgot the parachute and the hole the crewmember made in the roof. Even now, I remember when I pass the 'Bull's Head'. Two of the crew were buried in Coventry cemetery (military section) just a few hundred yards from the balloon site that killed them.

During the Battle of Britain we were treated to a spectacle not to be missed. One afternoon I cycled to Greyfriars Green to see the German fighter displayed there for all to see. It was the much vaunted twin-engined Messerschmitt Me 110, known to the *Luftwaffe* as the *Zerstorer*. It looked quite a mess, with bullet holes in the fuselage, wings, engine cowling and one tail fin, and the engine thoroughly blackened. It had been forced to crash-land in Southern England during the Battle after an encounter with RAF Hurricanes or Spitfires. Written on the nose in Gothic lettering was the inscription '*Gott Straffe* England'. I thought, H'mmm, who sez? Get stuffed! Soon it will be '*Achtung Deutschland!*' Most onlookers seemed to agree. Many of them laughed and made similar comments.

Just after Christmas came the announcement on the radio, followed by comment in the national and local newspapers, that the Air Training Corps was to be formed. This was to attract boys of sixteen years and older and to train them for air and ground duties in the RAF. I still have an ATC recruiting leaflet.

The date set for forming the ATC was 1 February 1941. The basis of the new corps was to be the existing Air Defence Cadet Corps, previously privately run and privately funded. The ADCC was now to be incorporated into the ATC and would then receive official backing and funds from HM Government. The first Commandant was to be Air Commodore JA Chamier.

I noticed an article about the ATC in the *Midland Daily Telegraph* with details of when and where to apply. I went along on the very next Saturday at the end of January 1941. We'd had quite a fall of snow overnight so I walked up to Bablake School in my father's wellingtons. There was a cadet Lance Corporal on duty at the main entrance to the building. He asked me what I wanted and I said 'I've come to joint the ATC.' The Lance Corporal immediately corrected me. 'You mean the ADC! Come with me.' I didn't correct him or argue about it but followed this very swanky marching cadet to the Adjutant's office. The Lance Corporal saluted and handed me over to the Adjutant and departed, again saluting smartly. I secretly wondered if, later on, I would do any better?

The Adjutant took a long look at me and his eyes dropped. He stared at the 'wellies' and made no comment. I was given an application form for membership of the ADCC and was told that it applied to the ATC and would have to be countersigned by a parent or guardian before acceptance. This would also depend on satisfactorily passing the medical examination, which was given to all applicants regardless of air or ground crew category.

I was then taken off to the main hall where a lecture was in progress. It was being given by a Spitfire test pilot. I noticed that his rank was flight lieutenant and that, due to the snowy weather, he was wearing a pair of flying boots. All rather thrilling for us lads, all right up to the moment with the 'gear of the day'! I found, for perhaps the first time in my life, that my eyes were constantly drawn to the RAF pilot's badge above the left pocket of his tunic. Occasionally, I looked at the fur-lined flying boots but 95 per cent of the time it was the pilot's wings that drew my attention. This became the rule in the following days. I don't know how the other lads felt but I know now that this was always the focal point for me when looking at instructors in the future. Mostly, instructors would be NCOs or officers and, even more so, aircrew of some kind.

My service with the ATC was a very happy time, surpassed only by service with the RAF. We continued at Bablake School for some weeks, taking part in copious quantities of drill led by Cadet Flight Sergeant Bates and attending various military and airman-like lectures. Foot drill became quite a job at Bablake, since most of it was done on the sports field! Also, being winter, the grass had grown fairly long and was therefore quite tufty, making it nigh impossible to achieve the slightest resemblance to smartness out of a bunch of over-keen 'would-be airmen'.

It was at Frederick Bird's School that the tempo quickened and we began lectures in earnest, not forgetting some absolutely expert 'tuition' in drill by that wonder of the drill square, the now Cadet Warrant Officer Bates. Whatever we did as members of the ATC, you can be sure that at the very least, half of it was drill, so much so that, when the real day dawned, drill had no fears whatsoever, thanks to the ATC and Warrant Officer Bates. We also had periods of PT (Physical Training) but not as often as foot drill. Lectures consisted of Airmanship, Theory of Flight, Aircraft Recognition and Signals. These were all done at Frederick Bird's School. The Commanding Officer, Flight Lieutenant Dono, took us for Airmanship and Theory of Flight, the Adjutant, Flying Officer Elliott, for Administration and Air Force Law. Signals was organised by Pilot Officer (later Flying

Officer) Bonham, who used to teach at Cheylesmore School when I was a pupil there. Flying Officer Bonham, in company with one or two electrically minded cadets, rigged up a marvellous signals training unit in one of the sections of the large wooden hut that belonged to the ATC. It was a genuine replica of many an RAF signals training unit that I was later to experience.

The ATC work was going well by the summer. We received our uniforms in August and I remember that the waist fitting of the pair of trousers given to me was for a person almost half as wide again; fortunately the tunic covered up the error very well and no one ever knew. The ATC tunic of those days had a button-tight collar, not open neck as now. I managed to get hold of an old shirt that had the neck band but no collar, which fitted fine under the tunic.

The best of the ATC weekend always came on Sunday afternoon. This was our visit to No. 9 EFTS (Elementary Flying Training School), RAF Station Ansty, near Coventry.

In 1938 it was a close-up of the Bristol Blenheim day bomber or the almost new Avro Anson reconnaissance bomber that drew us youngsters to the show. There were also impressive aerial displays by the Hawker Hurricane, Avro's Tutor and Cadet, and Hawker Harts in Training Yellow flown by the local instructors. The most impressive part of the display came when a flight of Fairey Battles dive-bombed the airfield in a dynamic mock attack. I thought for many a month later just how powerful the Battles looked and what a noise they made when pulling out of their dive. I could never imagine myself as a crewmember of these presumably fast bomber aircraft, which they were, in that year of crisis and alarm.

One of the lectures we had from a civilian instructor was on the VGO (Vickers Gas Operated Machine Gun). This was a drum-fed aircraft machine-gun used in the Battle, Hampden, Anson and Whitley. The instructor rapped off smartly the names of all the parts as he stripped the weapon. He told us the operation of the mechanism, gun-loading, fire and safe switch – all in a very loud voice. Without warning he asked one cadet, then another, certain questions about the gun and, upon not getting the desired replies, became quite annoyed with us all for being so inattentive. He gave us a right rollicking. I think the average cadet was just recovering from the drill we'd had on the tarmac. It has occurred to me since, that the VGO was obsolescent then. I wonder why RAF Elementary Flying Training Schools were training aircrew on the gun? The Browning .303-inch was the main replacement and, being belt-fed, was mounted mostly in the turrets of bombers or in fighter wing sections. The VGO, also using .303-inch ammunition, may be useful if used singly, in hand-operated positions, being drum-fed, like the beam guns of a Beaufort and later in the nose of a Halifax III, where it was sometimes called a 'scare' gun. I never knew who it was really intended to scare – probably the bomber crew? As I was to learn later, the only gun to be of use in a bomber was a belt-fed turret-mounted gun. Hand-held guns were poor by comparison.

We sat for our ATC Proficiency Test just before the end of 1941. This was supposed to be equal to the ITW (Initial Training Wing) final exam – we were supposed to get the same rank, i.e., LAC, as RAF aircrew cadets reaching this stage. However, the ATC awarded us a Proficiency Star instead and a certificate to go with it.

One evening just before Christmas 1941, as my father and I sat by the log fire, I asked him if I could volunteer to join the Air Force as a pilot. He was very sharp in his reply, thrusting back the picture offered by me, of a bomber crew.

'You silly young fool, they are all sergeants! Do you think you will make sergeant?' he said sarcastically. I didn't reply; I felt very hurt at the time.

A month or so later, I asked my father again. 'You must see your mother about it. Otherwise it's all right by me,' he said, much to my surprise. I think he was just avoiding the issue, which was a pity.

A few days later I asked Mother if I could volunteer. Her answer was immediate.

'Yes, if your dad agrees.' So I told her he'd already agreed (which he hadn't).

'I see no sense in you waiting to be called up, possibly for a service you don't want, so you might as well choose your own.'

'You will be eighteen next year anyway. It makes very little difference. We don't want to lose you but I'd rather you did what you wanted,' she added.

I went to the medical examination at the time specified. I had to hand in the form that my father had signed, giving his approval, to the RAF recruiting section before the medical could proceed. (My father had already ensured the form had been mandatorily countersigned by a JP, Miss Jenny Lee. I was absolutely staggered by his forthright immediate action in this respect.)

Firstly the Corporal showed me the forms that I'd filled in on the Monday. It was now Thursday and across the top of the first one was written in red ink 'This man is under age and cannot be accepted for service'.

'How can you be a man if you're under age?' the Corporal said to me. 'These WAAFs, you know, are b.... stupid creatures.'

'I thought the age for acceptance was 17?,' I said.

'Don't worry lad, she's got it all wrong on the form and she's not up to date, is she?' the Corporal said.

He gathered up the necessary papers and took me downstairs and out across the yard and into Sibree Hall, where the medicals were already in progress. There, I filled in the usual medical questionnaire regarding serious illnesses, hereditary diseases etc. and joined the queue for the various cubicles.

The Hall was arranged like a one-way street. The applicants for all three services began at a reception table filling in the 'docs' and then went on to the first doctor and so on until all (about eight it seemed) had been attended. I managed the medical all right – it was a general fitness medical. The doctors were mostly older men; one in particular seemed interested enough to ask what I wanted to do in the RAF. When I told him I wanted to be a pilot he laughed.

'You will have to wait until you get older,' he said.

The final examination at Sibree Hall was completed by the President or Chief Medical Officer. This chap simply analysed the contents of the various forms to decide whether I was fit or not. While I was awaiting his decision, he must have had me under observation too. He asked me if I took after my mother. I said I didn't know. The President remarked that my upper lip was quite like a Cupid's bow. I thought it was a strange remark then. Now I can see quite clearly that he took his job very seriously indeed but, perhaps forgetting that one so young as I was, was not too appreciative about his remarks. It made me feel as if I possessed female features. I asked him how I'd got on and he replied with a smile that I had passed.

I took the relevant documents back to the RAF Recruiting Office.

'You managed the first stage alright then,' the Corporal said.

He told me to report in approximately a month's time and come prepared to travel to Birmingham for the Aircrew Selection Board and Medical. The date given was 2 February at 9 am. We were to call at the local Recruiting Office first to collect a travel warrant to Birmingham New Street Station. It was also mentioned that I should report in ATC uniform and take with me a Certificate of Service.

Tuesday 2 February dawned a reasonable sort of grey winter's day. I was joined at Sibree Hall by four other aircrew volunteers, the eldest was a lad of twenty-two who wore glasses. He seemed a well-educated chap. He had volunteered for training as an observer; due to his lower grade of eyesight he would have to wear his specs in the air. There had recently been a change in the recruiting requirements for observers (later known as navigators). This was that volunteers were acceptable with certain grades of corrective vision and up to the age of forty-one. The age limit had been up to thirty-two until then. The other lads all wanted to be pilots and were all around eighteen or nineteen years of age. The 'observer type' was given all the gen about how to get to No. 1 ACSB (Air Crew Selection Board) Birmingham and was given the travel warrant for the five of us. We set off from Coventry just after 9 am and on arrival at Birmingham we spent most of the morning filling in more forms. Family medical histories were required, as were details of past or serving family members of HM Forces. Lunchtime soon arrived and we were served a good meal: meat pie, beans and chips, plus fruit pudding and custard, all provided free by the RAF.

The afternoon was spent in attending written examinations. Mathematics was the prime subject, followed by a General Knowledge test and a General Science examination. We completed the day with a meal in the small canteen, after which we were allotted billets within walking distance. The Coventry group of volunteers had managed to stay together. This wasn't difficult for the first day, due to the general routine of form filling and educational exams.

After booking in at the main entrance we proceeded in various directions. I saw little of my colleagues from Coventry that day. We were shown to benches outside various small offices. This was the all-important Selection Board. I didn't have long to wait, I was one of the first in. As I entered smartly and gave the best imitation of an Air Force salute I could possibly muster (I was still in ATC cadet uniform) the Flight Lieutenant (a two-ringer) asked me to sit down. I noticed he was accompanied by no less a person than a Group Captain (a four-ringer).

The Groupie looked up and smiled.

'Hello lad. So you want to fly as a pilot?' he said, looking at various forms in front of him.

'Yes, Sir,' I replied.

'What for?' smiled the Groupie.

'Because I want to fly and fight in the air, Sir.'

'What sort of aeroplane would you like to fly, my lad?'

'A night fighter, Sir,' said I.

'Why?' asked the Groupie.

'There is plenty of scope for improvement at night, Sir, having been in the Coventry "blitzes".'

The Flight Looie asked if I knew the working of an internal combustion engine. I explained the theory. The Groupie asked what sports I took part in.

'Swimming and cycling, Sir,' I replied and he asked how far I could swim.

'About three lengths,' I said. He then asked if I had passed any certificates for swimming while at school.

'Three, Sir,' I replied, quoting the latest one.

'What distance do you cycle?' asked the Groupie.

'About a hundred miles Sir,' I said. The Groupie's eyes nearly popped out and the Flight Looie looked at him in amazement when I told them of my ride to Gran's in 1940, map reading the way too, all without a signpost. They seemed very impressed with how long it took and asked if I had found it tiring.

'Your exam marks are very good in Mathematics and Science, but your General Knowledge results are low. You should do some crossword puzzles, they will help you,' said the Groupie.

'Er, accepted for training as pilot or wireless operator/air gunner – do you agree?' the Groupie asked the Flight Looie.

The Flight Looie smiled and said 'Yes – pilot or wireless operator/air gunner, Sir.'

'That's provided you pass the medical, of course.'

I stood up and saluted.

'Thank you very much Sir.' As I turned to go they both wished me good luck with the medical. They'd explained that if I failed the pilot's course I would be retrained as a wireless operator/air gunner.

Two corporals told me and another lad simultaneously about the conditions of service. We signed the relevant documents. We were told that we had been accepted into the Royal Air Force Volunteer Reserve for the duration of the present emergency. We received our RAF numbers. Mine was 1582840.

As mentioned earlier, each ATC cadet was due for a flight in a Tiger Moth. When my turn came, I had to make my own way out to Ansty as the flights were scheduled for Sunday morning. I arrived in good time and presented myself at the Training Flight Hut on the flying field. My parents had to sign a chit to say that they were agreeable and that if any accident were to occur it would not be an RAF responsibility.

A flying officer pilot instructor soon sought me out and, together with a borrowed Irvin sheepskin-lined flying jacket, helmet, goggles and parachute, we found our way to a parked Tiger Moth.

It was a bright, sunny morning; there had been a hoar frost the night before, making the countryside a brilliant white in every direction. We took off into the wind – the take-off seemed very bumpy. There was considerable vibration from the tail skid until the tail came up when sufficient speed was reached. We were soon aloft. How marvellous it all felt. It seemed strange to look out of the cockpit and see the fabric, the struts, the wings, and to think that this supported us. It seemed unreal in this respect. We took a wide circuit of the airfield. The instructor had asked which part of Coventry I lived in and took me over Wyken where I was able to see our home in Farren Road (we'd moved from Gulson Road earlier in the year). It was a very pleasant flight and as this was my very first flight it was naturally of great importance to me.

We came down after approximately twenty to thirty minutes. The flight seemed to last longer. The landing was very good – very smooth. We taxied in to the parking lines and after 'switching off' the instructor got out, helped me to get out, and assisted in stowing the gear etc.

He asked how I felt about flying and did I like the trip.

'It was great stuff, Sir,' I replied. In fact, I was relieved that we'd done no aerobatics; although I had enjoyed my first flight very much, I was very apprehensive about the more professional stuff. I felt a bit of a cheat really and yet with the passage of time I realise that I only needed confidence.

'Did you manage to see your home? I flew over that part of Coventry.'

'Yes Sir, it was just down to starboard as we crossed the Ansty Road.' We'd been at about 1000 feet so it wasn't too difficult to spot, even if you were scared of looking down over the side.

The time was almost due for my call-up papers. I couldn't think of much else in those last few weeks; it was on my mind whenever I was alone, particularly in the morning, cycling to work. I left before the post arrived and so had it in mind that 'they' could arrive before I got back for tea. I also wondered if I would fail the course. I thought I'd got a good chance of completing the ITW course, due to the ATC work and certificate, but after that, who knows? Maybe I wouldn't like flying? It would be very different from a trip in a Tiger Moth around the circuit at Ansty.

One Monday evening on return from work, I came into the house with the usual expectation. There it was. I couldn't believe my eyes – the official-looking envelope on the mantelpiece. There was no mistake, the typed address read '1582840 AC.2 BROOME F D'. I rapidly opened the envelope and produced the mauve document it contained. Half was the instruction to report to Lord's Cricket Ground on 7 September 1942, together with a small amount of personal luggage. The other half was the rail warrant to London Euston!

I was overjoyed and proud to be called up for the RAF. It had been the main topic of conversation for so many of the past months, since joining the ATC in February 1941.

CHAPTER 2

Royal Air Force

'Arsie Tarsie'; Hardening Camp and ITW

At last it was 7 September. I was up at about 6.45 am, I had breakfast with Dad; Mother had already gone to work an hour before. She was the staff cook at the London Road Institution, perhaps better known as the Workhouse. She'd been a Poor Law Officer for some years and had met and married Father, also a Poor Law Officer, while at Rotherham Institution. I collected the small attaché case that I'd borrowed from Mother, which I'd packed the night before. A firm handshake and 'Good luck, Frank. Take care of yourself,' from Dad.

With some other lads I'd met on the train I arrived in London just before 11 am and went on the Underground to Lord's. We were only a matter of yards away when a young, dark-haired lad of about eighteen, wearing a dark navy gaberdine raincoat, asked if we were bound for the Aircrew Receiving Centre (ACRC) at Lord's. He joined us for a few moments as we headed for the entrance. I noticed he was shorter than the rest of us and rather a good-looking lad. We were greeted by a corporal at the gate who asked what trade of aircrew we had been selected for. The pilots went in one direction, as did the observers, but our young friend of a few brief moments said 'Air gunner?' and away he went in a different direction. I often wondered in the months that passed how he fared as an air gunner. One day I was to find out – almost for sure!

The four of us disappeared up some stairs in one of the buildings for our first FFI (Free from Infection). This was the first of the many naked inspections we were to have in the near and also distant future.

It was to become a matter of routine when changing station or unit, although it hadn't sunk in by then.

The corporal who took charge of our group, about sixty lads aged between eighteen and twenty-two, was a man of around forty-five years. This chap took us, or marched us, from one place to another. We had our first RAF lunch in the restaurant at Lord's. Later in the day we were kitted out with uniform, tin hat, respirator, anti-gas cape, wellingtons, PT kit (including pumps), two pairs of boots, three pairs of socks, three shirts, six collars, three sets of heavy woollen underwear (not long johns), mess tin, knife, fork and spoon (known then as 'Irons'), three towels, holdall, housewife, shaving brush, hair brush, button stick and a set of webbing (including belt, backpack, small pack and water bottle).

We stuffed this lot into a kit-bag as best we could, a joke really because unless you knew how, it was nearly impossible. Then we 'fell in' behind (our) Corporal Loader who marched us to our billets, which turned out to be Viceroy Court at Regent's Park. I noted that Corporal Loader had a room of his own some short distance down the corridor.

We then went for our first main meal in the Cook-house at Viceroy Court. This was in the basement garage, which had been modified by the RAF to become the Airmen's Mess. As we queued on the left down the ramp some lads were coming out up the other side.

'Whatever you have – do not complain! If the Orderly Officer doesn't agree with you, you get put on "Jankers",' one of them said in answer to various questions about the quality of the food.

'You get an egg for breakfast on Sundays with your bacon,' someone also said. Eggs were very scarce in wartime Britain.

The next day we had the tailors round in the afternoon and everyone was measured up in uniform. Mine needed some alterations, so did Cliff Wheeler's. We were told they should be back on Friday or Saturday, maybe before.

Meanwhile, at Regent's Park we had all sorts of tests. We had a full aircrew medical, a night vision test, dental inspection and inoculations. We also had tests in Maths and Signals. If you didn't reach the required standard you were posted to Brighton for three weeks to do a special course covering these subjects. If you passed, you went on to the ETW (Elementary Training Wing) at Ludlow and thereby saved three weeks' training. Most lads I knew were keen to pass these elementary exams, mainly to cut the amount of ground school they had to do and so increase the chances of getting to a flying school as quickly as possible. You wouldn't think that three weeks was worth bothering about, but I can assure you it was all taken very seriously.

We all knew that we had some six months' of ground training to do, and there was no way of getting around it. When we had finished we would be promoted to LAC (leading aircraftman) and our pay increased from 3s (15p) to 7s 6d (37½p) per day (plus 6d (2½p) a day Post War Credit). This would only happen if we completed the ITW Course (Initial Training Wing). Otherwise, there would be no posting to EFTS (Elementary Flying Training School). Aircrew cadets were generally expected to qualify on these early courses, although the examination marks required for a pass were quite high – 70 per cent minimum for most subjects with 95 per cent for signals and aircraft recognition.

Among our group of recruits was one chap who, every time the question was raised by an officer or NCO regarding our training classification 'pilot or observer', called out 'Radio observer, Sir.' We were then greeted with a remark from the officer or NCO that was to become the norm for the time: 'You must have some special qualifications for this sort of training?' The radio observer chap never seemed to give a perfect answer to this question, possibly because he was further qualified and didn't want to draw attention to himself. This went on until we left ACRC. I don't remember where he was posted to. We never saw him again. A radio observer was almost certain to be bound for night fighters. I thought he was a lucky chap. (NB A radio observer would operate the night fighter search radar.)

I seemed to have done well in the tests taken at 'Arsie Tarsie'. Apparently, I was up to the standard required for I was to be posted to Ludlow. One other interesting test was that for night vision, in which I gained twenty-three out of thirty-two marks. This was considered 'above average'. I didn't realise then just how important this was going to be in the future.

On 26 September we left London by train for Ludlow, Shropshire. Cliff Wheeler and Ray Twigger were with us; I am not sure about Stan Clarke. We arrived in Ludlow on a sunny autumn afternoon and marched from the railway station to the camp, which was about a mile and a half from the country town. There were many grunts and groans during this part of the journey, which was no wonder because, in addition to a full kit-bag each, we were all wearing full webbing and carrying a tin hat, gas mask, gas cape, dixie (cooking pot) and water bottle.

The journey seemed never-ending. It was quite a struggle to get up the rise in the road where the bridge spanned the river; it was a steady climb for some 100 yards further until the road levelled off. The corporal in charge rather enjoyed himself by calling us everything except 'rookie' airmen. I don't believe he gave us any sort of break. We were in three flights of about 100 men and so the front batch (my group) was not allowed by the corporal to be caught up by the second or third. We were more than glad to have arrived at the camp gates, except that the sight of the place dimmed all prospect of a happy time there.

After a short parade for roll call we were given a 'welcome' speech by a flight lieutenant engineer type. He told us in no uncertain terms 'If you play ball with me, I'll play ball with you. I want the building of this camp completed before the winter sets in and it's up to you lads to see that you do your share.' What he really meant was that if we didn't work according to his plan then the camp would close for the winter and he would lose his position, especially as he seemed to be the most senior officer on the camp.

We were shown to bell tents down by the riverside. We each drew three blankets and a straw palliasse; the tents were already equipped with duckboards as 'flooring'. The washing and shaving facilities were pretty crude. They were just galvanised bowls on wooden benches fitted with cold water taps and with no cover of any kind. There was no way of heating the water. On frosty mornings we were to find the taps frozen.

On 9 October 1942 we entrained at Ludlow Station, bound for Aberystwyth via Shrewsbury. The ITW was the main ground training establishment of the RAF. If we passed the course we would start flying training in about three months' time. We were met at Aberystwyth Railway Station by several enthusiastic corporals who swiftly lined us up in threes and marched us off into the town.

Our destination was the 'Hotel Lion Royal' in the main shopping street. It was an old-type hotel with rooms of varying sizes. Cliff and I were marched into a room with three other cadets: Johnny Walker, Ray Smith and Jock McFarlane and a Serving Airman, LAC Mansey. There was another cadet in a very small room adjoining ours. All I can remember is that he was a dark-haired lad of medium height and build, about nineteen or twenty, who always looked smart in his uniform.

We were given a very strong lecture about our untidy appearance on arrival at the 'Lion Royal'. Since we had come straight from the mud of RAF Ludlow, who would wonder? We still got a rollicking!

We were issued next day with white belts for 'walking out' into the town and for church parades. We had been told the day before about the regular blancoing they would need. They really had to be brilliant white, not off-white or greyish. (The normal colour of the webbing and belt was Air Force Blue).

The lectures began in earnest on the first morning. We needed to study Air Force Law, Hygiene and Anti-Gas straight away as there were exams set for six weeks' time. The rest of the course was quite good. We took Navigation, including elementary Astro-Navigation and Meteorology. These were taken at the college – the University of Wales. We were lucky to have the opportunity to study in such a beautiful building. We often used other buildings owned by the college, which were scattered around the town. One of the nearest was a chapel in its upper half, and the lower half (i.e. the basement) was used for navigation lessons.

We soon realised that No. 6 ITW Aberystwyth was a unit to be proud of. When we first arrived we learnt of the amount of 'bull' required from the new arrivals. At the time we found this rather frightening. We listened to tales from those already established in No. 4 Squadron at the 'Lion Royal'. We also had comparisons of 'bull' quoted from those cadets who had missed the hardships at Ludlow but had gone to Brighton for Maths and Signals courses. These lads had quite an experience and it appears that Brighton was so simply full of 'bull' that one wondered whether there was any benefit in the course at Ludlow. Mind you, from the comments that the lads from Brighton made (to those of us who had been at Ludlow) you could sense the *esprit de corps* after only five or six weeks of service life. They seemed to think that we Ludlowites had really missed out. Perhaps we had, although in the long term, once we were through the ITW course, neither Brighton nor Ludlow would count for much.

We became 'B' Flight of No. 4 Squadron, No. 6 ITW. Flying Officer Bishop was our flight officer, who took us for many of the early lectures, particularly Air Force Law, Hygiene and Anti-Gas.

On one occasion we were being marched to the college.

'"B" Flight Attenshun! By the left, quick march, 'eft, 'ight, 'eft, 'ight, 'eft, 'ight. Come on lads, 180 to the minute, quicken up a bit, you're not in the "Guards", you're in the RAF. 'Eft, 'ight, 'eft, 'ight, 'eft, 'ight.'

We belted off to the college at a good 200 ppm, past some old ladies, standing by the kerbside waiting to cross the road.

'They are like a lot of mad things. They don't need to march like that, do they? Thought they were supposed to fly?' one said to the other.

It caused a giggle among the cadets.

'There you are, lads. Got a few admirers already – cor lummy, what a blooming lot! Pick 'em there lads, quick time now, let's see those arms swinging shoulder high. Come along now, bags of swank. 'Eft, 'ight, 'eft, 'ight.'

We had some immediate tests on Navigation and Anti-Gas. The marks we got were quite good. My diary entries show the results of those days.

23 OCTOBER 1942
SAT FOR ANTI-GAS EXAM, AND PASSED WITH 74% (PASS MARK 50%).

6 NOVEMBER 1942
SAT FOR PROGRESS TEST IN NAVIGATION AND PASSED WITH 95%.

Our swotting for the final exams in the evenings became a necessary chore. None of us wanted to fail the course and, apart from that, our pay didn't allow for much jollity. If one didn't smoke and drink, one could perhaps see three cinema shows a week. Neither habit struck me very hard, although it seemed a pity to give the cigarette ration away. There weren't many takers for the 'sweets/cigs swap'. Most lads liked both!

When we returned to Aberystwyth at the end of our leave, Cliff and I found that we had passed our exams. Almost the whole course had passed; the odd bod who failed just one or two exams was given further training on the course following a fortnight later, and therefore re-sat the finals with them.

We stayed at Aberystwyth until 11 March, enjoying this extended spell of 'luxury'. I say this because, as one of our DI (Drill Instructor) corporals remarked one night in the WVS Canteen: 'You'll never get as good a place as this, lad. Your ITW days will stand out as the best you have had in the RAF.'

We didn't really think so at the time, thinking of our forthcoming Grading School at an EFTS and further to flying training in Canada, South Africa, or perhaps even the USA.

'You wait and see, lads,' said the corporal, a Yorkshire man. He was a fairly strict disciplinarian, like most of the DIs. During the years that followed I found he was absolutely correct. We didn't really have time to think about it, in fact we rarely had time to reflect then, on any period of training. Also, since ITW dealt only with the ground instruction, we could hardly be blamed for forgetting how we came by some of it.

Once the final exams were completed we expected to be posted within a few days to a Flying Training School. However, the winter weather spoilt the chance of any early movement. Flying training was always affected by inclement weather, at home or abroad, winter or summer.

Our waiting period at 'Aber' was put to good use, we were provided with a supplementary ITW Course. We moaned about it, of course, not that it did any good. It lasted eight weeks. We were given further training in Navigation, Astro-Nav, Met, Aircraft Rec and Armaments.

During our course we had instruction in firearms of various kinds. We were given a spell of arms drill and rifle practice. We spent approximately half a morning each week on the clay pigeon shoot, using 12-bore shotguns. The latter were good fun and quite a number of cadets were good natural shots with this sort of weapon. Unfortunately, I was not one of them. Our main gunnery training was on the Browning .303-inch aircraft machine-gun. The Browning was a splendid weapon as it could fire at 1180 rpm (rounds per minute). It seemed a very complicated piece of machinery to me at that stage of training. I had very great difficulty in describing the various mechanical operations of the gun and also fully understanding these operations in detail. However, much to my surprise, I passed the final exam with a fairly good mark.

'OK lads, get back to your flight – you're all on posting tonight to Flying Grading School.' Jeepers, we could hardly believe our ears. Really? At last, had it really come through? Gosh, the thought of the Tiger Moth and learning to fly really came home with a bang!

It was not until we boarded the train that we knew for certain that we were going to No. 9 EFTS Ansty, near Coventry. I couldn't believe my luck – of all places! Just fancy, flying training at dear old Ansty. Why did it all seem to happen to me, I wondered? There had been rumours and speculation about the posting – one could have gone to Brough or Carlisle or many other places.

CHAPTER 3

The Last Weeks in Blighty....

Ansty; Heaton Park; HMT *Queen Elizabeth*

We travelled via Shrewsbury and Crewe and, after a tiresome and slow journey, arrived at Shilton railway station about 6 am. The RAF lorries were drawn up near the bridge. We clambered aboard and our kit-bags were loaded on to an accompanying vehicle.

Ansty was to be a happy station for me; although some of us were on guard duty on the very first night! It seemed amusing to be issued with a rifle and bayonet, together with only one clip, of five rounds. The latter were to be carried in one's greatcoat pocket – not in the gun! What could we do with five rounds anyway? Evidently, someone at Ansty had decided the war was nearing its end.

The next morning some of our group, including myself, were posted to 'F' Flight, which was at the Relief Landing Ground (RLG) at Southam.

I was a little disappointed at first on being attached to 'F' Flight at Southam. Although I was a Coventrian I knew nothing previously of the RLG until I flew from there. Many cadets realised I was a local lad and asked for the places like pubs and dances to be recommended. I couldn't help really because I had not been old enough for those entertainments pre-RAF. There were many complaints about entertainment in Coventry and I got it in the neck regularly.

'Hey Broomie, this city of yours – it's a right dump! Was it like this before the bombing? Sounds as if it was already dead!'

It was intended that the Grading Course would cover twelve hours' of dual instruction on the Tiger Moth. Apart from actual flying, we took very little ground instruction at Ansty or Southam. There were no regular lectures; the only time we had anything like it was when the weather was too bad for 'sprog' pilots to fly.

One day we had a talk by a warrant officer pilot, one of our instructors. He was a pre-war regular, who looked very smart in his warrant officer's uniform with peaked cap. He told us of the early days of the Desert War, Sidi Barrani, Tobruk and Mersah Matruh. He also talked about how they foxed the 'Ities' into believing the RAF air strength was much greater than it was, by flying their Gloster Gladiator biplane fighters in and out, over the lines at well spaced intervals. It was hoped this would delay early offensives by the enemy in the desert.

We took in this war talk like the hungry kids that we were! This pilot wasn't just an instructor, we respected him for that, he was also an ex-operational pilot and that seemed very important to us at that time. Somehow, the more experienced a pilot was in air warfare, the more human he became and therefore more likeable in the lecture room, and in the air too!

Apart from this particular chat, on a rainy day at Southam, there was only one other lecture of importance. This was the flight plan circuit of the airfield, the method, speed and height of approach, LH circuit only. There were various landmarks, i.e. the slagheaps at Binley. Momentarily, I remembered the wall posters I had seen on visits to Ansty in my ATC days. One in particular showed a Tiger Moth that had landed beside two pyramids (desert and palm trees in background). A solo pupil, getting out of the cockpit, says to a nearby Arab on a camel: 'Eeee, I thought it twa't slagheaps at Binley.'

My only encounter with the Squadron Leader was highly amusing in some respects, although it didn't seem too funny at the time. I did my share of guard duties at Southam and was on guard at the main gate one night, armed with a rifle (unloaded), bayonet and a clip of five rounds. Some time around 10.30 pm I could hear the sound of voices and footsteps coming along the road from Southam. I'd had other airmen arrive from outings during that evening. As the voices and footsteps came nearer I could already tell who one person was, although it was a pitch-black night.

'Halt. Who goes there?' I called.

'Friend,' the answer came. I knew there were two and no more.

'Advance No. 1 to be recognised,' I called.

The person came up to me at a walking pace. I could see that it was none other than the Squadron Leader, the Commanding Officer of the RLG. I already knew this from the sound of his voice. The officer came right up to me, grabbed the rifle and wrenched it out of my hands!

'Now, my lad, what are you going to do about that? If I were the enemy, the camp would now be at my mercy. [For how long with an empty gun? The five rounds were still in my pocket!] What have you got to say for yourself?' rapped the Squadron Leader.

'I knew who it was, Sir,' I said.

'Rubbish,' said the CO. 'You couldn't even see me.'

'I knew you by the sound of your voice, Sir!'

'Rubbish, lad, you're just making excuses. I'll see you in my office, prompt at 08.00 hours.'

'Yes, Sir,' I replied.

I then called out for No. 2 to advance and be recognised. The Adjutant came up to the sentry box, the CO having departed some distance. The Adjutant halted in front of me.

'Pass, Sir,' I called. He gave me a grin.

'Don't take too much notice, he's in a bad mood tonight. He'll be better in the morning.'

Away they both went, leaving me thinking 'Stuff you, Squadron Leader!'

The CO was undoubtedly a good pilot but he was a stroppy little man in other ways and his night vision must have been at a low ebb, or was he just mildly 'khalied'? I did not think about either at the time. I thought it was just the sort of thing that would happen to me!

The next morning I reported to the Administrative Offices just before 08.00 hours and was reassured by the Adjutant not to worry too much. In the event, the Squadron Leader was almost the same as the previous night. I was given a mild roasting for not being a 'proper' sentry when on guard duty. I made a resolution that if it happened again, I would shoot before anyone had time to disarm me! The only reservation I had was that I would have to load my rifle first from the five rounds in my pocket.

When it came to flying, it turned out to be much better than I expected. I was allotted to Sergeant Pike, one of the instructor pilots. At a guess I would say he was about twenty-four years of age, although he had the maturity of an older man. He was a good instructor as far as I could tell. I had no doubts about him at all. He possessed a very friendly manner, even if you were flying like a brick! All cadets soon formed the opinion that 'their' instructor was the best on the unit and there was no point in arguing about it. I don't know how many of the instructors were sergeants, possibly half to two thirds. The officer instructors were good too, as I was to find later.

Flying the Tiger Moth was quite an experience, especially if you had absolutely no idea of what it was going to be like. On the first day we were taken up for a familiarisation flight. After take-off, flying to a suitably clear piece of sky, Sergeant Pike demonstrated what the various controls could do: rolling, pitching, yawing. He showed where the horizon was, or where it was supposed to be – a sort of vague 'no man's land' murky patch where earth and cloud met. It looked a very uncertain blurred mess, especially after being trained for all that ground precision at No. 6 ITW. This put me off flying slightly to begin with.

After a few minutes, I was asked to place my hands and feet on the controls. I soon found it wasn't as easy as it looked. It seemed difficult to keep the aircraft straight and level. It was near impossible at times, especially with almost no horizon. My instructor demonstrated how easy it was by holding his hands above his head; the aircraft, when properly trimmed, gave a good account of flying itself. It all seemed easy, but when I put my hands and feet on the controls, the aircraft objected like a mad thing. A three-dimensional environment did not help either. It seemed impossible to keep the aircraft's height, course and altitude stable, much to my absolute horror!

Taxiing quickly gave us confidence in handling the aircraft and operating engine controls while in reasonable safety. Starting the engine by swinging the propeller by hand was frightening to begin with as no one wished to lose a hand, arm or even a head, especially if they were your own!

The grading course gave a pupil sufficient time to settle down to flying an aeroplane and hopefully to go solo. The object of the course was to eliminate those who wouldn't make it finally on a complete course, usually in Canada, the USA or South Africa. It gave one a better chance of being selected earlier as either navigator or air bomber.

We learnt to take off, fly a circuit of the airfield and land properly. Also, we were required to show during two tests, one at eight hours and one at twelve, our ability to complete gliding turns, medium turns with power, stalling, spinning and recovery, a glide approach and landing.

We received instruction for engine failure on take-off, fire in the air and forced landing procedure; although all very rudimentary at this stage, it was absolutely essential for, as you will see, we were to lose several cadets in accidents later on, although not in the UK.

We soon learnt to do a reasonable take-off, circuit and landing. We were slow to realise that one could have 'on' and 'off' days, assuming instead that we were doomed to failure. Nevertheless, the approach and landing caused the main problems. A take-off could be managed quite well by most cadets in half a dozen lessons. Keeping on a definite heading until one reached either 500 or 1000 feet before turning crosswind at 90° at an IAS (Indicated Air Speed) of about 70 mph, then turning again on 90° to the downwind leg was usually a piece of cake, providing you didn't go too far and so lose sight of the aerodrome altogether. Turning 90° to bring you at right angles to your final approach, was still reasonably easy, except that at the end of it you had to decide exactly when to turn in for your landing approach and also to decide when you were 'dead into wind'. The latter was not easy for a pupil, especially with the small number of hours of the average Grading School cadet. Once into wind and heading for the airfield, the elevator trimmer had to be set for 'landing' and the engine reduced to a tickover. Depending on the strength of the wind, one had to judge when to throttle back the engine. This distance varied daily and so the problem was not easily solved. Once the airfield boundary had been reached, the pupil needed to level out at the right airspeed and height in order to touchdown correctly in the right place. Sometimes we did wheel landings and sometimes the preferred 'three-pointers'. The latter did not come easily or regularly for the average cadet.

There were some for whom flying came more easily. Johnny Walker, our room-mate from Aberystwyth, was one who apparently had this gift. He soloed just before his eight-hour test! A 'born pilot', we said at the time. About half the cadets soloed on our course at Southam.

We all hoped to go solo but the most important thing was to get good marks on the eight- and twelve-hour tests to ensure selection for further training as a pilot. Although we knew how important the other types of aircrew were, particularly the navigator, we all wanted to be pilots. There were exceptions, but they were very rare indeed.

I recorded my experiences in my diary:

28 March 1943 – I did only one trip today of 50 minutes' duration; the same thing – circuits and bumps. My circuits are much better and my approaches and landings are getting quite good and only occasionally do I get a rotten landing. I am beginning to think that there may be quite a good chance of getting a good mark for my 12-hour test and possibly a post-grading. [Extra flying time, usually to offset bad weather, which could be unfit for solo.] I have now got 10 hours 40 minutes' 'dual' in and I am feeling more confident.

29 March – Today we went on a spinning trip for 35 minutes. I did three good spins and a circuit and landing. Sergeant Pike did a loop and also showed me how a bad gliding turn may result in a spin.

30 March – Our day off again and, as usual, I went home.

31 March – I went up with my instructor and did a few 'circuits' for 30 minutes. This brought my total to 11 hours, 45 minutes. Just before lunch I had my 12-hour test with Flying Officer Boroughs in T6200 (10). I did much better than I expected. Firstly, I did a circuit and a very good landing, then I climbed to 3000 feet and did a spin (1 LEFT), then medium turns left and right and a gliding turn. After this I came back onto the circuit, landed and made a good job of it. To finish, I made another good circuit and was told I could have gone solo but for the bad weather (wind 20–30 mph) so I asked to be put on a Post Grading Course – and got it.

1 April – Bad weather and no flying. Started my guard duties at RLG Southam the night previous, 6 hours off and 3 hours on duty.

2 April – I went up with Pilot Officer Perkins for 10 minutes only and managed to do a circuit, although not a very good one.

3 April – I got in 30 minutes, 'dual' on circuits with Pilot Officer Perkins. Made a pretty poor show but managed one landing OK. Finished my guard duties.

4 April – Had another 30 minutes on circuits with Pilot Officer Perkins in T6200 (10). Made about 50% good landings, circuits much better.

5 April – Mother's birthday! The weather today was excellent, very little wind or cloud. I did 40 minutes' circuits and bumps. My first landing was lousy, the second I did with my instructor, the third one myself and not too bad, the fourth and fifth were quite good.

'You can go solo, we'll fill her up first. Then you can take your time,' he said. I could not believe that I was to be allowed to solo. It all happened so fast, I had really no time to worry about it! The instructor ensured the tank was full and then told me to taxi downwind to the take-off point. This gave almost a diagonal run across the airfield for take-off and just about the longest run possible.

It took just a few minutes to taxi into position prior to take-off. I did my cockpit check, a five- or six-letter code flashed through my mind as I checked the vital items. I looked downwind to ensure there was no aircraft making a landing approach. All was clear so I turned into wind and opened the throttle gradually until it was fully open. The Tiger Moth bumped along the field, faster and faster. I could see a fair-sized tree on the horizon and lined the aircraft up on this. Stick forward, to get the tail off, not too much or the prop may strike the ground. A glance at the ASI (Airspeed Indicator), now registering 55 mph, then, easing the stick back, the Tiger Moth and I were airborne.

The aircraft became 'unstuck' earlier than when flying 'dual', obviously because of the lighter, empty cockpit ahead of me. It was almost an unbelievable sight – the empty cockpit, very strange, very unfriendly, very, very vacant! What price now for courage? All the best wishes and prayers in the world would not fill that vacant front seat. I had four or five hours' of petrol in the tank, right above that empty seat. However, I attained the steady climbing speed of 65 mph, which I continued until I reached 1000 feet. Then, I looked left to port and turned on to the crosswind leg at 90°, a medium turn, airspeed still about 65 mph. Once the field had been cleared and I had made my turn at 1000 feet, the main thing was not to lose sight of the field. The general rule was to keep it just behind the tip of the port lower main plane. Very soon it was time to turn downwind so I commenced a rate 1 turn to bring the airfield squarely on the port side of the aircraft. We were now travelling at about 70 mph, straight and level. I could see quite clearly the two slag heaps at Binley Colliery. It was a good day for flying; the horizon was fairly sharp, the spring sun was shining and the visibility was good. It was on the downwind leg that I heard strange sounds.

I thought I could hear the angels singing. The voices, soft at first, rose to a triumphant crescendo, beginning at about the centre of the downwind leg, fading away just as I made the third medium turn to bring the Tiger Moth crosswind. The aerodrome then lay diagonally to port between wing tip and engine. I was reasonably close, perhaps half to three-quarters of a mile away, when I made the final turn into wind in preparation for landing. I closed the throttle and as the engine noise faded, I could hear the scream of the air through the bracing wires and struts. I lined up for the glide approach and landing. The wind was fairly brisk at about 20 mph. I managed easily to clear the furrows that had recently been ploughed by the local farmer and was some 50 feet up as we came over the boundary. The trimmer had been fully set for landing and all I had to do was to concentrate on the final run in. I gave a touch of rudder and aileron to keep her straight and level. There was no other aircraft ahead, so down we came. As we got close to the ground, I brought the stick slowly back, to level off at about 5–10 feet, allowing the Tiger Moth to make a 'perfect three-pointer', much to my utter astonishment. I taxied carefully to the dispersal point.

Before I had come to a halt, Pilot Officer Perkins came running across the field to the aircraft.

'Congratulations, Broome. Good show, lad,' he shouted with a tremendous grin, sharing the moment with me.

'Thank you, Sir,' I answered. 'How was the landing, Sir?'

'Very good,' said the instructor. 'Very good indeed.'

'Thank you, Sir,' I beamed.

'Damn good show, lad. Damn good show. Off you go now and stow your kit. Good luck with your selection for pilot training. You should have a very good chance now that you've soloed. Bye for now.'

'Thank you, Sir,' the new pilot replied.

I realise now, that the instructors must have appreciated just how young we were. As far as we cadets were concerned, we were men at eighteen. Well, we were in the RAF, weren't we? It is worth noting how keen the two officer instructors had been to get me to solo at that time. Some eight months later attitudes had changed considerably.

Part of our guard duty at Southam was inspecting the picket lines of Tiger Moth trainers. Armed only with a cycle lamp, it was our job to make sure that the aircraft, which were all parked in the open around the airfield perimeter, were securely staked with their cockpits properly covered. On one particularly dark and windy night in March 1943 I inspected the seemingly endless line of parked aircraft. They looked all very quiet and mysterious in their sombre camouflage paint of olive green and khaki. They were all OK, so down the line I went. I had all night had I not?

When the last aircraft appeared I walked a short distance further to make sure there were no more. Then, I thought that instead of going back the way I had come, I would cut across the aerodrome to shorten the return distance. (The kites were parked in a crescent-shaped line.)

I set off across the field. There was no danger of an aircraft coming in, even in an emergency, as there was no flare path, lit or unlit. It was a dry night, slightly windy. I walked in the general direction of the guardroom and kept on going and going. Still no buildings. After a few more minutes (it seemed like hours) I stopped, looked and listened. There was nothing in sight and not a sound, except the wind. I became more than a little concerned. I had walked a fair distance. It seemed longer than the journey to visit the picketed aircraft! I thought that by this time, since I was supposed to be taking a short cut, I should have been back at the guardroom! Unfortunately I had no watch, like many other cadets. Most would eventually bring back a watch after overseas training, but that was of no use now.

I put out the torch and crouched on the grass. I thought I might be able to see nearby buildings silhouetted against the skyline. No such luck! It was now a pitch-black night and there were no stars visible. Otherwise, I might at least have been able to determine the correct direction, being fresh from the elementary Astro-Nav taught at ITW. I realise now that I hadn't give my night vision much chance, as I had only just flicked off the torch. One really needs at least ten minutes, preferably half an hour, to adjust night vision. So I kept on walking and walking. I became quite mystified and puzzled by it all. The field wasn't that big. Or was it?

After what seemed a lifetime, I suddenly stumbled and fell into some furrows, freshly ploughed. I just could not believe it. These furrows were at the bottom end of the airfield. Instead of walking approximately south-west to return to the guardroom, I had slowly changed direction to end up roughly at the south-east corner of the aerodrome. I made the return journey up the tarmac road past the billets and administration block to the guardroom. The journey had taken at least double the time it should have done and was certainly double the distance. So much for my short cut and night navigation!

I completed my spell of guard duty at Southam and returned to Ansty, where I was immediately put on guard duty the same night. I began and finished my spell at No. 9 EFTS, on guard!

On completion at No. 9 EFTS, we were to go on fourteen days' leave before reporting to RAF PDC (Personnel Dispersal Centre) at Heaton Park, Manchester.

Heaton Park was nothing more than a despatch centre for overseas training. We had little or no training there apart from the odd lecture or so. Cliff and I managed to stick together on arrival and for billeting. We all craved private billets. Most of our intake was allocated a Nissen hut within the park grounds.

Heaton Park was a normal suburban park with lawns, gardens and shrubberies. It even had a bandstand, which looked quite like a stage. The area in front of the bandstand was a flat square, free of grass and made an ideal parade or assembly ground. (Perhaps the RAF had modified it.)

We assembled in front of the bandstand daily and were given an introductory lecture – all the dos and don'ts. Squadron Leader Turnbull was in charge of the postings. Everyone hoped for an early posting to Canada, South Africa, Rhodesia or the USA.

Heaton Park was not a popular place, mainly because its function was to post people as quickly as possible. If it were not possible, they needed to give you something to do. This usually meant some sort of fatigues, guards, fire picket etc.

On 26 April Cliff and I were notified that we could continue training as pilots. We were delighted. Our intake was fairly lucky; a posting came along for most in about a week. In the meantime we had various medical checks, inoculations and vaccinations where necessary. We were whisked off to Manchester for a swimming test in the local baths. Then, before we knew it, the whole lot of us were posted. On 27 April 1943 we were notified of a draft to the USA, to various BFTSs (British Flying Training Schools). Cliff, Ray and Johnny Walker were on the draft. I was only a reserve.

You will understand how I felt about losing my former roommates. Although I hoped I would be needed as a reserve, I was very disappointed at not being on the actual draft. However, I wasn't as unfortunate as some who were to be travelling reserves. These lads went on the draft and travelled right up to the dockside, only to return to Heaton Park because they were not needed. Those who remained passed the time doing various fatigues.

The prospect of a further early posting was in everyone's minds. I found myself devoid of mates. Fortunately I had met Edna by then so I wasn't too badly off in the evenings. However, the agony was to be short-lived for we soon found ourselves on another draft, much to our delight.

Perhaps I should explain that Squadron Leader Turnbull had promised all the unwanted reserves on the last draft ('travelling' or not) that they would all be on the very next draft. It seemed too good to be true. The Squadron Leader kept his word. We could hardly believe our luck.

We'd been kitted out for the last draft and then had to return most of our gear. It largely depended on the type of climate and geographical location of your posting as to the type of kit issued. We had been allowed to keep some of the more general stuff previously issued, which saved some of the bind.

Our posting was known as the 'Towers Scheme', something to do with flying boats at Pensacola! The name conjured up an image of a US naval air station in Florida, a memory of a Robert Taylor film 'Curtiss Helldivers' at Pensacola. I wasn't keen on the flying boat idea really. Spitfires seemed more my line, I thought, provided I could enjoy the aerobatics.

I had, by now, forgotten about night fighters and also, by way of a change, had even considered bombers. I suppose the majestic sight of the occasional Wimpey (Wellington aircraft) at Aberystwyth had contributed to this change of opinion. We frequently watched these apparently very solid-looking camouflaged bombers flying out over Cardigan Bay. They were OTU (Operational Training Unit) crews on cross-country exercises, sometimes complete with self-tow drogue streamed for air-firing practice for their own air gunners.

With our kitting out and medicals complete, the inevitable FFI, plus a bag of sandwiches, we were off 'for real' on our journey to Gourock and the *Queen Elizabeth*. We didn't know our destination at our departure from Heaton Park, only rumours.

It was a good feeling to be on our way at last. We were all too excited and cheerful about going overseas and the prospect of more flying to worry about the possibility of U-Boat attack. Strangely enough, although we crossed the Atlantic at the height of the German U-Boat war in April/May 1943, nothing happened.

CHAPTER 4

Flying Training in the USA

New York; Fort Slocum; United States Navy Grosse Ile

We arrived at New York in the late afternoon. The following is an extract from my diary.

21 May – Today was one of the greatest days of my life. In poor weather we entered New York harbour in a fog, which cleared later as we passed the Statue of Liberty and Brooklyn City. We had a splendid view of Brooklyn Bridge. The Statue of Liberty, looking unbelievably significant, the skyscrapers of Manhattan island, the Empire State, Rockefeller and Woolworth buildings. It is only when you sail past this spectacle that you realise you are really in the USA, a great country, hardly touched materially by war.

On entering our wharf we saw HMT *Queen Mary*, which had just returned from Australia. Also the *Normandie* in a pitiful state. She lay on one side, half submerged, the upper structure badly discoloured due to the effects of sea water. To me it looked like a good job of sabotage. She, with the *Queen Mary* and the *Queen Elizabeth* would have made a fine trio of large troop transporters and I hate to think of the loss we must have suffered by the tragic destruction of such a magnificent French liner.

As we pulled alongside our wharf, some of our chaps threw coins to the 'Yank' soldiers and dockworkers. Later, toilet rolls and electric light bulbs followed, much to our delight. After this, the US Military Police came aboard and everyone, including myself, booed and laughed at them. Consequently, we were ordered to quieten down.

We spent the night peacefully on board, the skyline a blaze of light. This was New York's 'dim-out', which was presumably to diminish the amount of skyline glare and so reduce the silhouette of Allied merchant vessels visible to submarines.

We disembarked just before lunch onto a ferry that took us away from New York to a quieter stretch, up river. I remembered to say goodbye to the MN (Merchant Navy) Steward the night before. I'd met him at the top of the gangplank as he was about to go for a stroll into New York City. He noticed our excitement and comments about getting ashore into the big city and said it meant nothing to him as he did it regularly every fortnight! He made it sound as if the journey was always a 'milk run' like we'd had. Not one word about U-Boats ever passed his lips. (I was told that the 'Lizzie' would take some catching at 30-plus knots by night with zig-zag courses by day. Also, she was fairly well armed. There had been the gunnery drill at about mid-Atlantic but apart from the noise, we were unaffected below decks.) My Merchant Navy friend wished us all good luck with our courses and departed down the gangway.

We arrived at Fort Slocum, an island in the Long Island Sound, after a trip of some three hours, in very warm sunshine and pleasant surroundings. The US Army Camp was pre-war built, it had many fine buildings, greens and gardens with tree-lined roads and pathways decorated with the odd ancient cannon.

Fort Slocum was to be the most splendid camp I was ever on. The barrack rooms were excellent, with really first-class fittings, superior bedding and toilet facilities. The messing too was very unusual for RAF cadets. Everyone on the unit ate in the same mess hall! Officers and other ranks, or as the Yanks would say, officers and 'enlisted men'! It was not unusual to find a US Army Captain or Major nearby, enjoying his meal, as if you'd always been there. The food was excellent. We couldn't have wished for better. We soon learnt to adapt to American tastes in both meat and vegetables. Our chips were their 'French fried potatoes', their steak was really 'T' bone steak. If you had eggs you had a choice of 'sunny side up' or 'easy over' (done both sides). Being mostly youngsters, we very soon adapted, perhaps too much and too soon. There was a tendency to take things for granted very quickly. We didn't realise how very lucky we were.

Fort Slocum appeared to be a sort of Transit Camp; presumably it dealt with arrivals from the UK, generally American Army personnel.

We RAF were there by chance. We should have gone to the RAF PDC at Moncton, New Brunswick, Canada (despite ultimate destinations in the USA). Fortunately for us there was an outbreak of Scarlet Fever at Moncton and it was for this reason that we were to get approximately two weeks of American hospitality and a new way of life, which we all enjoyed immensely.

Our FAA (Fleet Air Arm) cadets were a fine bunch of lads and made friends very easily. It was not uncommon at Fort Slocum, and later at Grosse Ile, to see pairs of RAF and FAA cadets becoming mates, some for the duration of their time in the USA.

1 June – We are all confined to camp. I suppose this means we're moving. Went to the camp cinema in the evening.

2 June – We were issued with tropical kit, six each khaki shirts, trousers, light underwear, socks and two pairs of shoes. We were also paid $5, very generous of them. Confined again, so I rang up Terry and cancelled our date.

3 June – Posted to USNAS Grosse Ile, near Detroit, Michigan. I rang Terry up for the last time just to say good-bye. We left New York on the 6 pm train.

We arrived in the early hours after travelling 600 miles by train. We soon found that the average Yank was far more patriotic than the Limey equivalent, although their war had only been going for eighteen months, compared with ours of nearly four years. At every stop there was the inevitable trolley of coffee, hot dogs, cookies and candies, surrounded by super-looking American women of *all* ages. These women were very well dressed, their make-up perfect. They all wore nylons and most wore light sweaters or blouses, since it was summer time. The average American female put ours 'straight in the shade', that is, by their appearance. Mind you, they just loved our accent. Some couldn't get over it and some never did!

The air base at Grosse Ile was at the southern tip of the island where the Detroit River flows into Lake Eyrie. It was very nicely positioned for a naval air station for, whichever way you took off in an aircraft, you went straight out over the water. (We never asked how deep it was!)

4 June – On arrival at Detroit, two naval lorries took us to the base. Our quarters are quite nice, plenty of room and good food. 'Bags of Bull' on the station – unfortunately. The aircraft here are Stearman N2S2s and Stearman N24s, Spartan NPs and North American Harvards or SNJs, i.e., three biplane types plus the latter a low wing monoplane.

5 June – Confined to barracks owing to being in quarantine. Had some PT in morning and afternoon. I got quite sunburnt.

6 June – Still in 'Q'. More PT so we won't get stiff.

7 June – The MO [Medical Officer] passed all of us out of 'Q'. We played a game of 'all-in rugger' during PT today. Visited camp cinema in evening.

We were fortunate enough to have a USN Chief Petty Officer in charge as a disciplinarian. He seemed hostile the first few days until he got to know us as individuals and then things were greatly improved. He was really quite a guy – we liked him a lot.

9 June – I drew a set of ground school text books on flying; meteorology; engines; navigation; aircraft and warship recognition. Also, had lectures and 'special PT', which included boxing and wrestling. In the afternoon we had aircraft maintenance in the hangars, and were introduced to American parachutes and life jackets.

10 June – More ground school, mainly on indoctrination and theory of flight. In the afternoon we started our Flight Board and Parachute Watches (assisting with Flight Notice Board entries and issuing of parachutes and life jackets to pupils and instructors).

After the parachute watches came the drill for flying on the circuit at Grosse Ile. We would be flying in the next couple of days.

The Stearman N2S2 was much larger than the Tiger Moth. It was more powerful with a 200-hp Lycoming radial engine. It was a heavier aircraft and more robust. In general, all the cadets liked the Stearman, remembering that it was summertime too. We had no idea how they coped in the winter with open cockpits.

The various Flying Regulations in use with the USN at Grosse Ile were very stiff in comparison with those of the RAF at home or the RCAF in Canada. There were really too many to remember and some were almost ridiculous.

One brilliant rule was that if you saw the red flag flying you were not supposed to land. Perhaps you can imagine how difficult it was to spot a red flag from anywhere, especially dead over the airfield at the regulation 500 feet up. Or we could be up to a mile away, keeping a lookout for other aircraft using that particular flying circuit. The flag was usually flown on or near the Control Tower or equivalent building. Many cadets were to fall foul of this rule and end up with some form of disciplinary action.

15 June – Had my cockpit check-out in the morning by Ensign South. Ground school lectures in afternoon.

16 June – Spent thirty minutes in the link trainer (a flight simulator) setting courses. At 11.50 I was due to have my first flight.

On the mornings or afternoons that we were due to fly, we always visited the Flight Section first. This was to ensure 'if and when' we were due to have a training flight.

The Flight Section possessed a very large set of black boards. They were 6 foot high and gave columns of information showing aircraft number, instructors' and pupils' names, flying exercise number and take-off time. All flying training was for one and a half hours per session.

On 16 June the flight board notified that I was to fly with Ensign Greig. The exercise number was A1 (straight and level, climbing and gliding turns). Greig, a great big good-natured USN officer, came into the Flight Section looking for 'Brome'. (It took a few days to get the Lieutenant Commander in charge of the flight board entries to accept that my name really was Broome.)

Ensign Greig and I walked to the allocated Stearman in the aircraft parking area. Almost immediately two Navy 'enlisted men' appeared from nowhere. These air mechanics were there to 'wind her up', as soon as we were ready.

Greig indicated how to check the aircraft over, while walking around with me, indicating the control surfaces, ailerons, elevators and rudder, following with wheels, tyres, struts and bracing wires. We then climbed into the Stearman, having put on the parachute harness, complete with seat-type parachute. We strapped ourselves into the aircraft. Greig checked the instrument panel with me, also illustrating how to check the correct movement of the control surfaces, using the control column and rudder pedals. He indicated the brake pedal movement by depressing the rudder bar pedals. The fuel cock, magnetos, switches and fire extinguisher were also identified.

'All OK for starting up Brome? Sorry, Broome?' I noticed the big grin in the mirror and the thumbs up, given by Greig's chamois leather gloved hand. I nodded in return.

'Well, let me see you start her then?'

'Christ,' I thought. 'Bloody hell!'

'Well come on then, lad.' Another big grin in the mirror! I gulped a couple of times, looked at the two mechanics, both enjoying the moment, one with a grin, the other an encouraging wink and thumbs up.

'Switches off.'

'Switches off,' I said, hopefully loud and clear.

The USN mechanics inserted the cranking handle into the socket behind the radial engine, just forward of the mainplanes and centrally in the fuselage. They began to rotate the handle, one mechanic on each side, both cranking away in circular motion. The generator began to whine. The prop began to rotate, slowly at first, then faster and faster!

'Gas on.'

'Gas on, Sir.'

'Switches on.'

'Switches on, Sir.'

'Contact.'

'Contact, Sir.'

The 200-hp Lycoming engine fired, coughed twice, belched blue smoke and then gave a roar, which blended into the rhythmic sound that was soon to become so familiar.

The mechanics removed the chocks on a signal from the instructor pilot. Ensign Greig taxied out to the runway in use, using the perimeter track from the aircraft park. The perimeter track was of considerable length, passing in front of the main hangars and Control Tower. It was in regular use by instructors and pupils and since the one and a half hour flying sessions all commenced at the same time, often the 'peri' track became overcrowded and plagued by queues of aircraft.

Once we reached the main runway, Greig lined her up and opened the throttle. We were airborne in seconds, climbing to 500 feet, the circuit height.

'We'll have to go back, Broome, I have some grit in my eye.' I noticed the Ensign was not wearing goggles, only sunglasses.

After landing and parking the aircraft we walked back to the Flight Section.

'Sorry Broome, I should know better than to wear these,' Greig said, rubbing his eye and waving the sunglasses. 'I'll see you later, after I've been to Sick Quarters.'

'OK Sir, hope all goes well,' I replied. Momentarily, I wondered if he would be treated by the attractive WAVES (Women Accepted or Voluntary Emergency Service) officer I had met on the previous day.

We flew again on 17 June. This was my first real flight in a Stearman. As soon as we were airborne, Greig (speaking through the one-way tube – instructor to pupil only) checked that I was OK in the rear cockpit. As he spoke, Greig looked into the specially arranged mirror for acknowledgement from his pupil. He was always sure to check that I understood his instructions, often backing up with visual signals, which I soon learnt to accept and answer rapidly. The latter I gave with grins or nods in the mirror!

We followed the flight plan of the aerodrome, a left-hand circuit, until we reached the outgoing line of marker buoys in the Detroit River. Turning then to fly over the water to the mainland, keeping to the marked route, we climbed to reach 1000 feet over land. (On our return we were to use a differently positioned set of marker buoys, descending to 500 feet, the air base circuit height.) We believed that the marker buoys were there to help locate our position in the river, should we have to ditch due to engine failure. More likely, it was to avoid collisions, especially with so many aircraft using the marked route to the base at the same time.

We always wore the bright yellow life jacket, USN flat pattern, air-cylinder inflated, which tied on with tapes around the waist and between the legs. These looked quite different from the 'Mae West' style life jacket issued to RAF aircrews in the UK.

Also, we wore the American seat-type parachute and harness, which had a crude type of fastening with three large dog clips. We thought these clips were a clumsy design when compared with the simple, quick-release box fastening that was part of the standard RAF parachute harness. We were never to fly without life jacket and parachute.

Once over the mainland, Greig said 'You've got her Broome', holding his hands above his head, with another big grin in the mirror. I flew mostly straight and level and also made the occasional medium turn as and when directed by the instructor.

We flew around to the various satellite fields to allow me to gain experience in handling a different aircraft and to discover the location of these practice airfields. They were Ash Field, just grass, for early solo flying; Newport, an all-concrete circular shape for power approach and landing; Custer Field, grass again, used for 'S' turns to circle; and finally, an 'L'-shaped field, more grass, for emergency landings, known as 'small field procedure'.

We returned to Grosse Ile after the normal one and a half hour dual instruction. I landed the Stearman without problem; the instructor seemed happy anyway!

The early flying lessons with the USN presented few problems for the RAF cadets as we had all flown before. The RN lads, however, were not so fortunate, having no previous flying instruction. They were expected, as we were, to solo after twelve hours' dual.

18 June – Flew again for one hour, thirty minutes and received more practice at take-off and landing using Custer Field.

19 June – Did spins, stalls and inverted flight. The latter I had always been afraid of. Surprisingly, it was quite OK – providing you are well strapped in, there is hardly any difference.

20 June – Flew again to Custer and as we approached my instructor saw some Curtiss high-wing reconnaissance aircraft so we joined the formation at 120 mph. We waved 'hello' and then returned to normal flying instruction. I did a few landings at Custer afterwards.

The Stearman was a good, strong aircraft, powerful in its role as a primary trainer. It was manoeuvrable too and fully aerobatic.

Ensign Greig soon noticed that I had a problem with rudder control on take-off. I had a tendency to over-correct the swing that sometimes occurred during take-off. Usually this was due to the wind direction and also the engine torque. Therefore, when I over-corrected, we'd 'S' down the runway with Greig bellowing in my ear to 'keep it straight'. Sometimes he seemed to be almost able to turn to look fully backwards in his seat and bellow at me over my windscreen, having slipped the speaking tube mouthpiece onto his chin. Only once did he get a little concerned, when I appeared to have taken longer to get airborne and swung towards a group of men working near the end of the runway. However, when we missed them by a few feet the Ensign turned to give me one of his self-satisfied grins, saying 'You certainly missed 'em – Brum, Brome or whatever your god-damned name is! You don't have to use all the damned concrete, just 'cos it's there.'

Once I had become used to going into and out of the Main Base and had a fair idea of the various satellites, Greig would simply say, after take-off, 'OK, Broome, you've got her.' Once clear of the base circuit, he would add 'Take me to Custer or Ash or Newport.' He specified the height too but after a lesson or so he would leave it to me unless I was too low or wasting time climbing.

> OK Broome, give me a spin to the left. Did you hear me, lad? Well, nod your head then — otherwise how do I know this god-damn tube is working properly? Got your strap tight? Then let's have it. Get the nose back more. Get the bloody nose up lad, god-damn it, how in the hell's it supposed to stall? She's going to the left now, there we go. Christ, don't whack the rudder over like that, you've got her in an opposite spin. Right, very good, now level her off. Make sure I see you look around before we commence any manoeuvre. Jeez, watch that bird. Didn't you see it? [I shook my head.] You'd better keep a good look out 'cos they'll make a real mess of us.

The bird looked massive. It resembled an over-large black gull, probably more than twice the size, perhaps an eagle of some sort, up at about 6000 feet! Thanks to Ensign Greig we had missed it by 30 feet!

When the test became due I looked forward with some confidence to passing. However, the fear of failure was never very far away. This particular event was just one of the many hazards of pilot training. We could fail for a number of reasons. If we messed up a test, sometimes we were able to get re-tested. This was a good thing about the USN because this was usually a certainty. (With the RAF and RCAF there was normally only one test.) We could also fail one of the fairly frequent medicals. We could fail the ground school programme; one subject was usually enough. We could have flying or taxiing accidents, which, if serious enough, could get a trainee eliminated. Breaking any one of the more serious flying rules meant certain elimination.

There was also what was known as 'attitude'. This is not easy to describe but it could be a cadet's aggressive attitude towards the discipline, flying rules or any instructor. A careless attitude to even the training programme could result in being CT (ceased training).

Ensign Greig seemed reasonably confident of my flying ability. On the last flight before the check, he wished me luck. 'Don't try so hard, Broome and you'll do all right.'

I was due to fly the solo check with Lieutenant (junior grade) Crawford. I became quite tense while waiting for him. I had not flown with, or even seen this guy before. Once we had got to the bright yellow Stearman I checked the aircraft over while the USN mechanics looked on. I climbed in, securing the parachute harness and checking the small compressed air bottle on the life jacket, fastened the silly lap-strap, a six-inch wide strap of khaki webbing. It had a very heavy buckle that locked when you pressed it flat. On some aircraft the buckle could be further retained by a local modification, a thick rubber band. Some of the bands looked like pieces of old motor tyre tube! Real safety stuff!

'Take her out when you're ready,' called the instructor after I'd started the engine. I waved away the chocks and taxied out of the aircraft park and along the perimeter to the runway in use. I had already made a note of the wind direction and also checked to see which runway was in use.

I opened the throttle, pushed the stick forward until the tail came up, corrected a slight swing to port with rudder and we were airborne. I circled the base, heading for the corridor over the river, aware that the instructor had given no further word.

Once we gained the mainland, Lieutenant (jg) Crawford requested 6000 feet. This height meant spins and medium turns, which were accomplished without trouble. A few minutes later down at some 2000 feet (we had lost the rest spinning) the engine cut. I pushed the stick forward and turned the fuel cock on and off to indicate that I knew the cause and then selected a large field ahead. This proved unnecessary as the check pilot had switched the fuel cock on; the engine restarted easily and we were under power again. A few minutes later, during a landing test, we touched down at Custer.

Crawford seemed satisfied and requested 'Take me back to Grosse Ile.'

The journey was completed in fifteen minutes, I made a further three-pointer at base and taxied back to the parking area. Nothing was said during the walk back to the Flight Section.

With his 'chute over one shoulder, like myself, Crawford commented, 'Just watch that swing on take-off, lad, and you'll be OK.'

Crawford walked to the blackboard, picked up a piece of chalk and marked an upward-facing arrow against my name. 'Great,' I thought, 'an upcheck.' This meant a solo flight tomorrow from Ash Field.

We took the waiting transport to Ash fairly early the next day. The satellite field was some miles away on the mainland. We arrived in good time, to be cautioned by the Lieutenant in charge about the red flag: 'Woe betide any of you if you don't obey the rules.' Each of the pupils was allocated an aircraft. It took a few minutes to get mine started, it was the last in the line. I waited for the oil pressure to reach 60 psi. It was still on zero after a further ten minutes, by which time I had the Lieutenant on the wingroot with his head in the cockpit!

'What's the trouble, lad?'

'Oil pressure gauge at zero, Sir.'

'Aw shit, don't bother about that – get the god-damn airplane off the ground.'

'But Sir, we were expressly told not to take off with less than 60 psi.' (We'd received this gen in the lecture on 'flying procedure', two weeks previously.)

'The gauge is wacky, it'll be OK, I don't want to see you here any longer god-damn it, so get this airplane into the air. You kids have some crazy ass ideas. You wear all this god-damn flying gear and it's not necessary,' said the Lieutenant, eyeing the flying boots and gauntlets I was wearing.

'Just get your ass out of here, right now.'

When the Lieutenant had climbed off the wing I opened the throttle and taxied a few yards away to be clear of aircraft on landing approach. I opened the throttle and away went the 'god-damn' aircraft.

Once airborne I took stock of the circuit and noted that the air appeared very bumpy due to slipstream from other aircraft. The oil gauge began to rise slowly and even nearly reached its minimum 'safe' pressure!

We were not supposed to actually land at Ash Field but to use the field as much as possible without landing and without cluttering the sky above. That is, until one and a half hours was completed, after which we landed and then took the truck back to base.

There was always quite a number of aircraft at Ash during a solo spell. The confusion both in the air and on the ground was pretty tumultuous, especially to 'first time' soloists. I was really pleased that I had soloed on Stearmans but was also very glad that I had already soloed in the UK. Otherwise, I feel it could have been a terrifying ordeal. Just imagine flying round and round the circuit for one and a half hours, practising approaches, touchdown and then opening up the throttle to take off again immediately.

The air bumps and slipstream from other aircraft were pretty unnerving to the inexperienced. It was like being part of a real live 'flying circus' staffed by eighteen- and nineteen-year-old pilots. Also, there were quite a few mature trees on one side of the field and there was also a forest of younger trees at the end opposite to the usual landing approach; these trees were mostly firs and were between 15 and 20 feet tall. We flew right over them, after take-off.

When we opened up the throttle to go around again the roar of several Lycoming engines made a stupendous din. We'd need to jockey for position to space ourselves out for safety's sake! 'Safety? What is that?' I thought. That's the reason they have all their god-damn rules! H'mm, no wonder there was no instructor to be seen at Ash. Perhaps it wasn't safe for them? Often on manoeuvring for a landing, somebody would be bound to steal your line of approach. All you got was his slipstream and you would have to overshoot and go around yet again. It was sheer lunacy to have so many solo pupils airborne at the same time. It was tempting disaster. It wasn't too long before it arrived.

I soon noticed that flying time was easily wasted near any of the satellite fields due to overcrowding. It was a very different matter if you were to practise spins, steep turns or wing-overs. For these you needed height and air space. So you flew away, climbed and found it.

29 June – No flying today for me. Lectures as usual. Received a letter from Cliff, who is at Miami, Oklahoma, No. 3 BFTS and flying Fairchilds, he has completed 2 hours solo. The unfortunate news is the worst I have received so far, that poor Cliff has been eliminated from future pilot training and has re-mustered as Straight Navigator and is to go to Canada for the new course.

30 June – Did my solos today, made some fairly good approaches and returned to Ash Field safely and on one occasion I nearly got put on report for landing when the red flag was lowered.

I find that soloing here requires a lot of concentration and alertness if you are going to live. My total flying time is now 28 hours, 10 minutes dual and 3 hours, 10 minutes solo (i.e., 14 hours, 10 minutes dual and 10 minutes solo at Ansty – 14 and 3 hours solo here at Grosse Ile).

2 July – Yesterday was the funeral of two Fleet Air Arm cadets, one of whom was on our course. We knew our colleague well. He was an extremely likeable lad, always so full of fun, never without a smile. He was the smallest of the FAA cadets, known to us all affectionately as 'Titch'. Both cadets were killed during very tragic flying accidents.

'Titch' was flying with his instructor and was being taught how to recover from a stall. During the recovery (a sharply executed, fairly steep dive) Titch's safety belt became unfastened. He was thrown out of the cockpit and apparently hit both the windscreen and top mainplane during his accidental exit. The latter stunned him, we believe, as he appeared to be unable to pull the ripcord of his parachute.

The other cadet had just finished his course and flew over to see his girl and did a few crazy manoeuvres to show off. One of them was a 'chandelle' (a wing-over). He stalled, spun and was too low to pull out and crashed into the beach on the edge of the lake.

The funeral was attended by their friends in the Fleet Air Arm. No RAF personnel were allowed to attend, much to our regret.

4 July – Had quite a good time in Detroit, went to a USO [United Service Organization] house party. Later Sid Oldfield and I spent the night in a USO dormitory and slept from 4 am until 9.30 am. Then a smashing breakfast – a dish of bacon and eggs (4 rashers of bacon and 2 eggs), finishing with strawberries and cream. I enjoyed it all very much and it only cost 67 cents, including coffee and toast. (An unknown Yank paid for the first course. It could have been one of the instructors? We never knew until we went to pay the bill, it was pleasantly puzzling!)

Returned to camp at 11 am, no flying in the afternoon owing to bad weather.

5 July – Went to Ash for one and a half hours solo. Made a few shots at circle landings, did wing-overs and steep turns. My attempts at circles were not too good as I kept getting 'cut out'.

The main points of 'B' stage on the US Navy course were: 'small fields', 'S' turns to circle and wing-overs. For the first two exercises an airfield was needed.

We were *not* allowed to practise the 'small field' emergency procedure without an instructor so we were unable to get enough practice! Whatever the manoeuvre, if we were not allowed to fly it solo for some of the time, we failed to get sufficient practical experience. The field was 'L'-shaped with very tall trees to one side. On some flights it was necessary to side-slip to lose surplus height and so, occasionally, make a good landing, this being necessary depending on the wind velocity. How we missed those trees each time I will never know. Sometimes they were really very close, with only feet to spare. We still did not seem to have any sort of phobia about the dangers! However, 'small fields' seemed to be quite the bugbear of the course.

I found side-slipping rather exhilarating because the airstream missed the windscreen and came almost directly in sideways at face level. It was quite a simple manoeuvre to get in and out of; stick over to a forward corner of the cockpit, port or starboard, and you were side-slipping. When you were ready to straighten, you simply centralised the stick and applied sufficient rudder in the desired direction to return to a straight line of approach.

The snag, of course, with 'small fields' was that the instructor always 'cut the gun' at the maximum position, upwind, i.e., in the dead opposite position to your line of glide approach! So it really wasn't funny, especially to lads with just a few hours' solo to their credit. (Perhaps one should remember that in World War I, pilots with as many flying hours as we had now were sent to front-line squadrons!)

The most important thing in 'small fields' practice was to whip the nose of the aircraft around sharply in a full 180° steep turn, wings vertical, while you still had a fair amount of forward speed, before the airspeed dropped to a gliding speed. Then, with nose down slightly, you kept the Stearman at a good glide angle, position and speed, until the final turn into the field. Very often a pupil's estimation of the position of touchdown, considering the variable wind strength, could be quite difficult.

I realise now that I hadn't learnt enough about the art of 'small field' procedure. It was one of my shortcomings, which gave trouble more than once. At the time it seemed surprising that we weren't allowed to tackle 'small fields' procedure solo. Now I realise that the field was dangerous enough as it was. It would have been more dangerous with solo pupils 'cutting the gun' all over the place. (Was it not bad enough on solo at Ash Field?) It was difficult enough to get into the field with an instructor present. The main danger lay in the small size of the field and the number of trees in the vicinity, particularly those right along one side of the 'L' shape.

The other major flying training bind on the course at Grosse Ile – 'S' turns to circle – sounds simple enough, especially when you learn that the circle size is 100 feet diameter! However, 100 feet ceases to be large when you approach into varying wind speeds, on different days and try to land the whole aircraft inside the 100 feet diameter. It is particularly difficult when you are required to make a glide approach from 500 feet on the downwind leg and execute a full 'S' turn on the final approach to touchdown (inside the 100 feet).

Half an 'S' was not good enough. Neither was a couple of 'wing waggles' to simulate an 'S' turn! It had to be a real 'S' turn or it didn't count. On *numerous* occasions I could have 'got in' without an 'S' turn at all! The general idea of circle shooting was to simulate the accuracy needed for aircraft carrier deck landings. Quite a number of the instructors, and a high proportion of pupils, were also inclined to land with a tail-down (arrester hook-type) attitude. Even the RAF pupils, myself included, soon came to consider this as an 'elite' way of landing.

In addition to judgement, range and lining up the Stearman, the 'S' turns and final tail-down landing, these manoeuvres alone were difficult enough for pupils to achieve correctly. There was also the inevitable 'cutting in', by other pupils in the main, but many times instructors were guilty and would take advantage of solo pupils. We were unable to react, except to retain our anger and try another 'shot'. One could hardly ball out an ensign or a lieutenant; besides, we feared getting put on report for flying too close to another aircraft, especially one that had an instructor on board.

There was also a certain amount of friendly rivalry amongst the instructors. They would, on busy occasions, shake their fists and make other rude signs at fellow instructors trying to 'cut in' on a circle shot. The most dangerous thing was to fly too close to another pupil – no one could stop that.

The wing-over was a really super manoeuvre – at least it was to rookie aviators. Apart from the spin and the steep turn we didn't do anything spectacular except for the side-slip at this stage of the training.

When I first began to try the wing-over I was far too tense. I was far too afraid of flying the aircraft in any banking manoeuvre beyond 45° *on my own*. The problem solved itself unexpectedly one day when I received a letter from Bill Hall who informed me not only of his graduation as a pilot, but also of his commission as a pilot officer plus a posting to a flying instructors' school. The letter had a morale-boosting effect and I went up solo twice the day after getting Bill's news. I flew out of Grosse Ile to well down south where I could easily fix my position by the main road running to Toledo and a selection of oblong fields and hedges at 90° to the road. It was here that I learnt to wing-over properly, purely because I had heard of Bill's success. It seemed to have a tonic effect. If he can do it, so can I.

The general idea of the wing-over is to change direction in a very short time and to retain the same height and airspeed. I was at about 4000 feet. I felt lonely if I went higher than 6000 feet, yet this was enough for all aerobatics, let alone wing-overs.

The main object, apart from the turn itself, was to keep the airspeed within certain limits. The climbing speed began at about 90 k, dropping to 55 k on the full 90° bank, before levelling off on the opposite course, having reached 90 k again.

The manoeuvre begins with a climbing turn, say, to port. You apply left rudder and aileron, while easing the stick back slightly to get into the climbing turn. Once the aircraft has reached the high position at 90° to the original direction and is now at a full vertical bank with airspeed at 55 k, with the control column centralised, then still with left rudder, the stick is pushed forward to the left-hand corner of the cockpit, to give a diving turn before levelling off at 90 k. The aircraft should now be at the *same* height as it began, but on a reversed course exactly. (Hence the flying practice over squared or oblong fields.)

Some of the instructors were very keen on the wing-over, they seemed to set great store by it. The RAF, I found out later, knew little about it except that some people consider it similar to the RAF's stall turn. (It wasn't really because in a wing-over the aircraft isn't stalled if flown correctly.)

The area I chose for actual manoeuvres was well clear of the various satellite fields and so was good for this purpose. The inevitable snag was that it took some minutes to reach from the base, so about half an hour of each solo period was spent flying straight and level to and from the zone. I could have practised closer but other air traffic would be a problem, similar to circle shooting. (It was quite normal for pupils to use about fifteen minutes each way to approach the various practice fields and to return to the main base.)

Ensign Greig seemed very pleased one day when I had flown the Stearman out of Grosse Ile.

'Do me some wing-overs,' he said quite idly and then appeared to drop off to sleep. I'm not sure whether it was the second or third wing-over, but quite suddenly he shot up in his seat and turned, giving that big grin.

Face aglow, he slipped down the mouthpiece and shouted 'By God, them's some wing-overs, Broome. Do me some more.' So I did. He was so pleased he beat 'seven colours' out of the aircraft fabric fuselage with his gloved fists!

A few days before, Ensign Greig had given his instructions about spinning, saying 'Go do some solo spins – you can do them, Broome. Yes, you can do them, don't start before 4000 and keep a good look out.'

I gasped inwardly and tried to look sincere when I said 'Yes Sir, OK Sir.' I thought 'Hell, he must be joking. Solo spins, in one of these Stearman screaming Banshees?' When you stalled an 'N-Two-S-Two' it went over on one wing and down in a deadly spiral like some writhing, protesting, live, wild reptile!

The next time I saw Greig he asked if I had done the spinning.

'Yes Sir,' I replied

'How many did you do?'

'Two right, two left, Sir.'

'All OK were you?' enquired Greig.

'Yes Sir, all OK.'

'Very good' said Greig. 'It will give you some confidence.'

I felt not only a coward, but a damned liar and a cheat by any standard. I wondered if I would have deceived him for long? Because what you can't do alone you can do with an instructor. There was just a chance with the spinning because I could do it with 'him' sitting ahead of me – so how could he know? I don't think I fooled Ensign Greig at all, he was far too smart a guy for that!

However, having received the good news from Bill in Canada, the boost it gave me was so dynamic that, on the way back from the solo wing-overs, I went into Custer and 'hit' two circles out of three. Then just before I returned to Grosse Ile at 4000 feet I let her go into a stall. The aircraft took its time to stall, being lighter with Greig 'missing' (his lost weight made the angle higher). She went over to the left so violently I hit the seat strap and cockpit enclosure hard on the right hip on just the slack. With the wail of the wind, screaming through the bracing wires and through the air-cooled Lycoming engine with the airscrew idling away she was terrifying! She came out OK, so I went into a right-hand spin with similar effect!

It's a pity we didn't give more details in our logbooks. (Usually all flying training manoeuvres were logged by exercise number only.) It seemed so commonplace because we lived in a flying environment.

The 'S' turns and 'small fields' proved to be the major snags on 'B' stage. Once I got through these I thought I would be OK. Many of our colleagues, both RAF and FAA, agreed on this point. Once through 'B' stage, which seemed to us all to be the hardest, the rest seemed fairly straightforward.

After the success with the wing-overs, slips, steep turns and spins, I felt much better about the prospect of aerobatics, which were due next on 'C' stage.

18 July – Flew my first solo from Grosse Ile. Satisfactory flight, weather bumpy, almost 'had it' over Custer while shooting circles at 100 feet. Air bump [slipstream from other aircraft] caused the aircraft to almost invert, rolled over but pulled out OK, lost some 30 feet in height.

First 'B' check with Lieutenant Mason, small field pretty bad, circles poor, two out of six. Got a down-check, wing-overs and steep turns 'shit hot' so the check pilot said.

19 July – Flew second solo from Grosse Ile. Pretty good warm-up. Second 'B' check with Lieutenant Byrd, got a 'down' only on 'small fields' – everything else OK.

There were one or two bright spots for me in the 'B' stage checks. The first was the general compliment that my wing-overs seemed to attract. This was great, especially as I was now a little more than keyed up over the 'B' stage check failure. The last thing I wanted was to be 'washed out' of pilot training.

It soon became known to the rest of the course that I was struggling to survive. However, the comments I received from the other cadets were magnificent. 'Bish' Bacon said I would do it easily, as did Carlyon, Sid Oldfield, Bill Tranter and others. After the second 'B' stage check with Lieutenant Byrd I went before the US Aviation Board and was awarded extra time. My colleagues on the course seemed as enthusiastic for me to pass as for themselves. One cadet, LAC Barton, suggested that if I had his instructor, Lieutenant (junior grade) Kujawa, I would not fail to pass.

'He is the wing-over expert and if you can do wing-overs he *won't* fail you!' was the advice. However, I couldn't simply pick an instructor. It was all done by the Flight Section Lieutenant Commander. It was therefore in the lap of the gods! In any case, these conversations, which were all very good natured and cheerful, especially in this sort of situation, made me hopeful and I wished I could be checked by Kujawa. Impossible, though? The attitude of most of the other cadets was rather special to me because it soon became the barrack room slogan.

'All 'ole Broomie wants is Kujawa,' said Carlyon with a wink and a knowing look.

'Shut up Bacon, leave the lad alone. Take no notice of him, Broomie, he's just pulling your leg. You get Kujawa and you will be on to "C" stage with me!'

24 July – Second solo from Grosse Ile. Practised circle shots, slips and circle landings at Custer. While flying back from Custer I noticed the blood wagon in the woods nearby. The wreckage of two Stearmans could be seen in amongst the trees, close to Ash Field. On my way back to the Main Base I saw the hospital plane, a Piper Cub on its way out. I learned later that Acting/Leading Naval Airman Ingoville (Fleet Air Arm) had been killed in a flying accident. His aircraft was in collision with another FAA student's aircraft. Both were believed to be on first solo. The other chap got off with a broken nose!

26 July – Flew 'B' stage review with Ensign Greig 'dual'. My instructor said I should pass the test easily.

The day of the third 'B' check dawned after completing the extra time awarded. I had looked at the board earlier: there was nothing to report. Later, someone came into the flight waiting room with a big grin.

'You're down to fly with Kujawa.'

'Rubbish, don't believe you,' I said.

'You are, go and have a look, you can't fail now. Kujawa will not fail a pupil who can fly wing-overs.'

'So everyone tells me,' I said and I nipped down the stairs to check the flight time.

Jeepers, they weren't having me on! It really was Lieutenant Kujawa's name on the board next to mine.

I was ready on the dot, with my parachute, life jacket, helmet and goggles, earphones and tube. I met Lieutenant Kujawa at the flight board. We walked out together to the Stearman. Kujawa was dark-haired, not tall but well built and very sun-tanned. He seemed a cheerful and likeable officer. I felt immediately at ease.

'Hello, so you're Broome. See yuh bin havin' a rough time lad? Got two downs already. Just forget it today. Greig says you're good, but you get very tense on these checks.' We reached the aircraft. I checked her over outside, while Kujawa climbed aboard. I then followed, strapped myself into the rear seat and carried out the cockpit check.

'Start her up and take me out to "small fields". Hy'am ready when you're ready.'

Kujawa said no more. I started up and taxied out to the 'into wind' runway and away we went. I turned left onto the circuit at 500 feet flying right around the base and was over the woods alongside our take-off runway. Kujawa was quite a guy. There he was taking a lad up for a check and it was obvious he was enjoying the trip because he began to sing. Yes, with the mouthpiece in position too! 'Siboney' was the popular ditty. 'When you're down Havana way, Siboney.'

I've never forgotten it in all these years. Whenever I hear it I think of Lieutenant Kujawa and of our flight together.

We flew to the 'small field' first, which wasn't too bad, then the wing-overs and steep turns. I got the same big grin and audible applause.

'Christ, kid, you're good on wing-overs,' said Kujawa.

We went on to Custer for the circles. I hit one and a half out of six or seven – very poor. The flight home and into Grosse Ile was uneventful. The check pilot had given me the impression that I would get a 'down check'.

'Sorry kid, I don't want to have to give you a down. I'll recommend you for extra time though. Those wing-overs were absolutely great.' (To get this comment from the 'wing-over expert' was really something.)

We flew on in silence. I landed at the base, taxied to dispersal. We got out of the Stearman almost simultaneously and proceeded to walk to the flight section.

Just before we got to the entrance of the hangar Kujawa turned to me and said 'I'm gonna give you an "incomplete" – due to the weather – understand?'

'Yes Sir,' I replied.

'Your wing-overs were great and if you can do wing-overs like that you can fly! Do you hear me? You've got very good co-ordination – the wing-overs prove it.'

'Thank you Sir.'

We parted, Lieutenant Kujawa went to the instructors' room, while I went to stow my gear.

The lads on the course, as they saw me, wanted to know how I had got on. I told them of Kujawa's remarks about the wing-overs and the 'incomplete'.

'Say Broomie, I told you he'd never fail you if you can fly wing-overs. Didn't I? Crafty beggar, giving an "incomplete"! I told you he wouldn't fail you,' said Barton. Such was the magic of Lieutenant Kujawa. My experience flying with him was the most magnificent and yet emotional moment I was ever to experience as a pilot.

Shortly afterwards I was able to obtain a re-test. Regrettably, the result was the same. I had come to dread the checks so much that I made a mess of them at some stage and from then on the test went badly, including things I normally did well.

My application for extra time seemed hopeful, especially as my own instructor, as well as Lieutenants Kujawa and Castor had put in strong recommendations. However, it was not to be. The US Navy Flying Training Board made very short shrift of my application to continue training with extra flying time. The very strong recommendations from Lieutenants Greig (Lieutenant (junior grade) Greig, recently promoted), Kujawa and Castor were completely ignored. Also, they ignored the recommendation for me to continue the course from two officers who were attending the inquiry. Both officers spoke up on my behalf. One was a USN instructor pilot and the other our own Flight Lieutenant Williams in charge of RAF at Grosse Ile. I was devastated at the board's decision!

Once I had been eliminated or 'washed out' (depending on whose air force you were in) the course and my colleagues moved on without me. I was left to do odd jobs until a posting came through to RCAF Windsor, Canada, on the opposite bank of the river from Detroit. The prospect of losing contact with all my colleagues on the course, especially Sid Oldfield, Bill Tranter, Carlyon, Barton and many others was particularly stunning.

Just before I left the base a mishap worth recording is that of a most spectacular accident that occurred to an FAA cadet due to fly solo out of Grosse Ile. I mentioned earlier that when flying from the main base there was quite a bit of taxiing to be done to get to the runway to be used. The runway on this particular day was the one that ran south, straight out towards the centre of the lake. This meant that in addition to taxiing around the perimeter track, one needed then to taxi along the shorter runway that passed in front of the hangars, Control Tower and other main flight buildings.

The FAA cadet had got as far as the end of the perimeter track and had just turned onto the first shorter runway, but not the take-off runway. He then spotted a pair of his RN mates standing along this runway, waving and making all sorts of rude signs. One of them appeared to wave him off on that particular runway. The cadet in the

Stearman must have thought that either the take-off runway had changed or that he was already on the runway in use. Without hesitation he opened the throttle of the biplane trainer fully and literally 'tore' into the aircraft in front, much to the amazement of the instructor and pupil in that aircraft! Although the solo aircraft ran into the dual at full throttle, the prop of the solo aircraft was shattered to a mere stub so quickly that the damage to the other aircraft stopped a mere six inches behind the pupil's cockpit. Miraculously, no one was hurt. The tail unit had almost completely disappeared and the fuselage behind the pupil was badly lacerated.

Fortunately, the wooden propeller chopped itself up as it screwed its way up the fuselage of the other aircraft. It was the strength of the tubular alloy longerons (i.e., the design of the Stearman fuselage) that saved the life of the pupil in the rammed aircraft. It must have been a terribly frightening experience for that pupil.

Both aircraft had been cleared off the runway to one side when I taxied by later on to fly a Grosse Ile solo. The two aircraft looked a gruesome sight, vacant and forlorn – a lesson to the unwary pilot and to over-enthusiastic sightseers!

CHAPTER 5

Canada

The RCAF; on to Moose Jaw and RAF Caron

I left USNAS Grosse Ile on 11 August 1943 in an estate wagon bound for Windsor, Ontario, with the same cadet that I'd been with on the laundry run. It was a lovely summer's day. We still wore our American-issue khaki and as we passed over the border into Canada, we tried to hide our cigarettes purchased at ridiculous prices just before leaving. This was unnecessary as the Canadian customs officials only glanced inside the vehicle.

'Hello lads, welcome to Canada. Carry on,' they said to the USN driver. We were soon driven to the RCAF station. Our kit was dumped on the gravel roadway outside the administrative buildings, beside a flagpole bearing the RCAF standard, sporting its maple leaf.

The driver bade us farewell and left to return to Grosse Ile. We, meanwhile, were shown to the billets without much fuss and given the mess mealtimes. The 'Discip' Flight Sergeant said we would be required for a Selection Board the next day and to be outside his office at 09.00 hours.

The camp looked pleasant enough. The chatter was 'all Canadian' – the accent, I mean. The grub was much the same. A pleasant change from the USN 'chow'. There was a considerable ease in discipline that I had never experienced before. This was my first RCAF station and I just couldn't believe it. The only real difference, a 'must', was that we were required to salute the RCAF Standard every time we passed the flagpole in daylight (when the flag was flying). We were shown the very stone (painted white of course) where we were supposed to bring up the right arm for the salute and the exact stone the other side of the banner to bring the arm down again!

During the evening of the first day, in the mess, mealtime passed very pleasantly as we listened to the Canadian cadet pilots talking about their experiences in their Tiger Moths during the day. They seemed just like the RAF lads at Ansty and Southam, full of life and enjoying every precious minute of flying time.

It was a very different set-up from Grosse Ile, a more relaxed atmosphere. The Canadian cadets were all very keen and the conversations were continually of flying. They seemed to have lots of confidence; failure was never mentioned.

The discipline was so relaxed that people like us (RAF in transit) were not considered to be on the strength of the unit. We were just passing through and, apart from making us very welcome and very comfortable, we were not really of much interest to the RCAF.

One morning at about 11.00 I was woken up by a Canadian flying officer pilot, the Orderly Officer of the day.

'What on earth are you doing in bed at this time of the morning?' he asked. (It was 11 am and I was in a top bunk of a row of bunk beds.) I explained that I was RAF and was awaiting posting. Whereupon, the officer immediately apologised for waking me up and walked away, saying he was very sorry. He simply left me to it. No one ever worried me again. Nothing had ever happened to me like that in the RAF.

My colleague and I from Grosse Ile paraded the next day for our Selection Board. This comprised three officers – all pilots – a Flying Officer, a Flight Lieutenant and a Squadron Leader. We were interviewed, one at a time. I was last. The officers were extremely courteous and understanding, especially when I was asked to explain my failure at Grosse Ile.

Apparently, I had been given a good report by Lieutenant (jg) Greig USNR and also by Flight Lieutenant Williams RAF, the Officer in Charge of the RAF cadets. There had also been a strong recommendation that I should be retrained as a navigator. However, the Selection Board were not by any means satisfied with the official reasons given for my failing the USN course. The Flight Lieutenant recommended that I be given a flying test in a Canadian Tiger Moth.

Within minutes I was given a flying helmet, goggles and parachute and was up with the same officer, flying around and above Ontario, Canada. I had explained that I hadn't flown a Tiger Moth for months. I was asked to do a steep turn each way, a couple of spins and to land it. I lost some height on the turns but was quite OK on the spins. Also, I put the Tiger Moth down on the runway in a real 'greasy' landing.

Admittedly, the Flight Lieutenant lined her up, and heading for the runway. He then said 'You've got her, do we have a landing?'

So I did just that and was probably more surprised than the instructor, who thought it was absolutely 'wizard stuff'!

When I returned to the Selection Board a few minutes later their minds were already made up.

'We don't know what the stupid Yanks are up to, so we're sending you to an RAF EFTS to do the whole course. We think you'd be OK to continue training as a pilot.'

I just couldn't believe it. Long ago, back at Heaton Park in UK, I'd favoured a flying course in Canada.

After one full day I received an immediate recall, which was sent to the USO at Detroit. I returned to Windsor to receive an immediate posting to No. 33 EFTS Caron, Saskatchewan. Everything had been made ready, including travel warrants and meal tickets for use on the train – a sleeper, direct to Moose Jaw, the nearest prairie town.

I was on the train early next morning with three full kit-bags, including flying kit plus webbing. As the weather was warm I had filled up my water bottle. I'd been taken to the station by an RCAF Corporal, in addition to the MT (Military Transport) driver. I was pleasantly surprised to find that while the Corporal saw me safely on the train, the driver attended to the kit-bags.

'Leave it, laddie. They'll be in the freight car when you get there. You've got your train tickets and meal tickets OK? All the best, lad,' the Corporal said when I went to assist.

Away went the Corporal and the MT driver and I went to find my seat. (I realised then that I was perhaps in the wrong Air Force. I should have been born a 'Canuck' or Canadian – lucky beggars!)

The journey took two full days and nights. I recall that I boarded at Windsor at about 10.00 and arrived at Moose Jaw at about 17.00 on the third day. In the meantime, we had travelled more than two thirds of the way across the North American continent, remembering that Windsor was over 600 miles from New York, our disembarkation port.

Once I had disembarked at Moose Jaw station I soon discovered that I was not alone. There was a whole group of about sixty RAF cadets coming off the train, straight from Moncton NB. These lads were to be my new friends and colleagues on the very next flying course. Most of them were able to collect their kit-bags from a massive heap on the platform. Mine couldn't be found anywhere. I was told it could be days before I got them. Very, very good, I thought, since I had only the clothes I stood up in. My small kit contained only shaving tackle, boot polish, towel and soap. I think I had some spare socks and that was all. It was very warm, being August, especially on the prairies, so the urgency of getting one's kit-bags was very real. Even so, the clothes they contained would not all be clean since several days were spent both at Grosse Ile and Windsor, where I was 'in transit' awaiting posting, and one was not allowed to send laundry at these times as there wasn't time to get it back.

My bags turned up three or four days later. It seemed an absolute age. However, it wasn't long before I possessed clean clothes, to some degree. I was at least capable of washing a pair of socks, a shirt and a set of underwear with toilet soap, which wasn't as bad as it sounds. The RAF in those days wasn't expected to wash its own laundry, it was all provided free at every unit. We only paid laundry bills when we wanted anything special done, like having our collars starched (at the Chinese laundry), a very popular practice.

I soon settled down to life at No. 33 EFTS Caron. It was an RAF station, quite comfortable with good RAF-type food as opposed to American or Canadian. A certain amount of American and Canadian food had been a change at Grosse Ile and Windsor. However, on USN or RCAF stations, quite naturally, the diet was based on their most popular national dishes. Generally speaking, their baked beans were foul, being mostly in gravy, so were their sausages, which had a cheesy taste that seemed 'off' to the UK palate. It was common to serve bacon with pancakes and then pour a ladle of maple syrup all over them! My dodge was to present a slice of bread for the bacon, which was usually served first, and so allow the pancakes to have the syrup to themselves (much to the utter amazement of the catering staff). A British bacon sandwich followed by 'flapjacks' with maple syrup tasted very good first thing in the morning! Especially as it had been preceded by a mug of delicious Canadian apple or citrus fruit juice, finishing with several slices of bread and marmalade.

The course started well with a lecture on the fitting and use of parachutes. I happened to be at the front of the group of trainee-pilots and a civilian parachute instructor thrust a seat-type parachute into my arms.

'Put it on, let me see how many of you were paying attention,' he said.

It was simple for me to put on and fasten the harness properly for I had been doing it for some months. The only difference between the

Canadian 'chute and those of the USN was that the former had the quick-release box into which all the straps fed.

I was asked to get up onto a table and demonstrate what I was doing. The instructor seemed very pleased with my efforts and allowed me to pull the ripcord. Later, all the cadets had a good laugh at my expense when I was asked how I would bale out of a Cornell aircraft.

'Roll her on her back and pull the pin out of the Sutton seat harness,' I said. (This was a four-strap harness, i.e., two straps over the shoulders and two from the seat base fastening approximately in the centre of one's waist).

It seemed too much of a professional answer for the instructor. He said 'Why don't you just climb out on to the wing?' I said I would if there were time. The rest of the class seemed to think the latter answer was very good!

We had the usual lectures on the Cornell aircraft (which had a 200-hp in-line Ranger engine). We were lectured on the action in the event of fire; bale-outs; weather on the prairies; dust storms and cumulo-nimbus cloud; thunderstorms; the effect of hailstones reputedly the size of golf balls; the practice flying zone; the circuit at Caron and the flashing beacon (a recall sign) for we were still without radio, as we were flying primary trainers.

We were given our flying map and spent some class time 'hatching' in our flying zone. We noted that RAF Assiniboine was to the south, RCAF Davidson to the north, Moose Jaw and Regina to the east, Swift Current and Medicine Hat to the west.

Our flying area was to the west of Caron, consisting mainly of wheat fields, the odd farmstead and grain elevator or other building. We had the main east–west railway line for the southern boundary. To the north-west we had a fair-sized river. We each marked this boundary on our personal flying map (the USN had not supplied an area map). I thought it was a grand idea. At least we knew where we were and there was little excuse for getting lost.

Nevertheless, one cadet on the course managed to do this. Just after lunch one day, most cadets noticed that LAC Lamb was missing. Later, there was a message from Flying Control that he was at an RCAF drome in the west. Apparently, poor old Lambie had taken off and climbed and climbed, up to 10,000 feet. Evidently, being up that high didn't worry him! When he looked around he hadn't a clue where he was. After some stooging around he came upon an RCAF Training Station and put down to find where he had landed. I'm not sure whether or not he flew back next day by himself. Sometimes an instructor needed to go to collect a pupil in this predicament.

I met my instructor, Sergeant Thom, and we flew together for the first time on 23 August. Thom was a likeable fellow. I liked him because he had a patient, yet carefree manner about him. Nothing was too much trouble for him. Whatever predicament one got into, one only had to ask Thom and he would immediately go into detail, both verbally and practically. Often, too, when you made a mistake, Thom promptly put you right, explaining and showing you 'how and why'. Yes, he was that good!

Although he was a sergeant and I only an LAC, he seldom pulled rank and, if he did, it was only as an instructor. He never became pompous like some of the officer instructors. If one had a bad-tempered instructor it was more likely to be an officer than a sergeant. The sergeants seemed to be 'one of us' and not a cut above you. There were many very good officers, both as instructors and later, as I found also, in Bomber Command but that's another story.

I suppose, being a youngster, I felt more at home with an NCO. One day in the distant future, but for the grace of God, this preference for NCO pilots could have ended my life.

As you will have guessed, Sergeant Thom was a good pilot and a good instructor. We flew the usual air familiarisation in the aircraft. The Cornell was unique as a low-wing monoplane primary single-engine trainer. She had enclosed cockpits, each with sliding hood, brakes, flaps and a steerable tail-wheel, the latter by virtue of its ability to rotate on its mounting shaft and re-centre itself in the tail-wheel socket. I thoroughly enjoyed flying the Cornell, especially as the pupil normally flew in the front cockpit.

The RAF Station and the Chief Flying Instructor (CFI) were all so much more acceptable to me than the USN had been. The ground staff, including some ground instructors, were civilians employed by the Boundary Bay Flying Training School. The Station was run entirely by the RAF and we ate British-type meals in the dining hall. The RAF flying discipline was exactly the same as at Ansty. The instructors, Flight Commander and Chief Flying Instructor were also all RAF.

I found Flying Officer Nathan, our Flight Commander, a very likeable and thoughtful person. On discovering my failure at Grosse Ile, he said he would make every effort to ensure that I would not fail at Caron. He really meant what he said. Nathan was a top-grade RAF officer and Flight Commander. He was to test me more than once during the course. His attitude was such that I would have followed him anywhere without question. He was without doubt the finest Flight Commander instructor I was ever to meet.

Sergeant Thom began by treading warily, or so it seemed to his new pupil. I think he expected something entirely different from what he got.

Thom soon found my faults when flying and speedily put an end to them. His patience was extraordinary. One day I flew the aircraft around the normal circuit, lined her up, selected half flap and 'aimed' the Cornell at the beginning of the runway in use. We approached fairly rapidly. I cut the engine over the edge of the tarmac but I didn't pull out of the descent until we reached what I thought was the precise moment. I then pulled the stick back sharply, levelled her off and sank onto the runway like greased lightning.

'Christ, Broome, don't do that to me again! You don't have to move that quick. Just take your time, not so fast but do it earlier. If you hadn't pulled out just when you did, we'd have pranged. I wouldn't have had time to do anything,' Thom called out.

Sergeant Thom and I got on well as instructor and pupil. The fact that he was a sergeant seemed to help. I often became tense when flying with officers, except Flying Officer Nathan.

The Ground School at Caron seemed a 'piece of cake' by comparison with the one at Grosse Ile. There was never any problem at Caron that I could not overcome. I obtained very good course and examination results in all subjects, especially navigation and aircraft recognition.

The weather was superb for flying. It was autumn, or fall to the Canadians. The corn was ripe, the fields a blaze of gold. The days were fairly long. We rose at 06.30, commenced flying at 07.30, continuing until lunch at 12.30, completing the day with ground school throughout the afternoon. Alternately, the ground school took the morning and we then flew in the afternoon until 19.00.

The flying training at Caron was nearly always good. Sergeant Thom, however, discovered a new fault of mine. After landing, especially at Boharm (a satellite grass field), sometimes the Cornell went into what was known as a ground loop. The aircraft goes into an uncontrollable full circle turn, swinging around on the ground with one wing scraping the field and the opposite main landing wheel off the ground. The Cornell usually spun around several times.

The ground loop was a common fault, which befell most cadets sooner or later. Once in this predicament, one had to more or less sit it out and apply opposite rudder and aileron, which didn't always work and seemed sometimes to make the aircraft spin around even faster. The remedy was more a prevention than a cure, especially to prevent any tendency for tail-swing after landing, which always preceded the horribly hopeless situation.

The 'small field' procedure and 'circle shots' of Grosse Ile came in useful during the course at Caron. I found I was able to estimate distances far better than I might have done without the previous experience with the USN.

In comparison with Grosse Ile, the forced landing procedure at Caron was a 'doddle'. As well as the precision landings, which were both based on estimation of distance and wind effect, the precision landings were just a simple 'landing on the spot' affair. Usually the pupil (if solo) or instructor chose the runway number. This was painted in large white figures near the end of the runway, the idea being to touchdown smack on the numerals. This was allowed with engine power 'on' and so making the job really a piece of cake!

The forced landing procedure consisted of making a very quick decision about the wind direction and finding a suitably large field in which to land. The field selection was easy because Saskatchewan was chock-a-block full of cornfields. The wind direction was not so easy. One could sometimes remember the direction from take-off, knowing that this could alter. Sometimes there was smoke from bonfires or chimneys and one had to ignore the smoke from trains using the CPR (Canadian Pacific Railway) that ran nearby.

Cloud shadow pattern could be useful but generally this took too long to be certain of their direction during an emergency. Once the pupil had selected both field and wind direction, the idea was to do a series of turns or 'S'-bends on the upwind side of the field at right angles to the desired approach. This was done to lose height and yet be within safe gliding distance of the field. It was simple to choose the right moment to attempt the 'forced' landing. It was very much simpler than the 'S' turns to circle or 'small field' procedure of the USN (where the rules were more complicated while achieving the same end).

I managed to solo from Caron in six and a half hours, which was about average. It took me almost as long as the average pupil to settle down on the course and to absorb the various drills on the new aircraft and also the circuit pattern, flying regulations and permitted flying area for No. 33 EFTS.

Just before my twenty-hour check we had a lecture about forced landing procedure by one of the Flight Commanders, Flight Lieutenant Maclean. The object of the lecture was to highlight the expected procedure and point out the usual errors of the pupil. One main error appeared to be very annoying to the Flight Commander. This was for the pupil to switch back 'on' the fuel tank or ignition switch that the instructor had switched 'off' in order to cause the forced landing exercise. We were most emphatically told to leave all switches and cocks that had been turned off as they were and to continue the exercise properly as if it were a real emergency. We also were not to open up the throttle (assuming of course that all switches and tank cocks were already switched back on) when we thought fit.

It appeared that many pupils did just that, much to the utter amazement of a particular instructor. What we were supposed to do was to continue the emergency throughout until told otherwise (which seemed fair enough to me). The fellow really had a go about this particular subject. His tone was quite bombastic and more like a Sergeant Major than a Flight Commander.

I could well see what the chap wanted; it seemed common sense anyway. We were in the Air Force and orders were orders. A very simple matter, no arguing allowed. I was most surprised that this sort of thing had to be brought up. A test was a test and as you were tested by an instructor, check pilot or Flight Commander, you carried out his instructions only. I didn't see how you could get it wrong.

On 22 September 1943 I was due for my twenty-hour test. According to the Flight Board in the crew room, I was to fly with none other than Flight Lieutenant Maclean! It didn't bother me much and, thanks to the lecture, I knew exactly what to do!

Maclean called me from the crew room. We strode out to the Cornell. We strapped in, started up, taxied out, took off and flew to the general flying area, the pupil flying all the way – all normal procedure.

We did a few medium turns, steep turns and then, without a word from the Flight Commander, the fuel cock was turned off (all controls being duplicated, of course). The engine cut in a few minutes. The fuel tap was indicated by myself and I then settled down to select a large field, just harvested, with only the wheat stubble remaining. I lost height in the approved manner, lined her up dead into wind and made the approach. No word came from Maclean. The ground came nearer. We crossed the field boundary at 45°, on a corner, with the landing run at 45° into the field, taking the longest possible distance available for safety.

Some 50 feet up, there was no word from the rear cockpit (the pupil was always in the front in a Cornell). At 20 feet, there was not a sound. I levelled out, not a sound. Tail down, not a sound. Three-pointer, whoosh! Down!

'Christ, lad, what are you doing, don't land her out here.' But I already had, so I turned on the fuel, opened the throttle and away we climbed.

'What on earth did you do that for?'

'What you told us to do Sir, at the lecture on forced landings!'

'You needn't have taken me so literally,' was the reply from the rear cockpit.

Better safe and sure, I thought at the time. I also thought I had done a damn good forced landing, right up to the point of a touchdown. It seemed perfect to me. There was no comment from the Flight Commander, either then or later! The rest of the test went OK and I was given a pass without further comment. I was disappointed. I thought I had flown well and felt that Maclean ought to have made a comment on the emergency touchdown. Because it really was a good one, I know I felt dead chuffed about it. It was obvious that I had unwittingly caused some sort of rebuff to the testing officer.

'What is the matter with him?' asked Sergeant Thom, eyeing the Flight Commander on our return.

'Serves the bugger right,' Thom said with a broad grin when I explained. 'I bet that won't happen again!'

Instrument flying (IF) was a very important part of flying training. The RAF took care to see that all its pilots were competent on IF and night flying as well as for day flying. This didn't apply to all air forces at that time. We had to do something like ten hours on the Link Trainer (instrument flying simulator) and some eight to ten hours on IF in the air. We eventually took an IF Test.

This was treated with some dread by most of the pupils, the reason being that good marks on IF were essential to complete the EFTS course successfully. The RAF set great store by it.

I'd had very little Link Trainer work, just an odd lesson at Grosse Ile. The Link at Caron, therefore, was as new to me as to anyone. I got on well with the Link instructor and therefore I had no particular problems at this elementary stage.

With the IF in the aircraft itself I managed to cope well. In fact, when I knew my IF Test was due I felt reasonably confident. I don't think I was too cocky about it, at least I didn't think I gave that impression.

You can imagine my delight when the day of the IF Test arrived, especially when the test instructor was Flying Officer Nathan.

I took off 'under the hood', a canvas arrangement designed to cover the rear cockpit completely. (IF was always flown with the pupil in the rear cockpit, for safety reasons.) Nathan told me to climb to 4000 feet and then took over himself. He threw the aircraft all over the sky while I sat peacefully in the rear, under the hood, smiling to myself, looking at the instruments: altimeter, turn and bank indicator, ASI. I knew almost exactly what he was doing, although the gyrocompass was 'caged' and the artificial horizon was locked. After about thirty seconds of twisting, turning, diving and climbing, Nathan returned to level flight. 'You have control,' he said.

So I kept her flying straight and level. The instruments appeared to be well satisfied. Occasionally he would say 'Good show' after some pleasing manoeuvre. I'm not sure now that we did a spin under the hood. I would think it very likely. The whole test went well, Flying Officer Nathan seemed very pleased on completion and I was given a pass.

The Link Trainer was nowhere near as good as the 'pukka' IF and, although I passed with 70 per cent in the final test, I was by no means happy about the Link.

The flying side at Caron went along all too fast. It went well too. I was happier at Caron than at any other flying training station.

Aerobatics soon became the order of the day. Although I could do most of the other flying practices quite well, there was a tendency for my instructor to insist on regular practice of these to keep my hand in, especially emergencies.

Originally, I had been worried about my reaction to aerobatics, but I soon realised that my fears were groundless. On the very first flight with Sergeant Thom we did some mild aerobatics. I'm sure he was trying to settle me into having confidence in the aeroplane in particularly unusual attitudes. The latter generally means inverted flying and virtually falling out of the kite!

It was great stuff to practise loops, rolls and rolls 'off the top'. We also did a number of other manoeuvres (flick rolls, wing-overs, upward rolls, vertical climbs and dives, vertical stalls) as well as those that were standard, like steep turns and spins.

I think it worth mentioning that, although I appear to have done slips and stall turns, I don't think that these were on the syllabus. Wing-overs, certainly, were not but I enjoyed 'showing off' to Sergeant Thom. I don't think the Sergeant thought much of them, but he took it all very calmly and made certain complimentary remarks.

We were never allowed or encouraged to do the 'bunt' (an outside loop) or inverted spinning. No instructions were given to get oneself out of an inverted spin, so it is perhaps as well that we didn't do them by intent or by accident.

One day, while practising various aerobatics solo, I tried a 'roll off the top' (which means you half roll the aircraft at the top of a loop and so finish the right side up). The aircraft must have been near to stalling at the top of the loop because the controls became sloppy and away she spun, fortunately not inverted!

It was the first and only spin that I had ever got into without intent. Imagine my surprise when, finding myself halfway round the loop, upside down, doing all the necessary juggling with rudder and aileron, suddenly the aircraft did not respond but did something entirely of its own.

My first reaction was to get out of the damn thing as fast as I could; my hand reached up and grabbed the handle for opening the sliding hood. 'Why bale out, try to pull it out first,' I suddenly thought.

My hand came off the handle just as if the handle were red hot! I applied stick forward and opposite rudder and out we came into a steep, controlled dive, pulling the stick back until she was level with the horizon and it was all over and all very much OK. The aircraft flew on perfectly, nothing wrong with it at all! Afterwards, I thought my reaction to a bale out was not all that bad. It seemed that I was going through the motions well enough, without any qualms about leaving the aircraft. I found some comfort in this reflection.

One of my favourite unofficial manoeuvres was to get up to about 6000 feet, put on climbing revs and then pull the stick back until the aircraft was as near vertical as possible. The Cornell would climb just a few hundred feet before she stalled in the vertical climb and then fall back, tail first (a 'tail slide') until the nose swung over to one side or the other due to the propeller torque or to a touch of rudder. The latter was little or no good in the stall for obvious reasons (i.e., little or no airflow). If we didn't spin, we pulled out of a steep dive as soon as possible. The slow roll was perhaps the most difficult of the aerobatics practised at Caron. This was because, if you did not execute it properly, you fell out of the sky, or very nearly.

The slow roll was quite a manoeuvre for testing one's co-ordination. One needed a smooth movement of the controls throughout to execute it properly and cleanly. With pupil pilots, the tendency for most, at first, was to come out of the roll slipping sideways and diving out of the manoeuvre.

Also, when one inverts there is the tendency to drop about two or three inches in the seat harness, for no matter how tight the harness is at take-off, it always seems to loosen when inverted. Not only this, but the intercom tube swings around your face, plus all the muck from the bottom of the aircraft. Most trainers collected their share.

Slipping into the slack of the harness when inverted, hampered rudder control at first. This was because one needed to apply 'top' rudder when rolling, to keep the aircraft nose from dropping, due to a change in the centre of gravity and also 'lift' direction during the roll.

The description 'top' rudder means that when you roll to the left you will need right rudder to keep the aircraft nose up, as the nose would normally drop without correction. The opposite occurs if you roll to the right: you will need left rudder to keep the nose up. The rudder corrections for rolling are always opposite to the roll direction and gravity, hence the expression 'top' rudder (i.e., uppermost when the aircraft is flying on one side). As far as applying rudder control when partially inverted, coming out of the roll, the fact that you've dropped some two or three inches out of the seat leaves you to grope with your feet to find the rudder bar and apply the correction! Also, as you may realise, one needs the opposite rudder to hold the nose up when coming out of the roll on the other (finishing) side. This still needs to be 'top' rudder.

Pilot navigation was a feature of the course at Caron that was completely new to me. There had been nothing like that anywhere on the previous courses.

Prior to getting an experience of Pilot Navigation (PN) with an instructor, we had a complementary lecture or two in the ground school. The idea of the class was to illustrate the pros and cons of pilot navigation: the Dalton Navigational Computer, map reading, course setting while flying in the air, as well as setting all the necessary 'guff' on the computer.

The word 'computer' these days conjures up the image of some sort of magic box that 'does it itself'. However, the ordinary and very simple aircraft navigation computer of 1943 was of no comparison to the present-day computer. It was just a flat box about 6 inches x 8 inches x 1.5 inches (150 mm x 200 mm x 38 mm), which strapped on to one knee. We could set up the course and airspeed, the wind direction and strength and get the track and ground speed after some manipulation.

When the day came to fly the first PN with an instructor, we were fairly confident about the exercise. Mind you, we only thought 'we knew how', because once we got into the air and the three-dimensional movement took effect, plus wind strength and direction, we could soon end up in quite a mess.

One of the first noticeable things is how difficult it is to fly an accurate course. It is one thing to set up a course on the aircraft compass, which is directly in front of the pilot at the bottom centre of the instrument panel. This is usually done on the ground before take-off. You set the required course of x° (magnetic), which includes the variation of that particular aircraft compass. The remainder of the calculation has come from your computer, which you have prepared already in the navigation room of the Control Tower or similar building.

When you get airborne you set course directly over the airfield at about 2000 feet so as not to interfere with aircraft on the normal circuit at 1000 feet. Setting course is not an easy operation for the pupil. If you turn the aircraft on to the course sharply, you then experience the compass needle over-shooting the desired course setting. If you turn on to the heading too slowly, you discover you have left the aerodrome behind and you are setting course some 2 or 3 miles away from it. Once on the course you need to keep the aircraft steady. This is not always easy because you have other instruments to watch, particularly the airspeed indicator and altimeter. While you are busy flying a reasonably accurate course, you could be losing or gaining a few hundred feet. The strange thing about this is that at this (Pilot Navigation) stage one is no longer a complete 'rookie' as far as flying straight and level goes. However, with practice and patience, in time one can fly a reasonable course.

In addition to Pilot Navigation, we also did similar exercises in the Link Trainer at Caron. I began the lessons on Link OK at first, then quite suddenly began to have difficulties. Flying a circuit pattern in the Link proved quite troublesome. The basic flight pattern was no problem, but to get the corresponding diagram drawn correctly by the Link remote equipment onto the instructor's table was a different situation altogether. Invariably, I finished with the starting and finishing point inches apart on the paper. It seemed that the instructor thought I could have done better! Although I managed fairly well in the end with the Link at Caron, I was not out of the wood, even though I passed the final exam.

We had our own share of crashes at Caron, although not as many fatal ones as at Grosse Ile. One of my colleagues on the course, LAC Machin, who slept in the bunk opposite mine, had quite a 'shaky do' one day. Sergeant Thom and I were on the approach to land at base in our favourite Cornell, FH876. I was flying the aircraft and was about to land. We were using 'the field' that day for landing due to the wind being across the runway and therefore too dangerous for the less experienced pupils on solo flying.

An aircraft that was landing immediately in front of us suddenly disappeared in a cloud of dust! There was a shout from Sergeant Thom, 'I've got her,' as he continued to land himself, landing as close as possible to the damaged Cornell. We did a fast taxi past the crashed aircraft; the solo pupil pilot seemed OK. He opened the hood and climbed out. The undercarriage had completely disappeared, the propeller sheared to splintered stumps. There was no fire. LAC Machin had immediately switched everything off. The look of utter amazement and consternation on his face was one I will never forget. Machin walked around the aircraft, scratching his head and just looking at the mess he'd made of the Cornell.

'Are you all right, lad?' shouted Sergeant Thom, who received just a curt nod in acknowledgement. I imagined that my roommate must have wished the ground could open up and swallow him. In fact, it very nearly had done! He was very lucky to finish the right way up! It could so easily have been terribly different, over-turning with the added risk of fire. We would have been too late to do anything, although we were the first there!

The crash tender and blood wagon rolled up, so we left to continue the day's work.

LAC Machin continued to fly on the course for a few more weeks. Unfortunately, he was eliminated later from further pilot training. Later on he re-mustered to another aircrew trade, as did LAC Lamb. I believe both re-mustered to air bomber. I was sorry to lose these comparatively new colleagues after some forty or so hours' flying training. Both of these lads had bunks adjacent to mine in the barracks building. I knew them well and felt very sad at their loss.

Sergeant Thom had a girlfriend nearby and on two occasions we 'shot up' her parents' farmhouse. On one occasion we celebrated by climbing to about 10,000 feet on the outbound journey. On arriving directly over the farm buildings, Thom opened and closed the throttle several times, to attract attention from below, then commenced a series of vertical dives, flicking over on one wing so that we went down sharply with the nose pointed straight at the ground. This was followed by an equally vertical climb, repeated some five or six times.

The Sergeant enjoyed showing off. I know I enjoyed it as much, if not more. I found the vertical diving and climbing exhilarating. I liked to feel the force of 'g' pushing my head into my neck and my neck into my shoulders. My bottom felt as if it were being buried into the seat-type parachute pack and beyond, into the bucket-type seat. We finished doing a low level run at about 50 feet and threw out a message. The slipstream blew the paper ball, weighted only with a pencil, swiftly behind. I do not know whether the girlfriend ever found it. I supposed it was likely she did, for we were merely 'hedge-hopping' over the garden fence. We seemed close enough for her to see the message dropping from the aircraft.

We had only one fatality at Caron during my time there. Fortunately, no one was killed in our mob. The unfortunate pupil was a member of the following course. I didn't see the accident happen, but I heard the siren alarm. There didn't appear to be any fire from the wrecked aircraft, which had crashed on some spare ground not too far from the canteen. The engine of the Cornell cut at about 500 feet on the climb, just after take-off. The pupil was flying solo, we believe, and not his first. The pilot did exactly what we were all told not to do! He turned back towards the aerodrome and presumably stalled on the turn, spun in and was killed.

It seemed amazing to us that a pupil should do this. It was regularly drummed into us that you always put the nose down and went more or less straight ahead to land in as clear an area as possible. At Caron, this was very easy to do, since the base was set in the cornfields of Saskatchewan. If the pupil had not chosen to turn back he would not have stalled. Also, he would have a clear landing ahead, well away from aerodrome buildings.

The day of solo pilot navigation arrived. On 28 September 1943, after course preparation in the navigation room at the flight offices, I took off for Dunblane armed with map, computer and course notes.

It looked a dead straight run to Dunblane. The track was relatively easy to follow – out over the bright orange-yellow cornfields to pick up a prominent river as a landmark and to fly alongside for a considerable part of the journey.

There was a tendency to drift more than expected as the met forecast wind had obviously changed. Or had it? The training value of a slightly incorrect wind at the beginning of a pilot navigation trip might be considered beneficial. We often thought that the navigation section gave us incorrect gen for this purpose.

Before I left the river path, I was greeted with a most amazing sight. There, slap in the middle of the river on the only visible islet, was a crashed and abandoned Cornell at about 60°, tail in the air. The aircraft stood on its nose, all alone on the island! There appeared to be only minor damage to the propeller, the nose and engine cowling.

It couldn't possibly have flown into that position, otherwise the damage would have been considerable. The aircraft's longitudinal axis (i.e., fore and aft) was in line with the river. It didn't look as if the pilot had tried to land on the surrounding cornfields, unless he found that he ran too far and fell off the bank onto the island. The river was too wide to get onto the island anyway. It could only have happened like that if the aircraft wing had struck a solid object on the island, which could have turned it through 90° to its apparent position. The puzzle was never solved.

I continued with the flight, eventually spotting several grain elevators ahead. There were just one or two houses nearby. I approached the prairie village from the south-east and flew alongside the elevators, perhaps a quarter of a mile clear, making a good steady turn of 180° to set course to return to Caron. I could now see the name of the village painted on the roof of a long building adjacent to the elevators. The lettering looked some 10 feet high – black letters on a white background. There was now no mistake in my navigation: the name on the building made it all seem too simple and yet reassuring. I covered much the same ground on return, passing the lone, crashed aircraft and on to Caron.

After landing, I made my way to the Control Tower to report to the Navigation Instructor. Later I discussed the trip with cadets who had already completed the flight. We seemed to be in agreement about the simplicity of finding the turning point.

Regarding the crash, apparently the aircraft had been there a day or two. The pupil pilot from a nearby RCAF Station was unhurt in the incident. We were relieved to hear that a 'Canuck' had crashed the Cornell and not one of our own RAF lads!

The next pilot navigation solo was to the RCAF Station at Davidson on 9 October. It was a different navigational exercise, including a landing at a strange aerodrome and reporting to the Navigation Office within the Control Tower buildings.

Once at Davidson, we needed to satisfy their Navigation Officer that we had reached the aerodrome with reasonable ease and also that our return course with their wind (RCAF Met, Davidson) was to his satisfaction. The return to RAF Caron was a replica of the successful outgoing flight.

I completed the pilot navigation part of the course shortly after this and fared fairly well in the subsequent test. This was a three-point exercise – Caron–Bridgeford–Craik–Caron.

What we gained from this part of the course was threefold. Firstly, the practice of keeping the aircraft flying exactly where you wanted it, i.e., flying a compass course and maintaining the height you were set at the start of the exercise. (For safety reasons this was decided upon by the Navigation Officer who had knowledge of the local terrain. This would be 4000 feet for all or most Pilot Navigation from

Caron). Secondly, knowledge of the variation in the Met wind and the actual wind and its effect on the track of the aircraft. Thirdly, the value of keeping a good lookout, both for map reading and for other aircraft. These later items were not too easy for the pupil who was concentrating on flying an accurate compass course.

It was always essential to have your 'homework' done before the event. This was the way we were taught by the RAF and the only way to really be sure of your own navigation. Once you were in the air, it was not easy to do much more than glance at the map or compass, in addition to other instruments, the altimeter and airspeed indicator. You would almost certainly have to do some slight alteration of course, work out any wind change and get your new course with the aid of the computer. However, it is all too easy when on the prairies to see what is going wrong and do some wild cheating like keeping the Canadian Pacific Railway on your left and the Indian Creek on your right, or starboard, almost under your wing tip! This sort of DIY navigation was easy and understandable in Canada, but it would be of little use when flying in the UK because at home one would hardly be able to distinguish one small town from another, let alone the odd village. They were all far too close together. A further air navigation course would be necessary for this reason, on return to UK.

The ground school appeared to be going very well. I was to get good mid-term final results for navigation, signals, aircraft recognition, engines etc.

Although we flew every day and the accent at EFTS was most definitely on flying, the ground school examinations were still an essential part of the training. Pass marks of above 70 per cent were still required for most subjects, with signals having a 95 per cent minimum pass.

I had one pleasant surprise in store for me while at Caron. I knew Bill Hall had completed his flying instructor's course and was stationed at an RAF EFTS near Assiniboia, some 60 or 70 miles south of Caron. Bill wrote fairly regularly. He mentioned something about trying to get over to Caron. I didn't take the remark seriously. In fact, I gave no further thought to it.

I had been out on a solo exercise and had landed perhaps about ten minutes' earlier, when there was a Tannoy demanding 'LAC Broome report to the Control Tower!'

'Christ, Wha' you been up to, Broomie?'

'You must be in the deep, having to report to Flying Control?'

'I bet ole Broome's "shot up" a bit of "crumpet".'

Off I went to the Control Tower, wondering what on earth it was all about. What could I have done, I wondered? Did I cut up another aircraft on the circuit? Perhaps I'd had a near miss with a 'Canuck' instructor on a training navigation session? I certainly couldn't think of any such incident. (I kept a fairly good lookout, didn't I?)

'H'm, we'll soon find out,' I thought as I climbed the stairs to Flying Control.

I knocked on the door, went in and saluted the Flying Officer on duty.

'Ah, Broome, someone to see you, an old friend of yours, I believe?' I turned to face the pleasant smiling face of Pilot Officer Bill Hall. I 'banged him one up' as smart as I could – one of my best salutes, I hoped.

We chatted for some minutes. Bill was quite calm, reserved, it seemed. He took the situation for granted. He asked how I was getting along on the course. He seemed pleased to see me. It was a short meeting, far too short really. Bill had brought a pupil over and had just made it a routine training flight, probably an hour each way.

I felt quite 'chuffed' at seeing my old 'cobber' from Sterling Metals, a Pilot Officer too, who'd taken all the trouble to fly over to Caron just to see LAC Broome! I thought it was a wizard show!

Our reunion was to last about twenty minutes. Regrettably, I was called to the crew room to fly a further solo. (Sometimes they just put odd bods up without warning to complete the flying programme.) I said goodbye to Bill and went to collect my gear.

A few minutes later I was taxiing out to the runway when I saw Bill and his pupil sitting in their Cornell, getting ready to start up for their return journey. There was a friendly wave, a cheerio from Bill, which I returned as I taxied by and took off. Bill seemed most interested in watching the take-off, which was to be expected of a flying instructor. Somehow, I did not think of him as an instructor, like I did our own at Caron. Instead, I thought of him purely as an old friend, a person from another world.

I have thought since how lucky I was to have the meeting. Bill planned it as a surprise for me. We both were lucky that it worked as well as it did. He would have found it necessary to consult his Flight Commander and get approval for the flight. He would have been away from his home unit too long to have just 'buzzed off'. Yes, had I thought about it, I should have been more pleased than I perhaps appeared; I was especially thrilled by the visit. Enjoy it I did, but I took it all for granted in our naive wartime flying world. Almost anything worked in those very special times.

Night flying was an interesting speculation. Most of us at some time, had problems during day flying. Among these was the high standard required for instrument flying (under the hood). Also, there was the high performance one required in the Link Trainer. Night flying still seemed to have its peculiar fascination. Perhaps it was being out all hours of the night? Or the prospect of a late supper? (This was not to be confused with the bacon, egg and chip specialities that were to come along with operational sorties.) Perhaps it was because it was a new experience? Like flying in a darkened and sometimes pitch-black night sky, looking for any sort of ground illumination to give one the comfort of knowing where you were or perhaps to counteract that sometimes lonely feeling?

Most cadets treated the forthcoming 'night' events as something special, perhaps with awe and not without boyish excitement. Almost everyone looked forward to it. It seemed to be a subject that was not to cause many failures on the course. Most of these, strangely enough, came from daylight-flying exercises.

It was just 'my luck' when the night flying programme was drawn up. I was to fly from our satellite field at Boharm. The relief landing ground was about 4 miles south, south-east from Caron. This was unfortunate because the lights in use at Caron were the more modern electric system with various colours. We noticed this immediately we flew to Boharm. In comparison with the brilliance of the circuit lights at Caron, the lights of the long-necked 'goose' flares at Boharm, were just a flickering pale yellow from the oil-fed lamps. These were much dimmer, and a dead loss, I thought!

We each had a different instructor for night flying, not Sergeant Thom in my case. Also, we didn't keep to the same one. It could change for each night on the night-flying programme.

The first time I drew Sergeant Farmer, who took the aircraft over to Boharm. I gasped when I saw the 'goose' flares.

'Blimey, are we supposed to land by that sort of light?' I thought. It didn't seem possible. It was little better than candlelight!

We put in about two hours' circuits and bumps before going back to Caron. The flying seemed just as easy as in daylight, except that the approach and landing was a much more 'hit and miss' affair. That is, actually putting the aircraft onto the grass. The 'grass detail' present in daylight hours was not visible. In daylight I used this to tell me exactly when to level off. All I had now were these wretched flares and only about six of them, in a line, with another added at the end, at right angles to the last flare, making a crude sort of 'L' in lights.

Believe me, I was damned glad of the company of the instructor in the rear cockpit! Being young, and inexperienced in life, had its compensations. We didn't worry too much about the risks. There weren't any, we were told, and by people who knew better than us.

'Just do as you are told. Follow the simple rules. Watch your altimeter on the approach. Check that the altimeter is at zero before take-off. Keep the aerodrome lights in sight and you cannot get lost.'

All good common sense, of course, which works very well if everything goes to plan. Sometimes, minor last-minute changes can alter everything. The old saying 'safety first' is always a good one and applies to pupils flying solo at night, especially if you only have 'goose' flares on the field. The next time I flew at night it was to Boharm again.

On 27 September I was due for further night-flying training, this time with Sergeant Shaw. We flew over to Boharm. I did my circuits and bumps; the instructor seemed very satisfied after only one landing and one over-shoot. (The over-shoot procedure was practised almost as much as the landing procedure!) I was quite surprised to be told I could solo so soon! The instructor got out and disappeared into one of the temporary buildings, leaving me to taxi around the field to the point ready for turning onto the take-off position. I hadn't a clue where he went or where to pick him up. He never bothered to tell me!

I taxied around the field in a fairly wide rectangular circuit and began to head back towards the landing flares at the take-off point. I was on the last leg, where the blood wagon and crash tender should appear at any moment. I continued to taxi forward, looking through the windscreen, straight ahead, left and right, with the hood opened. Suddenly, I sensed something almost dead ahead, something not definable, through the Perspex. I stopped the aircraft, with the engine still running. There wasn't anything or anybody about, or so I thought! I undid the safety straps and stood up in the cockpit to get a good look ahead, outside and above the cockpit cover, through the revolving airscrew.

There, just 20 feet ahead and very slightly to the right was a windsock tripod mast, some 30 feet or more high with bracing wires, staked around in various positions like points of a compass. If I had not stopped I would have taxied into the mast and its supports and, without doubt, smashed up the airscrew and at least sliced into one wing with the wire cables.

The windsock was completely unlit, with no warning of any kind. There were no lamps – not even on the adjacent hut! At the time I just thought I was lucky to have stopped. If I hadn't, the resulting accident would have been my fault. Later, I realised that there should have been lights around the site, particularly since pupil pilots were using the field. We always thought the RAF were always correct, never wrong, and that any accident was our own fault, generally accepting the blame! This attitude was to follow most of us all through our training, including operational flying. It was quite understandable, but sometimes there were terrible consequences.

Having determined the position of the windsock tripod, I altered course towards the left and this brought me to within a short distance of the end of the flares, crash tender and blood wagon.

I waited some minutes for my turn to turn on to the runway. There was no one in front waiting and no one to the rear. There was, however, another Cornell with pupil and instructor on the circuit. I noted the aircraft's progress during the final approach. I could see its navigation lights very clearly. It passed the rescue vehicles at about 20 feet high and then, while landing, pranged on the field almost directly in front of me! There was a great cloud of dust but fortunately no smoke or fire, just plenty of commotion while pupil and instructor climbed out amid shouts and warnings from the 'crash crew'. It seemed that the field might not be cleared of the crash very quickly. Therefore, all solo flying was cancelled. The instructor I had flown out with joined me after a few minutes, explaining the situation as we taxied for take-off on the opposite side of the line of flares. We returned to Caron and were down within fifteen to twenty minutes of leaving Boharm.

If the crash had occurred after I had become airborne – it took some time to clear – what would have become of a first-time night solo pupil flying at Boharm? Normally the fuel tanks were filled each night before take-off from Caron, so fuel might not have been too much of a problem. There was no provision for a pupil to return to Caron without an instructor. The Cornell carried no radio. The runway lights at Caron could not usually be seen from Boharm, at circuit height. It makes interesting speculation. It must have happened somewhere, at some time.

During the late afternoon of 3 October, I flew with Sergeant Thom on a night-flying air test. This was to ensure that any aircraft used for night flying was in perfect condition. We flew in formation with Sergeant Mahoney and his pupil. Later, during that night's flying, Sergeant Mahoney and his pupil crashed during a night landing. No one was hurt. That same night I was due for night flying at Boharm. Imagine my surprise when I realised who the instructor was. It was the Pilot Officer who had been the instructor in the Cornell that pranged in front of me while I was waiting to take off on my first night solo a couple of nights previously. My logbook makes simple reading of an exceptionally 'hairy' experience:

3 night landings, 1 over-shoot, 1 hour.
2 night landings, 2 over-shoots, 1 hour (solo).

But it wasnt quite that easy.

The Pilot Officer flew the aircraft out to Boharm, made the first circuit and demonstrated a night landing, except that he didn't get down properly. The Cornell bounced so badly that the instructor opened up the throttle, saying 'I'll go round and try that again. Better luck next time.' We flew a normal over-shoot, resumed a normal circuit and approach, came into land, repeating the performance with a bump, several bounces and an over-shoot.

'Christ, you'd better have it, I just can't get the bloody thing down,' the instructor said We then flew a reasonably good circuit and I managed to land the kite on the 'goose' flare-lit field.

'Christ, that was greasy, very, very greasy,' said the Pilot Officer. 'You can fly this thing better than I. Taxi up to the hut and I'll get out. You can have her.'

The instructor had gone in a flash. There was the 'goose' flare path all for me, with not another aircraft in sight. The blood wagon was on one side and the crash tender on the other. I was utterly amazed. There was nothing I could do about it. The Pilot Officer didn't know that I had witnessed the previous night's prang from possibly the closest position. Nor did he realise that my 'greasy' landing was but pure fluke. Or so I thought at the time. There could be no arguing – the instructor had already gone. I taxied forward, looked to starboard, which was all clear, turned onto the flare path, opened the throttle, and took off, and away into the pitch-black night.

The Cornell went very nicely. I levelled out, turned crosswind, left-hand circuit as usual, turning downwind to find the flares well to port, beginning to look quite distant. It was surprising how soon they got so small. I turned the aircraft crosswind again, prior to the final approach, continuing until the flares were almost level with the port wing, and turning just before to line them up, dead ahead.

I seemed a long way from the field; the wind seemed to have strengthened. I kept the throttle on for a power approach, watching the position of the lights. The altimeter read 300 feet. I was still some distance away, a mile, I guessed. The lights got larger and larger. I could see the blood wagon and tender clearly. As I reached them, at about 20 to 25 feet high, I cut the throttle. Down I came with a bang, a bump and a bounce. Not particularly good, I thought, rather like the first solo at Southam! The aircraft seemed so much lighter with only one occupant.

I taxied around the perimeter and carefully missed the windsock. I felt uneasy about the landing; it wasn't bad but it wasn't good. I thought of the old air force slogan 'Any landing you can walk away from is a good one'. I wasn't in the mood for jokes and this seemed a poor excuse for any sort of landing. It may be OK for sprogs, I thought, but now I had a few hours in on Cornells and I should have done better.

I reached the take-off point safely and looked around for other aircraft. There were none. I turned into wind, opened the throttle and took off, climbing as before to 1000 feet. I flew the normal circuit and once more, when downwind, I wondered why the flares seemed so far away. Nevertheless, I kept them well in sight and made a normal approach.

The flare path seemed miles away again, perhaps 2 miles, about double the normal distance. With the throttle just over half open, the flares approached very slowly. I was most concerned about the altitude; I seemed to be around 200 feet. The flare path seemed as if it were about to disappear. I kept getting the sensation that I was flying too low. A few seconds later the flare path, blood wagon and tender were flashing beneath the wings. I cut the throttle, dropped some 20 feet, and bounced badly to my dismay, so I opened up the throttle for an over-shoot.

The over-shoot procedure gave no trouble and was simple enough. It was just a question of taking off the half flap, which was normal for the Cornell on landing, day or night, then, trimming the aircraft for normal flight. One had to climb to about 300 feet minimum prior to taking off the flap. The aircraft took much longer to climb to the desired height for this operation.

The reader may realise that the object of using flaps is to get down quickly and to shorten the landing run. So on over-shooting the field or runway, the pupil is faced with the prospect of climbing for some distance with something like half or one third flap on the aeroplane, the very opposite to what is desirable for climbing. Once the flap is removed or lifted, the aircraft 'mushes' forward, losing some height in doing so, perhaps 50 to 100 feet, depending on the airspeed, hence the need to climb to 300 feet at least.

I resumed the circuit pattern, repeating the earlier performance, keeping the flares constantly in view and making similar turns as before. Consequently, much the same situation arose. In addition, I appeared to be the only aircraft left on the circuit. The field seemed to be really deserted, except for the blood wagon and crash truck. There wasn't anyone in sight.

Continuing the approach, I still seemed too low. The altimeter read 300 feet on this quite long approach. The flares, when viewed through the windscreen, appeared to be only an inch or so above the engine cowling, and remained so until just before touchdown. I could not understand why I seemed to be so low and have such a long approach. Was the altimeter correct? Was it sensitive enough to be relied on at those heights? Perhaps it could not be trusted within 50 or 100 feet? I now think this was very likely.

I was determined to 'get in' on this particular approach. I felt tense and, although I liked flying very much, this particular night's flying seemed more than a bit 'hairy' as there seemed to be no one visible on the ground and no other aircraft appeared to be on the circuit. This made the situation more tense for me. If I were the only pupil on the circuit then all eyes must be on me. If this was so, why? What was so different?

There were no red Very lights being fired from the crash vehicles or hut. Presumably they were happier than I was with the aircraft's height. They weren't looking at *my* particular altimeter, were they? Later, I discovered that the wind velocity had increased considerably. Also, I wasn't at all certain that the altimeter had been correctly set for ground level at Boharm.

I continued to keep the Cornell at the same height until I was at about 20 feet over the crash tender and then cut the throttle to descend, touching down at about the second flare. The aircraft slowed up very quickly after passing the last flare and there was no trouble in stopping or in turning off the flare path to taxi back to return to the take-off point. Just as I drew near the flight hut the Pilot Officer instructor appeared. He waved me to halt and pick him up.

He seemed unconcerned except to ask 'How many circuits and over-shoots did you do, Broome?'

'Two landings, two over-shoots, Sir,' I replied.

'Ah, that's the stuff, lad. Plenty of practice is good for this night owl caper.'

We flew back to Caron and the Pilot Officer did the flying, which was a pity because I would have liked the chance of landing on a 'pukka' flare path. (Perhaps he needed the practice?) It also occurred to me that the Pilot Officer had no idea of how many landings I had done. He obviously had no worries. I wondered why.

Regretfully, I knew the course at Caron was coming to an end. Our ground school exams were underway and most of us were due to take our final flying test, the '50 hour', as it was known.

The weather was beginning to show its other side. Instead of the glorious summer sunshine that had brought the wheat fields to a blaze of gold from horizon to horizon, we began to get snow showers, sleet, wind and rain. I had hoped for some good weather for my '50 hour', in particular so that I could demonstrate my aerobatic capability. However, it was not to be, for when the day dawned it was very dull and the cloud base was down to 800–1000 feet.

I took to the air with Flight Lieutenant Budd and seemingly performed very well. I achieved a good pass mark, which wasn't disclosed. The RAF seemed keen on keeping one in the dark on the results of many subjects, as is seen later. I was disappointed not to be able to perform my usual loops and rolls, mainly because I had really learned to fly at Caron and had become completely confident of handling a light single-engined trainer.

The ground exams were soon completed and most of us came through with good marks. I completed the Link Trainer final test to some satisfaction. The instructors on the Link at Caron were very keen. Their enthusiasm made the course not only worthwhile but enjoyable too. When the final results were known, some of us were quite surprised. I noticed with regret that my flying logbook record was as follows:

As Pilot   – Average
As Pilot Navigator – Average

I had hoped to get 'above average', which should have been easy when one thinks of my additional experience at Grosse Ile. We were then told that 'average' was best because if one got a higher result one was expected to continue at that standard!

When the posting to Carberry on Ansons (twin-engined trainers) came through I was again disappointed. This may have been based on the '50 hour' test when no aerobatics were flown due to low cloud. I was particularly disappointed as I had been recommended for 'singles' (i.e., the Harvard) on the next course at 'Service' (Service Flying Training School) by my instructor. It seemed a poor show to find that Sergeant Thom's recommendation had been completely ignored.

Thom always seemed happy with my flying. I had asked whether he thought I ought to get 'singles' or 'twins'.

'You'll be all right on "singles". I wouldn't think you will do so well on "twins". You might have a job to manage. My recommendation will be for "singles",' he said.

It seemed to me then that the only possible posting would be to RAF Weyburn or similar. Just my luck to go to Carberry. My diary doesn't reflect how I felt. In fact, it gives the opposite impression. Lord knows why. I wasn't pleased with the posting and I think I made the entry to reflect my decision to make the best of a bad job. The decision to post me to 'twins' meant that I would not now fly either the Spitfire or Mustang fighters.

CHAPTER 6

RAF Carberry

Manitoban Side Steppe

We packed our kit very quickly at Caron, ready for the move to Carberry. I had been very happy at the former and left the unit with regret, accepting that it was an essential move in pilot training.

We entrained and travelled overnight, arriving in the early morning at Carberry railway station, not far from Brandon on the main CPR route across Canada. We were greeted by a number of open lorries, which conveyed us, together with our kit-bags, to the RAF Station.

On arrival at the camp, we noticed with some approval the bright yellow Avro Anson IIs parked outside the hangars. It was just getting light so the mechanics and engine fitters were taxiing the kites into a long line on the main tarmac in front of the hangars. (Later I was to learn that cadets of some experience also performed this duty.)

The MT 'wallahs' dumped us, together with our kit-bags, outside the Orderly Room. A Flight Sergeant appeared and marched us off to our billets not too far away.

It was common practice in Canada to have the wooden barrack buildings equipped with bunk beds. My favourite was the lower bunk; one could at least sit on it with one's feet on the floor. If you had the top bunk it had its disadvantages, like making one's bed up and down in the approved training fashion (i.e., 'liquorice allsort') during the day, later to be made ready for sleeping, after 6 pm. As you may imagine, making or stripping the top bunk bed was not easy, especially when compared with the lower one.

The billets were heated by two large coal-burning, automatically fed stoves, one at each end of the hut. These, with the aid of a thermostat fan, forced hot air through overhead ducts with vents at intervals, to heat the whole building. They were very efficient and made nonsense out of the single UK coke stoves.

The ground school started the very next day. We had course photographs taken – the first since ITW. A welcome talk was given by the Station Commander. We didn't like his tone and in particular the phrase we had all heard before, 'You play ball with me and I'll play ball with you'. When translated, this meant that you were usually in for a hell of a time! Many times we were under the threat of losing our fortnightly weekend 48-hour pass if our billet did not pass the CO's inspection.

We commenced flying almost straight away. My instructor was Flight Sergeant Partridge. My diary makes it clear that I could not have had a better tutor.

The Anson II was quite a steady aeroplane. It wasn't all that powerful. It just lumbered around the sky, which meant that on one engine it was a dead loss! It had no vices otherwise. I suppose when you compare it with some operational aircraft it was just too good and too easy to fly.

I was far from happy at Carberry. The gloom settled very early. The camp was more of a 'bully' place than Caron, which had been far too easy-going.

The choice of 'twins' was bad luck. Had I gone on to Harvards it would perhaps have been very different. How I longed for the posting that some of my colleagues got to Weyburn. Some of these 'lucky' guys had even been recommended for or had requested 'twins'!

However, in spite of some initial depression I very soon settled down on the course. The main reason for this was, of course, Flight Sergeant Partridge. He was an indomitable man! Man he was, for he appeared older than most instructors. He was a dedicated instructor and should have been commissioned long ago.

Flight Sergeant Partridge was very sincere and committed in everything he did as an instructor. On the very first day we had just climbed aboard the Anson. He indicated the left-hand seat.

'That's your seat, you're the aircraft captain. Remember that, you're the captain! I'm just the instructor sitting in the seat on the opposite side. Also, you're here to get your "wings" and get your "wings" you will – because that's my job and I'll make sure you do! Remember that my lad and you will have nothing to worry about. Just fly her like I tell you and there will be no problems, as long as you pay attention. OK?'

'Yes, thank you, Flight Sergeant.'

'If we have to leave the aircraft in the air for any reason, that's your escape hatch,' indicating a hatch above my head. 'Don't forget to clip your 'chute on!'

We were now equipped with bomber crew-type chest parachute packs. We wore only the harness in the aircraft; the parachute pack was in its stowage nearby. It had to be clipped on to the harness before jumping. (The Avro Anson had been designed and previously used as a reconnaissance bomber. It had already seen operational service with Coastal Command. Later, I was to fly with an aircraft captain that had done just that – flown the good old 'Annie' on ops.)

The Flight Sergeant was very thorough in his explanation of how things operated in the aircraft. He went to very great pains to describe everything in detail. He explained the dual throttles, the coarse and fine-pitch levers for operating the variable-pitch airscrews. He covered other points like the twin fuel tanks and cocks; the flaps and their operation to half and full flap position; the undercarriage lever for retracting the undercarriage; the audible warning (i.e., klaxon horn), which came on if you attempted to land without operating the undercarriage lever; and the undercarriage visual warning (on the instrument panel) – a set of green lights for verification that the undercarriage was down and locked. The instrument panel itself was much larger and carried more instruments, as one would expect for a much larger aircraft with a wingspan of 55 feet and two engines. We discussed many other aspects, from flying on one engine to operating the brakes on a flapless landing.

The first flights on the Anson were quite an experience: two engines, two throttles, two rpm indicators, two oil pressure gauges, two fuel gauges, etc. I soon found that I could fly Annie round the circuit in a competent manner. She was quite a beggar to stall – she was so good at not stalling that when deliberately put into a stall she simply recovered by herself! She just 'mushed' along until the nose went down and the airspeed increased suitably. You could keep the stick back and continually stall. There was little or no tendency to spin. We were never expected to spin the Anson.

We were taught almost straightaway to do single-engine landings, even before going solo. This was a natural precaution that was accepted easily. The only thing was that, for newcomers, flying a 'twin' on one engine was a bit of a handful! The Ansons at Carberry were not the best of aeroplanes. Many had minor problems like having a fast tickover when it would have been preferable to have had a slow one (especially during flapless landings). Sometimes the brakes would bind and sometimes they just didn't work. Some aircraft appeared to be nigh impossible to fly around the circuit on one engine!

My solo came at eight hours and was quite special to me as my diary records:

> **22 October** – I took my solo test with the Flight Commander, who wasn't satisfied with my approach and closeness to another Anson (NO 'red' from the caravan). Technically I failed, but Flight Sergeant Partridge wouldn't hear of it and after some discussion between the two instructors the Flight took me round the circuit and then sent me solo himself. (Normally unheard of!)

Flight Sergeant Partridge had insisted that I could solo and solo I did. He seemed angry with someone and it didn't appear to be me. It seems strange now that he was so insistent. He was very sure of his decision. It appears, too, that he took a great deal of responsibility on himself, for normally an instructor would not be responsible for sending a pupil solo without a check flight by another pilot. It seemed the Flight Sergeant did not see eye to eye with the Flight Commander on a number of things.

Shortly after our arrival at Carberry, we had a number of exams as a preliminary to the ground school course. It was very strange to get these because we had just passed out at EFTS on all examination subjects so why had further exams on these same subjects been initiated?

We were given the results of these exams within a few days. I was absolutely staggered to find that I had achieved a mere 40 per cent for Navigation! I just couldn't believe it. I spent the rest of the day thinking about this impossible result and the reasons for it. I thought that I had perhaps become confused in my written answers, referring to a 'course' instead of a 'track' – a possible throwback to the navigation training at USNAS Grosse Ile? This reasoning did not really make any sense at all as I was good at Navigation (final exam at Caron 84 per cent) and I liked the subject. My weakness, if any, was in the technical subjects like Engines or Armaments and perhaps Wireless Theory, but all only to a small degree. All subjects commanded my whole interest. I just felt good about *all* aircrew subjects, although I never felt much of an engineer at that time.

The effect of such a low mark for Navigation brought my morale down to an all-time low. Similarly, my training time on the Link was not bringing the expected results. I kept getting mildly admonished by the Sergeant instructor.

'You're not concentrating enough, you should be better than this on the Link.'

I didn't really trust the damn thing! Smart as it was, I did not get on well with flying the courses and flight plans on the simulator.

The beginning of a navigational trip on the Link should have joined up with the end, whatever pattern of flight plan we flew. The exercise was supposed to take one back to the beginning (like a normal flight from take-off to landing). The instructor was visually able to check the pupil's errors on a traced copy of the flight plan that the Link Trainer's co-ordinated trace had drawn on his table.

24 October – Flew 1 hr 10 min 'dual' instruction, mainly low flying. We went to see a certain little girl, flying several low passes over her home. Later, I flew 1 hr 10 min solo, mainly circuits and bumps, plus an hour on the Link Trainer.

25 October – Went up for 1 hr 15 min 'dual' on single engine flying, medium and steep turns. I was surprised at the amount of pressure required on the control column to hold the aircraft in a steep turn! I could hardly hold it with one hand. I was due to fly another solo later to practise but the trip was cancelled due to weather.

1 hr on Link Trainer. Lectures in afternoon: Armaments, Signals, Aircraft Recognition and PT.

27 October – I was informed that I was to lose my instructor, 'Chiefy' Partridge. This was quite a surprise and an intense disappointment, especially after being so lucky to have acquired such a dedicated instructor and then to lose him without previous warning.

Apparently, 'Chiefy' had been transferred to the Beam Flight. I guessed that this was because of his special qualities as a flying instructor. You had to be really good to teach bods to fly on the Standard Beam Approach System!

I came to rue the day I lost 'Chiefy'. There was little doubt that with him in the right-hand seat and myself in the 'Captain's', the result at Carberry would have been very different. 'Chiefy' Partridge was certainly quite a man. He was the sort that if he didn't like something he was 'straight in' about it, whether it be pupil or the Chief Flying Instructor! He was no softie, nor was he a patronising man. 'Chiefy' would not have sent me solo in an Anson if I had not been capable of flying it! He knew what he was doing: he wasn't the sort who took unnecessary risks but if *he* thought *his* pupil was good enough, that was it!

My new instructor was Pilot Officer Taylor, a relative youngster when compared with the Flight Sergeant. We believed he had come straight from Flying Instructors' School. The new chap seemed very tense with his pupils. He seemed to be a 'typical officer type' and kept us at a distance.

Most of his flying seemed to be by the book. He appeared to be as rigid a disciplinarian in the air as on the ground. He seemed very nervous when we were doing any manoeuvre that required special care, like single-engine circuits and landings. In general, we thought that Pilot Officer Taylor was a bit of a 'bind', to say the least. My diary bears out this fact. Also, I wasn't the only pupil that thought so! (Looking back, we were expecting too much from a brand new instructor.)

We did quite a bit of instrument flying on Ansons. I wasn't bad at all on IF but Taylor never seemed satisfied. We didn't do IF solo because of the danger of collision. Generally, as the course progressed the Pilot Officer became quite human, whereas when he first arrived he had seemed quite an 'alligator'!

We did a height test one day. We climbed to 15,600 feet, without oxygen! After I'd climbed on IF for about 8000 feet Taylor took over to climb the rest. He said he needed the practice on IF (I didn't argue). My job was to keep a good lookout while he was under the hood, which made a change.

The hood was not a complete hood like on the Cornell (which covered the whole rear cockpit). It was a sort of large canvas cap with a very long peak. The peak was like a miniature tunnel about 18 or 20 inches long. The whole device was canvas, supported by a sewn-in wire frame. We looked quite a sight I am sure, wearing an elongated granny hat of olden times. Pilot Officer Taylor looked great. I couldn't stop tittering.

9 November – Flew for 2 hours solo and had a wizard time as the cloud base was pretty high. I was able to go to 6000' and do some medium and steep turns. Also I practised precautionary and single-engine landings.

Put in a very good hour's work on the Link Trainer, got my first red which is 80–90%. My Link is now 20 hours, 10 here and 10 at Caron.

My full flying time is now 177.25, of this 27 hours is on Ansons (10 hours' solo and 17 dual).

10 November – Flew an hour's dual doing IF take-offs and flapless landings. Soloed for 1 hour 5 minutes doing single-engine landings and a precautionary. Weather was quite nice for flying but on 9 November there was 'ceiling unlimited' and it was just right for steep turns etc.

11 November – Dual for $1\frac{1}{4}$ hours doing a spot of navigation, such as setting courses and resetting the gyro. Did a couple of good flapless landings and a single-engine circuit and landing.

The wind was extremely strong today, accounting for all the flapless landings. 40 minutes' solo followed the above 'dual' and did a spot of course setting etc., returned to base and did another flapless landing, which wasn't too bad.

12 November – Went up in the afternoon for 1 hour 20 minutes' solo. Did steep turns, single-engine flying and course setting for navigation practice.

I caught the 4.30 train from Carbury and arrived in Winnipeg at 7.00.

18 November – Pilot Navigation went well. I flew two hours with Sgt Moody on a low-level navigation flight. Rather exciting, I thought, as it was quite different from navigating at 4000 feet in a Cornell. We flew at about 250 feet for this exercise, some of it following a winding river through valleys surrounded by the Manitoba 'Steppes' ['Steppes' was the RAF cadets' term for the stepped terrain over which we flew].

It became pretty clear that to fly at that height, one had to remain very alert! The navigation itself and the various pinpoints were one thing. The undulating terrain and obstructions were another! We were forbidden to do solo low-level navigation.

Single-engine flying was a regular practice, both solo and 'dual'. Taylor was continually checking my ability to handle the Anson on one engine. I seemed to be able to cope fairly well, but it was no certainty; I sometimes failed to 'get in' on one engine, having to use both occasionally to make the last few yards to the runway. There was never any trouble in making a good touchdown.

One day when practising solo single-engine and precautionary landings at Petrel, our satellite field, the starboard engine began to smoke badly, mainly inside the cabin. So I decided to return to Carberry. I throttled the engine right back. There was no flame visible.

I hoped it could be something to do with faulty exhaust piping. I continued the journey to Carberry on one engine, in earnest this time, not wishing to open up the other in case it became a 'flamer'. There was no other problem. I landed OK and taxied to the parking lines, reporting the fault to the engine fitters on arrival.

Sometime later, an Anson went missing on a night cross-country. It carried a crew of four: a flight lieutenant pilot instructor and three pupil pilots on a night navigation exercise. They were from a more senior course. The Anson wreckage was eventually found in a stubble cornfield, burnt out; all the occupants were killed. This was the only fatal accident that occurred while I was at Carberry. (At that time there was no radio communication with Anson trainer aircraft.) To the best of my knowledge, no reason was given for the accident.

Pilot Officer Taylor's mood mellowed a great deal in the last couple of weeks. Maybe we now understood each other better. Also, the Pilot Officer instructor had by now probably settled in at Carberry.

On 20 November we began night flying from Carberry and for once I had my day instructor. I flew several circuits, four landings and one over-shoot. They seemed OK; we had no narrow squeaks or near misses. I was surprised at how much flame we got from the exhausts. The port engine exhaust flame damper seemed useless. I found the amount of white-hot flame being emitted very disturbing. Pilot Officer Taylor could not see the port exhaust but agreed it looked too bright a light. The starboard flame damper appeared normal to the instructor. I was unable to check other aircraft as a comparison at that time.

On one particular occasion, while I was practising at Petrel, mainly for single-engine approach and landing, I became alert to the sound of the rear door opening and closing. I was queuing along with other Ansons awaiting their turn to take off. I was joined in the aircraft by an LAC ground tradesman requesting a flight.

'Can you take me back to base, Chief? It will be ages before the transport turns up.'

'It's OK by me, but you realise I am only a pupil?' I replied.

'That's all right, Chief. You can't be worse than anybody else,' the LAC said.

'You've no parachute either?' I queried.

'That don't matter, I wanna get back to Carberry, otherwise I'll be here all night!' the airman, many years my senior, replied with a laugh.

We took off. I flew him straight back. We landed on the grass and taxied round to the perimeter towards the first hangars, which were the engine fitters' workshops.

'See you Chief, I'll be off now before the Control Tower see me,' the LAC said cheerily. He was gone in a moment, running towards the maintenance huts.

No one ever said anything about it so I presumed no one had noticed. It only needed a Flight Commander watching your return or perhaps someone at Flying Control to wonder why you stopped momentarily on the peri-track outside the 'flights'. They were not as stupid as we sometimes thought and very often turned a blind eye to these things. The Flying Control types usually didn't miss anything!

One early morning job was starting up the Ansons stored in the hangar overnight. All pupils who had about thirty hours' on the type were duly certificated for starting up the aircraft in the early mornings. The 'erks' used to plug in the trolley/accumulator and we did the rest. Once we were clear of the hangar we taxied the Ansons to form a long line in front of the Control Tower. One had to be careful not to damage aircraft, hangars or injure personnel. Severe disciplinary action could await the unwary or the unlucky. (Today we all sometimes have difficulty parking a car. Just think what it was like parking a 55 feet (17 metres) wingspan, twin-engine aircraft? We had to do it properly, parking within 3 to 6 feet (1 to 2 metres) of the next aircraft wing tip. Your viewpoint was $27\frac{1}{2}$ feet (8.5 metres) minimum, from your own wing tip.)

One of our pupils was involved with a Canadian trainee in a taxiing accident. 'Our lad' was taxiing past a hangar when the RCAF pupil taxied from in between two hangars and ran into our colleague. Both cadets received punishment from the Groupie – our lad got fourteen days' detention and the other chap a month! It seemed a tough way to learn about taxiing an Anson with time spent in a Detention Barracks, right in the middle of flying training.

Another chore at Carberry was the job of Duty Pilot. This meant spending at least a morning or afternoon in the Airfield Control Pilot (ACP) Caravan, armed with a Very pistol, together with red signal cartridges and a red glazed Aldis lamp. The job was simple enough. We were expected to keep our eyes on all aircraft using the aerodrome, the idea being that we allowed enough 'safety' space between each aircraft and also to prevent 'wheels up' landings, as well as other possible accidents. It was good training for the pupils, for it gave us the opportunity of viewing things from the ACP Caravan. Most of the time there was not a lot to do, except to keep a constant vigil! If two or more aircraft were too close when on the approach for landing, one had to give a 'red' with the Aldis to the offending aircraft. This was not easy to decide, although the rule that generally applied was 'first was foremost' and to eliminate those who followed too close. Sometimes pupils and even instructors ignored the caravan signals. Usually, reactions were good from both. In the main they were *very* good. It gave some satisfaction to hear an Anson that you'd just given a 'red' to, open up both engines simultaneously in fine pitch to make quite a roar on the over-shoot. If the red Aldis signal failed to be noticed or was ignored, the red Very pistol (always kept loaded) was fired across the nose of the offending aircraft.

Later on in the day or evening my colleagues on the course made comments good and bad, the latter often of a sarcastic but jovial nature, regarding the signals received from the caravan on that particular day.

'Bloody hell, Broome, you must have known it was me, I'd got full flap on when you slammed that "red" up at me! The instructor nearly shit a brick! "Whosatt flaming' idiot mate of yours in that bleeding caravan?"'

There were times when Taylor had mercy on me when I was doing my ACP. He sent LAC Lethbridge (his other pupil) to relieve me while I did an hour or so on single-engine approaches, IF and so on. It seemed a great idea to me, although I'm not so sure that Lethbridge thought so!

One morning I discovered I was due to fly the thirty-five-hour test with Flight Lieutenant Blezard, which I passed without any difficulty. About a week later I was informed of yet another test. The Flight Commander was due to test another cadet, LAC Lewis, and me. We were to do the test together in the same aircraft. It was just a spot check, or so we were told. Nothing to worry about. It could happen any time!

Who was kidding whom? Was the axe about to fall? Spot checks were not done for nothing. I found this extremely demoralising, especially at such short notice after the thirty-five-hour test! Flight Lieutenant Blezard, a very pleasant instructor, had made no complaint but the solo test, prior to Flight Sergeant Partridge's intervention, had disturbed my confidence during flying tests and so brought memories of Grosse Ile.

The testing officer should have been a squadron leader, but we were both in for a leg up. We were to do our check with the CFI, a Wing Commander. The test was delayed a further day due to weather.

Lewis was tested first and passed. I found this encouraging. I followed immediately. The first thing I noted was that the testing pilot did not appear to know why I was being tested! The next thing I knew, after a straightforward take-off into low cloud (800 feet with snow showers) was that the Wingco cut the starboard engine. I applied opposite rudder, opened the port engine to full power and did the normal cockpit check of all instruments to ascertain the engine fault. The fuel cock for the starboard engine had been turned off (this I indicated to the Wingco). Next thing the controls were snatched out of my hands.

'You're stalling, I've got her,' the Wingco shouted. I was taken completely by surprise.

I was then asked to make a normal circuit, approach and landing with both engines, which I did.

Just before touchdown the Wingco said 'You're drifting to starboard.' I thought it looked very slight and applied port rudder to straighten the approach. We landed a second or two later, a normal three-pointer, with no swing.

'Good God man, you nearly ripped off the undercarriage!' (My flying logbook confirms I had never been taught how to land crosswind.) I was staggered at this remark and his earlier comments. Previously, there seemed no problem that I wasn't capable of handling. I realised much later, that there was something wrong with this test!

We taxied to the parking lines. I cut both engines after parking and braking. The Wingco seemed in a hurry to get out. I wondered why. He disappeared rapidly, not looking at me.

'We'll have you CT – if you go on like that you'll kill yourself,' he said as he left the aircraft.

Earlier, he had asked why I had used rudder to correct the slight crosswind approach. I replied that I had been taught not to use aileron to correct near the ground, especially as the wing is then near to stalling, therefore to use rudder only, to straighten an approach, the wings were level, at least I thought so.

'Do you always do as you are told?' the Wingco retorted.

Earlier still, I had been cautioned about the closeness of another Anson (again, there was *no* 'red' from the ACP). I felt the aircraft was well away from ours. In any case, it takes two pilots to present a possible collision course. The other Anson did nothing. I at least altered course!

I wasn't happy about the test at all. I felt very nervous throughout, especially after the comment about a possible stall and also the drift correction on landing. (It had never happened before on a single- or twin-engine circuit or approach in any aircraft, nor was I ever cautioned by an instructor.)

It was certainly a sad day for me. I wasn't sure which way up I was for the rest of it. It was a tremendous disappointment to be eliminated for the *second* time, especially after such a good show at Caron.

There was no time lost in getting a reselection board. A full aircrew medical was arranged for the very next day (someone seemed to be fully clued up). The following day I attended a reselection board.

The Wingco said it would be a very long wait for a Bomb Aimers' Course, twelve months at least. He added they couldn't recommend me as a Straight Navigator, especially with my recent low navigation exam marks. (The USN had been quite happy to recommend me for such a course on finishing at Grosse Ile.)

The Wingco then recommended Straight Air Gunner. (A 'Straight' Air Gunner is trained only as an air gunner, whereas a 'Wireless Operator' Air Gunner is trained also in all wireless and signals operation.) It appeared that he was backed by the rest of the Board. There was no mention of any recommendation by my instructor – I gathered he had not been asked for one. I was in no mood to argue. I was too fed up with the whole situation so I accepted the Board's recommendation. I was really quite 'cheesed off' with all this training bullshit. Let's get onto ops fast and be damned! I wonder how many other CT cadets at Carberry were to feel the same way?

I made no fuss about various comments made by the Board, e.g., the poor navigation result and the apparently poor results on the Link. The Wingco added 'you can get around on an Anson all right but we are training you to eventually fly the Lancaster or Mosquito.' (Later, a Bomber Command Squadron Leader pilot commenting on the latter remark, said that this was not the job of the CFI at SFTS.) I realise now that I accepted defeat too easily. My navigation and other marks at Caron had been well above the acceptance level. My flying was good on Cornells, and it was not likely that I was that bad on Ansons. Also, I'd been astounded at the low navigation exam mark. The Link performance too, seemed strange. These results were completely out of line with my previous exam marks at Caron.

Later, however, I was to learn there was a lot more to the story, for something like 30 per cent of the course was to follow me to the RCAF Station at Macdonald.

Pilot Officer Taylor made quite a few guarded comments, but perhaps let the cat out of the bag when he said 'There are just too many pilots, we had to get rid of some of them.'

I didn't believe this at the time.

'Your flying's not bad, you were no worse than the others. Don't take it too hard, best of luck at gunnery school!' he added.

I did not realise at the time (November 1943), that when my instructor, Pilot Officer Taylor, told me that there were 'too many pilots under training' *that this was true*! (I thought he was just being kind.)

Much later, when I was back in the UK in 1944/5, I was to meet two former pilot training colleagues. One was Sergeant Johnny Walker (6 ITW and 9 EFTS, Southam) and the other was Sergeant Martin (33 EFTS, Caron and 33 SFTS, Carberry). Both of these lads had *retrained* as flight engineers, after previously qualifying as pilots!

Even worse, some who similarly qualified as officer pilots were put onto railway engines as 'Second Stokers' (Ref *Pursuit Through Darkened Skies*, p227, by Michael Allen DFC, Airlife Publishing Ltd).

I spent the last days at Carberry painting the 'bogs' with LAC Robertson, a Scots cadet some years older who had been made CT the week before.

Just before I left the unit I met Flight Sergeant Partridge with an NCO colleague at the main guardroom. We were all in the process of booking out.

'How are you progressing? Everything going OK?' 'Chiefy' asked. I quickly explained what had happened.

'Have you had your Selection Board yet?' 'Chiefy' asked. I replied that I had and was going to Macdonald as a straight air gunner.

'Oh Christ, I wish I had known earlier, I would have had a word with the Wing Commander. It is too late now if you've been before the Board. It is a pity. I wish I had known.'

I thanked 'Chiefy' for all he'd done. He was a very genuine person and I am sure he meant what he said about seeing the Wing Commander. 'Chiefy' was so vigorous in his remarks and so pro 'his cadet' that if anyone could have done it, he would.

The time spent at No. 33 SFTS wasn't the happiest; it had been the most tense next to Grosse Ile. Also, I now knew I would definitely not be making the aircrew trade of pilot. Inwardly I felt upset, more deeply than the first time, probably because this was the final blow.

I could have pushed for an Air Bombers' (Bomb Aimer) course and so retain my PNB (Pilot/Navigator/Bomb Aimer) identity and pay. It seemed a pity to waste all that training.

Accepting a new course as 'straight' air gunner only came easy on the rebound. It was a fatalistic approach. I had really very little interest in the job. I didn't know much about gunnery other than that learnt already on past courses, and not from an air gunner's point of view. If I could become the rear or tail gunner, so much the better – best to get it over with. The course itself was to be a doddle, especially when compared with pilot training! The possible simplicity of the course was also in my mind when making the choice.

Various other cadets, including LACs Lewis and Lethbridge, were to join the rest of us already at Macdonald in the coming weeks. Some of these I had thought to be better pilots of Ansons than I was.

About three weeks before I finished at Carberry (while still on the course) we were all treated to a preview of the aircraft and trainee crews from Macdonald. (This was without realising that many of our fellow cadets from Carberry would soon join them. I've wondered since whether or not it was a sort of recruiting drive, i.e., was there something more behind this spectacular visit, or was it just chance?) The weather had apparently deteriorated rapidly in the vicinity of RCAF Macdonald (near Lake Manitoba, 70 km west-north-west of Winnipeg). Quite unexpectedly our aerodrome circuit was filled to overcrowding with twenty to thirty Fairey Battles.

Some of us had not seen a Battle since the pre-war air shows, certainly not the Battle II turreted version from the nearby Air Gunnery School. There were also the target-towing Battles – the old version (without turret) but possessing the fully streamlined cockpit of the Battle I. This cover enclosed both staff pilot and drogue operator; the latter aircraft were painted black and yellow in diagonal stripes on the wings and fuselage to distinguish the drogue-towing aircraft from the plain yellow gunnery trainer.

There were many sarcastic comments from our local instructors and pupil pilots regarding the landing discipline and flying skill of the visiting Canadian pilots.

The trainee gunners, we noted, were fully kitted with flying boots, gauntlets, outer and inner flying suits, plus the usual helmet, goggles and crew-type parachute harness. We noted too that most of the flying kit was pretty filthy, evidently from the grime and grease collected by the Battles during their gunnery training service. In addition, the undersides of the aircraft were severely blackened, presumably by exhaust smoke. This had rubbed off on to the recently issued new flying suits, making every trainee look like a 'flying chimney sweep'.

The entry into the Battle single gun turret was via an open hatch situated almost central in the bottom of the fuselage between the wings. We later discovered that each Battle II trainer carried two gunners. One gunner operated the turret, the other (awaiting his turn) sat on the floor, aft of the ever-open hatch (there was no door). Also, they carried in the fuselage two ammunition boxes containing 300 rounds for each gunner. Each allocation of 300 rounds was brightly painted a different colour to enable 'hits' on the practice drogue to be recorded for each trainee.

The visit of Fairey Battles from Macdonald was an experience some were never to forget, especially as many colleagues on the course at Carberry were later to join those already at Macdonald. We would perhaps benefit to some degree and be more prepared for our new training after the visit by the RCAF.

During the remaining days at Carberry we filled the time attending lectures on air gunnery for half of each day. The remaining half-day was spent painting the photo lab (we'd finished the 'bogs'). We were lucky to be left on our own to do the fatigues. The 'Discip' Flight Sergeant didn't seem to mind how much work we did, as long as we kept out of his way. He was another great guy!

4 December – Worked all day on the Airman's Toilet in the GIS (Ground Instruction School), painting and decorating the place throughout.

5 December Continued with our previous job and finished it about 16.30 hours. Made it quite nice. More like a lounge than a 'bog'!

6 December – Spent the morning doing lectures on air gunnery and a small amount of aircraft recognition. The afternoon was spent painting out the Photographic section.

7 December – Carried on with lectures – aircraft recognition, gunnery sighting etc. Painting as usual in the afternoon.

8 December – Got notice of our posting. We are going to No. 3 B & GS. RCAF Macdonald, Manitoba. Spent the day getting our clearance chits signed, only 3 of us are going – LAC Rogerson, LAC McBride and myself. Had my logbook returned. Flying time is as follows:

	Day		Night	
	Dual	**Solo**	**Dual**	**Solo**
DH82A Tiger Moth	14.10	00.10	–	–
Stearman N2S2	32.40	24.00	–	–
Cornell	32.50	40.35	4.00	1.00
Anson II	28.00	15.10	1.20	–
	107.40	79.55	5.20	1.00

	Link	**IF**
33 EFTS	10.00	7.55
33 SFTS	12.00	7.30
USNAS	1.00	
Total	23.00	15.25

The gunnery lectures were given by a Corporal Armourer. We discovered later on how high a standard they were. We didn't know what to expect at Macdonald. The Corporal was a splendid fellow, transmitting his keenness to us both. There was nothing to match his patience and consideration!

We didn't have long to wait for our posting to No. 3 Bombing and Gunnery School. It was a very quick move, which suited both Jock and me. Fortunately, the usual posting to the PDC at Brandon had been bypassed so we missed the extra bind of waiting around at yet another station doing useless jobs. What never occurred to us at that time, was the very possible explanation – someone, somewhere, still desperately needed air gunners, not pilots!

Epilogue to Part I

During my flying time as a single- and twin-engine pilot (nearly 200 hours with over 80 hours' solo) I had never pranged, got lost, or been cautioned by an instructor for flying dangerously. I was competent on IF. I had night soloed, was fully aerobatic to RAF standards and had qualified as pilot/navigator. My ground school marks were never lower than 80 per cent for any flying training subject (except for the recent navigation exam). Finally, I was nineteen years old and had been a trainee pilot for fifteen months. Something like £2000 had been spent by the RAF on my training. (UK wages were then approximately £5 per week.)

In just three months' time I would be promoted to sergeant, having qualified as a straight air gunner. Less than two months later I would become a member of a bomber crew. In that crew I was to occupy, voluntarily, what was considered by many at that time to be the most dangerous and unprotected position in any bomber aircraft.

What I didn't know then was that by becoming an air gunner, I was destined for the 'time of my life'. Also, eventually, I was to meet and fly with some of the best guys I was ever to know! Sometimes, life has its compensations.

PART II

Reluctant Air Gunner

CHAPTER 7

RCAF Macdonald, Manitoba

Sprog Air Gunner

8 December 1943 – Received notice of our posting for the gunnery course at No. 3 Bombing & Gunnery School, RCAF Macdonald. Spent the day getting clearance chits from RAF Carberry signed. LACs Rogerson and McBride are to accompany me on the course.

9 December – Finished our 'clearances'. Started packing our kit. We are leaving tomorrow at 06.00.

10 December – We left Carberry as arranged. RAF transport took us to Portage la Prairie. We arrived just after 07.00 to have breakfast at the Mayfair Hotel. RCAF transport arrived at 10.00 to convey us to Macdonald. We were there, all three of us, plus kit by 11.00. We were soon allocated to an empty and recently vacated barrack hut.

We spent a relatively easy day exploring the camp, visiting the canteen and later the NAAFI for candy and cigs, Sweet Caporal. We also discovered that there were WDs (Women's Division of the RCAF) on the base. In the evening we visited the cinema, which had a new show about three times a week.

11 December – Up at 10.00, lunch at 12.00. In the afternoon we cleaned up the billet. In the evening the new course arrived from RCAF Quebec. In the evening the three of us went to the WD's canteen. (One of us had received an invitation; otherwise we would not be able to visit.)

12 December (Sunday) – A very easy day. We became acquainted with the new course intake and soon learnt that the barrack block that we had been allocated was next door to the one occupied by the current graduating course of air gunners.

Very soon, we were invited by some of the excited and enthusiastic occupants to inspect their best blue tunics, complete with new sergeant's stripes and air gunner flying badges. It all looked too simple to ex-pilots who had enjoyed the hard work of previous courses. It seemed too good to be true that in twelve weeks' time we would be in a similar position, awaiting 'wings' parade.

Over the weekend there were further arrivals of new trainees. The first group was a small contingent from the RAF PDC at Brandon, making a total of eleven RAF lads on the course. Then came a batch of 'Newzies' and 'Aussies' (RNZAF and RAAF). These were either direct entry air gunners or those that had failed the radio part of a WOP/AG (wireless operator/air gunner) course.

Later, the billet filled up with the arrival of Canadian direct entry, straight air gunners from the RCAF Centre at Quebec. These lads were the backbone of our course. They had received basic training at an RCAF equivalent of our RAF ITW for air gunners. They represented some 80 per cent of the course and were a very mixed bag, mostly very young. Some were only just above the acceptance age of seventeen for the RCAF. (The RAF entry was still eighteen.) There were a few Americans who had purposely volunteered for the RCAF to take advantage of the lower age limit. (At that time, I believe the minimum entry age to be twenty-one for the USAAF and USN.)

We soon got to know each other and spent the weekend swapping experiences, as well as exploring the camp. The RAF trainee gunners included Alf Compton, Peter Bone, Al Lock, 'Tim' McCoy, Ken McBride and 'Jock' Rogerson.

There was one French and one Belgian trainee. All the RAF lads were LACs, including the Belgian who was 'RAF'. The Frenchman, André, was a corporal in the Free French *Armée de l'Air* and wore a very smart, dark navy blue uniform trimmed with gold, including peaked cap, so typical of the French forces. The Belgian was Johnny Passegea.

Upon inspecting the camp, we found that a new ground school was under construction. This was in addition to the buildings already in use by the more advanced courses who were taking their gunnery training in the air. The latter spent half a day flying and half a day in ground school.

Being new boys, we would have to do six weeks' 'full time' ground school in the new buildings. Then after an exam on all subjects, we would move to the flying and air firing part of the course for the remaining six weeks.

We kept the same billets for the whole course, which was good because we didn't lose touch with people, especially personal friends in nearby bunks. Only course failure could do that. I don't think any of the RAF guys from previous courses had any worries there.

Peter Bone had failed a navigators' course at the AOS (Air Observer School) at Winnipeg. LACs McBride, Compton and Rogerson had also failed as pilots at Carberry. Lock, McCoy, Passegea and André had failed at various stages of pilot training in Canada. None of these lads were to fail the course at Macdonald in either the elementary or advanced stages.

At the beginning there was a reluctance to accept the bind of yet another course, especially as we had already completed a similar course at ITW. Perhaps we were afraid of being 'once a failure, always a failure'. We had all been so keen in the past that nothing should have stopped us. Now, we were studying a course that appeared to be an absolute 'doddle' – it seemed too good to be true! To even think about being sergeants in twelve weeks' time seemed immoral! We'd all thought like that before, especially those from Carberry. We should have been sergeants or pilot officers twelve weeks after commencing the Anson course, subject to the weather. This is why a completely new course that looked so simple caused a supercilious reaction in most of us.

We commenced ground school on the following Monday morning and were speedily sorted out into groups alphabetically and allocated to classrooms with a class number for each group. Peter Bone, Alf Compton and I were all in the first class. I didn't know either very well then; Peter was a complete newcomer and so was Alf to some degree as I had not seen much of him at Carberry in a course of some sixty bods. I had lost my colleagues at intervals in the past due to postings of one kind or another. One made new friends rapidly but there was still the tendency to keep with former colleagues if possible.

Many of the subjects that were taught in the early weeks of the ground school course had been done by the RAF lads at ITW. It was nothing short of a solid bind to do something like 70 per cent all over again. The level of maths was very simple (no algebra or trig). The navigation was the same; we learned to map read, take drifts and sort out simple courses. A few of these things went down fairly well a second time. The subjects that didn't were Air Force law, administration, hygiene and any other unpopular subjects like PT and, later on, belting ammo!

Aircraft recognition was a bit of a joke at first, as there were about sixty-odd 'kites' on the list! We had 'any old bod' as an instructor for this subject to begin with. Then one day a Sergeant WD (Canadian WAAF) arrived and things took a different line. The *lady sergeant* was deadly efficient and so taught no rubbish. She shook the daylights out of some of the 'Canucks' and 'Aussies' too. Neither was she slaphappy or yet intolerant of boyish air gunner cadets. Lady she was – she wouldn't stand any nonsense. She was about thirty-five to forty years old and wore the Canada shoulder flash denoting she had been on overseas service. We sarcastically kidded ourselves that she had done her 'bit' in Newfoundland but in general, as the course progressed, we all treated her with the greatest respect. As for aircraft recognition, she really knew her aircraft, unlike her numerous male predecessors, sergeant instructor AGs, who seemed to be for ever talking a load of 'bull' about the merits of various aircraft. A popular ending by these types to many an aircraft under discussion was 'a stinger in the tail'. I never understood why this description should enter the subject of aircraft recognition, especially since the pupils were all trainee gunners! What use was it to know the armament of bombers, Allied and enemy, to that degree? Air gunners were not often to be found in the nose turrets as these were normally operated by the bomb aimer in heavies. It wasn't a general thing for bomber to attack bomber! If it came to armament of the enemy, we should have had much more detail of the fighter armament and armour, especially the night fighter arm of the *Luftwaffe*. Nevertheless, we came to greatly appreciate our RCAF Sergeant WD. She was the tops!

Aircraft recognition had always been a favourite subject of mine. Lord knows why I was attracted to it. It seemed natural enough to me that if one were to be a 'real airman' one ought to know one's aircraft! Many cadets were not so keen and had problems. However, it was probably one of the easiest subjects for us all. If I didn't manage to get 100 per cent on each test, I honestly thought I had been twisted. My usual reaction was 'Shit, I don't believe it. Damned "Canucks"!'

The usual trip-ups were aircraft like the Dornier Do 215 and Do 17z. Also, the Martin Baltimore and Martin Maryland were both extremely similar aeroplanes in silhouette. So, if one got both of these wrong in a test of fifty aircraft then it accounted for marks like 96 per cent.

The ground school was not very special. There was a tendency for people to get bored, the exception perhaps being the new boys of the RCAF. Clever sods (like myself) often paid little attention in class in the early lessons and consequently we occasionally got caught out.

I have mentioned already that I was not too mechanically minded in a technical sense, so armament theory became more than just a bind. It didn't take long for this to be noticed by the class instructor, usually a particular RCAF Sergeant AG. One of the favourite means of using up the last few minutes of a lesson was to ask questions of each pupil in succession, around the classroom. This was a certainty during lectures on the Browning machine-gun.

At the beginning of the course I found, when my turn came, that often I couldn't answer the question. This was usually because I hadn't remembered all the gen from ITW or because I hadn't been paying sufficient attention to what appeared to be a complicated mechanical function. Rather than try to flannel my way through by having a go at all sorts of 'waffle', I always answered 'Don't know, Sergeant.' After a few occasions, the instructor, pointing a finger at me, would say 'Ah, you don't know' before quickly passing on to the next cadet without waiting for an answer. Honesty never did pay off, whereas to waffle about it was supposed to show that I cared about the answer. Also, being ex-pilots and nineteen made some of us rather cocky when one is honest about it. This is very natural in youngsters of any decade.

We did our spells of PT in a hangar that had been converted into a gym, besides being fitted with galleries each side. These galleries contained numerous compartments with desk, top and stool, open-fronted to face a duplicate on the opposite side of the hangar. The compartments in the galleries were for Aldis lamp practice and were very acceptable considering the weather in December was usually poor with low temperatures and regular heavy falls of snow. One day I was called out of a classroom lecture to be confronted by a very angry Canadian Warrant Officer. He wanted to know if I came from Coventry, England. I thought at first that perhaps it was bad news, which it was in a way.

'Why have you carved your name into the new woodwork?' the Warrant Officer asked.

'Not me, Sir,' I replied.

'Why would anyone else carve your name, Broome?'

'I don't know, Sir, sometimes people do.'

'I don't believe you,' retorted the Warrant Officer.

'If I see it again, I'll put you on a fizzer for damaging Air Force property. Now go back to your class.'

I returned to my class, knowing that I was a liar too. Lots of people had put their names on those gallery ledges and tables. How stupid we were and how easily found out! FD Broome, Coventry, England. Yes, I deserved to be a 'dim air gunner'!

The new subject on the course for most was turret manipulation. We were aghast when we learnt that something like fifteen hours of 'turret manip' was needed to complete the course. (It seemed a lifetime.)

There were various turrets – all makes, types and sizes imaginable. There was the Bristol Mk III as fitted to the Blenheim IV and the Battle II trainer. This was most important at Macdonald because we needed at least some familiarity with the turret in which we were expected to fire our training ammo in the air.

The prospect of firing an aircraft machine-gun while flying on the firing ranges was not only an exciting prospect, but could also be quite a dangerous one. There would be other aircraft nearby so one could not fire willy-nilly. The drogue aircraft would be fairly close, 200 yards or so, and if not carefully positioned by both drogue pilot and gunnery trainer staff pilot a ghastly situation could easily develop – a trainee gunner in the turret, in charge of a death-dealing weapon firing 1180 rounds per minute! We didn't worry too much, but took our drills quite seriously. Most, if not all, the trainees were very conscientious in this respect. We were all desperate to get our turret manipulation hours in as soon as we could, although most of this would come in the latter part of the course. At this earlier elementary stage it was necessary to complete two hours in the Bristol Mk III single-gun turret before commencing air firing during the advanced and final part of the course.

One of the most colourful of our instructors was a young and vigorous Canadian Warrant Officer, about twenty-three or twenty-four years of age, of medium, stocky build. He was absolutely 'mustard', especially about being an air gunner. There was no other instructor like him. Warrant Officer Tate knew his stuff on elementary air gunnery. He stood no messing about or inattentiveness in class. He really taught by the book and he believed implicitly in the book. If he suffered from anything at all, it was perhaps 'the book'. After all, who were we to judge him? We were only rookies, not even qualified rookies.

If you asked him a question you simply got an answer as if from the book. If you asked one that wasn't in that particular book, then the sort of answer you got was to suggest that it couldn't happen! For instance, according to Warrant Officer Tate, the rear or tail gunner could not possibly miss seeing a fighter at night unless he was asleep, not searching properly, having his coffee or smoking a fag. No one ever queried the answers! (Most of the elementary training we had at No. 3 Bombing & Gunnery School on tactics was completely outdated.)

However, if one was to survive the course one had to watch out for Warrant Officer Tate or else you simply wouldn't. He was the best elementary gunnery instructor we had. He was commissioned just before we finished the course. We heard a rumour much later, when we were at OTU or Conversion Unit, that Tate was in the UK. Much later we heard that he had been severely wounded in action, as a result of a combat with a night fighter over Europe. We hoped that it was just a rumour.

Sometimes, when the class had to be left without an instructor, perhaps for some sort of a meeting or if someone was ill, one particular person was regularly chosen to take charge, especially if the subject was armaments. That person was 'Old Bogie', an ageing Warrant Officer. He was a Canadian armourer who had, at about forty plus years, decided to volunteer to become an air gunner!

Warrant Officer (2nd class) Bogart was a much-liked person. He seemed to have taken stock of everyone in the class. What he didn't know about the individual cadet wasn't worth knowing. Also, 'Old Bogie' knew the Browning gun inside out. I am sure that with his enthusiasm the class improved its knowledge of the weapon a hundredfold. He was a right old wizened-up guy in comparison with us 'kids'. How on earth he ever stood us, I will never know!

'Old Bogie' sometimes suffered from a temporary loss of memory, like naming a part of the gun. His spontaneous substitute was always the same word: 'dimafricket'. Other instructors called it a 'whatsit' or a 'gubbins', and sometimes an 'oozit'. 'Old Bogie' certainly knew his guns and quite definitely the Browning gun. We were all absolutely delighted at the end of the course when he earned himself a commission as Pilot Officer Air Gunner. Poor 'Old Bogie' was posted to Instructors' School. All he did for the remaining few days was to bind and rave that he wanted to go 'overseas' and we all knew what that meant – operations in Europe. 'Old Bogie' was absolutely wizard so we didn't want him killed. We respected him far too much to doubt the sincerity of his request to 'serve overseas'.

We had just settled down to the course when the Christmas break arrived. We had six days' leave, which I thought was pretty good, although it meant letting the New Year in back at the Station.

There was a waiting train in a siding outside the camp for those who were going into Winnipeg. From Winnipeg, those Canadians who could get home in the time went their respective ways.

Peter Bone sat opposite me in the carriage and spoke of visiting a girl in Winnipeg. I told him I thought he was a lucky beggar having a girlfriend so near. I presumed he would stay with her family for the whole of the holiday.

I hadn't been so lucky. I still wrote to Terry in New Rochelle, New York, and to another girl, Gerry, in Detroit. Since Detroit was the nearest I had asked Gerry if I could visit her and her family. I had received an immediate invitation and later I had to name a guarantor because I was visiting the United States. I understood from other cadets that the guarantor had to send sufficient money for the journey. This seemed strange, since we hopped over the border quite frequently without this problem while at RCAF Windsor. However, I was unable to get the guarantor and so had to cancel plans at the last moment.

I said cheerio to Peter Bone as he left the train at Winnipeg and then made my way to the Airmen's Club to see what I could do with six days' leave. Little did I know how lucky I was that evening to meet the Kirbys and have a most special Christmas with a wonderful Canadian family and one I was never ever to forget.

There were two other Air Force guests at the Kirbys for the Christmas period. A party had been arranged for Boxing Day and one of the guests was Jonesy (his own nickname), a Canadian hell-bent on getting into a gun turret! Let's hope he made it in the end and, more so, survived to tell the tale. The other was a Canadian WD, a very attractive girl, about twenty-three or twenty-four, already engaged. They both helped, together with the Kirbys, to make Christmas what it ought to be and I suspect that Mrs Kirby had invited them to make up a nice party atmosphere.

I took to Mrs Kirby straight away. I had hardly stepped inside the door, well at least she had shown me the room I would use, when she apologised for not having any daughters. I thought this was very good of her and I'm sure she meant it. Her only son, Halder, was seventeen. He was a likeable chap and near enough my own age to keep us on the same level. He was at college at that time.

Mr Kirby was a likeable person. He had a responsible technical position with a fire extinguisher company. Most of these extinguishers were fitted to Canadian-built or modified aircraft.

Much later he was to lose an eye when a fire extinguisher on test exploded. It was a terrible blow to Mr Kirby and a great tragedy for the whole family.

I bought some popular records in Winnipeg and then took them 'home' to the Kirbys to drive them mad with the repetition of 'Moonlight Serenade', 'Moonglow' and 'Paper Doll'. These were played on their radiogram. I enjoyed this special privilege and just hope I didn't wear out my welcome. No one ever complained; they were all saints at patience.

I used to sleep through the morning till a late hour. No one ever seemed to mind. I wonder how they took it all so well. I imagined that Mr Kirby seemed to only half-believe my lineshoots about the Coventry 'blitzes'. Nevertheless, he never challenged me or complained about it. I realised how lucky I was having spent Christmas with such a magnificent family. (I had stopped at three other homes previously on 48-hour passes from Carberry. They were all excellent.)

One of the visitors to the Kirby household was an oldish man of approximately sixty years. He had been an air observer in the Royal Flying Corps during the 1914–18 war and had been flying on operations on the Western Front. He seemed to think that our modern aircraft like the Spitfire and Lancaster were far too fast for him. He seemed unable to believe that one could travel through the air at 300 mph plus. He spoke of the terrible cold when airborne during the winter over the Front in the early flying years. He made us all laugh when he said that the best thing for such low temperatures was a hot water bottle, strategically placed on the tummy. According to him, it acted like a central heating system and warmed the whole body!

Our Christmas leave soon passed and once the New Year festivities were over we became embedded in the course once more.

The Canadian instructors were mostly sergeants, straight from the Air Gunner Instructors' School. They were not a bad bunch and it took a great deal of patience and understanding to teach classes of headstrong youths like us. There was never a complaint and there wasn't anything that appeared to be too much trouble for them. Almost any subject was explained very painstakingly. Even the dimmest of us were able to understand.

Our mid-term and course final exams soon came around. Everyone passed with ease, the pass mark in many subjects being as low as 50 per cent. Again, we should have realised – somewhere, someone needed air gunners. One guy got a 100 per cent for aircraft recognition and only 58 per cent for maths. No wonder they put him on a gunners' course!

CHAPTER 8

The Fairey Battle

Airborne Gunnery; the Station Commander; Ammo in the Lake

We were all looking forward to flying. For the direct entry gunners it would be their first flight! There was no familiarisation flight, although the first two exercises were with a cine camera gun, which was probably why.

I was certainly keen to fly in the Battle, especially the turreted version known in Canada as the Battle II. However, I was not too keen on firing a gun in the air. It is likely that I was no more nervous than the rest of the course. The Battle had a must about it for me, for while I was still a schoolboy in 1938 I had seen this aircraft at the Empire Air Display at Ansty. It was very impressive, I thought. Sadly, it was not to be very successful when it was used in France in 1940 as part of the Advanced Air Striking Force.

I had been at work six months by the time the *Wehrmacht* broke through on the Western Front. One of the jobs given to Battle squadrons was to destroy the Maastricht bridges to hold up the German advance. One of the squadrons chosen for this was No. 12 Squadron, the low-level attacking force, led by Flying Officer Garland, whose Battle aircraft was seen to crash onto the bridge. Both Garland and his observer, Sergeant Gray, were to receive the Victoria Cross posthumously. LAC Reynolds, who was WOP/AG, received no award.

The Battles fought a brave but hopeless battle in France. They were eventually withdrawn at the end of the land campaign in that country.

Battle squadrons continued to operate with No. 1 Group from the UK, bombing targets such as airfields, invasion barges and port installations. They were eventually replaced in late 1940 and early 1941 by heavier bomber types, such as the Wellington. One of the squadrons so equipped was No. 12 Squadron based at Binbrook and finally at Wickenby, Lincolnshire.

At Macdonald, the early days in the 'Battle' were full of fun, albeit hairy at times. We found that the Battle was a fine, reliable aircraft for this particular job. This was the general opinion of most trainees.

We soon learnt the simple daily drill for gunnery training. We reported to the Gunnery Flight Crew rooms fully kitted up and ready to fly. We drew parachute harness only, the parachute itself being already stowed in the aircraft. A glance at the blackboard in the crew room would inform one of the names of gunners, time of take-off, aircraft number, staff pilot and type of gunnery exercise – weather permitting, which it didn't, much to our dismay, on too many winter days.

Once we knew we were flying, the next thing was to draw the training ammo, 300 rounds each. A separate colour paint marked each set of rounds for each gunner. Usually, the round noses were painted red, green, yellow or blue. It was a greasy paint and hardly dried, otherwise it would be useless. It came off very easily and so daubed everything it came into contact with, including the trainee gunner and his flying clothes.

Once the ammo had been drawn, the two gunners made their way to the allocated aircraft. This was always approached from the rear (since the single airscrew was almost certainly revolving), climbing in via the trap door under the fuselage. The first trainee to enter took the turret, becoming No. 1 gunner. On reaching the firing range over the lake, he would fire all his ammo at the appropriate target. Gunner No. 2 followed, repeating the exercise.

The first flight in a 'Battle' was a cine camera gun exercise. It was quite an experience watching another Battle 'attack' your own in a standard 'curve of pursuit attack'. The gunners, lining up the Browning machine-gun with camera attached, followed the 'enemy' aircraft through the ring sight. This was the modern reflector sight, similar to that used in operational aircraft. We were expected to apply the appropriate 'deflection' (lead) to compensate for the speed and position of the oncoming aeroplane. Deflection varied from 3 rads measured on the luminous ring of the reflector sight on the full beam position to zero rad at dead astern. Alternatively, it depended on the position of the attacker, i.e., 60° from the tail = 2 rads' deflection; at

30° it was 1 rad; at 15° it was half rad; dead astern, zero rad (point blank).

It was simple to decide the approximate position of the attacker when flying in the Battle, for the single fin and rudder of the aircraft marked the dead astern position. (The same applied to the Bolingbroke.)

We flew two camera gun exercises in the Battle and also two in the Bolingbroke (the Canadian version of the Blenheim IV). We did not have the opportunity to see the camera gun film. I thought this was poor, as the whole point of the cine camera in air gunnery was to show the *result*! If you could not see that result and so improve on possible errors, then apart from the turret manipulation and sighting in the air, the exercise was useless!

The weather in which we flew, from the end of January 1944 to early March, was appalling. We had consecutive snowfalls and visibility was so poor that we were unable to fly the planned timetable on many occasions. The cancelled flight time was usually spent waiting in the crew room, often practising dismantling and re-assembling the Browning gun, wearing dark goggles, and I mean dark! You could not see a foot ahead. It was good practice but not necessary as it was not operational practice to strip guns in the air. (The reason for this was not given until we reached an Operational Training Unit.)

Normally, we flew two gunners to a Battle or four to a Bolingbroke. (The latter were only used for cine camera exercises on our course, but were intended to eventually replace the Battles for all duties in the near future.)

As the gunners flew in pairs, this enabled the two concerned to carry the large ammo box, containing 600 rounds, out to the aircraft. It wasn't, therefore, too difficult to load the box into the Battle through the floor hatch. By the time we had settled in, the aircraft would be already airborne. Meanwhile, we struggled to load the single gun and operate the turret in the bitter cold. As you can imagine, on the early flights minor problems became major ones. It was always a race against time. We needed to get the ammo fired at the appropriate target in the smallest space of time. Time became the main consideration; certainly we fired at the drogues whenever possible, hopefully allowing the correct deflection. However, some guns were just plagued with stoppages, mostly No. 1 position (duff ammo).

Also, we had gun and system malfunctions galore. Sometimes the drogue-towing 'kite' simply did not turn up. If we were to complete the exercise, we needed to fire at least 100 each out of the 300 rounds issued per gunner. This situation could be greatly improved if the trainees dumped some of the rounds in the lake That is, if we were over the lake! In winter there was little to indicate positive demarcation between land and water, everything being white below. The practice of ammo dumping was passed on from the senior courses. It appeared to be a regrettable necessity in the winter time, in order to complete some or all of the exercises.

It was my fortune to fly with the same trainee on a number of occasions. He was a grand chap and typical of his race. He was a New Zealander, LAC Brookes ('Brookie'). He became my example trainee of the RNZAF. There were no better personnel anywhere in the world. They were at their best in war; they gave a very good account of themselves at other times too.

Brookes and I had our problems in the Battle on the various firing details that we flew together. We managed to sort out most of the stoppages to our combined satisfaction. I flew once with Peter Bone. He seemed quite a competent fellow. No problem arose that we couldn't overcome.

The keenness of both these trainees impressed me immensely. Their main object was to get the exercise completed properly, to expend all the ammo and to hit the target drogue as much as possible. So much so that sometimes we 'shot it away'. Two gunners cooped inside the fuselage of a Battle working like the very devil to keep the gun working, loaded and firing, not forgetting competent turret operation, was a memorable situation.

There was never a moment's hesitation to sort out any stoppage, of which we had many, so many that it was supposed to be a fact of life. We soon discovered that duff ammo was deliberately put into each belt by the armourers. If we fired off the lot, all to the good. If not, out the exit door it went. This was all in joint agreement in seconds, with just a nod and a cheery grin. There was no such thing as an argument, split decision, or any other dissatisfaction. We were all rookies but, as such, had enough sense to stick together.

When it came to handling guns, there were never any accidents, certainly not on our course. No one fooled with the Browning or any other gun. No one pointed guns at each other like kids sometimes do. The gun discipline of the trainees, like the instruction, was absolutely first class. We were, however, only at the elementary stage of air gunnery. Even the air firing side of the course was very simple stuff. We were to find considerable differences later at an OTU.

One of the surprises that occurred at Macdonald was the day the Groupie flew. Group Captain Gibb, AFC (Station Commander of RCAF Macdonald) flew quite a number of training exercises, certainly as many as his other duties would permit.

The surprise came when 'Brookie' and I discovered, much to our absolute horror, that we were due that very morning to fly 'an exercise' with the Groupie. Indeed, as lowly LACs, we were both shaking in our flying boots. We had no time to think about it. Out we went to the Battle, which was already warming up; the slipstream and exhaust gasses blasted us as we tussled with our ammo box in the biting gale and snow flurries from the airscrew.

Who would be first in the turret? There was no mucking about; I was nearest the wing-root as we prepared to duck under with our box. I looked up to see the Groupie give us a nod and a most reassuring smile as he watched our struggles. I entered the hatch first and so went into the turret.

When I had plugged in, the Station Commander asked 'Are you ready for take-off?'

'Yes Sir,' I replied.

'Are you sure? Just take your time, no need to hurry.'

The calm unhurried voice was very reassuring.

'All is OK, Sir. Ready for take-off, Sir,' I said.

We climbed up into the sunlit blue sky. We could hear the staccato roar of the Battle's Merlin, a most comforting sound to young, inexperienced flyers. True, we had a few hours' in by now. I was really thinking of the Group Captain's flying time, probably into 1000s of hours.

'OK, Gunner. Can you see the drogue aircraft?' sang the Groupie!

'It is on the port beam.'

'Open fire when you are ready, do not hurry. We have plenty of time.'

'Very good, Sir.'

I pressed the trigger, simultaneously sighting the gun ahead of the drogue. Ratatatatataaaa! Thump! Damned stoppage! Re-cock, press trigger, thump. Re-cock, press trigger. Ratatatatatat! Thump! Christ, more stoppages! Re-cock, press trigger. Firing gear not working, solenoid plug disconnected, re-fit, re-cock, fire. Ratatatatat.

'Cease fire, Gunner. Now turning to port, commence firing when we are in position with the drogue.'

'Very good, Sir.'

'Open fire, Gunner.'

Ratatatatat. Thump. Stoppage, cock, fire. Re-cock, fire. Re-cock.

'Goddamit, this bloody gun, how the heck…!'

I felt a tugging at one leg. 'Brookie' was pointing to the link bag. Jeepers, I thought, no wonder the gun wouldn't fire. The cocking lever had been in all three positions on the repeated stoppages. The link bag was ram bang full of links, so much so that it was quite a fight to get the bag off the gun. It took all the strength of the two of us. Once emptied, it was a simple thing to 'cock and fire'. Anyway, it was 'Brookie's' turn and I sat down near the ammo box, which was now partly full of links. (The two previous gunners had not emptied the link bag!)

The Groupie confirmed his patience and flew several times up and down the lake in an endeavour to enable us to clear our ammo. The stoppages received earlier had used up vital minutes; there was a limit that even the Groupie could not overcome, that of fuel and also training time on the range.

'Brookie' appeared to have trouble towards the end of his spell. The link bag was OK? Yes. How about the solenoid? It seemed OK. Perhaps Canadian gremlins had got at the gun, or perhaps someone was content to give us even more duff ammo? We were never to find out. We dumped the last 100 rounds through the trap door and, let us hope, into the lake. The calm, patient, resolute Groupie took us home to a landing that matched only his superb flying. It had been the best training flight we had flown. What a magnificent trip! Regrettably it was not to be repeated.

This performance was to be equalled in the future. It was by an RAF Bomber Command, Flight Lieutenant Pilot (later promoted to Squadron Leader), flying a fighter evasive combat manoeuvre known as the Lancaster 'corkscrew'!

The ground school, now the advanced stage, dealt mostly with gunnery tactics, pyrotechnics, the Browning gun, turrets and servo-feed (i.e., ammo supply to the four-gun tail turret currently fitted to the Wellington, Halifax and Lancaster). We also covered turret manipulation, more aircraft rec and took part in indoor skeet shooting in one of the hangars, especially adapted that purpose. We did the occasional spot of PT and also route marches. The weather prevented much of the latter.

We were getting the worst of the weather: deep, drifting snow, low temperatures and biting winds from across the open prairies. It gave us an opportunity to test our Canadian winter gear: the lined mittens, the long underwear, the snow cap 'cum balaclava', without which you could feel the blood in sensitive spots like the ears and nose 'ping' as it started to freeze in a few minutes.

We continued to fly whenever possible, reflecting on how pleasurable it must have been to fly the course in the Canadian high summer instead of the current sub-zero temperatures. The flying kit was very practicable for keeping out the cold at the comparatively low height needed for gunnery training. The kapok inner suit protected by the blue or dark green weather-proof outer suit was ideal for training duties and the current weather. We never needed an excuse for wearing the ever-popular flying boots and gauntlets, plus the soft leather flying helmet and goggles. The helmet, equipped with intercom leads and earphones, the goggles with sun visor, were worn mainly for protection in case of accidents or fire. A girlfriend's scarf or a mother's hand-knitted one finished the job. It was no wonder that we only felt cold on the ground and not in the air!

The turret manipulation was a bind at first. Fifteen hours seemed an age to airmen of tender years. However, the time was well spent in various turrets, which were installed in special buildings that contained the essential hydraulic or electric power supply for full turret operation.

It was to be the best opportunity we would get to try out the various types of turret then in operational service. The installation at Macdonald was to have each type of turret fitted into an internal half-sphere about 12 feet in diameter. The vertical half-sphere (approximately 4 metres) represented the sky and ground around the turret and the object was to superimpose combat cine film motion pictures onto the sphere. The idea was to give the trainee gunner the absolutely vital experience of sighting, identification and operating the turret in simulation of combat conditions.

The gunner was also expected to give a running commentary during the simulated attack, such as he would to his captain during the real thing. A typical commentary was as follows:

'Tail to pilot. Fighter! Port beam level, commencing attack now – 600 yards port quarter – 400 yards, port fine quarter – 200 yards dead astern – 150 yards, breaking away to starboard – 100 yards, *now.*'

Fortunately this wasn't operational gunnery patter. If it had been we would all have been dead by the time the attacking fighter reached 400 yards (in much less than ten seconds). The gunnery patter at Macdonald was fine for turret manipulation. We were in for a pleasant surprise at OTU!

I found the tracer demonstration disappointing. The staff pilot flew the aircraft through a series of climbs, dives and turns, while the trainee gunner fired off a burst from the Browning. The tracer allocation was one in five rounds. It should have been *all* tracer ammunition to give the required effect of bullet trail etc. The display effect of one in five was that each time you fired, you were just in time to see the tracer disappear at 600 yards (extreme range of normal day tracer). By then, the next tracer round had just started on its similar path. Consequently, with only one tracer alight at a time you didn't see any appreciable path in the sky. If you fired all tracer ammo you would have a better appreciation of the bullet path, trail and gravity drop.

The end of our course drew near. Most of us expected to pass and were looking forward to getting our air gunner brevet and stripes or, as the Canadians called them, 'three hooks'. The weather again took a turn for the worse, adding to the length of the course by two and a half days. We completed our ground school exams and now only needed to complete the gunnery exercises in the air.

CHAPTER 9

Graduation

Sergeant Air Gunner; Embarkation Leave; HMT *Louis Pasteur*; RAF PDC Harrogate

We attended our Graduation Dinner the evening before. It was a splendid 'do'. We could hardly believe that it was all over. Tomorrow would mean a flying badge and three stripes. Nothing seemed so important, nothing was more important!

12 March – Graduation Day

The weather cleared up a little this morning. I managed to get two G5 Air Firing Exercises (quarter-cross-UNDER, drogue target) completed in one flight. This was done by taking up 600 rounds by myself and firing off the lot!

After dinner I completed my last G5. All my air firing is now complete.

We had packed our kit the night before and at 4.30 pm we had our 'Wings' Parade. I came 34th on the course and so was in the front rank. After the Parade we drew our pay – I received $65 (Canadian dollars).

We had already attended a practice 'Wings' Parade so it all went easily enough. The Groupie made pleasant conversation with each graduating cadet. We had been briefed to appear in our 'best blue' uniform, complete with stripes.

When my turn came the Groupie said 'Congratulations, Sergeant. Where are you going for your leave?'

'We are off to New York.'

'I expect you are looking forward to returning home?'

'Yes Sir. Very much.'

'Best of luck for the future, Sergeant.'

What a splendid fellow the Groupie was. There he was, attending a regular fortnightly occurrence, the 'Wings' Parade (our course consisted of 104 cadets) as if it happened to him only once in a lifetime. He seemed to treat every man very personally and it sounded as if he meant every word, which I am sure he did. People like Group Captain Gibb, AFC, were few and far between, even in those days. The Groupie treated all the newly fledged sergeants with importance, as if it really mattered to him. It was this sort of spirit, especially that of the Group Captain, that made one feel really good, that you were about to do a job worth doing because people like him made you feel proud of that fact.

Becoming an air gunner hadn't meant much to me. Having to be reclassified stung my pride. I was quite happy to be a sergeant. Only one RAF cadet was to be commissioned on each course, that is, if there was one suitable. Wise 'Old Bogie' was encouraging all the RAF lads to apply, saying a commission in the RAF meant a lot more than in the RCAF! It seemed to be the practice at Macdonald to commission about 15 per cent of the Canadians on the course. The RAF's top cadet was of course Pilot Officer 'Tim' McCoy. Peter Bone also applied but was not successful this time. At least one silly guy didn't even try.

The train was waiting in the siding as it had done for Christmas leave. We left bang on time for Winnipeg. Peter Bone was to spend most of his leave there visiting the Hooper family, with whom he'd spent his Christmas leave

Both of my girl pen friends were in the States, many miles away. However, I intended to spend a couple of days with Mrs Kirby and family in Winnipeg before catching the Trans-Canada (sleeper) Express. My colleagues from Macdonald decided that I would travel with them to Montreal and New York before reporting to RAF Moncton, New Brunswick, at the end of our fourteen days' leave.

Mrs Kirby was most disappointed that I wasn't staying longer and said she had hoped I would spend half of my leave with them. It was a great pity, as the chance would never come again. Sometimes RAF comradeship, unfortunately, spoilt life outside.

During our stay in Montreal we bumped into André, now a Free French Air Force sergeant. He was in a fine mood. Apparently, he had gone along to the French Embassy for some special reason and got himself a real telling off by one of the Embassy staff. They had objected to him wearing an RCAF air gunner brevet. They told him in no uncertain terms to take 'that thing off' and wear instead a bright silver badge, the French Air Force insignia for air gunners. André was quite upset by all this. He had taken quite a liking to the RCAF air gunners' 'half-wing' and naturally assumed that, as his brevet had been officially given to him, he should be able to wear it.

Quite a number of the RAF lads had taken a fancy to the RCAF brevet too and some had sewn it onto their tunics. The Canadian issue was popular because it was larger and of a different design. The RCAF brevet carried a king's crown above the main lettering 'AG' and 'RCAF' in small letters below. All this contributed to a larger emblem. It was generally considered more attractive by most lads at that time. However, these brevets were taboo to our Air Force and no RAF bod wore them in the UK.

During our stay in New York we saw all the sights through the courtesy of the American USO. We were also able to find very comfortable 'B&B' accommodation at the Salvation Army Red Shield Club.

One evening I telephoned Terry at the Larchmont family home and arranged a full evening together with her family.

21 March – Went to Larchmont in the afternoon to seeTerry. Spent a pleasant evening but it could have been better if she had not been engaged!

She's a great kid, lovely to look at! Boy, does my heart beat when I see her.

It was a pleasant reunion after almost twelve months. Her parents, sister and younger brother were all present. The younger lad was convinced that I was to fly (over Europe) in an American-built B17 Flying Fortress, as ball turret (under) gunner. He was surprised when I told him that if I were lucky I would perhaps become rear gunner (tail turret) of an RAF Lancaster. He just couldn't believe it.

'Only the best guys fly tail,' he said.

'Maybe you're right,' I apologetically replied.

Meanwhile, Terry did a grand job sewing a button on my shirtsleeve. We were, unfortunately, not left alone at any time for she had become engaged to a United States Marine Corps Officer Pilot. Later she married him before he left for operations against the Japanese in the Pacific. (Terry continued to write until her wedding, by which time we were flying Lancasters in the UK. I never heard from her again.) She was a lovely girl and I felt very disappointed when she became engaged. Let's just hope the guy she loved made a safe return. My parents were quite disappointed when Terry's letters ceased. My father's comment was 'You lost a good one, she wrote such a lot for one so far away.'

The leave went very well. We all seemed very satisfied and reported to Moncton on time, 27 March. We were very pleased and surprised to be held at the PDC for only a few days. We had expected to remain there for some three to four weeks at least, like certain other bods did. For once, the grapevine was wrong. The rapidity of our posting to the UK did not cause any alarm to any of the newly trained gunners.

It was more than just a little sad to report to the first RAF station since Carberry and to rub shoulders with many old colleagues with pilot and navigator brevets. I bumped into Pilot Officer Carlyon from Pensacola while on a shopping expedition in Moncton town centre. Carlyon spotted me first.

'What-ho Broomie lad. See you made it then?' he called out.

'Ah yes,' I replied, half ashamed. 'Not like you lucky buggers, pilot's wings and a commission too.'

'Well let's see it then,' said Carlyon.

'What?' said I.

'The bloody half-wing, you idiot,' he replied.

'Never mind, you got these,' he said, tugging at my 'three hooks'.

'They are the most important, they're what counts.' Good old Carlyon, I thought. He never changes, does he? Hiding his own successes and not breathing a word about my failures but striving continuously to buck me up. We swapped yarns, I made enquiries about other old friends from Grosse Ile, like Sid Oldfield, Bill Tranter, Bish Bacon and Peter Shannon. Three were sergeants. Bish was now a pilot officer. The time passed quickly, we parted and I never saw him again or heard of his progress. He was a fine guy; one could only gain by the momentary acquaintance.

Two days later we boarded HMT *Louis Pasteur* (nicknamed by the crew 'the Past Whore') at Halifax. We left in the early hours of the morning on 5 April. The coastline of New Brunswick slowly passed out of sight, my air gunner colleagues and I manning the six-inch stern gun (reputedly World War I vintage). We were the auxiliary gun crew. Other air gunners performed similar duties on the ack-ack (anti-aircraft) positions. Some manned numerous 20-mm Oerlikon, which were mounted on flak towers along each side of the ship.

The purpose of the auxiliary gun crews was to act as a supplement to the RN gun crew for each gun. This enabled the 'pukka' gunners to perform their duties with a third of their own gun crew plus two-thirds auxiliary, enabling full watches on and off duty to be maintained. We were to help the Navy gunners get the gun into action should the occasion arise, until the whole RN gun crew arrived on station, during an attack by submarine or aircraft.

We were supposed to fire at any periscope sighted or any suspicious aircraft!

'If you see a torpedo aircraft on an attacking course, we shall only have time to fire one six-inch round and then get the hell out of it and under cover,' the RN gunners said with a wild grin!

I could just imagine that ruddy great gun, which was mounted on an open platform without armour shield, firing with one bloody great bang followed by another when the low-level flak shell burst about 3 to 5 miles out. I hoped that the marine engineer responsible for the platform and structure under the gun had done their job OK. If the gun and all of us had not disappeared in one great cloud of smoke I would have been the most surprised, that is, if we had had time to fire it. We never did, so the gods were kind to us aboard the *Louis Pasteur*!

There was gun practice laid on for us approximately mid-Atlantic. The stern gun was not scheduled to be fired, which pleased the RN gun crew as they would not need the gun-cleaning session afterwards. Those of us who were not required on the stern were temporarily posted to assist on other gun defences. It was my lot to help man one of the Oerlikon flak towers. This turned out to be quite the exciting event of the afternoon, for up in the tower one got an almost unrestricted view all around the ship, especially ahead and on the beams, and when she rolled or pitched, which she did frequently. Hence the nickname!

The first flak to be tested were the 4.5-inch forward guns, which first of all fired a parachute target skywards and then proceeded to knock it down with 4.5-inch flak. When this exercise was complete the 4.5s put up more parachute targets for the 20-mm Oerlikons. The full-time gunner manning our flak tower wasted no time in opening fire on his particular target, the 20-mm tracer shells making a distinct path towards the parachute. Our gunner wasn't able to shoot down the parachute (neither did any other), but he gave a very good demonstration of how accurate one could be with a 20-mm cannon.

Life aboard the *Louis Pasteur* continued at a rapid pace. We seemed to really clip through the seas and were home sooner than we had expected. One person who was pleased to see 'Blighty' again so quickly, perhaps just a little more than others, was Peter Bone. Peter served the same stern gun as myself and was on the same watch. He was no sailor and therefore had quite a grim trip, spending a great deal of his time hanging over the rail, wretching his tummy up.

He really did suffer badly from seasickness, so much so that after the first day he ate little or nothing at mealtimes. Peter could be seen hanging over the rail on nearly every watch, sometimes two or three times per duty. Just how he stuck it I don't know. None of us will ever know his agony. He was so pleased at the thought of getting ashore on good old mother earth. He swore he would be simply delighted to kiss the ground, once ashore.

I also met Bob Wilson, now a sergeant with pilot's wings, on board the *Louis Pasteur*. I had last seen Bob at No. 6 ITW Aberystwyth where, among other things, he was one of the local bandsmen and played for the dance at the King's Hall. Bob lost no time informing me that he and Jean were to become engaged on his return. Bob was pleased to show me the ring he had bought in Canada for the occasion. I was happy to hear that he and Jean had got along so well. I remembered her as a very lovely young woman of eighteen. Bob had been very thoughtful at Aberystwyth in asking if I was sure I did not want to continue to see Jean before she became his girlfriend. It was a very noble gesture indeed. Bob and Jean married after the war and have one son, Peter.

The spell on board the *Louis Pasteur* was short and pleasant for we docked on 11 April at Liverpool. On the same day a train took us to Harrogate. We were billeted in a detached house not far from the Majestic Hotel, which was our main HQ for the RAF PDC at Harrogate. The time could not go too fast for us. We spent only five days on documentation, FFI and medicals before going on disembarkation leave.

Most of the RAF bods from Moncton would get three weeks' leave before reporting back to Harrogate. Not so for André Vernon, the French aviator of the *Armée de l'Air*, now a full sergeant in the Free French Forces. Becoming a sergeant in the FFF was, according to some, as good as getting awarded a commission in our own British services. (This was reputedly because the step between corporal and sergeant in the French Army was like that of sergeant and pilot officer in our own.) André was on an immediate posting to a French Boston Squadron attached to the RAF Tactical Air Force. He was to be allowed only five days' embarkation leave, which he would spend with his mother in England before reporting for duty.

Once we left Harrogate we never saw André again. We all felt that the job he was going to do would not be enviable. Flying at low level on Army Support would not necessarily lead to a long life! We all wished André the very best of luck and a long life. Let us hope he got it, for he was a grand lad, like all the Free French (especially if you made allowance for their easy excitability). We tried to assure André about his leave, saying that he would get more allowed later. André wasn't convinced and was in poor humour about it all. He spent the rest of the time at Harrogate grumbling and becoming generally fed up. Who wouldn't be? We had all expected three weeks' leave for that was what the grapevine had decreed. Five days was a poor exchange, especially if it meant ops straightaway. Let us hope that it was a Boston OTU that André was posted to and that he would have more leave after his arrival and before going on ops.

In those days we took these things very seriously. Three weeks' leave was really something, but to go on ops straightaway didn't seem very funny. It wasn't the risk or the short life expectancy on a squadron, so much as not getting the leave one expected! The average airman lived for his leaves. It mattered not, or so it seemed at the time, that you might get the 'chop' (killed) after a leave as long as you didn't get it *before*.

During the documentation at Harrogate we had the rare opportunity of stating our preference to serve in our choice of command (i.e., coastal, bomber etc.). Most of the AGs from Canada almost certainly chose first, coastal, second, TAF (Tactical Air Force) and third, bomber (quite definitely last)! Indeed, *all* except two were to get their first choice. These two received an immediate posting to a Bomber Command OTU on return from leave. The rest were posted to a Coastal OTU on Sunderlands including one poor beggar who didn't realise that other commands would need gunners and so he only put *one* choice on the form – bomber. The dim sod didn't deserve such luck did he? (Note that Moncton, NB Canada, was essentially an RAF-PDC. Therefore, Canadian, New Zealand and Australian gunners would have gone elsewhere before posting to UK.)

During our stay at Harrogate I met my former colleagues from Aberystwyth – Ray Smith, Johnny Walker, both sergeant pilots, and Cliff Wheeler, now a sergeant navigator. It was very pleasant to shoot a few lines and to get news about others from No. 6 ITW.

No one made any fuss over the fact that I had passed out as a gunner. It was all very gently accepted and instead I received lots of bright and encouraging remarks. There was no talk about '10 seconds to live', at least not while I was present. They were a grand lot from our old room at the 'Lion Royal' in Aberystwyth.

I still felt I had let the side down quite a bit. It seemed that everyone else from No. 6 ITW finished up PNB (Pilot, Navigator or Bomb Aimer), although there could have been the odd bod about whom I knew nothing. This business of being a failure was not going to be easy to ride off. For one thing, being continually surrounded by successful guys didn't help. Harrogate was simply stiff with pilots, navigators and bomb aimers. Very few were trainee failures like the eleven sergeants from Macdonald.

16 April – Handed in spare items of overseas kit. Received pay £6.00. [NB Pay for a sergeant air gunner was 8s (40p) per day, pilots, navigators and bomb aimers received 13s (65p) per day.] Also drew ration cards for three weeks We were also issued with anti-gas kit, steel helmet and rubber boots – more junk to carry around!

17 April – Got up at 05.30, breakfast 06.30, followed by various parades until 09.30 when, armed with travel warrant, we left for the station.

My train left for Leeds at 10.20. Eventually, after much messing around, waiting for connections, I arrived at Coventry Station and took a taxi to carry all the gear home to Wyken, arriving at 7 pm.

18–30 April – Spent my leave visiting old friends, everyone seemed pleased to see me. On the first night Dad was at the Working Men's Club in Wyken. Mum took me over, Dad was all smiles! He couldn't get over it, kept introducing me to all his friends in the club. 'This is my son Frank, now a sergeant, straight from Canada! He's an air gunner, you know!' (They could all see that.) Dad enjoyed himself. He seemed so pleased, so full of it all.

The next day we went to Stirling Metals, saw Von (Veronica). She seemed as lovely as ever. She is now engaged to some 'jerk' of an officer in the Army Cadet Corps.

Les was surprised when I called at his home. We had some fun together – a few drinks and the occasional picture show.

Things went well. I spent a very happy time on leave. The last week was the best, as I started to take Von out once more. This time we got on a lot better, it was simply great! She mentioned two guys, whom I didn't know, who had left Sterling Metals before me to go into the RAF. Both were WOP/AGs with Bomber Command.

Both were 'missing in action'. Perhaps that was why she let me take her out?

1–7 May – Received a week's extension on Wednesday the 3rd. Seemed too good to be true! Later I found out that it was, for on Saturday the 6th I received a telegram recalling me for 'posting'. I left for Harrogate on Sunday the 7th.

On returning to Harrogate it was my misfortune to join a train at Birmingham that already had aboard a small number of sprog aircrew sergeants, all going to Harrogate. In the opposite corner of the carriage sat a sergeant air bomber who began to tell everyone else present, paying most attention to me, what would most certainly happen after arrival in Harrogate. He was absolutely sure that we would all wait about for weeks and months. (A regular feature at most PDCs was just waiting. This was dreaded by all aircrew, from LAC to sergeant and pilot officer.) This fellow obviously knew all the gen and told our fellow passengers, including a middle-aged married couple, two girls in their late teens and a woman with a baby, that I would be posted to Filey for a Commando Course! No one, simply no one, was able to escape the Commando Course, which lasted about four weeks. Some of the others would do supplementary navigation courses before more waiting, then on to AFU (Advanced Flying Unit). Poor old Broome was in for a very rough time of it by all accounts, with definitely no prospect of flying for some two, three or even four months. But the Commando Course was a must – no one had ever been known to 'skive' off it. I was assured by this obviously very clued-up sod of an air bomber, blast him, I thought. He simply couldn't be wrong, it was all I wanted after the pilot fiasco. Now the endless wait, binding courses and positively *no bloody flying*! He had been all through it. He knew by practical experience, so we were very lucky. He'd just given us all the very latest gen!

We arrived at Harrogate around 11.00 pm. I followed the rest of the bods and headed away from the station in search of the 'Majestic Hotel'. We arrived eventually at the guardroom in the hotel main entrance and were duly booked in. A 'Discip' Corporal took eight of us up two flights of stairs and into the main corridors. The hotel was in complete darkness except for the guardroom lights and the torch the Corporal was using.

When it came to my turn, after many a twisting route through the various passageways, the Corporal just shone his torch through into a room off one of the numerous corridor cul de sacs, indicating a vacant bed, complete with blankets. With a cheery 'Goodnight Chiefy' he was gone.

There was not a glimmer of light anywhere. It was after 'lights out' and I had not thought of the hazards of a late night return in the UK blackout. Why should I? I had been away for a year and had forgotten what it could be like returning from leave in wartime Britain. We had been rather molly-coddled in Canada.

There I was in a strange room, with no light and a bed to make. I managed to arrange the blankets and got undressed. I just flung my gear anywhere, most of it on the floor or on my kit-bag. Apart from a grunting and snoring noise in the next bed, all was quiet. The two other occupants of the room were fast asleep. It was now almost midnight.

Just before I got into bed I asked the 'noise maker' in the next bed if he was awake and got strange sounds in return. 'Drunk or daft' I thought. Could be both, he's aircrew isn't he?

'Any idea where the bogs are, Chief?' I enquired. There was just a grunt, followed by one or two short words that I could not understand.

I lay in bed for about thirty minutes or so, but could not get off to sleep. By now the desire for a pee was quite definite. I wasn't exactly at bursting point but I knew positively I wouldn't last the night. I tried again.

'Any idea where the bogs are, Chief?' All sorts of grunts and nondescript words followed. I just couldn't make any sense out of the very short conversation.

I searched for and found my Ronson lighter (bought at Fort Slocum), got out of bed and found the door into the empty corridor. I had imagined as I lay quietly in bed that I had heard the sound of a dripping tap, very, very faintly, nearby. Now I was in the corridor I could see a door on my immediate right, from which the dripping sound seemed to be coming. Luckily, in the light of the Ronson, I could see that when I opened the door it was a bathroom, complete with flush toilet. Saved by a Ronson! Of all the good luck. Mind you, I could fail a pilot's course twice and yet end up with a bog next door. Let's face it, there needn't have been one on that floor. (They were peculiar hotels then, and nothing like the standard expected today. For instance, the 'Lion Royal' at Aberystwyth only had one toilet per floor, and only two bathrooms for the whole hotel housing some 150+ bods.)

I was soon off to sleep and as usual the morning came too soon. I awoke to the sound of movement in the room. I asked about breakfast and was told I would get some if I hurried; it finished at 8 am and it was already 7.50 am. I then discovered that my 'noisy' colleague in the next bed was Polish! There, above his bed, hung an Air Force blue tunic, complete with three stripes and the Polish aircrew silver emblem, suspended by chain, above the left pocket. This explained the previous night's untranslatable conversations! I ran down the stairs into the Sergeants' Mess, having had a quick wash – there was no need to shave as I still only required one shave per week!

It was the usual transit Sergeants' Mess, like at Moncton NB. That is, there were no special comforts, only a few tables and chairs in the dining room and similar in the anteroom and bar next door. I didn't realise then, but this was to be the 'norm' for wartime aircrew Sergeants' Messes. Generally PP and bloody cool in winter!

The main parade of the day was for roll call at 9 am. After this it was announced that some 'postings' would be effected. A batch of names were called, various bods fell out as instructed and were then marched away. Then came a pause. We naturally thought that it was the finish for the day. Being new bods we knew no better! Then, quite suddenly 'Sergeant Bone and Sergeant Broome' was called out. Peter Bone and I duly fell out.

'Get your clearance chits from the Orderly Room, you are both posted to No. 83 OTU. Your travel warrants will be issued tomorrow providing you are "cleared",' the Parade Officer said. We could hardly believe it, especially after all that guff from the air bomber guy on the train!

Peter and I spent the rest of the day getting 'cleared', which was fortunately very simple since we had only just arrived. Mind you, there was enough to do and very often being a newcomer didn't always help. For example, you had to get a signature from the person who was in charge of issuing sheets. It did not matter if you had not been issued with any. We still had to get signatures to say we were 'clear'. Therefore, in some cases it took just as long. Fortunately we'd got them all by late afternoon so at teatime in the Sergeants' Mess I was able to make arrangements to see Cliff and have a few drinks in various pubs in Harrogate.

Cliff seemed quite concerned about the very early posting as we had both considered the prospect of a longer stay and the opportunity of continuing our friendship.

'You posted to an OTU already? We've been here for weeks. You haven't been here five minutes and now you're off to get the "chop". Christ Almighty, just leave it to the next man!' Cliff remarked.

We had an enjoyable evening and took a long walk back to the hotel via the lovely park, which seemed centrally situated in Harrogate.

Next morning, much to my great pleasure and surprise, all my old ITW colleagues were up early and already having breakfast when I arrived in the Sergeants' Mess. There were many happy and yet ribald comments made with firm handshakes all around as Peter and I went to find the RAF transport to the station.

We left very early with packed kit, travel warrants plus a long list of stations to make rail connections in order to get to No. 83 OTU, Peplow, Salop. We'd already drawn our travel rations from the Mess (a couple of cheese sandwiches each) to put into our special canvas sandwich bag. The latter was a rarely used item and being canvas it always dried the contents terribly.

Peter and I surveyed the list of stations.

'Cripes, Peter, we're really doing a cross-country. Do you think we will miss any of these connections?' I asked, indicating the list.

'We've got all day,' said Bone with a wry smile.

'Yeah, we might need it yet.'

We took the RAF transport to Harrogate Railway Station. We hadn't long to wait for our first train to Otley and then another into Leeds. There was an almost immediate connection to the next and then on to Stalybridge Station, a place I had never heard of. Then the lady ticket collector told us we had over two hours to wait and suggested we might like to have a walk in the park!

There was nothing of special interest in Stalybridge and the park was only ten minutes' or so away so we had a walk around. It was a misty morning, pretty cool for the time of year. We were both wearing our greatcoats. We ate our sandwiches sitting on a park bench and later we had a cuppa in the nearby station snack cafe.

We caught our connection out of Stalybridge and changed at Stockport, Crewe and Shrewsbury. The train was waiting at Shrewsbury on the buffers so we climbed aboard. We spent more time here waiting and then a Flight Sergeant WOP/AG appeared and asked if we were bound for No. 83 OTU Peplow. We said we were and he then joined us in the non-corridor compartment of the local train.

The Flight Sergeant told us he had done a Coastal OTU course. When we asked what sort of OTU it was at Peplow, he answered 'It's bound to be Coastal, after all, they wouldn't waste time on giving a certain type of training and then changing it, would they?' Apparently he'd been taken ill on the previous course somewhere, hence the posting to Peplow. This seemed a puzzle and I wondered why he didn't go on to the following 'Coastal' course, as this was normal after illness.

Peter and I kept a look out for signs of aircraft as we drew nearer to Peplow. We saw nothing to enlighten our curiosity.

After a while we stopped at a country village station. It was Peplow at last. We speedily unloaded the kit-bags and the train departed. Journey's end, or almost, we thought. We must telephone the camp to obtain transport, which was normally provided for postings.

CHAPTER 10

Bomber OTU

A Flight Lieutenant; Crewing Up; the Wimpey; a Nickel; a Diversion and Bull's-eye

Before we had time to pick up our gear, a train steamed in from the opposite direction and halted to unload an absolute 'shower' of aircrew. The din as they detrained was unimaginable. A smart Flight Lieutenant called them to order; some were busy unloading kit, others just looked across at us, making rude signs.

We rapidly concluded that these bods must be bound for Peplow. A few questions across the tracks confirmed the situation, so over we went rather unceremoniously, struggling with two full kit-bags plus webbing and full packs. We joined 'the mob' and soon gathered that we ought to report to the Flight Lieutenant who was busy taking charge of the situation.

This officer stood out from all the other officers and NCOs on the platform. He was very smartly dressed, wearing full uniform, not battledress, and a field service cap rather than the usual aircrew officer's favourite, a flat hat. I noticed he wore the NAAFI gong (1939/43 star) underneath the pilot's wings, above the left pocket, indicating that he had seen operational service. A roll was called, after which Peter and I, followed by the Flight Sergeant WOP/AG, notified the Flight Lieutenant of our presence. The officer appeared to be about thirty years of age (he was twenty-seven). He did not hesitate to use his authority for he was the senior officer present. Perhaps he had been given the job of bringing this 'shower of bods' from the AFU. Maybe he just took charge as he would do, with his seniority. There appeared to be no question of this. All the aircrew from the train 'jumped to it' whatever his command.

He wasted no time in dealing with Peter, McClelland and me. He was completely unperturbed by our appearance from the other side of the station, although he didn't appear to be expecting anyone extra. He didn't show any concern.

'Right, Sergeants, just join the rest. Oh, have you got your kit?' We told him we had.

'That's more than I have. It should be all together in the same van,' he said with a wry smile.

'H'mm, I thought, this chap knows his job all right, doesn't he. Lord help the poor fellow that annoys him.'

It didn't occur to me just then, that sometime later he would need a crew to fly with!

There was also a Flying Officer Observer who seemed to be a friend of the Flight Lieutenant. This chap looked older, perhaps thirty or thirty-five years. He wore the observer brevet, indicating perhaps that he could aim a bomb as well as navigate! He seemed a pleasantly quiet person in many respects.

While we were waiting for the transport a twin-engined aircraft flew over, quite sedately. It had camouflage-painted upper surfaces, black sides to the fuselage and tail fin and also had black undersides. There was a gasp from the crowd of OTU 'recruits' for the aircraft type left no one in doubt as to what Command it belonged. Gone were all the hopes that had prevailed when our WOP friend insisted that it 'must be a Coastal OTU'. Lord knows what he felt like. I thought, perhaps like Peter, 'Ugh, a bloody Wimpey (Wellington), so much for a Coastal OTU.'

'Coastal? Course it's not,' said some wag nearby. 'It's bloody Bomber Command, you nitwits. Ha, ha, ha.'

Maybe they knew already, or was it just boyish enthusiasm? This was a point we were to learn so well later (i.e., treating a semi-disaster as a joke).

Momentarily, I thought of home and the cycle rides out to the airfield at Wellesbourne – Mountford. I remembered the day when, around lunchtime, I cycled up a narrow lane bordering the airfield (a bomber OTU), weaving in between on my cycle to narrowly miss some of the young airmen, all sergeants. They were 'Aussies', 'Newzies', 'Canucks' and RAF. They were wearing flying brevets of all kinds, on their way perhaps to the Sergeants' Mess for lunch. They were so busy chatting to one another that they didn't notice the idolising boyish figure on the cycle! Now, here we were, Peter and I.

Well, I had always fancied a Wimpey. I felt quite thrilled at the prospect of flying in one, so the moment had its compensations. How good it was to be young. The 'bloody Bomber Command' comment had gone in one ear and out of the other!

Our kit had been delivered to one of the many dispersed sites about a mile or so from the airfield. The Sergeants' Mess was in between somewhere, perhaps a quarter of a mile from the main entrance to the 'drome. Our site comprised Nissen huts with half-round, corrugated metal roofs, camouflaged. The ablutions were similar, but of a larger size. The notice above the barrack hut read 'Airmen's Quarters' in bold white letters. We drew sheets, dumped our kit in the hut, selected a bed and dashed off to find the Mess and, if possible, get a meal since it was now nearly 19.00 hours.

The aircrew Sergeants' Mess at Peplow was poor by most standards. However, as we knew no better at that time it was easily accepted. The best thing in the anteroom was the cheap-looking utility radio! This piece of wartime wisdom emitted a constant supply of music in the form of records played by the AFN (American Forces Network). The Canadian trainees on earlier courses seemed to have it all taped (i.e., clued up). We were treated to ceaseless programmes like 'Duffle Bag', which specialised in the music of Harry James, Glenn Miller, Joe Loss, Ted Heath and Hoagey Carmichael, not to speak of the fantastic stream of Boogie Woogie, much to my delight. The anteroom became so popular at lunchtimes it was necessary to sit on the floor or stand, in order to listen to the AFN programmes.

It was now early summer. The nights were quite light, especially with double British Summer Time. The dispersed billeting sites looked serene among the leafy green of the oaks, elms, hedges and the rapidly maturing grasses.

Peter Bone and I stuck together, simply because there was no one else we knew. We had flown together at Macdonald but only once. I had known him best from the *Louis Pasteur* since we shared duties on the 6-inch gun on the same watch.

We had little time to consider who was who: it seemed sensible to stick together. We billeted in the same hut and had adjacent beds. We were tired from our journey and turned in early. Peter shaved before bed. I didn't bother for I had shaved three days ago while still on leave!

Next morning came soon enough, the chat of bods getting up soon brought us to life. We nipped out smartly to the bogs and the ablutions for a wash and speedily dressed in battledress to dash off to arrive in time for breakfast. I never flew without breakfast and I don't think Peter would either, so it became a 'maximum effort' at that time of the day.

We reported to the training section, where there was a general mob of aircrew, most of whom had arrived with us the previous evening.

The first morning we were treated to the usual documentation that occurs on arrival at a new unit. During the process I came to learn a new term used on one or more forms – 'screened'.

'Are you a trainee or are you screened?'

'Screened? What the devil's that?'

Peter didn't know either. Some bod nearby did and told us that it meant tour-expired aircrew and usually applied to instructors (an aircrewmember who had completed an operational tour). I never really found out why the term was used. In later years I wondered whether any sort of screening was done with tour-expired aircrew to determine their suitability as instructors at an OTU or HCU (Heavy Conversion Unit). Perhaps that was the reason for the title.

After the documentation we were told the length of the course would be approximately twelve weeks. We would be formed into our own choice of crew where possible and that to complete OTU training we would fly either a Nickel (leaflet raid to enemy occupied territories), a Diversion (which was to assist the main force of Bomber Command by becoming decoys for enemy radar and fighter tracking), the latter flown as near to the enemy coast as practicable, or, alternatively, a Bull's-eye, which was a Command exercise flown in conjunction with RAF night fighters and our own flak, radar and searchlight defences. The Bull's-eye would also include a photograph or similar record of a bombing beacon.

We finished the morning with a talk given by the Station Commander. This consisted of a severe warning to keep away from the WAAF quarters, or else. We were told to walk about properly dressed at all times. Just because we were aircrew and flew at various times of the day or night didn't excuse us from being properly dressed.

The Groupie ended by telling us about an aircrew NCO he encountered one morning while he was exercising his dog. The unfortunate sergeant was taking a short cut across the fields to the Sergeants' Mess. The poor guy was not wearing his cap and the Groupie proceeded to 'tear him off a strip'.

'Excuse me Sir, I lost my cap while flying last night,' the NCO had replied. This had apparently angered the Groupie further.

'Don't excuse me, Sergeant, go and bloody well find it,' the Groupie had exploded. 'Fancy the cheek of the fellow – excusing me like that. Who did he think I was?' the Groupie said to us.

Poor guy, all he wanted was his breakfast and it appeared that he didn't get any that day. I wondered whether he found his hat! It probably blew out of some goddamned Wimpey on night circuits.

The remainder of the day was spent getting accustomed to the ground school programme. We learnt that we would do two to three weeks' ground training before flying commenced.

The following morning Peter and I joined the rest of the course at the ground school site. Here we assembled most days while the roll was called and individual crew categories were sent off to do various specialised training, according to their trade.

It was during these early morning and afternoon assemblies that Peter and I soon noticed other trainees were forming into crews of their choice. I thought we should do something before it was too late; fortunately Peter agreed. I mentioned that I had fancied crewing with any of three NCO pilots on the course; Peter didn't object.

I asked Flight Sergeant Dawson, an ex-Spitfire pilot, first.

He thanked us for our enquiry but replied 'Sorry chaps, we have already chosen our two gunners.'

Next, we tried Sergeant Paley who gave us a similar kind answer.

'Jeepers,' I thought. 'These guys certainly have got moving.'

Peter was just as puzzled and suggested we try the strict-looking Flight Lieutenant and his Flying Officer Observer chum.

'They look as if they are on their own,' said Peter.

'Good God, Peter, you can't be serious?'

Peter just grinned and jokingly replied 'They would be better than no crew at all.'

'Lord above, Peter, you are a keen type,' I replied.

Nonplussed, I said 'I'll try the Canadian, Flight Sergeant Beatty.' I did, and I received the same reply as before.

'Sorry lads, we've got our gunners. Thanks.' (They were Canadian gunners too, of course.)

'You're right, Peter. We'd better try the Flight Lieutenant, and may the Lord help us (or him)!'

'You never know, someone else might pinch him.'

'Huh, you're joking.'

Another day passed. Peter seemed interested in one or two officer pilots, but we still had no luck with them either. We noticed that the Flight Lieutenant and his Observer friend still hadn't attracted any attention. They remained on their own most of the time. It appeared that no other aircrew had approached them. The Flight Lieutenant seemed rather amused by it all, as if it were some kind of joke that no one wanted to crew up with him. Peter and I appreciated this apparent sense of humour.

After a further day it became clear that the only captain left was the Flight Lieutenant! Peter and I must have thought the same and neither of us were keen on the idea. We joked about it, the two of us. Something was said about waiting for the next course. I didn't think that very funny. We didn't want to miss out on crewing up. The main snag with the Flight Lieutenant was that he seemed such a disciplinarian. Another point was his more senior rank compared with the rest of the course. There was no other officer above flying officer. To us sprog sergeants it seemed too much to accept.

We both fostered the idea of a friendly sort of crew. I thought it was highly desirable, if not essential! The real compensation was in what we already knew. The Flight Lieutenant was an experienced wartime pilot, we knew that from the NAAFI gong. He hadn't lived through whatever he had done before for nothing or because he was no good! We didn't know then just how experienced he was, or what sort of man he was, pilot or navigator.

He appeared to be a leader of men and a disciplinarian to some considerable degree. We didn't know how far that went, it could be too late to back out on that score if we were to have any misgivings. The fellow might be a real bind. He might even be a right 'basket'. Maybe he would expect a lot from his crew. Maybe Peter and I would not be good enough. Perhaps he wanted really 'shit-hot' air gunners. Well, we would like a 'shit-hot' pilot and captain too. Who wouldn't? Dare we ask him? We hastily agreed. We had nothing to lose, we thought. The Flight Lieutenant might think differently!

Peter plucked up the courage, I just went along as a 'paper tiger'. We both 'banged him one up' (saluted) with all the other crews looking on.

'Do you still require air gunners, Sir?' Peter asked.

I stood firmly behind him, shaking, waiting for the answer. I'm not sure how Peter felt but I am sure he felt something. What if he turned us down? What if he didn't? My God, he looked such a stern type close up. If he turned us down we might even get a week's leave.

The Flight Lieutenant looked at us both and with a cheery grin said 'Christ, I thought we'd had it, that we'd have to wait for the next course.'

'Sure, I haven't any crew except for Freddie here,' indicating the Observer-type.

The Flight Lieutenant introduced himself and asked 'What are your names?'

Peter and I quickly gave them.

'Bone, Sir.'

'Broome, Sir.'

'Ah,' said the Flight Lieutenant. 'How about your Christian names?'

'Frank and Peter, Sir.'

'This is Freddie Dirs, our navigator. Freddie, meet Frank Broome and Peter Bone.'

'Cripes, Broome, did you hear that?' Christian names, good God!

Peter looked very pleased with himself.

'By the way, I'm Dick Lane,' which we instantly ignored and chose to call him 'Skipper'.

The tension dropped immediately for Flight Lieutenant Lane had a way about him that made you feel important. He also possessed a very friendly manner providing one didn't attempt to 'try it on'. We were to discover later that he stood no nonsense from anyone.

Skipper asked about our training and where it had taken place. His eyes opened in wide amazement (we found out later that this was a Lane characteristic).

'You trained in Canada? How come? Ah, you failed pilot and navigation courses. How far did you both get? H'm, you both seem to have been very unlucky. Frank, you soloed on Ansons and they still chucked you off? Well, I don't think it was their job to teach you to fly Lancasters and Mosquitoes. That was someone else's. How the devil could they have known that at "Service"? [SFTS]'

'All we need now,' said Skipper 'is a WOP and a bomb aimer.'

Next day we appeared to have acquired one of each, both sergeants. These guys had been part of a crew on an earlier course. Their Wimpey 'went in' on a night circuit! One engine caught fire on take-off or soon after and it ended up in a field. The bomb aimer brought out his injured pilot and earned himself the GM (George Medal) for his courageous action. The rest of the crew had escaped uninjured and it appeared they had later continued to train as part of other crews after the prang. Both these lads had been hospitalised and had been on leave. Their skipper was still in hospital, they told us with some regret!

They were a grand pair, the bomb aimer and WOP. They were good lively types, always ready for a joke, yet taking their aircrew roles seriously. A few days later they were surprised by the appearance of their old skipper, a flight sergeant pilot, newly discharged from hospital. Quite naturally, they wished to crew again with him. Our skipper and the Training Officer agreed and so we lost them almost as quickly as they had arrived.

It was with intense regret that we learnt several months later that the bomb aimer and WOP, with their cheery pilot, were reported missing from air operations. We understood that they had been posted with the rest of their new crew to a Special Duties Squadron flying Wimpeys in and out of the occupied territories and had FTR (failed to return) from one of their sorties.

Meanwhile, we were fortunate to discover another bomb aimer without a crew. Peter noticed him first, describing him as a 'tubby' chap who seemed to be on his own. We both went to see him. It was quite true; he had not yet crewed. Also, the bomb aimer was aware of a WOP who also seemed to be without a crew. They obtained the Skipper's approval to join the crew. The Skipper must have been inwardly amazed, forming a crew from all these 'odd bods', yet he never commented on it.

Of the newcomers one was Fred Till, air bomber, just fresh from AFUs at Moreton Valence near Gloucester and Upwood near Peterborough. Fred was a quietly spoken man of about thirty-two years and therefore became the eldest member of the crew. He was also a family man; he had three children who, with his wife, lived in their own home in Bognor Regis.

The other was Bert Bray, a wireless operator/air gunner from Hereford. Bert knew his wireless and could also knock back a few pints. He had done his radio course at Madeley and his air gunnery at Bridgnorth. He was proud of the fact that he was a WOP/air gunner rather than just a straight WOP. Later courses arriving from Madeley were to wear the Signaller's 'S' brevet and took little or no gunnery. Bert referred to the 'S' Wallahs as 'stokers in a jet-propelled aircraft'.

So, at last, we were all ready to fly as a Wimpey crew. No one said anything about who was to be rear or mid-upper gunner. I fancied the rear turret, purely because it had four guns and they made more noise! Also, the tail turret gave an unrestricted view from the beams, covering fully from 180° and through dead astern. The view below was fairly good, downwards to about 60°, with 80°–85° down through the moveable side panels. Later, during ops I was able to improve on the search below and dead astern.

Peter didn't seem keen on the rear turret, that is, as a permanent home. He would need to use it on training sorties while at OTU and didn't object in any way. I think he felt happier and perhaps more secure in the mid-upper position. That is, when we got to an aircraft with a mid-upper turret! The Wimpey had only nose and tail turrets, although some had a position in the mid-aft fuselage for beam guns, complete with swivel seat. However, when we flew on cross-countries Peter usually stood under the astrodome, just behind the WOP's position and approximately mid-wing. He was a very patient type and only occasionally mentioned his keenness to get into a real mid-upper turret.

On certain local training flights, mostly circuits and bumps, we took it in turns to man the rear turret. The unnecessary gunner reported to the gunnery flight for special training, like air firing or cine camera, including combat manoeuvres. These exercises were carried out in a Wimpey that was crewed by a screened pilot and screened air gunner instructor, with possibly four or six OTU trainee sergeant gunners per aircraft.

I was pleased there had been no opposition to the turret choice. It could have been a very awkward problem to solve, had both gunners wanted the same turret. As it was, we were just happy and fortunate.

Once the fortnight of ground school preliminary was complete, we were ready to fly. We still continued ground school for approximately half a day each day. For most of the remaining part of the course, once the Skipper had soloed on daytime circuits, we were able to go further afield. Sometimes we did bombing exercises at various practice ranges nearby. The R/T call sign of the main range was 'PEACE TIME' and our call sign would be the station call sign followed by the aircraft phonetic letter like 'Willie', 'Oboe', 'Jig' etc. We spent many long hours over bombing ranges, day and night, while Fred patiently obtained the required number of successful practice drops.

A high percentage of hits or very near misses of the bombing target was required by the Bombing Section at OTU before an air bomber was considered good enough to continue. Fred knew his stuff, obviously enjoying all the practice over the bombing range.

In addition, it was necessary for the navigator, Freddie Dirs, to get all the practice he could on cross-country training flights. While Freddie was on these 'stooges' the WOP, Bert, would be at his TR 1196 radio getting QDMs, QFEs and other forms of bearings, weather information and listening out for a recall or other instructions.

Skipper got all the practice he needed on the Wimpey; he was due to night solo at any time. It was just a matter of fitting into the night flying programme. Meanwhile, for Peter and I, the gunnery 'stooges' were useful even if flown and accompanied by screened instructors.

We felt happier about the prospect of working together with our own crew.

The big day came for the gunners when we were flying a navigation exercise. Having received a message from Skipper, Peter and I prepared to launch a self-tow drogue with about 150 feet of cable. We had just managed to stream the drogue when we were informed that the navigator was airsick and we would have to return to base. We quickly reclaimed and stowed the unused drogue.

A few days later we were very sorry to learn that Freddie Dirs was to be taken off the course due to his recurrent airsickness. We understood that he would be found a less turbulent job somewhere, perhaps on Liberators, which were reputedly steadier aircraft than the Wimpey.

A day or so later we were allocated another navigator. He came direct from a following course. He was an RCAF sergeant, a nice, bright, easy-going Canadian. No bull, he really was a very quiet lad for a 'Canuck'. The fellow took to his (almost) all RAF crew very easily and soon moved his kit into our billet so that he could be with us at all times. He was quite a guy; he always appeared completely unruffled on the ground or in the air.

We began our cross-country flights once more. We had to start at the beginning due to our new navigator. These trips usually brought us over Cardigan Bay so that we could fly a northerly or southerly course over the Bay and thereby get our air firing exercises completed on the longest possible leg over sea.

The next time we took up the self-tow drogue was a flop. It took both Peter and I far too long. By the time we had streamed the drogue at the correct cable length it was time to 'cease fire' and turn around. Skipper was pretty understanding for he frequently took great pains to do the run again and again, thereby giving each of us a double chance of using the four rear guns.

I found this to be the sort of situation in which our captain excelled. He seemed to thrive on making decisions of this sort. Frequently, the encouragement we received was to 'fire all four guns' (*not* two as recommended by the Gunnery Section). I'm sure it was as much a delight to Peter as it was to me. Mind you, we were also pretty good at asking the right question.

'Do you want us to fire all four guns, Skipper, or just the two as recommended?' Skipper's reply never failed.

'Go on Frank, fire all bloody four. Ha, ha, ha, ha.'

Our friendship with our new navigator was not to last long. Skipper was not satisfied with him on the cross-countries. I'm not sure whether a screened navigator was present. It was normal on the first navigation exercises. I think our quiet 'Canuck' lasted about two or three cross-countries. We felt very bad about it; I know all the NCO members of the crew were very sorry to lose him.

Failing at OTU almost certainly meant loss of aircrew rank and status. Our Canadian navigator said very little and complained very little about it. One day he said 'I think your skipper had it in for me. Perhaps someone wanted me off the crew.' Nevertheless, the fellow took it all very well and when his posting came through to Eastchurch he wished us well as a crew and hoped we 'made it on ops'.

Skipper said later that he had not been happy about having a Canadian sergeant navigator making the comment (like Warrant Officer Bogart at Macdonald) that to be really good in the RCAF, a navigator needed to have a commission! The navigator's job was far too important to risk just anything or anybody.

A day or so later Skipper informed us of another new navigator. He was apparently pretty good; he was top of his course at Air Observer School in South Africa.

Skipper added with a grin 'He's a Scotsman, a sergeant, but looks more like a navvy than a navigator.'

H'mm, we thought, he's picked just what he wanted! We were quite correct, it seemed he had been allowed to do just that, pick the best bod from the latest course. This meant that our new navigator would jump from being some month or so behind us to join a crew with quite a few hours' flying on Wimpeys.

Sergeant Duncan McLean was just what Skipper said he was, a tallish, dour Scotsman from Edinburgh, with high intelligence and intellect. Whatever 'Mac' was to us and his other mates in the Mess, he was to be the equal as a navigator to Skipper as a pilot. Thus, without realising it at the time, we had been most fortunate in obtaining two first class bods who between them were to mean such a great deal to us in the future.

We continued with our course and with Mac's aid we didn't take too long completing our share of cross-countries. There were no further problems of airsickness, poor navigation or anything else. As gunners, Peter and I completed our 'self-tow' and 'air to sea' firing, both taking turns to use the FN20 rear turret. Fred was also expected, as bomb aimer and front gunner, to fire off some practice rounds. However, as he was 'only a bomb aimer' he just managed to fire a few hundred rounds 'air to sea' from the rear turret. Bert, too, was expected to keep up his air gunnery and also amused himself firing off the odd couple of hundred rounds or so. I noticed that not one of them expressed any love for the tail turret. They seemed to be glad to get out of it as fast as they could. Mac also tried it once. He seemed keen to try out the turret. He did and came out afterwards looking very pale, saying 'You can stuff that, Frankie lad!'

We completed our required number of training flights to the bombing range. Fred had been able to obtain his quota of hits and/or near misses, i.e., minimum acceptable error in yards from the practice bombing target. Bert had completed the WOP's course at OTU and had obtained his quota of QDMs and QFEs and other messages received from base, mainly while on our cross-countries. He also obtained weather reports, recall signals from base and, when required, he obtained radio bearings for the navigator. Bert was a keen and competent WOP and it wasn't long before the crew realised that any electrical fault that occurred on the aircraft or our equipment was soon accurately diagnosed and remedied.

I am sure that our navigator, who was to go through his OTU in a bare six weeks (as opposed to twelve) enjoyed the long training trips as we all appeared to do. Mind you, it is easy to enjoy things when the effort is mostly made by two crewmen only, the skipper and the navigator. The rest of us did our jobs perfectly but so far it had been a 'doddle' for me. I very soon realised that both the captain and navigator had the most exacting of jobs in a bomber crew.

Having performed the air-firing part of the course, Peter and I had only the cine camera combat manoeuvres to do. We had already completed the 'elementary' cine camera exercises. These were in every way similar to the exercises in Canada, that is, a simple curve of pursuit attack by a fighter, usually a Martinet. We used Hurricanes only for combat manoeuvres.

We soon discovered that our British air gunner colleagues who had trained in Britain already knew the exact deflections to allow in the 'corkscrew' manoeuvre. We did not! We had not even heard of the 'corkscrew' before reaching OTU! It did not take us very long to get the latest 'griff' from the others.

The gunnery deflection for the 'corkscrew' seemed very simple, so simple it was 'wizard'. One rad up or down to port or starboard, or simply point blank. It couldn't have been better. I thought it would give the *Luftwaffe* night fighters a run for their money. It was time the poor air gunner had his chance; perhaps this was it. Or was it? Only time would tell.

We did a spell of combat manoeuvres with a screened pilot first, followed by Skipper at the controls. From the tail turret there appeared to be very little difference; the reactions of the two pilots were similar.

Flying the 'corkscrew' manoeuvre was an exciting business. The rear gunner usually felt great with the breath-taking, heart-throbbing thrill of the chase, to the fullest effect. Skipper relied upon his gunners to give him directions because it was of utmost importance not to 'corkscrew' too early and, more obviously, not too late either!

The other major point in the 'corkscrew' was that it was necessary for the captain to inform his gunner(s) exactly what part of the manoeuvre he was flying. This was extremely important because no gunner, however good, could know *exactly* what position in the 'corkscrew' the aircraft was, that is after the first few diving turns, rolls and climbing turns. If the gunner knew his aircraft's position in the 'corkscrew', he could then apply the correct deflection. The deflection needed to be changed only when the bomber's flying altitude or movement changed. Hence, the earlier comment regarding deflection of one rad up and down and/or point blank.

The Hurricane flown by Sergeant Cake or one of his colleagues would make the normal curve of pursuit attack. He would begin with the essential double bank of a fixed gun fighter, in order to gauge the correct gunsight deflection to be allowed by the fighter on the bomber. The fighter, approaching from astern and usually from the beam or quarter, gave the gunner the essential clue. As soon as the fighter made the double bank (in fact, as soon as he made his first bank towards the bomber, followed by his second, and as soon as he started to make the second bank), the commentary from either Peter or myself (with the Hurricane fighter attacking from port) commenced.

'Corkscrew port go.' The direction depended on from which direction the Hurricane came, the rule being always to tighten the turn, to make it more difficult for the fighter to apply his deflection.

Skipper would reply quite coolly 'Diving port.' (Own gunner's deflection, 1 rad up on starboard wing-root of fighter.)

'Rolling.' (Deflection point blank.)

'Diving starboard.' (Deflection 1 rad up on fighter's wing-root.)

'Changing.' (1 rad level on starboard wing-root.)

'Climbing starboard.' (1 rad below port wing-root).

'Rolling.' (Point blank, i.e. no deflection.)

'Climbing port.' (1 rad below starboard wing-root.)

'Changing.' (1 rad level on starboard wing-root.)

'Diving port.' And so on. (The reader should note that at OTU we flew the Wellington 'corkscrew', which was not exactly the same as the Lancaster 'corkscrew'.)

We soon noticed that unless the Hurricane pilot throttled back to follow us through the 'corkscrew', he could not keep up his attack because at normal attacking speeds he was unable to bring his sight and fixed wing guns to bear on our Wimpey. (This was due to the tightness of the turns, dives and rolls made by the bomber in an expertly flown 'corkscrew' manoeuvre.)

The 'corkscrew' enabled the bomber to keep approximately on course as well as to make it almost impossible for the fighter to hit the larger aircraft. (At the same time the rear gunner was able to hold the correct deflection continuously, firing at will.) The only disadvantage was that prolonged 'corkscrew' manoeuvres tended to make some crewmembers sick! Better to be sick than dead, I thought. I was lucky really, as no doubt the aerobatics during pilot training helped. I was perhaps more used to unusual positions than most other members of the crew, except Skipper.

The essential thing about the 'corkscrew' was that provided you got into the manoeuvre fast enough on sighting a night fighter about to attack, you would almost certainly get away with it. At least that is what we learnt and understood. It seemed a reasonably effective tactic and one that would pay off perhaps, especially if both gunners were able to open up! (Considering there are two rearward-facing turrets in either the Halifax or Lancaster, i.e., with eight or six guns to bear on the attacker.)

From a morale point of view, the 'corkscrew' gave the heavy bomber a fighting chance. Without the 'corkscrew' we were most certainly sitting ducks. The gunners, therefore, had a greater sense of importance, due to the opportunity that the 'corkscrew' manoeuvre gave to the enterprising, keen, sharp-sighted captain and crew of the modern, heavy night bomber. In contrast and by comparison, the lessons given at Macdonald for the deflections during a curve of pursuit attack, were quite outmoded.

Peter seemed to have a rough time during the fighter affiliation exercises. However, at no time did he duck out of an exercise and very often he put up a good show until the 'corkscrews' made him too ill to continue.

We went into a nearby town frequently for wet dinghy drill. This consisted of a visit to the swimming baths, which were normally deserted apart from the RAF on those early mornings. We then had the unpleasant task of donning wet flying clothing over our swimming trunks. Only those who were lucky enough to be the first crew 'in' were able to dress up in dry gear! We were only lucky once. When dressed in flying suits we were expected to launch the dinghy – a six- to eight-man circular-shaped bomber dinghy. This was always thrown in upside down. Usually Peter was the first in; his job was to turn it the right way up. He did this by climbing onto the upturned dinghy, then standing on one side while grabbing the ropes on the far side, then trying with all available inertia to topple backwards, bringing the dingy with him. If it worked, and it usually did after one or two attempts, the dinghy turned over to its correct side up and with Peter underneath it! He always seemed to enjoy it. I noticed there was no one else in a great hurry to relieve him of the job. While Peter was turning the dinghy over, the rest of us climbed up to the top diving board and then jumped in, wearing inflated Mae Wests, as well as the outer flying suit. Fred was our non-swimmer and many times he bravely jumped in the 'deep end', briskly paddling his way to the dinghy. It was always a struggle for most of the crew to get into the dinghy. Fred's efforts were often speeded up by many helping hands. Poor Fred found himself bundled into the dinghy very unceremoniously, often upside down, always without complaint.

Skipper seemed satisfied with our efforts as a crew in the dinghy drill. At least, he didn't criticise anyone. I noticed that he gave me quite a sure, steady look the first time he saw me in swimming trunks, for I was a very boyish-looking skinny lad, some five foot seven inches tall and weighing nine stone, stripped. Possibly Skipper thought for a moment that I wasn't up to the job of rear gunner? Perhaps he expected someone with a more athletic frame. Perhaps it was just my imagination. He never made any sort of comment.

During our stay at Peplow we did practise dinghy drill (dry) in one of the hangars. The aircraft used were the older type of Wellington, Mark Ic with twin gun turrets fore and aft (as opposed to operational Wimpey IIIs or VIIIs with four gun rear turrets). We also used this aircraft for 'bale out' procedure. There were mattresses at strategic points. Mind you, mattresses or not, Peter and I 'baled out' through the rear fuselage hatch 'feet first' instead of 'head first' as it would be for the real thing. The rear hatch was in a peculiar position, situated two-thirds of the way down the fuselage and halfway up from the aircraft flooring, i.e., it was neither in the side or in the bottom, but half in each.

When it came to 'dry' dinghy drill in the Wimpey, most of the crew got out through the astrodome situated mid-wing in the upper fuselage. The skipper and air bomber got out through the pilot's hatch in the top of the cabin. The navigator, WOP and MUG (Mid Upper Gunner) went through the astrodome. Yours truly turned the tail turret on the beam, climbed out onto the tail plane and inched past the fin onto the back of the Wimpey (upper rear fuselage). From there I walked along to the wings where I joined the rest of the crew. We then slid into the dinghy, which in normal ditching would have inflated itself from its internal wing storage. The walk from the tail to the wings was a hairy experience and not one I enjoyed, even under the 'dry' training conditions. It was the only 'funk' I had in the Wimpey (not forgetting that no one else in the crew had such a walk). I was never very keen on anything resembling tightrope walking! I did not mind heights under most circumstances, being quite happy climbing up and down ropes and swinging along beams in the gym. Anything approaching a narrow parapet above ten feet high always scared me half to death. Flying in the tail turret, never did!

Another experience for us was the decompression chamber. This glamorous-sounding item looked little more than a large boiler with a door at one end and a porthole or two in the sides. The interior was simply fitted out with bench-type seating and was not too large; we could just about seat six without flying kit. Skipper and Peter volunteered to take off their oxygen masks, to test their reactions under such an emergency as oxygen failure. The two guinea pigs, one at a time, took off the equipment while scribbling various sentences on a pad. We had an instructor in with us and there was also one outside watching through the portholes. Both Dickie and Peter could hardly believe that they had all but passed out. The scribbling pads backed up the true account and neither could believe what they saw on the pad.

It was thoroughly brought home to us that oxygen failure was a real problem, especially as the individual crewmember would feel highly elated, not realising the danger. Every second without oxygen meant really dicing with death (depending on the altitude). The test in the decompression tank was intended to simulate an altitude of about 20,000 feet. We had all known for some time that the need for oxygen is usually from above 11,000 feet. One can fly fairly well up to about 15,000 feet without oxygen but it was not recommended.

In addition, it was recommended on ops later on, that when flying the rear gunner 'took off' on oxygen and remained on it for the whole flight. It was supposed to improve night vision.

We didn't have any oxygen problems in our crew at any time, so we were very fortunate. The odd crew experienced oxygen failure at some time during their flying. Sometimes it could be serious, particularly if a single crewmember was affected, especially if that crewmember's position was remote from the rest. We heard of the odd gunner dying from lack of oxygen. The only cure for this situation was to always check the supply before the flight. One could hear the oxygen pulsing quite clearly. It was just a matter of holding the tube to an uncovered ear. If the system failed in the air it is likely that all positions would be affected and perhaps one crewmember would notice the effect in time. It was recommended practice that the captain called each member of his crew on the intercom at regular intervals to check if everyone was OK. In our crew Skipper regularly called up both gunners throughout the flight. Also, as individuals, it was up to us to check our oxygen connections periodically during each flight.

We were not allowed to smoke while flying. It was a safety measure in view of the inflammable nature of the aircraft, the high-octane fuel and pyrotechnics. One of the gunners on our course was severely reprimanded for smoking in the rear turret. The guy concerned was a likeable fellow, Sergeant Rhakola, a Canadian. We had seen him before somewhere, most likely he had been with us at Macdonald. There was no mistaking his pugilistic but happy face; once seen, you never forgot him. Peter and I met him on odd occasions in the crew room, on the airfield or back at the Nissen hut sites. He invariably acknowledged our names as he passed, giving us both a grin, pleasantly muttering 'Brum and Bowen'.

I don't think 'Rak' was too put out by his reprimand for smoking. Presumably, it had been on a training flight with a staff pilot and screened instructor. I couldn't see his own skipper putting him on a charge for smoking in the rear turret. For example, Skipper Lane would have really 'rollicked' any of our crew behaving similarly. We wouldn't have risked repeating the offence, so there would be no need for the charge.

Soon, our final exams were due; we learnt for the first time that the RAF, at an OTU, didn't give results of the finals to the individual. The skipper of each crew and the course instructors knew how we had done! Some days after we had completed the exams, one or two instructors were asking 'Who is Broome?' I was rather mystified by the question. For once I wasn't afraid of failing! The gunnery tactics and other allied subjects had been a piece of cake!

One Scots air gunner (this was either Sergeant Mason or Sergeant Murray) said to me later 'You must be "top of the course" Broomie.'

I answered with a grunt of disbelief, to which he replied 'That's why the instructors were all asking "Who is Broome", you fat head.' I thought I could just as well have been 'bottom'.

We completed our studies at Peplow with the ground school screened instructors discussing tactics and any other up-to-date bomber defence topic. The screened gunners had all done a 'tour of ops' and were extremely keen to pass on any additional benefits they could to trainee crews.

During one of these late sessions one of the pupil gunners asked one air gunner instructor 'What position did you fly in, Sergeant?'

'The rear turret.'

'How many ops to your tour?'

'Thirty,' he replied, adding 'including thirteen to Berlin.' Most of the sprog gunners let out a gasp or some other appropriate exclamation!

'How many combats did you have?' asked another.

'None, we were never attacked.'

A complete hush fell over the lecture room. The answer had not been the one expected! A light, nervous laugh went around the room, more out of relief than criticism or sarcasm! I thought to myself that it seemed absolutely unbelievable that one could fly as rear gunner on a tour of ops and not get attacked.

We didn't live on cloud nine, nor did we hope to hide in it either! It was perhaps as well, for a few days later, having completed all our day and night navigation and bombing, we found ourselves on ops for a Nickel (a leaflet raid from an OTU).

Strictly speaking, a Nickel doesn't count towards a tour of ops (the latter was usually thirty trips), they were merely considered 'operational training sorties'. They were not often considered to be as dangerous as normal bomber ops, although they were usually only flown over enemy-occupied Europe. We only carried leaflets printed in the language of the country below and perhaps a photoflash, a Very pistol, complete with the 'colours of the day'. The front and near turrets would have the guns loaded and on 'fire' but that was it. There were no bombs!

A few weeks before there had been a tragedy during a Nickel exercise. One Wellington, complete with its newly qualified OTU crew, failed to return. The news that 'one of ours was missing' was greeted with much amazement and disbelief. The idea of a Nickel was to give the trainee bomber crew an experience over enemy territory that would give them confidence to face sorties over such places as Happy Valley (Ruhr), Berlin and similar hotspots. The FTR of one Wimpey and crew from No. 83 OTU Peplow could hardly have improved the local morale. It made us all dead cold sober. There were many comments of disbelief. 'Christ!' 'Jesus!' ' 'Poor sods.' A few days

Sergeant Frank Broome whilst at OTU in June 1944

No 163 Squadron Air Training Corps on parade in Coventry in June 1942

B Flight, 4 Squadron, 6 ITW at RAF Aberystwyth during December 1942

A de Havilland Tiger Moth of 9 EFTS in March 1943

Stearman N2S2 at USNAS Gross Ile in Michigan during June 1943

A Fairchild Cornell at RAF Caron, Sask, Canada in August 1943

Avro Anson MkII, RAF Carbery, Canada, in November 1943

The author with various friends in the park at Moose Jaw in September 1943

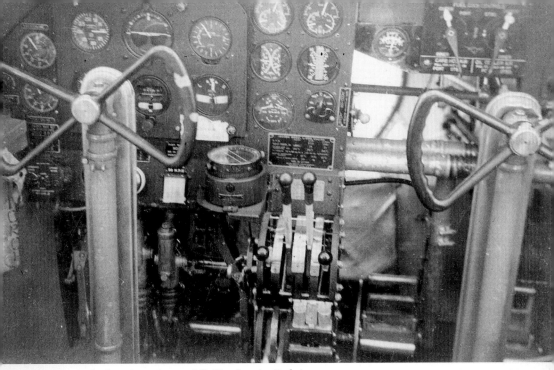

The control panel of an Avro Anson Mk II, taken in flight!

Frank in front of an Anson with some of his fellow students in November 1943

Ansons lined up every morning by cadet pilots at Carbery

One of Frank's great pals, Eddie Coogan, a US Navy cadet in New Rochelle, New York in 1943

The Mayfair Hotel in Portage, La Prarie, Canada

A Fairey Battle Mk II used for gunnery training seen at RCAF MacDonald in Manitoba

Fairy Battle Mk Is used for target-towing

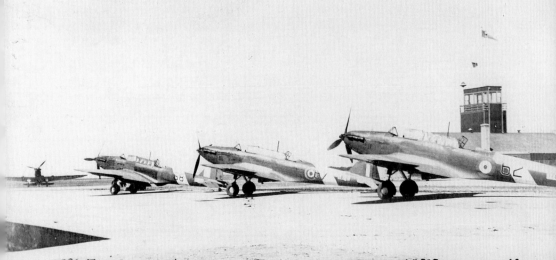

Left to Right: Sergeants Fred Till, Peter Bone and the author at 83 OTU, RAF Peplow, Salop

Lancasters flying in Gaggle formation in a bomber stream

Sugar Two viewed from the port rear quarter

Sugar Two, Flying Officer Ensiso's Lancaster

Tare Two, Flight Sergeant Broome, Rear Gunner

Flying Officer Ensiso's Flight Engineer, Sergeant Den Butler in the cockpit of *Sisco's Scamps*

Left to Right: Flight Sergeants Bray, McLean and the author, 626 Squadron, Wickenby, June 1945

Below Left: The 'Lane' crew, 626 Squadron, Wickenby, Lincolnshire in May 1945. Left to right back: Flight Sergeants Till, Bray, Thompson and Bone. Front: Broome and McLean

Warrant Officer Duncan McLean DFM

Sergeant Dennis Butler, Flying Officer Ensiso's Flight Engineer

Tare Two's Wireless Operator, Bert Bray and the author in May 1945

Sergeant Cliff Wheeler, Navigator, 150 Squadron

The author in August 1946

A 626 Squadron reunion in London in 1950

Frank and Edna enjoying Christmas in Australia, 2007

later a notice appeared among the usual DROs (daily routine orders) stating that an aircraft had been lost from No. 83 OTU while on a Nickel. It was stated that other crews on the Nickel reported that an aircraft was seen to explode in a ball of flame. No reasons were given. Presumably it wasn't flak, otherwise the reporting crews would have noticed other shell bursts.

Someone offered the explanation of a crewmember possibly smoking! No one thought of the possibility of a night fighter immediately below the Wimpey using a technique we were not to know about for many, many years. One might at least have seen tracer in the sky from the normal (expected) attack but there was no report of such. The fact that enemy aircraft could be modified to take upward-firing cannon using no tracer (in order to keep the secret) never occurred to anyone!

Like any other mid-summer day, 12 July dawned. We got through the day just like any other. Then just before teatime we were called in for briefing. It was a Nickel and we were to fly it together with only *three* other crews from Peplow.

The navigation briefing took place slightly earlier so we were able to have a good look at the chart that Mac was preparing. The route took us from Peplow straight out over the south coast not far from Weymouth, then down towards and narrowly missing the German-occupied Channel Islands, turning into the coast near St Malo and proceeding to Laval, our dropping point, almost 70 nautical miles due south of the battleground at Caen. As I gazed down at the route on Mac's map I noticed that his release point for the leaflets was west of Laval by some miles. Mac grunted and said 'Christ, Frank. You're right. I'm a chump!' He proceeded to extend the track to Laval and reworked his ETA (estimated time of arrival). I was to realise a few hours later that I should have been minding my own business, leaving Mac to do his own job, which he could do far better than I. Anyway, what could you expect from a 'dim air gunner' on that night?

We went along to the Mess for our flying meal. All of us felt pretty good at the prospect of such a treat for in wartime Britain an extra egg was like gold, not to speak of extra bacon with chips too. It never failed to increase our morale, not that morale was low. On the contrary, we all felt absolutely great! We had the prospect of flying over enemy territory at last. Perhaps being a real bomber crew instead of just talking about it did most of us a power of good. Gone were the fears experienced on the day of arrival at Peplow railway station when we saw the solitary Wimpey fly over.

I sincerely believed that if the crew had been offered a posting to a Coastal Command squadron right then, at the moment of preparing to fly the Nickel, we would all have turned it down. The confidence that the operational training had given us was such that we felt right up to the mark. We knew our training and aircraft were the best in the world, and that *nothing* could stop us operating over enemy-occupied Europe.

My own 'chip on the shoulder' attitude (i.e., being a 'failed pilot and only a gunner') had now completely disappeared. Fortunately, something had got through at last. Perhaps the message was 'Broome, if you don't bloody wake up you and the rest of the crew are already *dead*.'

After our meal we went to the main briefing at which the Groupie was present. Later we emptied our pockets of all personal items, particularly anything that would give information to the enemy, should we have to bale out and become POWs. We put these items into simple canvas bags, which were to be returned after the trip. To me, that seemed perhaps the grimmest experience of the whole operation. It seemed as if I was tempting fate, leaving all those precious personal belongings in a simple canvas bag, the contents of which one day may be sent back home to Mum and Dad. I hoped the day would never come and I felt very low just at that moment. Into the bag had gone my wallet, fountain pen, watch and the Kirbys' identification bracelet, followed by RAF identity card and loose change. I had kept my cigarette case and service issue dog tags. The latter were already around my neck on a piece of string.

The Intelligence Officer, a flight lieutenant, gave the latest gen about the Normandy landings and the forward positions of our troops in and around Caen. Our leaflets were to let the French nation know what was happening on the beaches and, in particular, what sort of a pasting we were giving the Boche! We were warned of various flak areas, particularly not to stray over the Cherbourg peninsula, the Channel Islands and to *stay on track* when over France.

Fighter opposition was mentioned. We were informed that there were several night fighter units based in France. These were either Ju 88 variants or Me 110s, both twin-engined and multi-cannon armed. There was no mention of these being radar-directed. We were not at all put off by the possibility of night fighter attacks. France was considered a soft target and therefore not very well defended. One could alter that opinion when one thought of the Normandy landings, only five weeks' old. Surely the *Luftwaffe* night fighter arm could not afford to leave the battle zone and surrounding areas to the invader to do as he chose?

After the briefing the Groupie wished us 'the very best of luck, chaps.' It really seemed as if he meant it. He no doubt wished the same the other week when the Wimpey failed to return.

We collected our flying gear, parachutes, Mae Wests and flying rations: sandwiches, coffee, Fry's Chocolate Cream and PK chewing gum. I carried two talismen inside my battledress, a pair of USN wings – a gift from Bill Tranter – and Dad's Army issue identity disk from World War I, clearly stamped Broome, A J 55533. I thought an extra pair of wings might come in handy. Also, Dad's identity disk had come to no harm, him neither, in over four years' of World War I. Perhaps it would protect me as well?

We were issued with escape kits to assist us in evading capture. They contained European money, compass, handkerchief map of Europe, concentrated foods and tablets etc. There was also a rubber-encased four-inch long hacksaw blade. You will perhaps easily realise the only place where this could possibly be hidden? We were also given a phrase book in five or six languages. We carried identity card photographs of ourselves in civilian clothes, which had been taken at Peplow by the RAF photographer and were to be given to the underground movement in Europe should we be able to contact them after abandoning the aircraft.

The crew bus took us to the far side of the drome. There we saw the four Wimpeys neatly lined up, bomb doors open, awaiting their crews. The sun was setting in the western sky and the Wimpeys looked dark and foreboding, their matt black sides and tail fin clearly silhouetted by the setting sun. It was a moment I was never to forget, the menacing look of the Wimpeys. I had never seen them like that before, fully prepared for war!

We stood around in groups, each crew beside the assigned aircraft. Ours was LN 286, GS-N (NAN). The first two letters were the unit coding of No. 83 OTU, the last letter the aircraft identification. We had dumped our kit nearby and were not yet fully dressed as it was summer time. Later I put on the yellow buoyancy suit, which had replaced the kapok inner and waterproof outer suit that I had worn on previous flights. It was a new scheme to issue buoyancy suits to gunners. These suits had kapok-type buoyancy pads inserted into pockets each side of the chest, the collar and each knee. I wasn't very impressed. Skipper made us all laugh; he told of an earlier Coastal Command experience with new types of buoyancy suits. He said quite dryly that he and several others at that unit were expected to test various types of buoyancy suits in the swimming baths. An admin type attended, to record all the data. I asked Skipper what happened.

'Well Frank, some of the suits were OK but most just sank, taking the poor beggar down in them. We had to jump in fast to save some of the poor sods. Ha, ha, ha.' Everyone seemed to enjoy the laugh.

I never wore my buoyancy suit again after leaving No. 83 OTU. I had not liked it anyway; the joke was great but that settled it. Give me the good old Mae West any day. If it went down, providing it wasn't damaged, you could always 'blow it' up.

It was reassuring to note that the rear turret of the Wimpey for the Nickel was the FN120 model, which was fitted with folding armour plates. This armour arrangement was simple and yet rather ingenious. The armour plates folded up if the guns were depressed, flattening out to form a vertically protective screen of $1/2$-inch (12-mm) armour when the guns were elevated.

The screened gunners at Peplow had already told us that this armour was *not* standard on the Lancaster, which to me seemed a great pity. I would think that a resourceful and keen air gunner would become even more so, when protected by such armour. However, it seemed the Air Ministry didn't agree. Someone said that it was because we might hide behind the elevated armour and therefore not use the guns! (Armchair warriors? Bloody rubbish!)

We never thought to query any of these baffling regulations or design requirements specified by those who decided what we flew. We had such a high opinion of RAF tactics that we accepted whatever it was without query. In fact, to query was frowned upon, even by one's own mates. I once asked if the Perspex covering of gun turrets was 'bullet proof'. It caused quite a howler among the other trainee sergeants, not to speak of 'tut tuts' from the screened gunner.

The main morale booster for most of the crew on the Nickel was that we had real operational ammunition in the ammo tracks and servo feed of the rear turret. This fact was displayed boldly to all who gazed into the turret, for between the two banks of guns was a colourful display. Operational ammunition was always painted with different colours (on the noses of the bullets). Peter and I were quick to note that we had been supplied with one tracer (pink paint), three incendiary (blue) and six armour-piercing (green) in every ten rounds supplied. There were at least 1000 rounds per gun in the feed tracks up the fuselage. I didn't check what quantity the fuselage ammo tanks carried. These could have been up to a further 4000 per gun, although for night ops 1000 rounds per gun was normal.

We stood around in a group as a crew, watching the last of the setting sun. It had been a really beautiful summer's day. The navigator reached up into the open bomb bay to secure a copy of *Courier de l'Air* for each of us from our load of leaflets. We hastily scanned the four-page document we were about to deliver. It gave the usual guff and pictures about the Normandy battlefront, knocked out German tanks, pillboxes, lorries, dead Germans and those more fortunate to survive as POWs. Yes, we really were giving the Boche a pasting! Pity we hadn't a bomb or two to go along with the leaflets. I don't mean for the French obviously, but wherever our leaflets landed there would be some of Adolf's *Wehrmacht* nearby. If they were SS or *Gestapo*, all the better!

We gathered around to have our final fag. Peter was the only non-smoker. Good old Peter, just stood there beaming at us in his absolutely inimitable way. His job that night would be a bit of a bore, for he would fly the whole trip standing in the astrodome. It had already been decided to have him there – another pair of eyes to look rearward. Fred would be up front and would man the twin-gun front turret when he wasn't map reading, windowing or 'bombing' with the leaflets.

Skipper looked fit and in great shape. Seemingly, he was taking stock of his crew and their reactions to their first op. Skipper won our admiration when he appeared in a super pair of black leather flying boots, very well polished. They were obviously boots he had cherished for some time, perhaps from his Coastal tour?

Our navigator was all ready for the sortie, his homework well done. Soon he would need to concentrate on his Gee fixes to check his track against that already worked out with the Met wind in the Navigation Room. Upon Mac would rest the responsibility of avoiding enemy flak positions such as Cherbourg and the Channel Islands, that is in addition to taking us to and from Laval accurately!

Bert would listen out on his R/T continuously from take-off. He would advise Skipper of any change to the flight plan, weather reports, *Luftwaffe* night fighter Intruder Warnings, possible cancellation and whether we would be diverted to another airfield on the way home. In addition, he would be ready for any emergency with the Very pistol, together with the colours of the day. Also, if we ran into trouble he would send an SOS, if there were time. At briefing we had already been warned of the possibility of diversion to another airfield due to mist or fog.

Skipper started and ran up the twin Hercules radial engines. We tested all our gear, sights, guns (on safe), intercom, oxygen and taxied out to the caravan. Skipper patiently waited for the Aldis lamp signal. Soon we got the 'green', and were off down the runway, airborne, bound for occupied France.

The airfield soon disappearing behind us, we circled to gain height before setting course. It was important that Mac received a good starting point and from the conversation on the intercom Skipper made every effort to turn accurately onto the heading required at exactly the correct time.

I knew that most crewmembers would be checking their equipment once again. It was doubly important that the gunners checked their turrets, sights and gun mechanisms when airborne. All these items were previously checked on the DI (Daily Inspection) and also on the Air Test and the pre-flight or pre-op check at dispersal.

Nevertheless, it was necessary to re-check from time to time. It was easy to check the traverse of the turret, the depression and elevation of the guns and the operation of the sight at all operating positions. It was most important to check that the guns would fire. To do this we were supposed to set each gun to 'safe' and then manually operate the gun using the manual release lever instead of the gun triggers. This was to ensure the remaining guns were left on 'fire'. These three guns would only fire if the triggers were pressed. The gun on 'safe' would operate but the round was made safe because the firing pin in that gun's breechblock would not operate with the others, i.e., when a gun was put on 'safe' its breechblock mounted firing pin was rendered mechanically inoperative.

Manually operating each gun in turn on 'safe' only checked the mechanical operation of the weapon. The hydraulic firing system, trigger-operated, had not been tested. The old system of firing guns into the air to test all the aircraft defensive armament was now considered dangerous and was discontinued. It was a great pity! Too much faith had been put into the manual check of each gun on 'safe', which *in no way checked its hydraulic firing operation*. The Frazer Nash FN120 in which I was flying was a fully hydraulically operated turret. Knowing no better, I checked each of four guns by the book, as described above. From time to time I checked also the oxygen and intercom connections in case of disconnection due to movement of self or aircraft. The oxygen check was a 'must' if one were to survive in the tail turret at altitude!

Fred called to Mac that we were crossing the English south coast and gave a pinpoint for Mac to fix our position and to enable him to check his Met wind. Several times during our OTU flying, Mac had asked if I would get him a 'drift' from the rear turret. This was simply what it implied – the gunner took a sight (through the reflector gunsight) onto a prominent landmark or, if out at sea, a 'white top', keeping the object dead centre of the sight for a few seconds. The degrees of drift can be read through a Perspex visi-panel in the turret mounting ring. This was helpful to the navigator on trips where no recognisable pinpoint appeared. The navigator could therefore calculate any alterations in wind strength and direction from the drift angle.

By the time we had crossed the coast it was getting quite dark, it was probably dark already on the ground. Soon the daylight began to fade completely. It wasn't long before the south coast faded into the mist that was already forming around the coasts.

Skipper cautioned Mac about the presence of enemy flak on Jersey and Guernsey. We seemed to be closer to these islands than to the French mainland. We were at about 14,000 feet, well above the height of light flak (i.e., 12/13-mm heavy machine-gun and 20-mm anti-aircraft cannon) so we needed to be wary of 88-mm and 105-mm heavy flak. Should we be near enough we could be subject to a barrage of really heavy, radar-predicted flak. So far our trip had been quiet. Neither Peter nor I had sighted any sort of opposition since leaving Peplow. I saw the odd dark shape but it did not materialise. There was broken cumulus cloud beneath us through which the sea could be seen at intervals.

Mac informed Skipper of our ETA at the French coast and seconds later confirmation came from Fred in the nose. We appeared to be dead on track and in good time. It seemed that Mac's Gee set was functioning perfectly. There was no comment from Mac about Gee being jammed by German radio countermeasures.

We altered course according to Mac's instructions. Skipper checked all the crew on the intercom and gave a warning to Peter and I to 'keep a good lookout for fighters'.

'How are you in the back there, Frank?'

'OK, Skipper thanks.'

We continued *en route* towards Laval and to port of our track we could see flames from buildings on fire to the north.

'Probably Caen,'said Skipper.

'Everyone keep a good lookout now, keep your eyes peeled for fighters.'

'ETA in six minutes, Skipper,' called out Mac.

'OK Mac, give me a course for home before we get to the target.'

'OK Skipper.'

A few seconds sped by, perhaps a full minute. Then '290, Skipper.'

'OK Mac, 290°.'

'Target coming up, Skipper,' said Mac.

'OK Fred, all set.'

'OK Skipper, all ready.'

'Bomb doors open,' repeated Skipper.

'OK Fred, press the tit,' said Mac.

'Bang over Laval release point.'

'OK Mac, very good. Turning onto return course 290°.'

Skipper completed the 180° turn. We were facing homeward at last. Peter and I scanned the enemy sky. We were the only two crewmembers facing aft and trouble, if it came.

We flew on for some minutes. A shadow to port downwards caught my eye.

'Fighter, Skipper. Prepare to "corkscrew" port.'

The shadow disappeared so I called 'OK Skipper, resume course.' It was the standard patter. We had not altered course.

'What was it Frank?' asked Skipper.

'Just a shadow I think, Skipper, thanks.'

'OK gunners, keep looking.'

'OK Skipper,' came the dual reply.

Just before we crossed the French coast I called for 'Prepare "corkscrew" port' and later over the sea 'Prepare "corkscrew" starboard'. Both were false alarms due to shadows, black smudges in and around the broken cumulus cloud. I hoped I hadn't alarmed the crew too much. Maybe it showed how keen (or scared) I was. Who knows? I was surprised how clear it looked below. This was due mainly to the white cloud beneath.

The spaces between the broken bits of cumulus tended to look like fighters. I didn't worry about it, or think I was too nervy, for I was just doing my job. I always knew the odds were often against the bomber, but from the OTU training received at Peplow, I had become very confident and truly believed that provided we 'corkscrewed' before the enemy opened fire we would survive. Hence, I had to be doubly sure to spot him first, especially before the fighter opened fire.

Away to starboard on the route home we could again see the fires and explosions from high-explosive shells being used by troops in and around Caen. Also to starboard a little later I could see some heavy flak bursts in the sky over the beachhead. I reported this to Skipper, adding that it was some 10 to 15 miles away. This was to be our nearest flak and we could not be certain that they were enemy guns firing. We assumed that it was because it was well to the south-west of Caen and much nearer to us.

We continued homeward uneventfully. The intercom was quiet except for occasional navigational jargon between Mac and Skipper. Fred came in occasionally with the odd pinpoint or 'crossing the coast' comment.

We'd been expecting to be directed to another airfield (Ossington) on return but it did not become necessary. Peplow appeared clear and so we were able to land there. As we joined the circuit, Skipper announced our presence. We were given an immediate 'Pancake NAN' from the WAAF duty officer. Skipper replied immediately bringing the Wimpey into the circuit, calling 'Downwind NAN.'

Then it was 'Funnels NAN.' Each phrase was repeated in acknowledgement by the WAAF on the R/T. Finally we touched down, bounced a little, slowed towards the end of the runway and then turned off, with 'Clear NAN, out', taxying towards the aircraft dispersal points.

Our Nickel completed, I unloaded the guns (now on 'safe') and disconnected the four belts from the guns. I fired and re-cocked (each gun still on 'safe') to eject the round at the breechblock face, then fired again (still on 'safe') to return the breechblocks to their forward positions without rounds. I unplugged my intercom and oxygen connections and collected my gear and uneaten flying rations of sweets and chocolate. The gum I had chewed furiously since take-off, now horribly stale, I got rid of just before boarding the transport.

Interrogation was a pleasant and satisfying experience. We satisfied everyone that we had flown successfully to Laval, especially as we had dumped enough 'bog paper' for the occupying power to last him until VE Day.

We went off to our eggs and chips at the Mess and then to the billets. I had parked my cycle near the Briefing Room, which was quite handy for the dash to the Mess or billets on return. I rode back along the dark leafy lanes of Peplow, reflecting that a couple of hours earlier we had been 14,000 feet over occupied France. I felt pleased with myself; so did the rest of the crew. We felt elated with our experience, proud and satisfied with a job well done. Well, nearly well done!

I expect Skipper felt the same as he returned to the officers' quarters. He'd had his meal with us as always on the night flying programme at OTU. I wondered how he felt dining with a load of sometimes scruffy sergeants. Whatever his feelings were on these occasions he never complained. Generally, he had that big 'Dick Lane grin' and always seemed satisfied. He rarely made idle comment. If he spoke about anything it was usually to say he was confident in our individual abilities. What he thought of the Nickel we never knew or what he thought of our individual performances as crewmen. I wondered whether he was as happy about it all as we obviously were?

He'd been on ops before in Hudsons, Blenheims and Bothas. Just how Coastal Command sorties compared with our Nickel we would never know. He seemed as keen as we were and as nervous, excited and thrilled as we were. Perhaps he looked on us as just 'sprogs' and thought the Nickel just another 'piece of cake'. He rarely criticised any of the crew. He seemed always pleased with our performance.

Present-day reflections on the Nickel question why the *Luftwaffe* night fighters didn't attack Wimpeys on such sorties. After all, a continuous loss of OTU crews would be unacceptable to Bomber Command and any remedy, such as abandoning the sorties, would lead to less experienced crews on first real bomber operations over Europe. Also, intruder sorties by the *Luftwaffe* over OTU bases such as Peplow and Hixon would have wrought havoc with the local flying and one cannot abandon night-flying training of a night bomber crew. OTUs sited in North America, as an alternative, would not give men the opportunity to gain expertise from operational training sorties such as Nickels or Diversions. These are only two very obvious outcomes but a third, that of lower morale as a result of either or both of the above could have been catastrophic to the bomber effort.

During one of the night cross-countries we flew we were notified to expect interception by one of our local Martinets, flown by Sergeant Cake. It was supposed to give gunners the experience of night interception and to gain knowledge of how the Martinet or similar radial-engined fighter (i.e., Fw 190) would look under night conditions. At the navigational briefing there was an instruction to the Wimpey crews that we should switch on our aircraft navigation lights as soon as the Martinet was spotted. It all looked extremely hopeful, helpful and perhaps exciting.

When we joined the circuit after our trip, Skipper called up Flying Control. He received the immediate reply 'Hello "Charlie"', can you see the Martinet?'

Skipper was about to ask me the question when I saw the Martinet astern and on the port quarter at about 300 yards. Unfortunately, he was only too plain as he had *his* navigation lights on and flashed the lights several times until we had acknowledged the interception. It seemed a pity that we were not able to find him ourselves without navigation lights; it would have been much more useful, made more sense and been a worthwhile experience. Perhaps it was rushed along like many other things in training to enable all crews to get a bit of practice rather than none at all.

It is likely, too, that there were several aircraft in the circuit, stacked, awaiting their turn to 'pancake'. This exercise was the nearest we ever came to experiencing night fighter affiliation. We could have done with much, much more. Day fighter affiliation with Hurricanes was all very good stuff but to do it at night with a Beau or a Mossie would have been just absolutely great – really an invaluable experience!

We had a pleasant surprise one night when Peter and I were just leaving the Briefing Room after a night cross-country. We saw a familiar face – Sergeant Baker from our course at Macdonald. Apparently Baker's Wellington had been diverted to Peplow in an emergency that included an engine fire.

From what our old friend said, we gathered their Wimpey had been iced up. Their skipper had given the order to jump and seconds later cancelled the order when he regained control of the aircraft. When a check was made of the crewmembers, their rear gunner, Keith Heslop, was missing. The rear exit door had been jettisoned and Keith's parachute had gone too. He had baled out over Birmingham.

Both these lads were RNZAF – among the best of the 'Newzies' that we had met. Baker was reputed to be of Maori extraction and proud of it. We never saw them again. It had been a pleasant reunion if only for a few minutes. We sincerely hoped that Keith 'made it OK' and that both of them and their crew survived their time with Bomber Command.

One day when we were out on the airfield waiting to fly, there appeared, just on the horizon, a large plume of black smoke, away in the direction of Stafford.

'Hixon!' said one of the crew. 'Somebody's pranged. Looks quite a blaze.'

I hadn't a clue who would be in the Wimpey, for we presumed it was a Wimpey from the OTU at Hixon, which was situated near Stafford.

Shortly before the apparent prang, I had heard from my old ITW and Grading School colleague Cliff Wheeler. We had kept in touch, just about, mostly by writing to each other's home address when we were not sure. Cliff had written to say he had been posted to the OTU at Hixon. He mentioned in this letter that he returned 'the boots compliment', which was rather amusing as it was a reminder of an 'official secrets' message. When I arrived at Peplow I had written almost immediately to Cliff, then still at Harrogate. I wrote mainly to keep in touch and to give what gen I could that might be helpful, should he be following in our footsteps – which is exactly what he did.

When writing about the aircraft type we flew I thought then of the lectures on the Official Secrets Act. We were not supposed to disclose to anyone what aircraft we flew or the unit identification and whereabouts. Our correspondence should be addressed: 'Sergeants' Mess, RAF Station, Peplow, Salop' – *not* '83 OTU'! Our letters were liable to censorship and therefore, in order to communicate to Cliff that we were at Peplow and flying Wimpeys, I added a PS to one of my letters: 'By the way Cliff, you left your Wellington Boots behind when we were on leave in Coventry.' He didn't get the message until some later date, by which time I had had to explain to him my ridiculous code. It was after this that I got the 'boots compliment' in return.

When we met again, quite some time later, I discovered to my horror that Cliff and some members of his crew had been slightly burned when escaping from the very same Wimpey cremation we witnessed from Peplow on that day!

Apparently, the aircraft had developed an engine fire on take-off and had crash-landed, wheels up, in a nearby field. There was some delay in some of the crew escaping via the astrodome. The fixing attachments were a bit stubborn, so much so that the crewmembers trying to use that hatch had almost given up. Fortunately for Cliff, the offending clips gave way and so everyone got out OK finally.

A main surprise at Peplow was to find that two days after our Nickel we found ourselves on the night-flying programme for a Diversion.

On 14 July 1944 we attended the Briefing Room where it was explained that Bomber Command main force would be attacking various targets in Europe. The OTU groups were to provide a diversion, which would hopefully draw enemy night fighters away from Main Force Heavies, as well as alert all the enemy defences, flak, searchlights, Wurzburg and Freya radar units. We were to fly to a position just a few miles out from the Dutch coast.

We had our flying meal and once again I dressed in that damned awful yellow buoyancy suit. There wasn't so much care taken with the 'special exercise' as there was with the Nickel. The ammo was ordinary training ammo, i.e., ball and tracer. Ball ammo was only good for training and or killing personnel. It was almost useless for bringing down an enemy fighter.

The turret was an ordinary FN20 with no armour plating. We were using window again, presumably to make a few Wimpeys look like a hefty force of 'heavies'. We received our Fry's Chocolate Cream, barley sugars and PK chewing gum as before and were transported to the various dispersal points and to the aircraft allocated. This time it was Wimpey HE 459. We lost no time checking over the engines, controls, hydraulics, electrics, guns, turrets and survival equipment.

We stood around for the usual smoke, chatting and joking together. Skipper came forth with his special recitation of 'Our Poor Willie' accompanied by many grunts of approval, whereupon Mac gave us a few bars of 'Eskimo Nell'.

Bert told him to 'Can it Mac, you're not in the air yet. We may get a recall.'

'Oh, hell Bert, I've got all my courses done, we've gotta go now.'

Peter looked a bit glum and said 'Hope we don't draw too many fighters, Frank.'

'Hope the beggars wait till you've got your mid-upper,' I replied, thinking of the additional two-gun back up. (Two guns for a Lancaster and four for a Halifax.)

Fred was busy checking the parcels of window bundles. Skipper and he had arranged them in the interior of the aircraft. Just imagine the innumerable parcels, sometimes nearly fifty in number. Each parcel contained twelve bundles of valuable radar-jamming, life-saving, black and silver paper slips, restrained by elastic bands. These parcels had to be carried within the aircraft, mostly 'in the office' (the forward area in or near the flying controls containing the captain, navigator, air bomber and WOP). Probably for the Nickel and Diversion we would carry and use only twenty to twenty-four parcels throughout the trip. Later on, when on ops, we would use fifty to sixty on the longer trips. A point worth thinking about was how the crew would cope with an emergency situation leading to bale out with all these parcels in the way. Confident youngsters that we were, we had only to be told that 'You'll have used half of the window before you get there.' So that made it easier! How blissfully ignorant we were and happy to be so inexperienced.

We might have had to jump for half a dozen different reasons: being iced up, collision, our own flak, engine failure, instrument failure. I was perhaps the most fortunate for window was never to be a bother to me. I was just too far back down the fuselage, just past the Elsan toilet. Let us hope that the position of the Elsan and the rear gunner was no reflection on the importance of the Elsan. Let us hope that no one had two helpings of prunes at lunchtime. (Prunes or dried fruit salad were a popular sweet at Peplow.)

Soon it was time to go so we climbed aboard. We plugged into the intercom, the engines were started and we taxied out and lined up on the main runway. Skipper had done all his checks at dispersal and was away on the 'green' from the caravan. Throttles wide and up into the gathering dusk. There was some light cloud overhead as we climbed over the airfield. Looking down as we gained altitude, I could see the ground haze forming and away to our port the outskirts of Stafford seemed even more murky.

Skipper set course at the appropriate time in conjunction with Mac. We set off across England and later crossed the East Anglian coast. Fred gave a pinpoint for Mac to log and to check his Gee. We altered course for the Dutch coast. The visibility below the aircraft was now very poor. How Fred was able to get his pinpoint was a credit to his observation and superb ability to map read at night.

Fred started to window (chaff) on reaching the required geographical position as briefed and when advised by Mac. I looked downwards from the rear turret but could see nothing below – no window, no visible ground, only a very murky, smoggy blackness.

After about an hour Mac called out that we had reached position 'X', the turning point for the Diversion. Skipper executed a very smart steep turn, nose down to increase our return speed.

'OK Mac, on course,' he said.

'OK Skipper.'

'Keep a good look out for fighters, gunners.'

'OK, Skipper,' was the joint reply.

I thought at the time that the visibility was absolutely useless. It appeared to be so black out there astern of the aircraft. I had the impression that we were completely surrounded in black smog. I could see absolutely nothing within the 180° rotation of the turret, up or down. I wondered how Peter felt seeing possibly even less and standing almost bored stiff in the astrodome. He would be able to see 360° in a half-sphere, like my view, but for him upwards and to the beams. I had never felt more useless, I just sat back and resigned myself to the situation. I was wearing the yellow buoyancy suit and noticed, as on the Nickel, that at our operational height I lost body heat steadily. This was not really surprising as the suit was just a glorified waterproof outer. It had nothing in it for warmth. Whoever had been responsible for withdrawing the kapok inner and green outer suit had really miscalculated. There was no electric heating within the buoyancy suit. We would have done better to have kept our original flying gear and then added the heated suit that was to come later.

We returned to base almost without a hitch. Skipper called up the Control Tower on return and was immediately given 'Pancake', which surprised us all. We were even more surprised to find when we got down we were the last to land.

'Huh, the rotten beggars, must have opened up the throttles to get home that early,' Skipper said.

It was to become a common thing later for us to be late and the others to be early. The Skipper was as good at obeying the operational rules as he was at dishing them out! We'd been briefed to fly at various airspeeds, courses and heights in order to maintain the 'stream'. This was to be the 'norm' for us in the weeks ahead.

We had our flying meal on return together again. We all seemed to enjoy tucking in to the glorious feast of bacon, eggs, beans and chips. Skipper seemed to enjoy our company. He was always a very jovial person on these occasions.

We split up after the meal and cycled towards our respective billets. Dawn was breaking in the eastern sky, although the horizon in the direction of Stafford seemed as thick as ever. I reflected that the trip had been disappointing in many respects – the preparation of the aircraft, for example, with no operational ammunition. The inky blackness of the sky, most particularly, as we turned for home had been disappointing. Spotting a fighter in such visibility had been hopeless. I was never to forget the feeling of being quite so useless. This thought came to me the moment we turned for home when the tail faced enemy territory. I don't think I had ever flown on such a foul night. It was opposite to the Nickel when we had almost unlimited visibility. Fortunately, although we had some bad nights to come, we never again had one with quite as bad visibility rearwards.

'Christ' I thought. 'Can't see a bloody thing, so here's hoping we make it home quick.' I half expected to be shot down by some unseen fighter at any moment, chewing my PK more furiously than ever.

In the training Wimpeys the rear turret Perspex was complete apart from a small sliding Perspex hatch, 8 inches (200 mm) wide and 18 inches (460 mm) long, positioned dead central and to approximately 45° up. This meant that the rear gunner was completely surrounded by Perspex except for the sliding hatch. Visibility is always impaired at night when looking through glass or Perspex with dirt, grease smears and condensation. The 'clear vision panel' on some operational aircraft (i.e., the whole rearward-facing panel of Perspex except for about 18 inches (460 mm) of it directly overhead) was removed. This improved the rearward vision more than 100 per cent over that of a totally enclosed turret (i.e., mid-upper on the Lancaster and the OTU rear turrets).

While we were at Peplow it was a common sight most mornings during our walk up to the flights to see several operational aircraft such as Stirlings, Lancasters and the odd Halifax parked at intervals around the perimeter track, these aircraft having been diverted to our airfield due to weather or other problems. One morning, as our whole crew walked up the main road and passed a parked Lancaster, Skipper remarked hotly, pointing to the obviously missing panel in the rear turret, 'Christ, Frank, you aren't half going to be damn cold in there. Just look at that, you guys. It's going to be really b— draughty. Poor old Frank will freeze to death. Ha, ha, ha.' Everyone joined in the mirth, the joke was well and truly on me. I wasn't at all bothered, I had already heard talk of such panels being removed from operational aircraft in the gunnery classes and valued more the vision advantage. However, I had not tried it out yet but felt no real apprehension. That particular night on the Diversion proved without any doubt the value of real clear vision.

With the Diversion completed sleep came quickly. We awoke next morning to find another sunny day. We were very fortunate at Peplow to get a good number of 48s (48-hour leaves). These we put down to Skipper's fortuity and our good luck! Perhaps Skipper was glad to get home to see his wife Joan, as often as possible. The crew were always pleased to go on leave so everyone was well suited.

It was on one of these 48s that I met an old colleague from the ATC and of the RAF at London and Ludlow. It happened while waiting on Coventry Station. I noticed an officer pilot. We glanced casually. Then, there was instant recognition by both. It was Ray Twigger!

'Hello Frank,' said Ray with a smile.

'Hello Ray,' I said, banging up a salute.

'How are things going with you?' asked Ray, returning the salute.

'Not bad, I'm at 83 OTU on Wimpeys.'

'Did you hear about Ken Essex?' asked my former colleague.

'I last heard he was in Canada flying Cessna Cranes.'

'Yes, that was true but sadly he's been reported missing Duisburg, ninth op, 21st May. He was on Lancasters,' informed Ray.

'Let us hope he is a POW?' I ventured.

'Yes,' said Ray. 'His Commanding Officer wrote to his mother and said he may well have survived. It takes time to get news from the Red Cross.'

A few minutes later the train thundered in.

We said 'Cheerio, best of luck.'

I took a third-class compartment while Ray was more privileged as an officer and took a first-class carriage.

I never saw Ray Twigger again while we were in the RAF. Our paths only crossed once again, so briefly, after the war. I understood Ray to have become a flight lieutenant, captain and pilot of a Lancaster before he left the RAF.

Back at Peplow, we expected our posting any day. We knew that almost certainly we were to go to Lindholme, near Doncaster, to convert to four-engined aircraft. Meanwhile, we waited around a few days until Skipper got fed up of the waiting and promptly got us all seven days' leave.

Skipper was like that. If there was any sort of a delay, like waiting for another navigator or another course, off we went on leave. We had more leave passes at Peplow than anyone there or anywhere else. No one in our crew ever complained about the stern-looking flight lieutenant.

CHAPTER 11

The Halifax Four-engined Bomber

No. 1667 HCU Sandtoft; 47 Crashes; No. 1481 Bomber Gunnery Flight

After a reasonable and happy leave I left home, complete with three kit-bags, bound for Doncaster via Birmingham, Derby and Sheffield. Mother came with me to Birmingham. Evidently she didn't think much of the service who sent its aircrews on leave with three kit-bags!

It was a typical RAF posting – to be on leave between postings — so that you personally had to lug everything you possessed, including that goddamned buoyancy suit, which needed a kit-bag of its own! Mother, always there first with help and ideas, especially in those days, was fit and seemed proud enough to help load her son's kit into the guard's van at Coventry and then *insist* on travelling to Birmingham, purely to help with all the gear.

She very thoughtfully bought lunch at Lewis's during the wait for the connection to Derby. She then helped get all three kit-bags out of 'left luggage' and into the train, also helping to get her slim son onto a corridor train through one of the long narrow ventilation sliding windows! Yes, the train was so jammed full it was impossible to get in by the doors!

The British public were out in force that weekend. I could have sworn it was a Bank Holiday (it was the Friday before the August Bank Holiday). The journey, standing up with kit in the train, was long-winded and tiring. I failed to get a seat at any change because of manhandling the three kit-bags.

The last leg of the journey up to Doncaster was spent in the corridor of a train in company with a Corporal wearing a bush hat of the KOYLI (King's Own Yorkshire Light Infantry). He was on his way home from the jungles of Malaya, very sun-tanned and looking full of meppacrine (anti-malaria drug).

We swapped a few stories during the journey. He told me some of the things the Japs did in the Far Eastern war, like tying a bod over fast-growing bamboo shoots. I told him I wouldn't fancy his job.

'You can keep your job too, Sergeant. Too dangerous for me,' he instantly replied. I thought he was joking or being pleasantly complimentary. He could keep the Malayan jungle for certain.

The arrival at RAF Lindholme was unceremonious. We were to spend the first week or so at a holding unit before starting the course. I had arrived in the early evening and after finding a Nissen hut and a meal at the Mess I began to look for the rest of the crew. I had kept a good lookout for them since arriving.

We managed to find each other although some members arrived after dark. Mac always seemed to find someone he knew wherever we went. It was quite common to find him settled in a card game at the Mess or a nearby hut. Nevertheless, Mac was always pleased to see most crewmembers. Bert often went out with one of his numerous WOP mates and it was while we were at the Lindholme holding unit at nearby Boston Park that some members of our intake found themselves in a 'dust up' with the local 'Bevin Boys' at a dance hall at Thorne.

Apparently, the 'Bevin Boys' took exception to the presence of so many good-looking, fit and energetic young airmen. The latter were being quite busy polishing off the local talent. There was quite a scrap; most of the RAF lads bore evidence of the sortie next day for on parade we were treated to a vision of something that looked like a hospital casualty department. Poor old Kennie Austin, one of Bert's WOP colleagues, had his head and eye well bandaged. Others had arms in slings, fists and wrists bandaged; the odd bod even had a walking stick.

'Stupid beggars, did you ever see such a forlorn mob? Good job poor Willie wasn't there,' was Skipper's remark.

It was strongly rumoured that the following night all aircrew types were to arm themselves with whatever they could – stout pieces of wood, angle iron etc. All self-respecting RAF were to make for the dance hall at Thorne as soon as the pubs threw them out. It was all to no avail. Somebody heard about it and all evening passes were scrubbed. We were confined to camp until further notice! The big fight never took place.

On one of the first mornings on parade at the holding unit we were formed up into a hollow square. We should have known something strange was about to happen. We had never previously experienced this manoeuvre on the parade ground. There was speculation as to what it could be. We didn't really have time to think about it for long.

Suddenly it was 'left, right, left'. Two aircrew sergeants, one an air bomber, the other an air gunner, were marched by the Station Warrant Officer (SWO) into the centre of the open part of the hollow square. The two sergeants looked very solemn. The SWO read out the charges of AWOL. The sergeants had been found guilty at a recent court martial and sentenced to be reduced to the ranks, followed by a period in an RAF Detention Barracks. The parade was attended by the Commanding Officer and Adjutant of the holding unit. The SWO called out one rank and name at a time.

'Sergeant, one step forward march.' The already loosened stripes were ceremoniously ripped off each arm.

'AC, one step backwards march.' The same treatment applied to the other aircrewmember, after which both were sharply marched away.

'ACs left turn quick march.'The pair of them were very red-faced.

We had never seen anything like it before or since. We were all numbed by the experience. Perhaps it was all for our benefit? Perhaps it was all a fake, I wondered? Skipper didn't have much to say about it but he appeared to be as inwardly moved as everyone else. Perhaps it hit us harder because we were all sergeants. Perhaps Skipper was concerned because we were sergeants.

Next day, true to form, we were told we had not been lucky enough to be on the first course at the HCU and, therefore, we would not be required for a further week. It was gently rumoured that we could lose ourselves from the camp. There would be no roll call until the following Friday. There were no leave passes issued. I expect the extra work of issuing passes was not wanted and yet it would have legalised the whole affair. Yes, this was after the AWOL-stripping spectacle! The whole crew opted to go on unofficial leave.

I decided to go to Manchester to see a girlfriend and it was on this leave that I became engaged to Edna. I discovered later that both my parents were annoyed that I did not go home for the leave and also for getting engaged and not telling them in advance.

In retrospect, it was a strange world. On one hand we saw two sergeants reduced to the ranks for going AWOL and on the other we were given leave without passes. It all seems so stupid now. If any one of the NCOs on our course had been stopped by service police and found without a pass, technically he would be AWOL and therefore the fact reported to his Commanding Officer. (Fortunately no one was.)

Once back from leave, time passed quite rapidly. The very night we arrived three Halifax aircraft pranged in the vicinity of RAF Lindholme. Two aircraft collided on the circuit during night flying and the other was destroyed by a practice bomb dropped by another Halifax using the same bombing range. The crews of all three aircraft perished. It was headline news in the local newspapers. It wasn't the best of introductions to a Heavy Conversion Unit or to the Halifax four-engined bomber.

On our return, we discovered that we were to fly from No. 1667 HCU Sandtoft, a nearby satellite of RAF Lindholme. We moved in quite quickly. Our Nissen hut site was surrounded by sun-ripe cornfields.

Skipper met us fairly early the next morning and we went with him to meet our flight engineer, Sergeant Stan Thompson. Stan was a quiet, polite, tallish fellow with lots of good humour. He was medium build, twenty-nine years' old and married. He came from Leeds and had been a sewing machine mechanic for Singer prior to volunteering for flying duties. We were to discover he was a 'shit-hot' flight engineer – our Skipper had done it again!

Peter and I then discovered that while the rest of the crew would be doing two weeks' ground school prior to flying the Halifax, we would be going to 1481 Bomber Gunnery Flight at Ingham on four-engined aircraft. It wasn't many hours before we were on our way.

Ingham appeared to be a pleasant place, which it was except for the plague of earwigs that invaded the Nissen huts after dark. I remember Peter striving to get rid of the determined little beasts by rubbing a bar of Lifebuoy toilet soap to make a line on the floor around his bed as a deterrent. Once the lights were out it wasn't long before you could hear the familiar crack as they fell off the corrugated walls onto the linoleum floor. This was unsettling but in itself it had its lesson for all gunners. You could not hear the one that landed on your bed (unless it landed close to your ear, on the pillow). This would be the one to enter your bed and cause discomfort, the lesson being that the one you heard caused no harm, although the sound demoralised the Nissen hut occupants. The one that mattered, you couldn't see or hear until it was too late. They were most unpleasant at the time.

RAF Ingham was quite a place even with the earwigs. The small Sergeants' Mess was quite good and efficiently run by the Mess Sergeant and his staff of WAAFs. We were looked after very well, the station having previously been used by Polish squadrons flying Wellingtons.

The ground school was done in the farm buildings built in the centre of the field. These buildings were perhaps unique because they were farm buildings, cowsheds and barns. Inside, they had been modified as classrooms. There were no runways for the six or so residential Wimpeys. They and the odd number of Martinets were dispersed around the field when not in use.

Half the course flew in the mornings and half in the afternoons. The air was constantly full of Wimpeys and Martinets. They really worked and flew the pants off us at Ingham. The instructors were a glamorous, bemedalled lot. All of them flew *without parachutes*. Evidently, instructing rookies was not dangerous when compared with ops. Who were they kidding, I wondered, especially when a Wimpey full of trainee gunners and instructors crash-landed, wheels up, after an engine fire on take-off? Two gunners, the two instructors and staff pilot escaped through the cockpit roof hatch before flames engulfed the centre section and astrodome. The gunner in the tail turret had his turret to port (the standard take-off and landing position) and, therefore, escaped too. But this left three gunners trapped in the fuselage. The fire at one end and the stationary turret on the full beam at the other, blocked any exit. The escaped gunners were prevented from going to the aid of their trapped colleagues by the instructors who held them back.

'You cannot save them, you will be killed if you try,' they said.

Then, as if to defy all odds, one by one the three gunners appeared from underneath the aircraft. Fortunately, when the Wimpey crash-landed, wheels up, the aircraft finally stopped, rolling on to one wing tip, the other wing high, therefore exposing the escape hatch in the floor of the operational trainer. Had the aircraft settled the other way, the three gunners would, almost certainly, have burnt to death!

For the two weeks spent at Ingham, we flew nothing else but camera gun training sorties with Martinets. On the following day we were able to view the previous day's cine film. This would be shown to the whole course while the gunner gave his own verbal commentary. The screened gunner in charge would then assess both film and commentary. Generally speaking, the number of hits, according to the instructor, was consistently high from all members of the course. We only did elementary exercises with Martinets. (It would have made much more sense to have flown the 'corkscrew' manoeuvre on advanced exercises with Hurricanes.)

During our spell in the classroom we had the opportunity to brush up on tactics. One way of doing this was to read through combat reports. These were the recent reports of combats by gunners of various squadrons throughout the command.

The gunner instructor who took us for this was a pilot officer air gunner, wearing the ribbons of the CGM (Conspicuous Gallantry Medal), DFM and NAAFI gongs plus two *wound* stripes!

It was the lot of each gunner to read out a combat report to the rest of the class. The gunner was expected to comment on the combat, then others in the class were permitted to join in with their views.

It was at Ingham during this particular lesson on tactics that I read an official review that clearly stated 'A survey of combat reports shows that in 70 per cent of night combats, the attacking fighter attacks from above.' No one said, at the time, that this summary was based upon *survivors'* reports! For as we all know now, *dead men tell no tales*!

Intelligence gained from recent combat reports was all we had to go on at that time. This particular survey gave the impression that 70 per cent of fighter attacks at night still came from above. We should thererfore concentrate our visual searches from mid or rear turret in that direction, i.e., upwards. Searching below was very difficult at the best of times. One could not see immediately below the aircraft and the only way to do this was to periodically roll the bomber (fully loaded or unloaded) to near vertical so that the gunners could look below. This search should have been carried out every three to five minutes (or less), the captain having first advised the gunners early, which side the bomber was to roll, in time to rotate their turrets to get the maximum view downwards.

Unfortunately, the survey carried no evidence of the *Schrage Musik* attacks that came from *immediately* below, as there were usually no survivors. Therefore, this sort of summary of combat reports gave the *wrong* impression entirely and also gave false confidence that most likely your bomber would be attacked from where you could easily see the enemy fighter, astern and above from beam or quarter. (This may well be true of daylight sorties.)

Years before, as a schoolboy fascinated by air war stories, I eagerly sought from the library books by PF Westerman and WE Johns (for 'Biggles' stories) and Father's *G8 Air War* magazines and many others. All these accounts of World War I gave the fighters' most successful attacking position to be directly behind and below the bomber, day or night.

I was never happy as a gunner trainee with the mostly negative attitudes of others. When raising the point of underneath attacks with gunner colleagues, I was often ridiculed (to say the least). Thank God I had my own search ideas and carried them out on night operations.

During one of these sessions reading combat reports, one trainee read out that the gunner concerned, a sergeant, had been wounded in the combats but had destroyed both night fighters that were engaged in the consecutive combats. Finally, he added that the gunner had been awarded the CGM, which is awarded only to NCOs and airmen. An officer wearing the ribbon must have been an NCO when he won it, i.e., before being commissioned.

Another trainee gunner, a Scotsman, in the class, as sharp as a tack, stood up and commented 'The CGM, Sir, what like is that?' he said in typical Scots accent.

I winced inwardly for the Pilot Officer Gunner instructor was the one with the CGM ribbon and other gongs, plus the wound stripes. The Pilot Officer looked up, his face expressionless.

'Anybody know what the CGM is like? Perhaps somebody can tell him?'

Quiet gasps of amazement ran through the class in due respect for the immediate responsive answer. 'Ah,' I thought. 'The Pilot Officer is all he is cracked up to be, he is even sharper than a tack.' I think that after this incident everyone's respect for him went up by heaps. He was a strict man as an officer gunner, stricter than most. He also appeared by far the most adept at lectures on tactics. He really took the pupil gunners apart if they were not really attentive. He knew, of course, more than any of us, that once we were 'over Europe' at night all alone, as the night bomber is, we would have the fright of our lives. In that quiet, safe classroom that was once a farm, the only person who knew what we were in for was *him*. Everyone knew that you didn't get a CGM for nothing. You might possibly earn a DFM for fifty trips (we hoped it was only thirty) but you had to fight for more than your life for the pale blue ribbon with black edging of the CGM! (The DFM was narrow purple with white diagonal stripes.)

Peter was a constant companion at Ingham in addition to his ops against earwigs. We spent many an hour in the intelligence library at Ingham under the ever-watchful eye of an attractive WAAF intelligence officer.

She was a flight officer and we always 'banged one up' whenever we entered her sanctuary. Invariably, this embarrassed her. Nevertheless, she seemed taken up by our interest in her domain. Perhaps our frequent visits stirred some emotion; perhaps she felt sorry for two very ordinary young sergeants who were perhaps steadily approaching their doom, or at least the day of reckoning?

It was here that, through her enthusiastic introduction, we were privileged to examine a photograph album containing a pictorial history of the previous occupants of Ingham, Nos 300 and 301 Squadrons of the Polish Air Force, flying their Wimpeys in the most madly courageous manner, as only Poles did. There were the usual scenes of aircraft with crews, prangs, crash-landings, all depicting the hairy experiences of days gone by.

It appears that the Poles were among the last squadrons to fly Wimpeys on ops in the RAF and were among the last to convert to Lancasters. Why they were kept so long on the older aircraft is a puzzle. They were good flyers and invariably believed in taking the fight to the enemy, which was what the bombing war was all about. True, somebody had to be the last on Wimpeys, but why the Poles?

The days spent at Ingham were fairly long and sunny. We were still on double BST, although it would not be long before the sun would set on our days of peace. The 'Bombers' War' was now just a few weeks away. Worry us it didn't. We were very confident youngsters; we were very fit and quite ready and eager to join in with those already on ops, to do our bit and take our 'bit' of destruction to the Third Reich.

One myth of long standing vanished at Ingham! A long time ago, when we were training in Canada at No. 3 Bombing & Gunnery School, a 'Canuck' instructor told us that on operational aircraft fitted with hydraulic turrets (Frazer Nash on the Lancaster) the rear turret, which was normally driven by the EDP (engine-driven pump) from the port outer engine, had an alternative and duplicate hydraulic system, which was piped to an EDP on the port inner engine. This alternative power system could be selected by the rear gunner in the event of a port outer engine failure, malfunction or damage. It was a popular idea to have an alternative power supply to the main turret.

The Canadian source of information was poorly informed. However good the idea was, the instructors at Ingham soon blew it. The standard Mk I and Mk III Lancaster, equipped with a Frazer Nash FN120 tail turret, operated only from the EDP on the port outer engine. This left one engine with an EDP and no turret to drive, hence the popular misconception.

The front turret (FN5) was driven by the starboard outer and the mid-upper (FN50) by the starboard inner. The FN64 mid-under turret with periscope sight had been abandoned long ago. It seemed to make sense to use a spare engine and EDP as a standby but it was no more than wishful thinking. Our morale faltered a little at the thought of losing power on the rear turret and losing the effect of its four guns. The prospect of no alternative supply seemed hard to swallow. There seemed to be no real reason for it, except saving time and money on the production line.

The two weeks at Ingham were really concerned with work, both class study and practical during the cine-camera trips in the Wimpeys. Peter didn't seem to be having too much trouble during the sessions. He appeared to be getting his film OK and as no official adverse comment was made about this, everything must have been good enough for the instructors.

We had quite a display of medal ribbons too. Most of the instructors had at least a DFM, a few had bars, two had a CGM and one or two had both the DFM and CGM. There were wound stripes galore as there were the NAAFI gong and the 'Spam' medal (Africa Star). To young sprog sergeants, all this paraphernalia had its effect. It was just what we needed. Perhaps to be trained by the 'elite' could possibly produce more 'elite'? There was no other RAF station that did as much to boost our morale as Ingham did. On completion of the course we really felt we were all 'crack gunners'. There were really no air gunners like RAF air gunners!

After Ingham, returning to No. 1667 HCU Sandtoft was like riding a bike with two flat tyres. We were just in time to find the rest of the crew ready for circuits and bumps, including our brand new flight engineer, Stan.

One of the immediate rumours at Sandtoft was the ghastly figure of forty-seven crashes in one month. All Halibags. We believed it to be correct then. Now, I wonder if it were true. It could have meant the whole base (three airfields), i.e., Lindholme, Sandtoft and Blyton. There were certainly enough Halis at the various dispersals and we saw plenty each day. It seemed as if there were, as a minimum, three or four aircraft at each dispersal. Sometimes they were not dispersed very well, being more like clusters of six or eight in a group, all facing any which way. They stood about on any sort of hard standing and we had to look around the groups of aircraft, trying to find which one was 'our' allocated kite. They seemed a right old bunch, some just about ready for the scrap heap. There were tatty old Halis, Mk IIs and IIIs, some with mid-uppers, most without. They nearly all carried guns in the tail turrets, which was handy in case of intruders! Skipper took his time sorting out our kite and if it wasn't to his liking he left it where it stood, which was really good stuff because we learnt to trust his decisions.

We must have discovered as many U/S (unserviceable) aircraft and therefore unflyable, as those we flew! We were always having to 'try another'. Sometimes we even got it into the air before Skipper realised the kite was no good. (Not often though – he was too hot for that!)

It was at one of these over-full dispersals, while trying to find 'our kite' that we spotted a brand new Halifax. On closer inspection we found that instead of the H2S blister, at the mid-under fuselage position there was an under-cupola, equipped to carry a gunner and a .50-inch (12.7-mm) Browning. The shape, colour and position of the cupola was exactly the same shape as the H2S scanner would occupy. I was quite delighted with the find and wondered why it had arrived at a conversion unit instead of a squadron.

I suppose to many people it was just another Halifax. To me, it represented the best effort I had seen so far to equip a night bomber with an under gun, especially a .50-inch (12.7-mm) calibre. The position for the gunner was not very good, demoralising would be the word. He just sat on an ordinary turret seat and cushion that may or may not have carried its usual $1/4$-inch (6-mm) thick armour plate between the cushion and the seat frame. The seat was simply bolted through the light alloy cupola. The gun mounting was fixed to one side and presumably the gunner would centralise the mounting and gun once he was aboard. There was the usual seat lap strap, which was fitted to all turrets but rarely used. (Neither Peter nor I strapped ourselves into the turrets on ops or training. It sounds silly now, but it had a lot to do with getting ourselves out fast, if trouble occurred.) There was no armour plating visible. This was normal in a British night bomber – we had very little.

There appeared to be access into the fuselage above the cupola via a very large wooden, circular trap door let into the fuselage. There did not appear to be any hinges for the door – the visible circular timbers seemed to slot into one another. If the door was not hinged but simply slotted, then I could visualise the 'whole lot' taking a ride when the aircraft commenced the first dive of a 'corkscrew' or when on the 'hump' in the 'corkscrew' (i.e., coming out of the climb port or starboard and then changing to a dive in the same direction). Nevertheless, it seemed a good idea and, if the gun were .50-inch calibre, all to the good! There didn't appear to be any ammo storage, although this could have been 'upstairs' in the main fuselage.

Among the ground school subjects dinghy drill became a regular item (as at Peplow). We learnt how to use all the equipment such as radio, the aerial, signal rockets, flares, Very pistol, leak plugs of assorted sizes (not very encouraging), a first-aid kit, rations in a concentrated and compact form. There was also a box kite with a longer radio aerial attached. This was to be launched by rocket on the 'crest of a wave' preferably. The instructing officer, giving an outside demonstration, fired the rocket, plus kite, three times on the airfield at Sandtoft and each time the kite soared with the aid of the rocket to about 100 feet, then plummeted to earth as fast as it could, without taking the air! Each time the kite thudded down onto the turf an enormous cheer rang out from the watching trainee crews. The Flying Officer giving the demonstration seemed very embarrassed and explained that at sea there would be more wind, which brought another roar of raucous disapproval from the assembled crews.

One morning when we assembled for the roll call prior to training sessions, Mac turned up a little on the late side. He looked just a little rumpled and in addition he had lipstick smears around his mouth and ears and his shirt collar bore similar evidence of a night's passion.

'What the devil have you been up to?' roared Skipper. 'Go and tidy yourself up immediately and get rid of that lipstick. Don't dare come on parade like that again. You are a disgrace to the rest of the crew.'

Poor old Mac was still half asleep. Evidently, he had just rolled out of bed and hadn't had time to wash, shave or even look into a mirror. He had arrived on parade buttoning up his battledress as he came up the roadway towards the training area.

The rest of the crew had a quiet snigger at Skipper's remarks, that is, when Skipper wasn't looking! Poor Mac, I felt sorry for him. He didn't know what to do with himself. He kept very quiet and just took the public reprimand on the chin. The incident never repeated itself for Mac was no fool be it that he was fond of a good evening down the pub with a local girl. A highly intelligent navigator at all times, his work in the air and in preparation on the ground was a credit to him. We were as lucky to have such a navigator as we were to have Skipper as a pilot. Presumably, it was Mac's untidy appearance and generally slack attitude towards anything but flying that kept him an NCO. Nevertheless, I am sure we were all endeared to him in one way or another, Skipper included. We all knew that we had the 'Gen Kiddie' at the nav table – 'God's gift of a first-class navigator'.

Flying the Hali at Sandtoft in the early part of the course was quite exhilarating; the day circuits and bumps were no problem. The night flying, particularly the night circuits, became hairy at times.

Most of the crew, except pilot, navigator, engineer and WOP, sat in the fuselage as we were not allowed to enter our crew positions until airborne. Therefore, during circuits and bumps it was not practical for either of the two gunners and bomb aimer to enter their turrets. True, we could get intruders at any time and our fears about this were quickly dispelled by our WOP stating that he would get an intruder warning first. We seemed always to trust whatever we were told as long as it came from an official source. The RAF didn't appear to be wrong and if it were, it wasn't very often and besides there was little or no proof either, if they were wrong!

The spell of night circuits was perhaps the most boring of our flying days. Fred, Peter and I sat facing each other on the rest-beds. We passed the odd nod, smile or other grimace to each other, depending on what sort of a landing Skipper was executing.

One night, while listening to the constant patter from pilot to flight engineer, it seemed that Stan reported to Skipper that we had 45 gallons of fuel left in the main tanks. Also, from time to time, Stan mentioned the fuel consumption rate, which was probably about 0.95 miles per gallon, commenting to Skipper that he would change tanks soon. The patter continued.

'Full power, wheels up, flaps 30°, flaps up,' etc.

This went on for two more circuits and I thought at any moment now Stan will say

'Changed tanks, Skipper. On outboards.' (Or 'inboards', whatever was the rule.) No such comment occurred. Neither Peter nor Fred had noticed. (Perhaps my pilot training was to blame once again?) I mentioned it to each of them at the rest-bed position. It was necessary to shout to get above the sound of the four Merlins, each person having to pull aside the helmet to by-pass the earpiece. Peter didn't seem very bothered, Fred seemed to think I should mention it to Skipper and Stan over the intercom. I didn't want to make a fool of myself and, after all, none of us had heard any further patter about fuel. We did another circuit and I remembered that many of these supposed forty-seven crashes were on the circuit at night, overshoots and such. In some, the engines had cut out unexpectedly. We kept on listening. We flew around again and bumped up and down the runway. Some typical Skipper Lane landings, more bumps than circuits, or so it seemed on these night landings in a Hali! (A guy I knew could do better in an Anson I thought!)

After four circuits and landings there was no comment from Stan or Skipper. We were getting tense about it now so I risked it.

'Hello Stan,' I said over the intercom. 'Please excuse the query. Didn't you say you had only got 45 gallons left in the main tanks?'

'Yes,' said Stan, evidently mystified. 'Well,' I said, 'We're all sitting here with nothing to do but listen to you and Skipper and we haven't heard you change tanks.'

'Oh, I changed them some while back,' said Stan. 'I wouldn't forget a thing like that, Frank. Don't worry.'

I felt a right clot and apologised to Skipper and to Stan for being such an idiot. The remainder of the flight continued uneventfully. Later, Stan was to repeat his assurance that he wouldn't ever forget to change tanks. Let's face it though, plenty of flight engineers had and they were no longer around to confirm or deny it.

We didn't get any intruder activity while we were at Sandtoft but when we visited the Intelligence Office one day to collect some escape aids in the form of pen clips, trouser buttons etc. (all these items were magnetic compasses in disguise), a *Luftwaffe* officer's cap caught our notice. In answer to questions we were told the following hairy but humorous tale.

Apparently, during the winter months earlier that year a Ju 88 intruder had followed a Halifax into the circuit at night. There had been an intruder warning sent to all crews on training but the Ju 88 was not known to be in the immediate vicinity of Sandtoft, otherwise the aerodrome lighting would have been switched off. The Hali had its navigation lights on and in due course called up base, gave the airfield and aircraft call sign and added 'downwind'. Base acknowledged, as is normal practice. The Hali repeated the procedure as it turned on to the final approach, adding 'funnels', and continued with undercarriage down and full flap when the Ju 88, a mere 300 yards astern, opened fire on the Hali with four 20-mm cannon and four 7.9-mm machine-guns.

The intruder pilot closed rapidly, giving the unfortunate Hali (a 'sitting duck') a long burst at point-blank range and *missed*! Meanwhile, the Halifax had put out its navigation lights and the airfield also plunged into darkness. The Hali slipped quickly away to hide in the shadows while the Ju 88 pilot, so angry at missing a large four-engined bomber trainer, flung out his peaked cap onto the runway in disgust.

After all, if he couldn't shoot down a trainee crew, what chance would he have with an operational crew? Still, it's a thought that it was *he* who was looking for the easy picking. If the Hali rear gunner had been on the ball too, with his guns loaded (if he were not on circuits and bumps) he may well have opened fire and even hit the night fighter intruder, which would have made *Herr Leutnant* even more angry.

Our billets at Sandtoft were the same sort as at Peplow, corrugated iron-roofed Nissen huts. The aircrew sergeants' sites were dispersed in the surrounding cornfields. We had rather an attractive walk to the Mess each morning and again after lunch. The only thing that spoilt the view was the rough planking that had been used to provide fences each side of the path. I was amazed to find that the Air Ministry or building contractor, on construction of the airfield, had constructed such routes through the fields. Such thoughtfulness was very rare. Generally, it seemed a lovely walk through these fields of golden corn. I thought the farmer on harvesting would have a bit of a problem getting around such obstructions and in places the simple pine paling with wire bracing had broken away and could foul the tractor or the plough.

We were not badly off on rainy days either for again some thoughtful contractor had laid duckboards the whole length of the paths. It seemed too that for once an illegal short cut had been eliminated by providing an official route straight through the fields. This is exactly what had been done and I was never to find it repeated on any other RAF station.

We had a certain amount of petty theft in the Nissen huts. We suspected one particular aircrew sergeant. All occupants of the hut knew that each individual was losing the odd toilet item – toothpaste, soap, hair cream, boot polish etc., nothing traceable. We found it rather distasteful that it could be one of our own kind. It never occurred to any of us that it could be an intruder from another hut or site. Presumably the offender took the odd item rather than buy his own. Although this seemed very petty at the time, air gunners were the lowest paid of all the aircrew trades, receiving 8/- (40p) per day (less Messing charges).

We flew numerous cross-countries and trips to the local bombing ranges day and night. These training missions enabled Mac and Fred to become experts with the navigational and bombing aids carried by most Conversion Unit Halifaxes. These would be the usual Gee equipment and in some aircraft we would have the rarer H2S, a combined navigation and bombing aid that gave a rough TV picture of the ground beneath the Hali.

We didn't do any air firing from the Halis although we did our share of fighter affiliation (F/A) at Sandtoft. The Halifax was bigger and heavier than the Wimpey and most had a mid-upper turret, which brought a pleasant change for Peter. We usually flew these trips with a Hurricane, which we met right over the aerodrome, commencing the manoeuvres when we were clear of the circuit pattern.

The crew had mixed feelings about these F/A training trips. I think most would have preferred not to do them at all. We were perhaps more fortunate than most for we had only one or two crewmembers airsick on these flights. To me, the evasive action employed by the Halifaxes and previously the Wimpey was the most important and thrilling part of the course. I quite honestly think that I could have flown 'corkscrews' all day long but guess that some of the others would have been objecting loudly by then.

We hopefully looked forward to flying a Diversion from Sandtoft but this unfortunately was not to be. Instead, we did two Bull's-eyes, which we flew with co-operation from our own flak, searchlights and night fighters. Both sorties were night navigational cross-countries, finishing with infra-red homing and a simulated 'bomb run' on Bristol. They were a little dull after the Nickel and Diversion at Peplow.

Although Peter and I kept a constant watch for night fighters, it was all in vain on both Bull's-eyes as we were not intercepted by anything. Bert kept a good lookout too on the Fishpond. This was the bomber's own radar fighter warning system, which operated from the H2S, using the same scanner but had a separate screen from that of the H2S. Sometimes it could pick out nearby aircraft and it took a diligent WOP to readily distinguish the echoes on the screen. This was most difficult when the set was operated while flying in the bomber stream as it gave numerous echoes, depending on the stream's concentration. If the bomber was on the outside of the stream or well off track, the echo or blips of any fighter would be easily distinguishable (and of course the bomber to any fighter).

Both nights flown on the Bull's-eyes were very cold, especially for the time of year, early September. The outside air temperature on one occasion was 47° below. It was on this trip that my oxygen mask froze up. It wasn't long before Skipper discovered this due to his frequent calls on the intercom. I had to signal 'yes' or 'no' on the crew communication light in conjunction with Skipper's conversation. Later, Stan, the flight engineer, using a portable oxygen bottle, brought along a spare oxygen mask complete with microphone. Stan was on his way back up the aircraft before I realised that as I was wearing three pairs of gloves I couldn't re-clip the mask on to my helmet. I then attempted, rather foolishly, to take off the helmet and disconnect the oxygen supply too, during the changeover. Quickly realising my mistake with very low temperatures at 22,000 feet, I hastily replaced my headgear.

It was also necessary to plug in the intercom and at the same time hold the mask to my face as I was not able to re-clip it to the helmet. Although I had removed my helmet and mask I had at no time taken off my gloves – the reason, the best in the world, would be seen later on. The new mask still didn't work and like the first became very quickly iced up, due to condensation forming inside the mask.

Not to be outdone, after we had done our practice bombing run over Bristol, using the call lamp, I gave 'corkscrew port' followed by a 'resume course' signal, a further 'corkscrew starboard' and finally 'resume course'. The Skipper sounded excited when he came through on the intercom.

'Was it a fighter, Frank?'

I regretfully informed him via the lamp that it wasn't and explained later that it was just practice. Everyone took it OK but there was a general feeling of disappointment that it had not been an RAF night fighter Mosquito. On the other hand, it proved that we could signal on the emergency call lamp and not misinterpret the signals, which was very important. We had done a couple of practice 'corkscrews' on a Bull's-eye exercise and I felt quite satisfied, especially with the co-ordination between captain and rear gunner. Not only that, I felt that Skipper's attitude about these things was always very good and that made an enormous difference to us all. Finally, these happenings had helped dispel the feeling of uselessness that I experienced when I discovered the oxygen mask and intercom had iced up.

There was little to choose from either of the Bull's-eyes – they were almost replicas. The two exercises certainly seemed identical to a weather, navigational and bombing exercise. The absence of interception was most disappointing for I would have liked to have had this experience. I have always felt that we should have had some night-fighter affiliation exercises while on the course. It would have been invaluable. Perhaps the Command believed that if we had been intercepted, our morale might suffer, whereas to tell us to expect interceptions and *not* get any was supposed to boost morale. That is if one could be hoodwinked into believing that if one of our own night fighters couldn't find us, what chance had the enemy? Like those crews who preferred a dark, moonless night. It reminded me of the ostrich who hid his head in the sand and got shot up the duff for his pains.

Our time at Sandtoft drew to a close. Skipper was enthusiastically looking forward to flying the Lanc at LFS (Lancaster Finishing School). One day he took great pride in telling us that we would almost certainly fly Lancasters as most crews posted from No. 1667 HCU were sent to No. 1 LFS based at Hemswell in Lincolnshire.

Skipper was dead right in his assumptions for we collected our clearance chits and packed out kit for the expected move.

CHAPTER 12

The Lancaster

No. 1 LFS Hemswell; the Lancaster 'Corkscrew' Manoeuvre; the 'Bomber's War' Draws Near

We all seemed cheerful about the posting to Hemswell, which had been a pre-war RAF station. We expectantly looked forward to the pleasure of peacetime-type billets, which were far more luxurious than our wartime Nissen huts. It would certainly be my first spell on a 'peacetime station' and I am sure we all looked forward to it quite eagerly. It seems strange now to accept that in 1944 by far the most important thing was to be comfortably accommodated. We worried far less about the coming ops, now barely four weeks away. It seemed as if any out-of-routine thing took any foreboding out of our minds.

At Hemswell we still knew nothing of the bombing war. We thought we had seen some action flying a Nickel and a Diversion. True, we had, but we were all still very inexperienced in the 'Bomber's War'. Our two OTU end-of-course sorties had been too much a piece of cake.

Hemswell billets were a shocking disappointment for we were allocated a dispersed site both for the Sergeants' Mess and the inevitable Nissen huts for sleeping. All we ever saw of the 'peacetime station' was the Station Cinema and that was built into part of a hangar.

We were still in company with some of our training colleagues from Peplow. Flight Sergeants Dawson, Paley and Beattie, with their crews, were all at Hemswell. It was here that the crew captains were, or would soon be, commissioned as pilot officers.

The Lanc proved to be the 'Four-engined Bomber of the Year'. At least, that seemed to be Skipper's impression of it. Our first trip was the 'familiarisation flight'. We went up with a screened Flight Lieutenant pilot who praised the Lanc from take-off to touchdown. Presumably, Skipper sat in the captain's seat and before we had been up ten minutes he was flying it. The aircraft seemed a pleasure to fly and was very manoeuvrable. According to Skipper it was really a dream to fly, especially compared with the Halifax or Wellington.

We tried two-and three-engined flying and from both pilots there was only praise for the aircraft's capabilities. We had a pleasant forty-five or fifty minutes. It even felt better in the tail turret, which was an FN120. It seemed the whole crew liked the Lancaster, which was all to the good since we were expecting to do at least thirty ops in one.

Thirty ops was the norm at that time. There was a slight tendency for the number to vary during the winter months (i.e., with slower training due to bad weather). Squadron crews would then be asked to do three or six ops more due to a lack of replacement crews.

The thing that didn't seem to dawn on anyone, at least none of the six sergeants, was the fact that at that time our Skipper was a 'second tour man', which normally meant only twenty ops were needed to complete *his* tour on bombers. Thirty ops would be expected from each of the rest of the crew. We were very soon to find the answer to this one, quite unexpectedly.

We did day and night circuits, during which our crew remained aboard the aircraft one night while other captains soloed. Mac also tried out the desirability of the tail turret during that session. He had always wanted a ride in the rear turret and on circuits there was no navigating for him to do except if we had a diversion for some reason, i.e., weather or 'intruders'. Skipper was instantly agreeable, later commenting that it was a good thing that Mac could handle the rear turret. It didn't take a second to draw a conclusion from this comment, although these remarks were all taken very seriously then. There was only one situation serious enough to require a navigator to handle the rear turret – a dead or seriously wounded rear gunner! Simple as the explanation was, it has a stunning effect now but at the time it was taken quite calmly. The situation was fully appreciated without any qualms whatsoever.

Later, I understood from Mac that he wasn't too keen and although, as I explained, not only had his 'ride' been his first at night, it had been at the hands of different first solo pilots. Consequently, they were not the best circumstances in which to be introduced to the rear turret. In addition, Mac was much bigger and taller than I. This alone would make life in the 'tail' much more uncomfortable and even unacceptable to some people.

After completing our share of day and night landings we had only one thing left and that, as far as I was concerned, was the most important – the Lancaster 'corkscrew'. However, some members of the crew again were not too enthusiastic.

My heart missed a beat when I noticed that we were on the training board for a fighter affiliation trip. It is also worth noting that two other skippers and two additional pairs of gunners were to go up with us, presumably to save time. We were down to fly with Pilot Officer Gallagher, DFM, which at that very moment didn't mean anything, but it would once we were airborne!

A day or so before I had gone round the crew to find out what their feelings were about fighter attacks. There was no real difference in the attitude of most crewmembers. Stan seemed the most helpful, but the rest didn't want to know. I had not put the question to either Skipper or Mac. They would be too busy and had enough to do.

I was quite staggered when I discovered the attitude of the WOP and bomb aimer. Bert said he would not be able to leave his seat for various reasons, i.e., listening out for recalls, 'intruder' warnings, weather information, SOS etc. Fred said that he would be busy helping to navigate, but mainly he would be doing his own job over the target. He also said that once we were on the bombing run a 'corkscrew' would be out of the question! I just couldn't believe it. Here was an intelligent, highly trained member of a bomber crew saying that we wouldn't be 'corkscrewing' on the bombing run, assuming we were attacked by a fighter at that time. Well, it wouldn't always be a Bristol Bull's-eye would it?

Stan's attitude was a little better. Although he said he would have various jobs to do, such as checking his instruments and keeping his log, and most importantly, keeping fuel consumption under surveillance, when he wasn't busy he would keep a lookout ahead and to the forward beams for fighters!

Peter didn't seem to be unduly worried by any of this.

Somebody said 'It is the gunner's job to look out for fighters.'

Peter seemed to think so too and was a little amused at my concern. Very true indeed, but how many pairs of eyes would one need when we were over the target itself? As many as possible I would think (and we still wouldn't have enough).

I was quite happy carrying out our normal beam to beam search, up and down and through dead astern, throughout the whole trip. It was just that I thought it would be a good idea to have all the other eyes open as well. They should all be wide awake. I had no doubt about that. However, I felt that over the target they could all help whenever possible because there is a whole lot of night sky to be searched and it can't all be searched at exactly the same time. For example, a fighter could attack in seconds from port while one or both gunners were searching starboard.

I was thinking about one of Major Hajo Herrmann's 'Wild Boar' cat's-eye, single-engined fighters diving down from above in a half-roll, half-loop manoeuvre, down onto our tail, firing as he came. We'd be gone before I would see him and before any gunner could get over the surprise, perhaps not having the time to 'corkscrew', line up the sight with the correct deflection and open fire!

The next time I saw Skipper in the crew room I popped the question very bluntly.

'Think we will survive a tour of ops, Skipper?'

'Yes, Frank, I don't see why not, why do you ask?'

'Well, Skipper, I have asked most of the crew if they could help out with the air search, particularly over the target and *en route* homewards. I was offered no assistance whatsoever and also the prospect of having to "corkscrew" on the bomb run wasn't acceptable at all.'

'Christ,' he said. 'We'll "corkscrew" first, a fighter attack is the most important, even on the bombing run. I'll have a word with all the crew except Mac, who should have his head down under the navigation blackout curtain anyway.'

It didn't take long for Skipper to get the crew together at the first opportune moment.

'Everyone except Mac will keep a lookout for fighters, except when actually doing their particular job, especially over the target and homeward route.'

I felt a great deal better after that and satisfied that I had got my point over finally. It was easy to see that each crewmember would be doing his job properly and would, therefore, wonder why the gunners weren't doing theirs too. The sky is an awfully large place.

'Thank God for Skipper Lane,' I thought, on that and on many other occasions.

The time arrived for us to do our first fighter affiliation in a Lancaster. We gathered our gear together and with the other two pilots and four other gunners, we took the transport out to a Lancaster Mk I awaiting us at dispersal.

In addition to the ground crew were two army types – Mountain Rescue/Airborne. Also, Pilot Officer Gallagher, DFM, a young, dark-haired, tallish chap with a pallid complexion, stood with them.

It was decided that the two bods 'up for the ride' (i.e., the 'brown jobs') would fly in the nose, Fred's compartment. I inwardly winced.

I thought 'Poor sods, what idiot has sent these nice guys up for an "air experience trip" on a fighter affiliation exercise in a fast, four-engined bomber doing a Lancaster "corkscrew"?' I just couldn't believe it, but I was not in a position to do anything.

The four pilots, including the screened pilot, discussed who would fly first and in what order. The six gunners would sort themselves out to be in their respective turrets when their particular skipper was at the controls.

It was the Lane full crew so I expect Skipper had some choice. As it turned out we were to do our 'corkscrews' last. I presumed that Gallagher took off as he then immediately instructed the individual pilots how to 'corkscrew' in the Lancaster.

The Lancaster 'corkscrew' was different from that which we had practised in Wellingtons and Halifaxes. The difference was that in the first dive to port or starboard the Lanc was fast and powerful enough after the first dive to pull straight up into a climb before rolling to starboard or port (whichever was required). In contrast, the Wellington or Halifax rolled the opposite direction to that taken in the first dive and continued diving before pulling up into the climb, in order to increase speed. The Lancaster – performing the climb immediately after the first diving turn – would therefore turn tighter and so become more difficult to be followed and fired at by the attacking fighter.

After making our *rendezvous* with the fighter – a Spitfire – over Hemswell and as soon as we were out of the airfield flying circuit, away we went into the first of some thirty-odd 'corkscrews', which were performed in just over ninety minutes.

My position was amidships on the rest-bed near the main spar (wing main member). The initial dives were so steep that I became 'airborne' during all the repeated diving movements of the 'corkscrews'. I could clearly hear the commentary as the rest of the crew and I were plugged into the intercom.

Apparently, the screened pilot wasn't satisfied with the speed at which the trainee pilots were putting the Lanc into the initial dive. Also, he criticised the angles of the dives and banks during the manoeuvre. They were nowhere near steep enough! Gallagher then took the controls and again performed his version of the 'corkscrew'.

I became airborne above the rest-bed as before, and kept company with the yellow dinghy 'emergency' case that had broken loose from its stowage and also my parachute pack. I lost sight of Peter but I knew he wouldn't be enjoying the ride.

'Get the nose down fast. You must get into the first dive really fast,' repeated Gallagher.

We continued the 'corkscrew' manoeuvre until the screened pilot became satisfied with each pilot's reactions. Then it was necessary to change pilots and air gunners.

The gunners came past the rest-bed to take up their turret positions.

'Christ, you should see up front, one of the pilots has been sick over the control column,' one said to me.

So far, I had been enjoying the Lancaster version of the 'roller-coaster', although I knew it was being performed with extra severity. The 'G' forces experienced on the rest-bed were quite considerable. I was perhaps in the best position in the aircraft, being approximately amidships, or rather midplanes. Lord knows what it was like in the turrets or nose. I never gave a thought at that time to the 'brown jobs' up in the nose for air experience. They were certainly getting that, poor beggars!

I believe both our WOP and flight engineer were sick and also our air bomber. Skipper was OK, as I had expected, so was the navigator. When our turn came to man the turrets I discovered how bad Peter was as I made my way aft.

I saw his unmistakable shape ahead of me in the darkened fuselage as I climbed over the main spar. He was hanging on to the aircraft structure on the starboard side of the fuselage and partly sitting on the step, i.e., the bomb bay step just below the mid-upper turret. I asked him how he was and whether he could take the mid-upper turret. He just grunted with dismay and shook his head. I could see that he was far too ill even to try. I climbed over the Elsan toilet and slid feet first down the chute-like planking into the rear turret. The air smelt fresh and clean; it was as draughty as hell after the hour or so spent on the rest-bed. I connected the intercom to my helmet. I didn't need the oxygen as we were at 6000 feet and didn't use the safety belt. We crewmen never used them. Skipper, like all pilots, was always strapped into his seat.

'Are you ready, gunners?' came the question from the screened gunner, followed by Skipper's enquiry.

'Rear gunner OK Skipper.'

'How about Peter, is he OK?' Skipper enquired.

'He's not too good but I can take the first attack. He may be OK later,' I replied.

The Spitfire was already making an attack on the starboard beam, which presumably had commenced while the changeover was in progress.

'Fighter 300 yards.'

'Corkscrew starboard go!'

'Diving starboard.'

'Changing.'

'Climbing starboard.'

'Rolling.'

'Climbing port.'

'Changing, diving port.'

'Break away Skipper, 100 yards.'

'Resume course.'

And so it went on.

Peter was unable to man his turret. I continued with the attacks until fighter and bomber, screened gunner and pilot had all had enough. I think most of the crew had, a long time before.

There had been no criticism of Flight Lieutenant Lane's 'corkscrews' by the screened pilot and the gunner instructor seemed pleased with the patter. Neither of these bods ever knew that Peter wasn't in his turret.

Nothing was ever said regarding fighter affiliation by the gunnery section about Peter's bouts of airsickness. He was a tough nut to be able to stick such an ordeal, the one just flown proved that beyond doubt. How about the rear gunner? Well, he was just 'too thick to be sick'! Or was he?

I remained in the rear turret while the Lanc rejoined the circuit and landed. As we taxied to the dispersal point I disconnected the intercom, opened the turret doors and proceeded backwards up the ramp. As soon as I came through the double doors across the fuselage, just forward of the rear turret the smell hit me. It was quite a horrible stench due to the positioning of the turret at the tail of the aircraft. The reek of mixed aircrew spew made me inwardly heave. My mouth went dry and then I had that awful feeling of saliva draining from the mouth and tongue.

'My God, I'm going to be sick.'

The main door was just a few feet further forward. I got this open quickly, gulping in the fresh, clean air. Peter was still crouching, half lying, near the bomb bay step, just forward of the door. He looked awful. His face appeared a greyish, whitish green. His battledress uniform had become streaked with vomit as he had rolled about the fuselage. Most of the crewmembers looked grey; nearly all of them had been ill. I never saw the 'brown jobs'. I understood them to be still up front, recovering.

I made the odd comment as the crewmembers came aft and went through the door. One of our crew said Skipper was annoyed with the screened pilot, presumably due to the severity of the 'corkscrews'.

'There was no need for that,' he was heard to say. I know that if I had not made the main door quickly and opened it to let in the fresh air, things could have been a lot worse. As it was, my stomach retched a couple of times before I had got to the door, I almost didn't make it. I remembered I had not been airsick since my first spell of spinning long ago, with Sergeant Pike at Southam. (Even then, I was out of the aircraft before I made a mess.) At Hemswell that day it had been a near thing, very near but not quite.

We didn't fly the Lanc again as we had finished the course. We expected to be posted in a few days. Skipper seemed very pleased with all of us as a bomber crew. We all felt very confident in him as our captain and pilot.

'We are certain to go on to Lancs and to a squadron of No. 1 Group, Bomber Command from here. Anyone got any ideas about which squadron?' Skipper said.

Apparently, we would be able to state a preference. There was a hurried conference around a map of eastern England, marked with bomber dromes. We settled on No. 100 Squadron at Grimsby. We thought Grimsby would make a nice change, the aerodrome being reasonably nearby. Bert seemed happy that we had not chosen No. 101 Squadron at Ludford Magna.

'Special Duties,' said Bert. 'I've an "oppo" on 101 and he doesn't say very much, all secret stuff, so we don't want any of that. Sounds too bloody dicey to me.'

We didn't ask for the Dam Busters because we didn't know then which squadron they were and, besides, it wouldn't have made any difference as 617 were in No. 5 Group and No. 1 LFS, I believe, only produced crews for No. 1 Group.

CHAPTER 13

No. 626 Squadron – 'The Fighting Sixes'

'Would You Like to Swing on a Star?'

As the reader may guess, we didn't get the squadron of our choice. Instead, the posting we received was to an insignificant squadron – 626 — at a similarly insignificant place called Wickenby, near Snelland Junction, fortunately still in Lincolnshire. The Gods had certainly lined it all up, had they not? The only other thing we discovered when we got off the transport with our kit, outside a Sergeants' Mess, was that this was '12 Squadron Territory'! It seemed we were to share the station with this shower, the *real* 'Dirty Dozen'.

Once inside the Mess, which seemed good for a wartime Sergeants' Mess, we had time to spend while waiting for the transport before proceeding to No. 626 Squadron. We soon spotted the painting hung over the main centred fireplace. The picture was simply entitled 'Sergeant Gray, VC'. I knew instantly that this was the unit that had attacked the bridge at Maastricht, Holland, in 1940 and gained a double VC. (The crew captain, Flying Officer Garland, also gained the VC. Both awards were made posthumously.) Good for 12 Squadron. They seemed then and always were a smart bunch of chaps!

Skipper, it appeared, was at it again, plugging for leave. How on earth did he do it? Getting us all these absolutely super and wizard spells of leave? Anyone who knew Flight Lieutenant Lane realised that he could keep a very straight face when necessary. Presumably that's how he got us our leaves, spinning a real good story or whatever. Nevertheless, we got it, possibly the only crew in Bomber Command to arrive on a squadron and get leave *before* ops.

Having been awarded the leave, we were quickly allocated billets and dumped our kit. Then it was off to nearby Faldingworth for *pay*.

'Can't go on leave without pay,' said Bert. We also received our railway warrants, ration tickets and subsistence allowance.

Transport soon took us over to Faldingworth No. 300 (Polish) Squadron for pay parade. We had to wait until after lunch and that was an experience in itself. The Sergeants' Mess was quite a comfortable place. It seemed better than ours at Wickenby, although still in a wartime Nissen hut. There was a number of blazing fires in the stoves in both the dining room and anteroom. The Poles were well and truly in evidence. Almost everyone we saw had three stripes and a Polish flying badge – the Silver Eagle and Chain. The counter staff in the Mess were all Polish too, although one or two of them attempted to speak English when we were recognised. We were offered a varied menu – Polish and English food. Poor old Bert seemed to collect everything being offered and ended up with a plate full of food that he couldn't recognise, let alone eat!

I was perhaps 'keeping a good lookout'. Thinking of Canadian food (like pancakes with bacon and maple syrup), I was a little more experienced and therefore took only what I recognised. We had some quite good fun and passed many remarks over that lunch at Faldingworth. Incidentally, the Polish WAAFs were simply gorgeous and I regretted not being able to speak Polish.

We were on our way, out of the Mess, trying to find 'Pay Accounts' (or wherever they chose to pay the odds and sods like us), when a Lanc at dispersal, immediately outside the Mess, started doing a 'run up', presumably in preparation for the night's operations. There were various ground types running around with chocks and things like 'trolley acks' (starter motor). There appeared to be much ado about the port outer engine, the skipper wasn't getting enough revs. There was lots of noise, shouting and gesticulating, all in Polish of course. It all seemed rather grim. Here we were at an operational station, the third squadron visited that morning, with all this bustle and hurry. The coal-black Lancaster revving up by the Sergeants' Mess, bore the red and white chequered national symbol of pre-war Poland on the port side of the nose, just below the pilot's position. These were young men, preparing for the Real War, not chucking out bog paper like our Nickel or making a feint like our Diversion. The Polish Lancaster doing its ground check and 'run up' seemed quite cold, dark and foreboding in the September lunchtime sunshine. It wasn't evil, it wasn't fear, there was just something quite uncanny about it. It just looked rather awesome and deathly. I thought of nothing else for some minutes. There was no going back; we were here with the Poles, in a fight to the death! It would be the fight of our lives that we would never forget.

We soon collected our pay and caught the transport back to Wickenby and then before we could make ourselves acquainted with No. 626 Squadron, we were on our way home for seven days' leave.

I left Lincoln on the 14.28 hours train bound for Manchester. Edna met me at the station and took me to her home. We spent the weekend in and around Manchester, leaving together for Coventry on the afternoon train, arriving at about 6 pm.

My parents were pleased to see me. This was their first meeting with Edna and it seemed rather strained. Something was not quite right. Perhaps I was still their little boy rather than a twenty-year-old sergeant with his fiancée, less than fourteen days away from almost certain death.

The leave passed well and we saw many of my Coventry friends. Most had heard of Edna but had not met her before. They all knew ops were due any time. Edna was cheerful but obviously uneasy about the immediate future. She made a brave, loyal show of it all.

My diary reveals a happy time in some respects, although there was something wrong at home. I was to find out, some months later, that neither of my parents saw Edna as a suitable partner for their son. I never knew exactly why, except they seemed to think I was far too young. Perhaps they preferred to forget that their son was rear gunner of World War II's heaviest bomb carrier – the Lancaster!

Unfortunately, our return trip to Manchester brought no better situation, for while Edna was out shopping her sister tore a strip off me. Something about being a 'young, toffee-nosed sergeant' and that 'three stripes have no effect on me, you know.'

Later, at Manchester station, while saying goodbye, we were saddened by a similar situation nearby; another airman, an RAF sergeant navigator, was saying goodbye to his family and girlfriend. He was on crutches, having lost a leg from the knee. Edna and I just looked at each other. We kissed goodbye. I took the 5 pm train for Lincoln and arrived at Wickenby on the last bus at 11 pm.

We had now reached the 'Bomber's War', each one of us after many months' of training. Skipper was about to commence his second tour and he would have two surprises in store for us, but more about those later.

We hadn't time to get to know anyone before our leave and when we returned we were expected to do a week's training before ops. The general idea was for the pilot and navigator to get used to the geographical location of Wickenby and for the rest of us to keep our hand in with our particular crew jobs.

A page in my logbook records the pre-ops flights made. It was the fighter affiliation, which again made my heart miss a beat, although rather selfishly. Peter probably wished he was still on leave!

We located the Spitfire eventually on the second flight, the first attempt being a complete flop. (Apparently, the first pilot reported his aircraft U/S.) The 'corkscrews' were magnificent, all flown by Skipper as we had no dual instruction at Wickenby. Peter established himself in the mid-upper FN50 turret but was unable to continue his running commentary due to further airsickness. After completing my own spell of some twelve 'corkscrews' with commentary, I was asked by Skipper to continue with Peter's share, except the first 'corkscrew', which Peter dealt with himself rather expertly, in spite of his bloody awful problem!

Later on, after we had completed the exercises, Skipper informed us that the Spitfire pilot's report was very good and that he (Skipper) was very pleased about it. The reports by the Spitfire pilots were always made after the training sortie (at the bomber's own airfield Flying Control). Apparently, the report spoke of good timing and co-ordination by both pilot and two air gunners. Later on, Skipper asked if, in view of Peter's airsickness, I could cope all right? I gave him the only answer I could at the time. We both should have known better. Fortunately, we were never to regret the decision. (Peter had never been airsick on anything other than 'corkscrews' and on the Bull's-eye 'corkscrews' he wasn't.)

We completed our training at Wickenby with an air/sea firing exercise and a spot of bombing for Fred and a nice long navigation stooge that included the Scottish Highlands for Mac. Presumably, Bert was getting his quota of QFEs, QDMs etc. Stan was patiently keeping his engine log and generally managing to keep everything running sweetly.

Skipper handled the Lanc like a veteran. Well, he was about to start his second tour! Occasionally, his landings would bounce and I would become airborne in the rear turret.

'How do you like that, Frank?' Skipper would then call up, finishing with his inimitable Dick Lane laugh!

I knew well that Skipper could execute both good and bad landings. The latter were due mainly to tiredness or perhaps he was becoming more than a little chocker at times. However, we managed to get our share of both types of landing.

We flew a drogue exercise with the Martinet trailing the drogue. I asked Skipper if he wanted me to use all four guns. His answer was always what all the crew wanted to hear:

'Fire all bloody four, Frank. Ha, ha, ha!'

It sounds stupid now but I really loved the effort the Skipper put into these gunnery exercises. After all, they were probably a solid bind to him. Even if they were, he always made sure his gunners got what they wanted!

We knew that our training was now complete and we looked forward to each day rather expectantly for signs of an operation. We had just returned from our leave as the Squadron returned from a daylight attack on the sea wall at Walcheren, Holland.

It was on the Walcheren sortie that our gunnery leader, Flight Lieutenant 'Willie' Whitehouse, DFC, flying with the Squadron Commander, Wing Commander Rodney, distinguished himself. Apparently, the Master Bomber had instructed all aircraft to descend below cloud for better visibility and in order to execute this quickly the Wingco had lowered the undercarriage and full flap. All was going well until two of the escort fighters decided to take a closer look, apparently performing a curve of pursuit attack, of all things, onto the Lanc. Taking no chances, 'Willie' opened up on the American P51 Mustangs who speedily broke their 'attack' off after some 100 to 200 rounds were fired by our enthusiastic gunnery leader. It was the talk of the Squadron Messes for some days.

Quite suddenly, there it was. *We* were on the Battle Order. Mac was due for the navigation briefing along with Skipper and Fred. The three of them spent the late afternoon and part of the evening preparing their charts, target maps, courses, bombing heights and winds. We lower fry, the two gunners, WOP and flight engineer, would only attend the main briefing.

The Battle Order (Orders for Flying) allocated our crew to Lancaster 'Charlie Two' UMC2. We had checked the aircraft the previous evening. We were all due for an early call at 02.15 hours. It was to be a daylight attack and it was rumoured that many aircraft would take part. The fuel load was known to the ground crews, as was the bomb load to the armourers. This gave rise to much speculation as to the possible target and which area of Germany we would be going to; the fuel load would determine the depth of penetration.

Later that night Mac joined us in the Mess. He seemed in good spirits for his first op. He had quite a twinkle in his eye, as if he couldn't keep everything secret, and yet he did. It didn't matter, I thought, I don't really want to know. I felt very apprehensive about what tomorrow might bring. We would soon see what it was all about.

Flying on air operations always seemed a great thing to do when I was at school in 1939. Later, in 1940–42, everyone at work talked about the bombing exploits of the RAF and the 1000 bomber raids, especially the daylight attack on the MAN works at Augsburg. Nothing seemed more correct at that time than to be involved in this type of air operation.

We turned in around 10.30 pm. We had been to our Sergeants' Mess on another site, comprising Nissen huts, as were all the living sites. They were well dispersed over the neighbouring fields. It was a good mile or more to walk from the Mess to the 'A' Flight accommodation site. We settled down quickly to an early night's sleep.

We were, it seemed, rudely awakened at 2 am by a dark-haired, good-looking Flight Lieutenant pilot, the 'A' Flight Commander. He was wearing the 'Spam' medal (Africa Star).

'Wakey, wakey, chaps. Flying meal at 02.30. Transport at 03.00, briefing at 03.30.'

The Flight Lieutenant soon disappeared. Mac, occupying the next bed, gave me a friendly dig.

'Wakey, Wakey, Frankie, you're off to the Ruhr.'

'Crikey,' I thought.

'Jesus, Mac, in broad daylight, the Ruhr.' I couldn't believe it. The Ruhr was the second most heavily defended part of Germany! (Berlin was the most heavily defended.)

We speedily dressed; there was no time to wash. We legged it to the Mess as fast as we could. It was cold, crisp and dark on that morning so we were wide awake when we arrived. We all enjoyed our meal of bacon, egg and chips. We said little, just looked at each other. One felt excited, yet apprehensive. It didn't spoil the young appetites. We always seemed permanently ravenous.

A few minutes later we could hear the motors of the crew buses or trucks assembling outside. These were the transport to which the Flight Lieutenant had referred. There seemed to be a buzz of excitement, a hurry and bustle out to the waiting trucks.

We clambered awkwardly aboard for they were just lorries with a normal drop-tail back with no steps, unlike the crew buses. Perhaps they had sent all of those to 12 Squadron? I hung on to one of the tubular frames of the roof canopy about two-thirds of the way into the truck. Most occupants remained silent during the journey to the Briefing Room. A few cracked jokes that met with nervous laughter. Others were sarcastic in their comments to other crewmembers and friends. There was a certain amount of horseplay between various bods who seemed to know each other fairly well so none of it was taken seriously. Some of these apparently happy guys would not return to the Sergeants' Mess.

The truck lurched to a halt outside a large Nissen hut complex. The main doors were already open, so were the internal doors to the right. As we entered the Briefing Room the hubbub of voices increased.

There was an excited babble from those already inside and a gasp from the odd crewmember as we entered, the reason being the large map of Europe on the far wall and the red ribbon that stretched out from Wickenby, Lincolnshire, to a German city! The map illustrated the flak and searchlight zones, coloured in red and blue respectively. The ribbon made as few alterations into Germany as it made out again. It appeared to be the normal sort of routing for a heavily defended German target.

'Christ,' said one.

'Bloody Duisburg,' said another.

'Jesus, the Ruhr,' said a guy next to me.

'In bloody daylight too.'

'Cripes, old "Butch"' must be mad.' Weren't we all?

The individual crewmembers made their way down the central gangway, looking for their allotted position, a seat in a particular row, together with the rest of their own crew. For one or two crews in the room it would be their last gathering in such a place. It would be their last operational sortie. Some would die, while some would complete their tour of thirty operational sorties.

'Frank,' somebody called out. 'Here we are.' I caught sight of five or six half-smiling faces. I went to the last seat, next to Peter.

'What d'ya think, Frank?' he said.

'Looks good to me,' I replied. 'We should get some fighters as they're a certainty in broad daylight.'

We quietly filled the canvas bags with personal belongings. The excited chatter continued until someone snapped out 'Attention.'

The Station Commander, Group Captain Haynes, strode down the gangway and took a chair to the left of the raised dais at the head of the long room.

'As you were, gentlemen,' he said, whereupon all the aircrew became reseated.

The briefing officer, was a dark-haired Flight Lieutenant, a very popular intelligence officer because of his jovial and pleasant attitude towards us and his aggressive attitude towards the enemy when discussing matters of the moment like targets, industries, PFF (Path Finder Force) marking, bombing heights etc.

'Gentlemen, your target today is Duisburg. More than 1000 bombers will take part in this attack.' I thought immediately of Ken Essex, reported missing from the May raid.

I wasn't happy at the prospect of our first real op being the same city that had claimed a former Coventry ATC cadet and colleague. (We still did not know the full facts at that time. Regrettably, Ken and all his crew were dead.)

The escort will be six squadrons of Mustangs and ten squadrons of Spitfires. You will note that H Hour is 08.45 DBST. This is so that you will be dropping your bombs at the time when most staff workers are in the streets on their way to join their shop floor colleagues who are already in the factories. You can imagine the chaos you are going to cause, with people trying to get into the works while those already in are trying to get out. Bomber Command have therefore timed your raid to cause maximum confusion in the city below when your bombing begins.

It all seemed very exciting to me and most of the crews in the Briefing Room. There were grunts and howls of approval. There was no mention of attacking innocent civilians. I am sure none of us at that time thought there were any such people in Germany!

PFF will open the attack with red TIs [Target Indicators] dropped by Oboe Mosquitos. PFF backers-up (in Lancasters) will be dropping green TIs throughout the attack. You will bomb the red TIs primarily; failing the reds, bomb on the greens. Conditions should be clear over the target but if cloud obscures, PFF Lancasters will drop Wanganui sky markers. Again, bomb on red sky markers. Failing this, bomb on greens.

Details of bomb loads were already known to each crew's bomb aimers. I was staggered to learn of the extent of our own incendiary load: 1020 x 4 lb, 150 x 4 lb 'X' (explosive), 108 x 30 lb, in addition to carrying a 4000-lb high-capacity bomb known to crews as a cookie and to the British public as a 'blockbuster'!

We received information from the Squadron Met Officer, followed by the Signals Leader, who gave details of 'spoof' and countermeasures being deployed by 100 Group Bomber Command and from 101 Squadron carrying ABC ('Airborne Cigar') from our own group based at nearby Ludford Magna. (101 Squadron Lancasters carried eight crewmen each, one of which was a German-speaking WOP who would transmit false instructions to German fighter crews.)

The Gunnery Leader then gave details of the possible enemy day fighter opposition in the form of Messerschmitt Bf 109s, Fw 190s and the odd jet fighter, the Me 262. The latter brought forth umpteen wry comments. Finally, the Station Commander gave an appraisal of the whole operation, wished us luck and dismissed the briefing. On the way out we collected our escape/evasion aid boxes and Stan collected the flasks of coffee, sweets, chocolate and chewing gum.

It was just beginning to get light outside the Briefing Room. The lorries had gone so we walked to the 'flights' (i.e., crew rooms and offices of the individual aircrew sections). We collected our gear from the parachute storage section. The two 'erks' on duty were both very pleasant, having something cheery to say to each aircrew bod on drawing his emergency equipment.

I took this all for granted at the time, being like most on the op, full of my own thoughts and thinking that the two ground staff airmen were on a cushy number. They were not like the aircrew wallahs who would be 'sticking their necks out' from the moment they taxied out of dispersal. Since then, I have thought of the boredom they experienced so cheerfully and the job they completed so carefully and efficiently, for it was occasionally necessary to change a 'chute or life jacket if a fault were suspected. They, too, would have been awake much earlier than the rest of the station and they weren't entitled to a bacon and egg special flying meal!

As we dressed for the op, Peter and I looked at each other. Nothing much was said. Someone in the same gangway was whistling the popular hit 'Would you like to swing on a star'. I thought Christ, that's about all that's left for us now, maybe we might just need to swing on a star.

I clipped the US Navy wings inside my battledress pocket flap. They remained invisible to the onlooker. They were never to be taken off during our stay at Wickenby.

Our flying gear normally consisted of a thick, white, roll-neck sweater, although I always wore an air force blue one, done in cable stitch. This item, along with the thick socks and balaclava complete with earholes, had been knitted by a dear mum and sent to me while I was still at No. 6 ITW Aberystwyth.

On top of this went the electrically heated suit with heated slippers and connections for heated gloves. We would be flying at about 17,000 feet and in October that would mean the temperature could be quite low. Finally, I topped it all off with a green/grey waterproof outer suit. I preferred this to the yellow buoyancy suit, now standard issue for rear gunners. I had borrowed the outer suit from Bert, our WOP, who said he had never used it since his position in the Lanc was adequately heated. Even so, he would have the choice of wearing his kapok inner suit, which could provide all the warmth he might need.

'Are we ready then?' asked Peter. I nodded, tying up the Mae West straps. We edged past the other dressing aircrew in the direction of the main exit, which led to a path adjoining the perimeter (taxi) track. Here we found several trucks waiting for us. They were being speedily loaded with bods dressed in all sorts of gear, depending on their aircrew position. The luckier ones, like the navigators, air bombers, engineers, WOP and pilot, wore only their issue polo sweater over their battledress uniform, fisherman's socks, flying boots and carried helmet, goggles and gloves, Mae West and parachute.

The waiting transport was soon loaded and went away to various dispersals. We were looking for the gun transport.

One gunner, on hearing this, said 'Good Lord, haven't you got your guns out there yet?'

'They're new blokes, Charlie,' said another.

'Christ, lad, best of luck.'

'What's the flak like?' joked one Canadian.

'Shall we tell them?' someone replied.

'Jesus,' someone else said.

'They'll find out soon enough.' Peter and I felt great!

'Gun transport, anybody want gun transport?' called a WAAF corporal.

'We do, Corp. Thought you weren't coming.'

'Oh, take no notice of those jerks,' said the bright-eyed WAAF.

'Don't worry, Sergeant, you'll be OK. They've only got two to do before they finish. They think they know it all.'

I bet they do, with twenty-eight ops in, I thought. Lucky beggars!

Peter and I climbed aboard; the WAAF corporal sped away in the direction of the Gun Room.

'Set twenty-two, Chiefy,' beamed the LAC armourer in charge of the gun room. The armourer was a bespectacled man of about forty years. A day or two before he had allocated to our crew a set of eight .303-inch Browning machine-guns. They were to be ours for the duration of our stay at Wickenby – at least that is what we thought!

The guns were speedily loaded onto the waiting truck. It was only possible for a gunner to carry two Brownings at a time. They were not very heavy but four guns were almost an impossible load for two hands. The truck tore away on to the peri-track and straight to the dispersal for 'Charlie Two', which was our aircraft for our first op.

Assisted by Peter, the guns were soon off-loaded and went into the Lanc. Fred's two guns had to be installed in the nose turret. They were left to Fred to mount and load. Peter took his pair for the mid-upper turret, while I slid two down the ramp to the rear turret and went back for the other two. Once seated in the turret, it was simple to mount and load the four Brownings.

Only a couple of days earlier we had to install those very guns in a Lancaster for the first time. We had been shown enough times in semi-practical demos but had not done it ourselves. One very soon got the impression that as this was 'the squadron' and everyone had been trained, we should know what we were doing. Well, new boys didn't and very often, as we found out, other newcomers after us didn't either.

The inboard guns, on 'safe', were loaded first because the belts from the servo feed passed over the inboard guns to the outer guns. Once loaded, all four guns were cocked, fired on 'safe' and re-cocked. The guns were now ready to be put on 'fire'; each Browning now had a live round on each breechblock.

'Hello, rear gunner,' called Bert.

'Ready to test your intercom?'

'OK Bert,' I replied, simultaneously turning the turret through 90° to the beam and then through 180° to the opposite beam, elevating and depressing the guns at the same time while looking through the reflector sight during the whole test.

'Testing, one, two, three' I called until all the positions were reached, while the intercom and gunsight remained switched on throughout the test. The intercom switch in the rear turret was on the central control column, between the dual triggers.

Bert repeated the test with Peter in the mid-upper turret. Again, all was OK. Bert then checked, in turn, all other crew positions for intercom serviceability.

The 'clear vision' panel in the tail turret (so-called because *all* the Perspex had been removed from the most rearward-facing panel) gave a wide-open window effect, i.e., there was absolutely *nothing* between you and the enemy.

'Charlie Two' had been further improved by a local modification that removed some of the light alloy sheeting adjacent to the gun ports. This gave a very wide view from the tail. The view downwards was still only approximately 60° degrees!

The local modification had also included a fairing arrangement covering the servo feed panel, sprockets and pawls. Someone had painted, rather expertly, a white skull and cross bones on this enclosure. From outside the Lanc this insignia stood out quite well and gave a very impressive picture. One never knew quite what to make of the painting. Was it intended to indicate that the rear turret was a deadly place to occupy or was it a death-dealing place to tangle with? I assumed the picture was intended to boost morale rather than destroy it.

The sun was just rising in the eastern sky. There didn't appear to be any cloud. In those days we didn't consider hiding in cloud. Why should we? We had the 'corkscrew' manoeuvre and never doubted its capability.

Skipper called up each crewmember, asking if we were OK.

Finally he said 'OK, Stan, brakes off. We'll join the rest. What time is take-off Mac?'

'06.45, Skipper.'

'We are in good time then. What's the deadline?'

'07.15, Skipper,' came the calm reply.

'Lots of time. OK, taxiing out, chaps. Keep a good lookout astern, Frank, don't let anyone get too close before letting me know.'

'OK, Skipper. Thanks.'

We taxied, following one or two Lancs that were heading for the main runway, which was 2000 yards long, running WSW/ENE approximately. Meanwhile, in the rear turret my thoughts strayed to Mum. She would be on her way to work at 06.15 hours and due to arrive about 06.45!

When our turn came, Skipper turned onto the runway, lined up the aircraft and called for Stan to open the throttles. The Lanc increased speed, the tail came up and then 'Full power' from Skipper.

We lifted off at 06.52 hours and at about 110 mph. Stan operated the undercarriage and flap selection, in turn, as required by Skipper.

We climbed steadily to gain the necessary altitude and to be ready to set course at the appropriate briefed time.

'Give me the course to steer Mac, so that I can be ready to turn right on time.'

'OK, Skipper,' replied Mac.

'241, Skipper.'

'OK, Mac. Let me know when to turn.'

'OK, Skipper.'

CHAPTER 14

The Lancaster – a Four-engined Flying Bomb

Looking from the tail, the sky behind seemed to be crammed with Lancs. They were busy climbing like us, out to sea on an easterly course and then back over land again, flying westerly. To see so many heavy bombers in the sky at once was a magnificent sight, never to be forgotten. We were very lucky in getting a daylight op to start our tour. We would never have seen such a spectacle at night.

I was too busy at this time looking for bombers on collision courses to worry about the operational sortie. Looking below, I could see Lincoln one minute, the North Sea the next and then Mablethorpe and so on.

'Reached 10,000 feet, Mac.'

'OK, Skipper, just under two minutes before setting course.'

'OK Mac. Don't forget to fuse the bombs, Fred.'

Christ, I thought, I forgot we were carrying bombs! Doesn't feel any different. Silly ass, you're sitting on them.

'OK, Skipper, I will fuse the bombs over the sea when we are on course.'

'OK, Fred.'

'Turn on to 201 degrees, Skipper,' called Mac.

'OK, Mac, turning now. On course 201.'

'OK, Skipper."

Behind us, as if guided by a magic force, all the Lancs in sight swiftly set course as one. Very soon we had converged into a fairly compact stream, stacked in layers of 1000 feet intervals, covering about four or five layers. Something like 4000 feet. As yet, which wave or height band we were in had not meant much to me. Later on in our tour I became more interested in these two points during the briefing.

We altered course at Reading before heading for the English coast.

'Crossing the coast, Mac. Three miles east of Brighton,' Fred called out, a short time later.

'Thanks, Fred,' came the reply.

Shortly afterwards came the similar remark 'Crossing the French coast, Mac.'

The navigator acknowledged as before. These comments were to become commonplace as our tour progressed. All conversation on the intercom was brief, to the point and always courteous. We never listened to the AFN, nor babbled to each other unless it was to do with the aircraft or the trip.

'Bombs fused, Skipper.'

'OK, Fred.'

'Log it, Mac.'

'OK, Skipper.'

I looked back through the clear vision panel and saw the English coast receding, clearly bathed in sunlight. It looked rather marvellous, serene and unspoilt.

'Lanc pretty close to port, Skipper, less than 200 yards crossing our stern from port to starboard.' (This was close for a fully bombed up, fully fuelled Lanc, weighing approximately 62,000 lb (28,000 kg).)

'OK Frank. I've got him.'

The heavies, Lancs and Halibags, were now in a tighter stream stretching behind for as far as the eye could see. We were now at 17,000 feet. There were some higher and some lower than us. They looked really magnificent, the early morning sun glinting on the Perspex cockpits and turrets.

The nearer the aircraft, the more one observed the detail. Individual crewmembers could be seen, their yellow Mae Wests standing out so clearly, the flight engineer standing alongside his captain. They always appeared to be surveying us as much as we were them. Everyone was wide awake, keeping their position in the stream, most maintaining the briefed height. Occasionally one would see the odd Lanc climbing well above the others. At this stage of our limited experience we did not know why. There was also the odd

Lanc well away on the beams, that is, well out of the cover of the bomber stream. This would be hazardous over enemy territory, as there was no window cover from other bombers still in the stream!

'Hello Fred. Nav here. Start windowing as soon as you like.'

'OK, Mac. Windowing. One to five bundles a minute.' (The 'window rate' increased to correspond with penetration into enemy territory.) I could just see the silver streaked puffs of window as they passed under the tail, streaming out behind like chaff caught in the wind.

Mac gave a final alteration of course to the Skipper.

'ETA Duisburg 08.45, Skipper,' he added.

'OK Mac. Can you give me a course out of the target and height to fly?'

'010 Skipper. Diving turn to 14,000 feet.'

'Fred, check that all the bombs have gone, especially the incendiaries, as soon as you can.'

'OK, Skipper.'

'Gunners, keep a damned good lookout for fighters.'

'OK, Skipper.'

Then, quite suddenly without warning, there were numerous awesome black puffs to port, perhaps 1000 yards away. None of your 'bok-bok' stuff, just 'whoomph' and some 100–150 shells burst almost simultaneously in a rectangular box-shaped area, all just within the outskirts of the stream.

I was quite surprised at the tactical awareness of the German flak! Also that it was coming up in salvo, not singly as I had foolishly expected. (Shades of Coventry flak?) I had not expected to see battery upon battery fire in salvo. This was certainly radar-predicted flak, fired by gunners who knew exactly our height band. Soon, we were enveloped in flak smoke. From these and earlier barrages we could smell the cordite as we flew through them.

'Jesus, just look at that.' A Lanc to starboard, way off track and trying to rejoin the stream, was ablaze from wing tip to wing tip. He had left it far too late and was some 1500 yards to starboard by the time I saw him and about the same distance astern. He was making every effort to stay straight and level, probably to enable the crew to bale out. The flames were about three times the length of the aircraft, say 300 feet; the plume of smoke following stretched for miles. This aircraft was one of our wave and height band. (I wondered later if this was our Flight Commander.) I was unable to read the Squadron identification letter codes on the fuselage due to flames and smoke. He wasn't that far away and in daylight at that range I should have been able to read the codes easily. Peter and I continued our search. We could see the odd pair of vapour trails high above us, most likely our escort of Spitfires or Mustangs at 36,000 to 40,000 feet. There was no evidence of enemy fighter activity, as expected.

I looked starboard again. There was no sign of the blazing Lancaster, just a trail of smoke ending in a downward spiral.

'What was that, Stan?' asked Skipper.

'A Lanc I think,' came the answer. 'Just blew up, dead ahead. They hit the bomb load, the cookie, I suppose.'

'Whoomph!'

A kite, almost dead astern, disappeared in a gigantic mushroom cloud of smoke. Another cookie hit?

God I thought. We are not there yet!

'How long for ETA, Mac?'

'Three minutes, Skipper.'

'OK, Mac. Switching over to VHF. I am steering into the centre of the bomber stream. OK? Are you ready, Fred?'

'Yes Skipper.'

'Can you see anything yet?'

'TIs dead ahead. Lots of smoke. Some obscuring the markers.'

'Smokescreens?'

'Don't think so, Skipper. Looks like incendiary fires.'

'OK.'

'Bomb doors open.'

'Bomb doors open, Fred.'

About ruddy time, I thought, looking at the flak and occasionally at the gigantic mushrooms in the sky. It seemed as if everyone was being shot down.

We could hear the Master Bomber on the VHF quite clearly.

'Calling Main Force – Bomb the centre of the red TIs.' The instruction was repeated throughout the attack. The Master Bomber's voice seemed very calm and unruffled. You would have thought he was sitting in a deck chair at the seaside, perhaps calling out to the newspaper boy or ice-cream salesman. Instead, he was flying a Lancaster round and round a heavily defended Ruhr target at 8000 feet or less, in broad daylight. (No scooting in and out of clouds like some people seemed to think.)

'Come on, Main Force. Bomb the red TIs, bomb the red TIs, bomb on reds. Bomb the centres and for Christ's sake ignore those bloody poor imitations to the west [German decoy markers].'

'Left, left, steady,' called Fred from the air bomber's position in the nose cone below the front turret.

'Left a bit, Skipper.'

'Right, right, right.'

'That's it, hold it. Bombs gone.' Away went our 4000-lb cookie, preceded by over 1200 incendiaries.

I didn't see the cookie but I saw the incendiaries, blowing away behind and beneath us. They looked just like the contents of a gigantic box of matches being opened upside down in a gale.

The flak was still taking its toll astern; the sky seemed full of black puffs. Sometimes we could hear the simultaneous 'crump' of nearby salvoes. I never dared to stop searching for those fighters.

I felt Skipper swing the Lanc over in a diving turn and rapidly lose height as he brought us on to the first leg of the homeward route.

'Bomb doors closed,' came the command. We were always to delay closing the bomb doors after an incendiary attack. Quite often odd incendiaries got blown into the back of the bomb bay and took their time to fall clear. This drill was supposed to prevent accidental ignition of these strays after the doors were closed.

'Everyone OK?' called Skipper. 'You OK, Frank?'

'OK Skipper, thanks.' And so on throughout the crew. Once we were clear of the immediate target area the flak ceased to be evident. Travelling at some 200 mph we were soon out of range.

The trip back was relatively uneventful, with brilliant sunshine all the way. Just before we left the European coast we had company. A Lancaster with 'PH' squadron codes (12 Squadron, Wickenby) formated on our starboard wing and flew most of the way back to Wickenby with us. We never found out who it was.

We came in to land after being stacked up in the aerodrome circuit for a few minutes. During this time, damaged aircraft were given priority, including those on three or fewer engines. (Any damaged or engineless aircraft would normally be given priority, whatever time they arrived over the drome.)

It was during the last leg of the trip, when the 12 Squadron kite had kept us company, that I realised we had completed our first op. In those days the grapevine or 'bush telegraph' had it that completing one op paid for the crew's training! After this, all should be profit! I then remembered the *G8* magazines read by Father between the wars, which suggested that World War I aircrew soon grasped that if they shot down *one* enemy aircraft then it covered their own loss. If they destroyed any more afterwards they were winning the war. We very soon took to the idea that our ops helped to win the war and the more ops one did the more it helped the all-out war effort.

After landing, the transport soon arrived to take us to interrogation. The WAAF driver asked what the target had been. There were always smiles of approval from all the ground crew at the aircraft dispersal. Everyone seemed pleased that Duisburg had been well and truly plastered by over 1000 Lancasters and Halifaxes in broad daylight. (It was the RAF's largest daylight op on 'Hitler's 1000 year Reich' to date.) All our crew felt very pleased about it too.

We climbed aboard the truck and were driven back to the main Briefing Room. As we left the dispersal I glanced at the Lancaster that had taken us to the Ruhr, the Happy Valley, for our very first op. She looked quiet and sombre standing alone at dispersal, with no engine noise and no intercom babble. She had 'done her bit' for the day. One night in the coming winter months she would be flown by her regular crew on a mining op. Next morning her dispersal would be empty. 'Charlie Two' and her favourite crew would never be seen again.

The interrogation was quite an experience. Almost every Wickenby celebrity was there. The padre, a wing commander, seemed to be everywhere, passing on to everyone the ever-present, ever-hot mug of cocoa.

'Cigarette Sergeant?'

'Help yourself, Sergeant.'

'How was the trip?'

'Was there lots of flak?"

'See any fighters, Sergeant?'

'How was it, chaps?' asked the Station Commander.

'Very good, Sir, all went well,' replied Skipper.

'Did you bomb the reds?'

'Yessir,' said Fred instantly.

A few minutes later we were called to our crew interrogation. The Intelligence Officer was brief and to the point. Most of the questions were directly for Skipper, our navigator and our air bomber to answer. The rest of the crew confirmed when and where necessary any particular point. I was asked about the blazing Lanc.

'Any parachutes?'

'No Sir,' I regretfully replied. 'I didn't see any.'

Someone suggested that some crewmembers may have made a delayed drop for various reasons, e.g., height, cold and lack of oxygen or to clear the blazing aircraft safely. Someone mentioned two parachutes. It appeared that there were losses from both 626 and 12 Squadrons. Four Lancs failed to return to Wickenby.

Later on, I discovered that Flight Lieutenant Aldus, our Flight Commander, the bright, cheerful officer wearing the 'Spam' medal who gave us the early call that very morning, was overdue. He and his crew had been reported missing. Was the blazing Lanc their aircraft? If it was, I had seen no one bale out; they couldn't *all* be dead? Surely someone was bound to escape? It would be many years before I discovered, to my dismay, that very few Lanc crewmen escaped. Flight Lieutenant Aldus and crew would never return.

We went off to the Mess for our meal of bacon and egg at about 13.00 hours and then back to the billets to sleep. We slept until about 5 pm, when we were woken by Skipper.

'Come on, chaps. We are on again tonight. Meal 18.30, briefing 19.30, take-off 22.00.'

Christ, I thought, are we going out there again, so soon too? I was completely taken by surprise, as was everyone else.

We speedily dressed and tore off to the Mess from our site on the hill. Being mostly youngsters, we soon became engrossed in our meal – more eggs, bacon, sausage etc. Three lots in one day. Cor, what luck, we thought!

How Fred coped with it I will never know. He was thirty-three years old and simply years ahead of the rest of us. Being a family man, he must have had much more to think about than the rest of us, although both Stan (twenty-nine) and Skipper (twenty-seven) were married. Being young, foolish and hopelessly naive, the remainder of the crew didn't give much thought to matters outside our own hide.

Vehicle engines could be heard outside the Mess.

'Transport,' shouted an enterprising sergeant. We hurriedly cleared our plates, disappeared outside and climbed aboard.

'Good God, not again!' was the almost unanimous statement as we entered the Briefing Room once more.

'So much fer yer bomb aimin' cobber,' growled one Aussie.

'Goddamn pommy bomb aimers!'

'Aw hell, go back to the bleeding desert, you Aussie beggar,' came the reply from nearby.

We soon found our allocated row. This time we had Flight Lieutenant Hicks with us as captain; our Skipper would be 'second dickie'. It was normal procedure for first op pilots to go as 'second dickie' on the first night op. If there was a procedure for daytime it had not happened that morning. Also, as we were doing our Skipper's 'second dickie' with him, it now seems rather peculiar for after all we were a new crew too. More often, the crew captain flew for the first time with another crew entirely who were experienced, the idea being to give the new aircraft captain a chance to see what it was like before he was chucked in 'ass over head'.

We accepted all this without complaint and often without question. Generally speaking, we discovered that any anomaly to the expected duty was often to our liking. In our case, it would mean that the Skipper would do the same number of ops as we would and not leave him one ahead, as with most crews. We hardly considered this point any more than the one of Skipper's twenty ops to our thirty. Reflecting on this situation now, I am mildly surprised that it didn't appear to worry us. Or had the RAF taken care of it already? We would see in due course.

The briefing commenced:

'Bomber Command are furious! You made a poor show this morning, so you are to go back tonight and do it again. Otherwise you will go back again and again until you do the job properly. Crews were not aiming at the markers; some bombed dummy TIs; some didn't carry out the Master Bomber's instructions.'

The officer who gave us the rollicking from Bomber Command was the same Flight Lieutenant Intelligence Officer that had given us all the gen in the morning. He then proceeded to give the briefing details for the night attack. His introduction was followed by the briefing for all the other trades. A 626 or 12 Squadron Section Leader was appointed for the operation, i.e., Navigation, Signals, Engineer etc. This officer was usually of flight lieutenant minimum rank. Next came the Met Officer; the weather prospects looked good and again it should be clear in the target area.

Evasion tactics were discussed in the event of a bale-out. We were to head into France or Belgium and try to contact the underground. The briefing came to an end. There followed a summary by the Wing Commander, after which we were wished 'Good luck and thank you, gentlemen.'

We handed over our personal items as before and collected our escape aids. We walked back to the crew rooms of 626 Squadron, the general topic of conversation concerned flying 'two raids in a day'.

Peter and I drew our 'chutes and Mae Wests and dressed in the locker room as usual. I noticed that Peter never flew with his collar and tie on, always preferring to remove them. This was a survival tactic that was recommended because most cloth material tends to tighten when immersed in water. I preferred to leave both on, as did the rest of the crew. Only Peter was wise enough to do as recommended. The rest of us were not altogether stupid for we all at some time practised certain survival techniques, i.e., checking the Mae West inflation capsule, the battery of the Mae West signalling lamp and, very importantly, the rip-cord retaining pins on the parachute pack itself. (These pins needed to be absolutely straight, not bent. They were retained by a fine red-coloured, breakable thread.)

Our guns were already out at the aircraft. Sometimes off-duty gunners would deliver sets of guns to each aircraft, especially if the gunners on ops had no time beforehand to do so.

At the dispersal of 'King Two' we were greeted by Flight Lieutenant Hicks and Skipper. Hicks was in a jovial mood. He spoke with an air of confidence, born of experience. It boosted our morale. He gazed up into the loaded bomb bay where there were 11 x 1000 lbs and 4 x 500-lb bombs.

'I wouldn't care to be under that little lot tonight,' he said. The rest of the crew gazed up in awe at the sight of so many heavy bombs.

'Cripes,' I thought. 'What happens if flak gets one of those blighters?'

'Not to worry,' said Hicks, tapping my shoulder, for I had been thinking aloud. 'My rear gunner used to take a few bundles of window into the turret so that he could sling the stuff out if the flak got too nasty.'

'How about that, Frank? Why not take a few bundles?' queried Skipper.

'Good idea, Skipper,' I said. Fred then grabbed six bundles from one of the parcels that were stowed temporarily near the rear access door. Later, the six were carefully placed inside the rear turret.

We stood around waiting for take-off, mostly gazing at the dark but starry sky. Unfortunately, take-off was delayed about an hour. We lit our last-minute cigarette, had our last pee and climbed aboard when Flight Lieutenant Hicks was ready.

The engines were started and tested. Individual crewmen checked their equipment and we taxied out towards the runway. When our turn came we turned on, throttles wide.

'Full power, Flight Engineer please.'

'Throttles through the gate.' We unstuck at 110 mph. Our take-off time was 22.42 hours. We climbed to our briefed height for that part of the trip. The night was fairly dark; there wasn't any moon at that hour.

From the tail turret I hardly saw a soul. The intercom was my lifeline, as I listened to the conversations of the crew going about their various jobs in the aircraft.

We crossed the English coast, Fred reporting the pinpoint(s) to Mac again when we crossed the French coast.

'Bombs fused, Skipper,' called the air bomber.

Once more the Lanc headed towards the Ruhr Valley. There was some searchlight and flak activity to port along the Belgian coast. It seemed too far away for any of our wave to be involved, although, with Gee or H2S failure, anything could happen!

I had cocked all four guns before take-off, switching all four onto 'fire' as we were airborne. I checked all four guns, singly, manually, by firing each gun separately on 'safe', using the manual release on each gun in turn.

Then I checked the electric gun heaters and their connections. These were rectangular 'warm wire' heaters, which were clamped to each side of each gun in the proximity of the breechblock when cocked. This heating was to prevent the adjoining metal moveable surfaces from icing up due to condensation forming on the various gun components during the climb to our operational height of 19,000 feet.

I had tested the guns hydraulically on the ground, both for manoeuvrability and the firing system. I rechecked the firing system when airborne. All four guns were put on 'safe' and then fired by using the triggers (not manually but hydraulically), re-cocking all four and re-setting the 'fire and safe' mechanism to 'fire'.

I did this because the standard check of firing one gun at a time on 'safe' (manually) in no way tested the hydraulic firing systems. The only way to do that effectively was to actually fire the guns. This would have been a morale booster to the gunners and the rest of the crew. Otherwise, we never knew whether the system would actually 'fire'. Because of the density of the bomber stream there was a Bomber Command ruling that guns were not to be hydraulically tested on 'fire'. Therefore, I had to be content with testing them hydraulically on 'safe'.

The trouble with this method was the time it took. It could take a couple of minutes to re-cock all four guns and reset four safety mechanisms. (This was the danger!) I could see astern and below very well from the tail turret and therefore had a really good look around before commencing the check. I didn't know then what I know now, that a bomber could be attacked from immediately below by a radar-guided night fighter carrying fixed upward-firing cannon. We now know that the night fighter could get as close as 100 feet and be directly underneath the bomber and invisible to the crew.

Fortunately, I was keen on carrying out my own personal check of the four tail guns and ensuring that all would work when the time came. As far as I was concerned, the standard recommended Bomber Command manual check of guns was useless!

On most Lancs the FN120 tail turret had sliding Perspex side hatches. These were windows that were approximately 12 inches x 6 inches (300 mm x 150 mm), which slid fully back to give an absolutely clear view of the beams. I always flew with these windows *wide* open. In addition, when the turret was turned on full beam the gunner got a good view astern through these side windows, plus an unrestricted view downwards of about 85° from horizontal. The latter was perhaps the best view downwards one could get from the rear end of a Lanc with eyes pressed to the open hatch.

We arrived at the target bang on ETA, both Skipper and Flight Lieutenant Hicks were pleased with the timing. Fred was able to bomb a concentration of red and green TIs without much trouble. There were fairly clear conditions below and from 19,000 feet Duisburg appeared to be well ablaze. One could see the cookies exploding with a gigantic white flash, one after the other! The bombing appeared concentrated. PFF seemed to have done a good job. Flight Lieutenant Hicks put the Lancaster into a series of very steep turns to enable all crewmembers to have a good view of the shattered city. There was still a steady amount of accurate and concentrated opposition from flak and searchlight crews. It was our first view of a city under night attack. We were all most impressed. How could anyone possibly live down there?

On the homeward trip Peter and I kept the steady search for the unseen foe. Presumably, we were ably backed up by other crewmembers, although no comment was ever made. I sincerely hoped they were carrying out Skipper's request.

The operation was relatively uneventful compared with the earlier daylight incursion. The target had been well and truly pranged in true RAF style. I reported to the Captain that I could still see the fires when we were some 80-odd miles away.

Fighter activity in our wave was non-existent. However, being quiet didn't mean it was going to stay quiet. All hell could be let loose on us at any second over enemy territory. The unseen night fighter, flak or searchlight could surprise us at any moment. All the gunners could do was to continue their constant searching. To rest on the homeward trip would fatal; even over England a German night fighter/intruder could be waiting for us. A Ju 88 at this very moment could be circling over Wickenby hoping to avenge the night's destruction of the Fatherland. Bert might, if we were lucky, pick up an 'intruder warning' on his TR 1196 from base before the fighter made us its first 'kill'.

Soon, we were leaving the Belgian coast behind; we could see clearly the reflection from the sea several thousand feet below. As I looked down, I wondered how cold the seas would be. We had been cautioned not to expect to live more than thirty minutes if we were immersed in the North Sea at this time of the year. In the tail turret of the Lanc I felt quite safe and nicely warm, some 16,000 feet up over this unimaginably horrible fate. So much so that at times it gave a very false sense of security.

The *Luftwaffe* intruder pilot would not think twice about bringing down the *Englische Terror-flieger* whether over land or water, should the opportunity arise. A bale-out in winter over water would almost certainly have only one result, assuming that we had lived long enough to abandon a blazing aircraft, possibly out of control and before it hit the sea!

The East Anglian coast appeared below, accompanied by Fred's comment to Mac in order to fix our position as accurately as possible. There had been no intruder warning so far and many bombers were switching on their navigation lights. This was mainly to avoid the risk of collision due to the concentration of aircraft when nearing the Lincolnshire and Yorkshire airfields.

Again, we found that we mixed safety with hazard. Once the navigation lights were on, the rear gunner's view astern was hopeless due to a double white tail lamp sited immediately below the clear vision panel at the dead astern position. With night vision now ruined, the gunner would be unlikely to see the twin-engined night fighter until it was at about 50 yards' range, if at all!

Looking to port, I could see the emergency landing runway of Woodbridge. A triple lane runway, each lane having its own coloured lights, it appeared to be floodlit and the whole airfield layout clearly marked by intersecting searchlights at each end of the runway. Not far away, somewhere near the airfield centre, was a sweeping searchlight that could often be seen for many miles, well out to sea.

Occasionally Mac's voice would come through on the intercom. He always sounded quite confident with his instructions to Skipper.

'Alter course two degrees port, Skipper. Base should then be dead ahead. ETA in about thirty minutes.'

'OK Navigator, thank you,' replied Flight Lieutenant Hicks.

It wasn't long before the Captain called up Base.

'Athurst King Two 4000 over.'

'King Two 2000 over,' called the WAAF controller on R/T.

'Roger King Two 2000 out,' replied Flight Lieutenant Hicks.

'King Two 1000, over,' a little later from Control.

'Athurst King Two wilco out,' answered Hicks.

'Athurst King Two downwind out.'

'Roger King Two,' came the acknowledgement from Control.

The undercarriage was lowered and later 'Half flap, Flight Engineer.'

'Athurst King Two funnels over.'

'Pancake Athurst King Two.'

'Roger King Two.'

'Full flap, Flight Engineer.'

A few seconds later, there was a bump, a jolt and scream of the tyres, then another bump and jolt in the turret as the tail came down. The speed slackened off and we turned off the runway in use.

'Athurst King Two clear, out,' said Flight Lieutenant Hicks.

We taxied to our dispersal, unbolted the guns and removed them to the protection of the fuselage. The transport soon appeared and was ready to take us back to the crew rooms. Invariably, Mac was the first to board the truck, swinging his ever-loaded, bulging navigation bag and parachute aboard. Stan was sometimes next with his engine log and Thermos flasks. Fred was probably next, along with Bert. Fred would have removed the front guns shortly after touchdown, probably while we were taxiing around the perimeter. Peter and I were generally last. I rarely began to unload until we had reached dispersal. It was all so easy in the rush to leave the aircraft with the haste of the young. It would be just too bad if an intruder followed us in! Who would listen to the explanation of the rear gunner who had unloaded, like many did, when still on the flying circuit, just to make a quick getaway in the transport? The worst thing one could do, it appeared instead, was to keep the transport waiting!

'For Christ's sake, hurry up Broome, what are we waiting for?' snapped a crewmember.

'Come on, get those sodding guns out of the turret.'

'Bloody dim air gunners, they've had nothing to do all trip and now they're keeping us waiting.'

'Why can't they get their guns out earlier?'

'Reckon they've been fast asleep, the pair of 'em.' Flaming office-wallahs, I thought!

'About time too.' They all shut up when Skipper arrived. Someone banged on the driver's cab.

'OK Chiefy, all aboard.'

The transport rumbled off in the direction of the flights, pausing to collect the odd crew, sometimes the odd bod from other dispersals.

At the Briefing Room the procedure was the same as for the daylight operation.

'Good trip, Sergeant?' asked the Padre.

'Everything all right, Lane?' asked the Groupie.

'Fine Sir,' was the immediate answer.

'Good show, chaps.'

The interrogation went much as before.

'Bombing? TIs? Colour? Master Bomber?'

'Flak, searchlights, fighters, collisions.'

'Any hang-ups?' (i.e., bombs failing to release, possibly jettisoned 'safe' over the sea or still in the bomb bay.)

'Aircraft serviceability.'

'Engines, hydraulics, H2S, Fishpond, Gee, radio, turrets, guns.'

'All OK?'

We made our own way back to the Mess for our post-op meal. This was always the eagerly awaited bacon, egg, chips and beans that was so popular with young and older aircrew alike. One often got the impression that it seemed all worth it just for the extra bacon and egg! It always worked wonders for tired, tense minds and bodies. Some of us would have flown for nothing, we were that keen. Some parts of aircrew life seemed to be a picnic. True, there was always quite a bit of tension prior to an op. Usually, this disappeared once airborne. There were the odd incidents that frightened the wits out of us. We were all like that to some greater or lesser extent.

Our second op behind us, we felt great. Having done one over the equaliser, we were happy to have one to our credit and towards winning the war. It was a magnificent feeling to be doing your bit, to really be helping win the war. As young airmen we felt quite chuffed at our achievement to date: a Nickel, a Diversion and two bomber ops, especially the last two to the Ruhr Valley! We had good reason to believe in what we were doing.

Before the next op Peter and I were able to put in some time doing the odd gunnery job, harmonising, gun cleaning (eight guns) and checking the ammo, the servo feed, the turret mechanical, hydraulic and electrical systems. We became accustomed to the layout of the drome and the new discipline, i.e., the expected duties like reporting to the 'flights' for daily roll call and to the Gunnery Section for duties of various kinds.

If there was nothing further to do, Peter's favourite 'skive' was to vanish into the Intelligence Office where I joined him for the latest gen on tactics, reports of combats, raid reports and bombing photos etc.

Peter's favourite 'job' next to gun cleaning was harmonisation. Quite frequently, he would doggedly persuade me to join him on a jaunt across the airfield to some distant dispersal, often accompanied by the usual English drizzle, in order to harmonise the guns of our particular aircraft.

This wasn't as easy as it might seem. Firstly, it was quite a walk around the perimeter to the No. 626 Squadron dispersals, particularly if your aircraft happened to be parked on the Snelland side of the drome (12 Squadron, based at Wickenby earlier than No. 626 Squadron, had pinched all the nearest dispersals). Then you needed guns as you couldn't harmonise without guns! So you chose a day when the guns would be out there, like the day after an op.

Sometimes, the guns you had left in the aircraft had been removed by someone else! No one ever told you. It was common enough to ask gunners who had flown in the Lanc the day before where the guns were. Sometimes no one seemed to know or care. This meant a walk to the Gun Room and then across the airfield to the dispersal. Occasionally, it was easy to get gun transport; it largely depended whether there was ops or training on that day. Generally, one lorry ran around all the dispersals for the purpose of delivering or collecting in the mornings. If you had missed it, it was no good trying to get a truck unless you were flying. This meant carrying the guns and the harmonisation boards yourself and that was real fun. Sometimes people have asked why my forearms are like Popeye's. Well, it is because I was the smallest bloke in the crew and sometimes carried four Brownings out to our kite, which was often parked near Snelland Junction, about 1.5 miles from 626 'flights', or so it seemed.

Although harmonisation was Peter's favourite, perhaps he wondered why it wasn't mine. Well, he was a much bigger bloke than I, and the mid-upper gunner on a Lanc had only two guns. Occasionally Fred came along to harmonise his front turret. He didn't carry this out as often as we did but at least he did it sometimes, which is more than you could say for a good many bomb aimers. Besides, who would be able to hit anything from the front turret with two .303-inch Brownings that were probably iced up anyway? What we really needed 'up front' was a 20-mm cannon. Fred would have been a damn good shot with that, day or night. (NB The nose structure and gun mounting would have needed a complete redesign.)

Returning to harmonisation, we needed to set up the harmonisation board for the rear guns some 25 yards from the tail. We then had to manipulate the four guns that we had already carried out and mounted in the turret, to line up approximately on the board with the aid of the reflector sight.

The harmonisation board comprised a diagram in colour, showing the theoretical position of all four gun barrels (coloured circle symbol) with the sight (cross symbol) set in the theoretical centre of the intended bullet pattern.

We then removed the back plate, main spring and breechblock from each gun. This enabled the gunner to look through each barrel and, by adjustment of the mountings and sight via various knobs, we were able to line up all four gun barrels and sight onto each of the applicable coloured spots and crosses respectively on the harmonisation board.

Generally, I thought the job was a bind but I also felt very pleased when we had done it. This job needed doing about every three weeks and on No. 626 Squadron we harmonised for 600 yards' maximum effective range.

Set 22 Brownings was a good set of guns. We never had any problems or stoppages due to faulty mechanisms. However, the hydraulic gun-firing system on the FN turrets was a menace and could never be trusted. Otherwise, most things from the armament position were very good.

I was quite happy cleaning guns and regularly cleaned four while Peter cleaned his two and often Fred's as well. Sometimes Fred came along when he could. There were too few air bombers who cleaned their guns.

The LAC armourer in charge of the Gun Room was an absolute wizard with Brownings. There was nothing too difficult or too much trouble. If we had any problem he had an answer for it. No matter what it was, nothing ever bothered him. He was a great help to all the air gunners. Sometimes we had difficulty completing the cleaning of a gun barrel. Our friend had the ability and the know-how to get the job right in seconds. There was no one quite like our bespectacled LAC armourer. He was a great favourite with all the gunners. He often expressed great sadness when any two gunners went 'missing'.

Peter Bone's zest for harmonisation was to his credit. We wouldn't have harmonised so often if it hadn't been for him. We both had a liking for the Gun Room and the Intelligence Library, although the latter required little effort except the all-important one of being wide awake to new tactics in the ever-changing night bomber war. True, we were doing a number of daylight sorties just then but these were reasonably well escorted. After all, Spitfires and Mustangs could make up a lot for the shortcomings of being a bomber air gunner.

A few days later on 19 October, the Battle Order informed us we were to fly 'Able Two'. The various assembly times were soon chalked up on the Mess blackboard, i.e., flying meal, briefing and take-off times.

Very soon we found ourselves in the Briefing Room again. The target this time was much further south – Stuttgart. The name meant nothing; I was only concerned with the possible length of the trip. We were to fly out over Allied occupied territory, deep into recently liberated France, fairly low at about 3000 feet and, while still some miles away from the 'bomb line' (theoretical front line). Our lower altitude was to avoid enemy radar until the last turn to port, climbing up into Germany until we reached our bombing height of 15,000 feet.

As we had taken off in darkness we were soon out of touch with the other Lancs. The trip seemed long and drawn out and when we finally reached the target area the attack was almost finished. Fred had to be quick on the bomb run and bombed a Wanganui flare dying out. It looked as if everyone else had gone home, until I saw behind and below, an unfamiliar sight (so far) on our night ops.

It looked like a shot from a Very pistol – a brilliant yellow light with a halo around it. It looked most uncanny. It was at least 5000 feet below and some 5 miles to the rear of us. It continued across our track until it fell lower and lower, the cloud gradually obscuring the object, whatever it was.

I was most disturbed by the sight of something I could not understand. It bothered me for a while. The answer was simple really for I had seen my first aircraft shot down by a night fighter. I never found out what aircraft it was. There were British intruders active around Stuttgart that night. It could have been one of them claiming a Ju 88.

It was a long haul home, our airspeed was probably 180 mph and ground speed not much better. When we finally arrived over Wickenby the circuit was empty. Skipper called up Flying Control and, receiving no immediate reply, he repeated the call with the same result.

On the downwind leg Bert, in answer to the Skipper's query, informed him that the R/T was U/S. Skipper then requested Bert fire off a red Very light immediately (standard emergency procedure) to inform Flying Control that we had no R/T. Shortly after the Skipper's request Bert fired off another 'red' when we were in the 'funnels'.

Skipper lined up our Lanc heading for the main runway. I could hear the intercom patter with Stan as they prepared for touchdown. We landed normally and then there was a sudden lurch to port.

'Christ Stan,' shouted Skipper. 'I can hardly hold her.' The tyres screamed and we skidded off the runway in the direction of 'A' Flight. Skipper had quite a tough time holding the aircraft and with something that partly resembled a ground loop, we finally came to a stop.

'Fire off another "red", Bert, will you please.'

'OK Skipper.'

We could hear the 'phutt' of the roof-stowed Very pistol as it fired and a bright red glow gave our position to the crash tender and blood wagon as they raced over to us.

'Anybody hurt, Chiefy?' asked one of the crash crew personnel, sticking his head into the turret between the guns.

'No, all OK thanks,' I replied.

We soon struggled clear of the Lanc, which was now stuck firmly down, slightly to port. We had a burst tyre.

The crew bus joined the two tenders and we were away from the scene in the middle of the field almost before it had happened. As we climbed out a duty medic asked if there was anyone wounded. I guess they had seen our 'reds' and wondered what was up. Sometimes some bomber units used the 'red' to signify wounded on board. In our case, Skipper was following Bomber Command procedure and firing 'reds' to indicate no R/T and also to indicate our position at intervals on the circuit pattern and particularly on the landing approach.

When we arrived at the Briefing Room for interrogation we found the place deserted. A note chalked on the blackboard read 'Flight Lieutenant Lane and Crew – Missing'. Soon someone was rubbing it out. Apparently, everyone else had been home some time before. Our new Wingco came in.

'Jerry got your tyre with flak, they say!'

'Sorry about the aircraft, Sir,' replied Dickie 'I was a bit worried when we were careering towards "A" Flight aircraft dispersals!'

'Good show, Lane. Good show sergeants.'

The new Wingco was JHN Molesworth. We noticed his DFC and AFC ribbon, plus the NAAFI gong. Later, he was to add the Air Efficiency Award, which was a much-respected gong in wartime. Requiring six years' wartime service with the VR to qualify, there were not that many AE medals about.

We discovered that Wing Commander Molesworth had done a tour on Whitleys earlier in the war. Skipper later explained that we were to do some of our tour with him. We could hardly believe it!

The next thing we knew, on 20 October 1944 we were on the Battle Order with the Wingco, much to our pleasure and surprise.

At the Briefing Room we found we were in for a further daylight op, this time to Essen. Again, there was a fairly strong escort of Spitfires and Mustangs. The number of heavies in the attack was considerable so we should be in sufficient number to attract enemy opposition, be it flak or fighter.

The Flight Lieutenant Intelligence Officer giving the briefing mentioned the importance of Essen and, in particular, the Krupps Armaments factories, which appeared to almost fill the city. It seemed that if you attacked Krupps, you attacked Essen. One couldn't be done without the other.

We soon completed briefing and found ourselves back at the crew rooms donning our gear. It seemed quite novel for us to get the opportunity to fly with the Wing Commander. Perhaps the other crewmembers had their thoughts. If they did they said nothing. Wing Commander Molesworth, to me, seemed a legendary figure, what with all those gongs and a tour on Whitleys too.

What more could a crew expect? Flying with a captain who was the Commanding Officer? Whenever we flew with the Wingco it seemed that we all bore charmed lives. To me with my boyish outlook, it seemed impossible to be shot down while the Wingco was flying the kite. I felt safer and immune from the enemy. This was a silly thought really because we were a complete and well trained crew, especially with our own Skipper flying the kite. We had been together for six months now and we always were a good team. But I am sure the Wingco was a powerful morale booster to us all and to me in particular. He was a superb pilot, as we soon found, and perhaps he had every confidence in Flight Lieutenant Lane's crew. Would he have flown with us otherwise?

The Wingco had apparently commented to the Skipper with some surprise 'Your crew are all sergeants!'

'Your rear gunner looks damn young,' he added.

We kept all this to ourselves, the crew had quite a chuckle at the time of the conversation.

Whatever either captain thought of us, we never knew. Neither made a personal comment about the quality and efficiency of the crew that remained sergeants and flight sergeants until the war ended.

Our automatic promotion took effect, which was normal aircrew procedure. When early promotion, if recommended, was mentioned by one of the crew air gunners, the Skipper quite rightly queried the navigator's early promotion date and as this had already passed, no one got a recommendation at all! We were all finally promoted to flight sergeant in the normal time span of twelve months. This meant our flight engineer had to wait until after the war ended to get his promotion to flight sergeant.

We had not flown long with the Wingco before I asked Skipper if we could do some fighter affiliation trips with our Commanding Officer. Skipper approved immediately, saying he would ask about it but apparently nothing came of my request.

I also wondered why we never had the opportunity to 'have a go' at night fighter affiliation. It would have been invaluable. I am sure the RAF night fighter boys would have enjoyed it. They could have taught us a great deal. Many years later in the 1980s I discovered that, according to squadron records, some crews were lucky enough to get night fighter affiliation. I was quite amazed that it was not common knowledge (in the 1940s) that this valuable training was available, especially when you consider that the crew of a flight commander and squadron commander had no such opportunity. Also, since there had been no comments from other gunners regarding their experience of night fighter affiliation, it could perhaps have only just begun? Let us hope that for those that took part it was a great improvement on our experience with the Martinet at Peplow.

However, back at the Briefing Room we heard of the importance of this great Ruhr city and the strong defences surrounding it. The Krupps armament complex was the target. The Yanks had shot down some fifty fighters a few days before when their Flying Fortresses attacked a nearby objective. It seemed to me that the chance of getting an Fw 190 or Bf 109 would be quite high. Perhaps he would get us? Not a chance, not if we got into the 'corkscrew' first and before he opened fire! He would then face the return fire of both bomber gunners. However, six .303-inch Brownings, effective at 600 yards, are unfortunately no match for the four 20-mm cannon and two machine-guns of the Fw 190, with an effective range of 1000+ yards.

The op was scrubbed just after briefing due to poor visibility at base. It was put on again three days later. The very next day (23 October 1944) ops were on but we were not on the Battle Order. We felt pretty miserable when the rest of the squadron took off at 16.00 hours. The target was Essen again – H-Hour 18.30. It was a very heavy attack, with 1055 aircraft taking part (Lancs, Halis and Mossies). Eight heavy bombers were lost. Two Lancasters flying from 576 Squadron at Fiskerton were crewed by our former colleagues at 83 OTU, Flying Officer Dawson and crew and Flying Officer Paley and crew. The latter crew returned safely but regrettably Flying Officer Dawson, flying Lancaster 'King Two', PB467, failed to return. We knew the crew well and felt extremely sad at the news. We naturally hoped they would all be OK or, at worst, half would survive. We learnt many months after the war ended that they were all killed.

My diary records that all the No. 626 Squadron crews returned from the op, although one Lancaster, flown by Sergeant Yule, was hit by a 4000-lb cookie causing damage to the starboard wing and tearing away the starboard aileron. Miraculously, Sergeant Yule managed to fly the Lanc back to base.

On 24 October our crew was again briefed at 14.15 hours for a night attack on Essen. The op was cancelled while we were dressing and kitting up.

On 25 October we were in the Briefing Room at 09.30 hours for a daylight attack on Essen. We took off at 12.30 hours in good daylight conditions and soon set course for Reading, which was our turning point. From there, we headed straight into France, flying parallel to the bomb line some distance to the west, hopefully to avoid enemy radar detection for as long as possible. Vapour trails of our escort could be easily seen overhead, mostly in pairs. The sight of Allied fighters providing top cover on these daylights always gave a tremendous boost to our morale.

Mac gave the Wingco the alteration of course to take us into Germany. I looked below at the thickening cloud and thought we may be well obscured from the flak if the low cloud continued far enough into the Ruhr Valley.

From the intercom chatter between navigator, captain and bomb aimer, I knew that it would not be long before our ETA target. Sure enough, we arrived over Essen a few minutes' early. There was no sign of PFF. I could hear the Wingco and Fred exchanging comments and then, quite suddenly, several clusters of Wanganui flares appeared astern of us.

'Skymarkers dead astern, Skipper,' I called to the Wingco.

'OK, Rear Gunner.'

Making our orbit to starboard, the Wingco tried desperately to turn our Lanc round and back into the bomber stream in the shortest possible time. After all, making steep turns in a four-engined bomber over the Ruhr in daylight didn't appear too healthy from the amount of flak coming up astern. Fortunately, it was exploding too low; evidently the amount of cloud below and the window, being chucked out by Fred at five bundles a minute, was having some effect (i.e., only when Fred wasn't on the bomb run. Seemingly, some was going out during the steep turn.)

However, Fred couldn't get a marker in sight, no matter how the Wingco juggled and turned the kite.

'Left, left, steady.'

'Left, left, left again, Skipper.'

'Can't make it, Skipper.'

'We'll have to go round again.'

Around went the Lanc almost on one wing tip, still over Essen, still out to starboard.

'Watch out for other aircraft, chaps,' called the Wingco to all crewmembers.

'Just look at that shower,' said Wing Commander Molesworth to Stan, both looking at the oncoming stream of heavy bombers.

'We might just make it.'

'OK chaps, only a slipstream,' as the Lanc bucked madly from side to side, almost half-rolling as we hit the prop-wash of the other bombers.

'Left, left, steady, Skipper.'

'Left, left, left, Skipper,' called Fred. I fervently hoped he was having time to window during the orbits.

Woomph, woomph came the flak, those wicked-looking black puffs creeping round behind us, radar-predicted flak without doubt! We could hear it burst and we could smell the cordite as we flew through earlier puffs. I could see the puffs following our turn, fortunately still a bit low.

'Left, left Skipper.'

'Blast you, bomb aimer, blast you,' came the reply.

'Bombs gone, Skipper,' said Fred, rather joyfully, not wishing to prolong the agony of suspense for the crew. We had bombed on the turn and, as Fred explained later, the Mark XIV bombsight was quite capable and well suited to such tactics.

The Wingco swung the Lanc onto the homeward course.

'Can you see the target, Rear Gunner?'

'Yessir, lots of black smoke coming up through the cloud to our height.'

'Wizard prang, chaps. Wizard prang! Those PFF types were bloody late though, damn them. On course for home, Navigator.'

Peter and I facing rearwards, scanned the skies deep into Germany for signs of life from the enemy. Away to port a formation of four Spitfires was attracting the flak. They jinked smartly out of it. I felt it was good to see someone else getting it, the tight box of Spits probably looked like a Lanc on enemy radar. It was amusing at the time as the fighters had no difficulty in avoiding the danger and were never in any real difficulty. Oh! To be a fighter boy, lucky beggars.

We continued our search towards the rear, with nothing suspicious over enemy territory. We soon settled to our homeward run. Then, quite suddenly, over the Belgian border, dead astern, considerably higher than us, ten or twelve dots appeared. They were too far away to identify, the range being at least 5 to 6 miles. They seemed to be closing very quickly and at about 3 miles' range I felt it would be wise to warn the Wingco because they were overhauling us at such a terrific rate. I could see no obvious escort nearby and certainly none behind or above the unknown formation.

'Tail to Pilot. Twelve unidentified aircraft dead astern up, Skipper. Range 3 miles.'

'Are they attacking, Rear Gunner?'

'No Sir, still overhauling us, now about 1 mile.'

I could now see that they were painted duck egg blue underneath with two large bulges, one under each wing.

'Range about half a mile.'

'Are they attacking, Rear Gunner?'

'No Sir, still dead astern up.'

I could not make out the type, the large bulges had me stumped; they were too big for underwing drop tanks. The aircraft appeared to be little larger than single-seat fighter size. The wing shape appeared strange, perhaps slightly swept back?

'Goddammit man, they are Spitfires!'

'Are they hell,' I thought.

'I can see them myself on the beams.'

The oncoming formation was nowhere near the beams! They looked as if they were going to fly over us, about 5000 feet up, going like the clappers, fortunately taking no notice of us, which was just as well. There were no markings underneath their wings, which was not uncommon. I took my eyes off them for less than half second; I could see the Spitfires on the starboard beam at our altitude. I hadn't seen these before. The Spits hadn't seen the mystery formation. Peter in the mid-upper was silent. He later confessed he never saw them. Quite suddenly they turned to port, losing height, all still in formation, in pairs or in fours, in line astern. They passed out of my vision, flying south back towards enemy territory in the direction of the Ruhr.

'Don't you know a Spitfire when you see one, Rear Gunner?'

'Yessir,' I replied, rather taken aback. They were not Spitfires, I thought. What were they? Where were they going and to do what? They seemed to have ignored the bomber stream completely. I couldn't get over the closing speed. I had seen nothing like that before.

The remainder of our journey was uneventful. We landed safely. No comment was made by anyone at interrogation. I was both puzzled and bitterly disappointed by it all. Was I just a jerk, a fool, or had I really spotted something?

We had our meal in the Mess, just ordinary chatter. No crewmember mentioned the fighter incident, which seemed strange. They certainly weren't Spitfires, I thought again. My God, didn't they shift. Try as I might, the matter wouldn't leave my mind. Peter said he hadn't seen them but had seen the Spits on the beam. Strange, I thought, how Peter and the others failed to spot the fast guys.

Next morning, after the usual roll call and parade at 'flights', Peter and I reported to the Gunnery Section, which was the normal routine. The Gunnery Leader, Flight Lieutenant Whitehouse, DFC, had something special to say to all present.

'The Wing Commander is disappointed in your aircraft rec. Some of you do not know a Spitfire when you see one.'

I thought, blow me, not again. Not more duff gen. A few moments later, when the Gunnery Leader had dismissed the Section to their various jobs, gun cleaning, harmonisation etc., I took the opportunity to enter his office, saluting as I did so.

'Excuse me Sir, was the Wing Commander referring to me yesterday regarding aircraft rec and Spitfires?'

'No, Broome, it wasn't you,' said the Gunnery Leader without hesitation.

I quickly explained the situation previously described involving twelve unidentified aircraft over Belgium. (Author's note: These were almost certainly Messerschmitt Me 262s and had possibly been recalled to intercept another Allied formation heading for the Ruhr.)

'It wasn't you at all, Broome. The Wing Commander was referring to someone else.'

'Very good, Sir,' I replied and left the office. I was not at all satisfied. No one else seemed very bothered. Just goes to show how you could keep a bloody good lookout, so good that no one else saw anything and then no one believed you. But then I was just doing my job and everyone else in the crew were doing theirs!

The incident passed without further comment and I have thought since that Skipper Lane would have mentioned it if he were bothered about the incident, but he never did, so I presumed he was satisfied, which was just as well. I always felt that our Skipper had confidence in us all and would have said so otherwise.

On 28 October we were briefed at 11.15 hours for a daylight attack on Cologne, flying with our own Skipper. We were to bomb the industrial area and according to the RAF Intelligence Office we were 'to do what the Yanks couldn't do' on a previous occasion.

We took off at 13.21 hours, escorted by Spitfires to and from the target area. We climbed to 22,000 feet to get above cumulo-nimbus clouds. It was very cold. There was frost on my eyebrows and eyelids and an icicle a foot long hung from my oxygen mask.

We bombed at 16.01 hours on red Wanganui flares, dropped by PFF, as Cologne was partly obscured by cloud. The flak was moderate to heavy. We were now flying at 16,000 feet; our bomb load was a 4000-lb cookie, 5 x 1000-lb and 6 x 500-lb HE (High Explosive). There was a huge cloud of smoke over Cologne, which reached above the cloud tops.

Seven heavy bombers were lost, but none from No. 626 Squadron. Flying Officer Landells' Lancaster was damaged by several incendiaries released by an aircraft above. Fortunately, Flying Officer Landells was able to fly the damaged Lanc back to Wickenby. For us, the return journey was uneventful and we landed back at base at 18.50 hours. We went through the normal return procedures, interrogation and our super meal on return from ops. Most of the crew spent a quiet night either in the Mess or billets. I wrote home and to Edna.

We were not on the Battle Order for the next day, although five Lancs from No. 626 Squadron took off about midday to bomb an enemy fortress at Domburg on the island of Walcheren. All crews returned safely.

On 30 October, after a postponement of a daylight op, fifteen Lancs from 626 Squadron, were part of a force that bombed Cologne again in another night attack. There were no losses from 626 Squadron. The raid was repeated the following night with no losses to 626 Squadron again. Two Lancasters failed to return to other squadrons. There is a note in my diary for 31 October 1944 that states 'Getting a little cheesed off with not doing any ops.' The other crews had operated for four days' running. We had missed three and we didn't like it at all.

When we were not flying we often took the opportunity to take in the 'high life' in Lincoln, i.e., Spam and chips, the 'flicks', a pint or two and then onto the bus back to Wickenby. It was on one of these outings that I met some of Flying Officer Paley's crew, complete with their skipper, in a Lincoln pub. Apparently, Flying Officer Paley often went out with his crew and it was on one of these nights that the two Scottish air gunners, Sergeants Black and Mason, told us of their encounter with a night fighter, a Ju 88, over the target some nights earlier. Their account of the action was particularly interesting to me since the attacking fighter was first sighted as close as 150 yards and firing!

Both gunners, steadfast and courageous lads, gave no doubt as to their feelings in the action. They didn't want the chance again, not ever, to have a crack at another *Luftwaffe* night fighter. In contrast, I, the inexperienced, felt that it must have all been very exciting and worthwhile. I certainly did not doubt what they said; I could not then understand the mortal terror that they faced on that particular night. (Both the Me 110 and Ju 88 outgunned the Lancaster, both in gun calibre and gun range with their four 20-mm cannon and usually four 7.9-mm machine-guns. The effective range of a 20-mm cannon was well over 1000 yards.)

The reader may perhaps recall that earlier, at 83 OTU, Peter and I had approached both Flight Sergeant Dawson and Flight Sergeant Paley with regard to crewing. The other crew that we tried was that of Flight Sergeant (now Flying Officer) Beattie, now serving with our own 626 Squadron at Wickenby. We had also been joined by Sergeants Rakola and Joslin, who were Flying Officer Stroh's gunners, all previously from 83 OTU. (The two gunners were also from No. 3 Bombing & Gunnery School Macdonald, RCAF Canada.)

On 2 November my diary states:

Got up at 08.10, just made breakfast on time. Reported to Flights for roll call – at last we are on the Battle Order. We went out to our aircraft 'Able Two' in the morning. The crew did the run-up, which is normal prior to an op. Everything was tested; engines, turrets, hydraulics, electrics, W/T. All was in good shape.

The briefing was at 13.30 hours. The target was Düsseldorf, Ruhr Valley, at a height of 19,000 feet (the diary says 'for a change'). The bomb load was 1 x 4000-lb cookie, 6 x 1000-lb and 6 x 500-lb HE.

We took off at 16.05 hours and were over the target at 19.15 hours in the first wave. The sky was clear so there were bags of flak and searchlights. Two aircraft were soon 'coned' by searchlights and subsequently shot down. Seconds later, two twin-engined aircraft crossed our stern below at about 600 and 800 yards respectively. They were not Mosquitoes – they disappeared rapidly and neither was in an attacking position.

We bombed red TIs and saw a large explosion at 19.17 hours. There were several large fires below as we left the city. Our return flight was uneventful. All 626 Squadron aircraft returned to base, although nineteen aircraft were lost on the op. My diary states that 'nine enemy fighters were shot down' and that all the crew enjoyed their bacon, egg, toast and marmalade. I was in bed at 23.00 hours and got up next day at 11.00 hours.

On 3 November we were on the Battle Order, flying with the Wingco. The target was Bochum, which was cancelled just before briefing took place at 13.30 hours. Peter and I went out to 'Able Two' in the afternoon to DI the turrets and checked the ammo. We spent the rest of the afternoon in the Sergeants' Mess, writing letters. In the evening we went to the camp cinema. It cost 6d (2½p) The film was 'Escape to Happiness'. That had already happened, at 13.30 hours.

On 4 November we were again on the Battle Order and this time all the aircraft managed to get off without the op being scrubbed, which was certainly a change. The target was Bochum in the Ruhr. Eighteen Squadron aircraft took part.

The Wingco was his usual morale-boosting self, his conversation to the various crewmembers giving constant assurance of his belief in our ability.

This trip took us into Europe and right over the Dutch coast. Just before crossing into enemy territory we had our first experience of witnessing an aerial collision. The first I knew about it, in the tail, was a tremendously bright pinkish light in the sky up front. I could hear the Wingco and Stan conversing.

'Christ! What was that?'

'Looks like a collision,' was the immediate reply.

'No flak or fighters evident.'

'Wonder who the poor buggers were? Log it, Navigator.'

'OK, Skipper.'

The pinkish light continued for some seconds and then died away.

'Crossing the Dutch coast,' Fred called out.

'OK, Fred,' replied Mac.

We stooged on into the inky blackness. A course alteration was given by the navigator.

'160° Skipper.'

'OK, Navigator, on course.'

A little later another course alteration would take us onto the final run into the target. Bochum was an important industrial town in the

Ruhr. Certainly, the amount of flak on the 'run-in' seemed to indicate that. The searchlights were extremely active too. We could see other bombers 'coned' by some twenty or more searchlights.

Once an aircraft was 'coned', it rarely got out of the concentration. It was quite likely that some of these were concentrating on their bomb run. We could see the flak sending a torrent of steel fireworks into the apex of the searchlight cone. One could see the black silhouette of a Lanc quite clearly; also, there was no mistaking the red, white, blue and yellow roundel on the aircraft's fuselage. The white and yellow bands of the roundel clearly stood out in the searchlight glare. The flak hosed into the aircraft centre-section in a merciless hail. There appeared to be no attempt by the Lanc to break out. There was no diving turn, no evasive manoeuvre of any kind. Then, quite suddenly, a bright light flared out from the wing-root – a wing tank on fire!

The flames spread rapidly, the Lanc beginning to go out of control. I lost sight of it but not before it plunged downwards, still in the searchlight beams. Then another Lanc was lit up and the same thing occurred – the flak was merciless. Even after the bomber was on fire the flak continued to stream into the apex of the searchlight cone.

'Miserable baskets,' I thought. 'Can't they see they've had it?'

'Bomb doors open, Skipper.'

'Bomb doors open, Bomb Aimer.'

'Left, left, steady, Skipper,' cried Fred from up front.

'Right, steady.'

'Right, steady.'

'Steady, steady.'

'Bombs gone, Skipper.'

'Good show, Bomb Aimer.'

We sped downwards and away from the flak and the searchlights in one of our now familiar steep, diving turns.

'On course for base, Navigator.'

'Everyone OK?' asked the Wingco, as every crew position was checked on the intercom.

'Seemed a good prang, Bomb Aimer.'

'Yessir, well placed on the TIs, Sir.'

'Let's hope the markers were in the right place.'

'Yessir, they seemed OK.'

We settled down to an uneventful run home, eventually arriving over Wickenby at about 22.00 hours. We were not kept long in the aerodrome circuit; perhaps the WAAF on the R/T was well clued up as to which aircraft was the Wingco's.

'Pancake "Able Two".'

'Roger, Athurst "Able Two", out.'

We attended interrogation in due course, Wing Commander Molesworth taking care to ensure he was interrogated by his favourite WAAF Intelligence Officer. The crew enjoyed this special association immensely. We began to look forward to this after every op, with our CO. Remember, we were all still only sergeants!

It appeared that the target had been well and truly pranged but was also very heavily defended. Later, we learnt that the Command had lost some thirty-one four-engined bombers. Flying Officer Cook and crew on their twenty-seventh op, flying Lancaster 'Willie Two', failed to return. (It was their rear gunner's thirtieth op.) Two Squadron aircraft reported combats with night fighters. It was a night to remember for many months to come.

On 6 November there were no ops for us again. The Squadron went to Gelsenkirchen to bomb the Nordstern synthetic oil plant in daylight. Five heavy bombers were lost, but all 626 Squadron aircraft returned OK.

Most of our crew went into Lincoln while the op was in progress. We were able to get egg and chips at a local cafe, followed by an evening at the Theatre Royal, Lincoln, for a super variety show. We loved the chorus girls; well, I did! Fred made some adverse comments. He knew what he was talking about, being a showman musician – I was still a learner, on the girls, I mean! Later we had a couple of drinks before going back to Wickenby.

Meanwhile, Mac and Stan went to a dance, returning much later by 'shared' taxi. They woke us up, of course, one with a dead rabbit, the other needing to borrow the taxi fare. Both were in a happy mood. It was the good side of being a bomber crew; we enjoyed it all. We flew, slept, ate and played together – six sergeants, young and not so young. Life was still young, life was good. We lived for the moment, for the day, while we could. We rarely thought of tomorrow. We thought a great deal of sweethearts, fiancées, wives and mums too. We may have become shit-scared at times, when airborne, but never did we think it would happen to us. *Achtung Terrorflieger* was still to come!

Fifteen 626 Squadron Lancasters flew to Wanne-Eickel in the Ruhr on 9 November. A total of 256 aircraft bombed the oil refinery in daylight. There were no Squadron losses but Flying Officer Eames landed at Hardwick due to bad weather. Two Lancasters from other squadrons were lost during the attack.

During the afternoon we had to move our living accommodation. We had been on 5 site, near Rand. We moved to 6 site, almost next to the 626 Sergeants' Mess near Fulnetby. We were pleased about the move for two reasons. The first was the proximity of the Sergeants' Mess as opposed to 5 site, which was a good mile further. The second reason was that Skipper had become Flight Commander of 'A' Flight. We thought this had something to do with the move, but we were not sure of the exact reasons.

That evening there was a Mess social evening and dance. Someone had decreed that a busload of nurses would brighten things up. They were a right old 'matronly' lot and didn't appear to be of much interest to twenty-year-old sergeants. Mind you, they didn't seem to care much for us either. Bert and I took one look, had a few beers and went back to the billet. Peter was already in bed, and not with a 'popsie' either!

Later, I heard that one or two of the more enterprising NCOs had taken their dancing partners for a 'walking tour' of the camp. Of course, everywhere was blacked out and it happened to be a pitch-black night. Next morning we learned that it seemed to have suited everyone involved!

On 10 November we were notified of ops for the following day. We were on the Battle Order at last. Good show!

Peter and I checked the guns and turrets in 'Able Two'. We found the servo feed to the rear turret was in a hell of a mess. Ammo belts were broken, rounds misaligned and links rusted. We did what we could in a short time, making the system efficient and workable. Next day the forthcoming op was scrubbed so we went back to our 'kite'. We harmonised all the guns and completed the work on the ammunition in the servo. We checked all the rounds, at least a 1000 for each gun in the tracks, right up to the main ammo storage tanks, which were sited amidships. The ammo tanks held 3000 rounds per gun when filled. This was just the ammunition for the rear turret. The mid-upper and front turrets, both with twin .303-inch Brownings, carried only 600 rpg (rounds per gun).

The content of the operational ammo at Wickenby on 626 Squadron was identical to that for the OTU Nickel, i.e., three incendiary (tipped blue), six armour-piercing (tipped green), and one tracer (tipped red) in ten. We did not carry any ball ammunition at any time. I have read recently that a portion of some operational ammo was ball. This type of bullet was only useful against personnel. It would be next to useless against enemy aircraft with armour plate, bullet-proof windscreens and self-sealing fuel tanks! The idea of air gunnery was to bring down the enemy aircraft as fast and efficiently as possible. Killing the crew was *not* the criterion!

Ops were on for the evening of 11 November. Regrettably, we were not to take part. Eleven 626 Squadron aircraft bombed the Hoesch Benzin synthetic oil plant at Dortmund. Three Squadron aircraft laid mines in the Kattegat. A total of 209 Lancasters attacked Dortmund. Fifty Lancs and Halis laid mines off Oslo in the Kattegat and the River Elbe. All aircraft returned but Flying Officer Dainty crashed north of Wragby shortly before landing. Both Flying Officer Dainty and his bomb aimer, Flight Sergeant Friend, were killed. The navigator was taken to Station Sick Quarters at Wickenby and the rest of the crew to Lincoln Military Hospital.

On 12 November I received a spell of training on the new FN121 rear turret, which was fitted with the new Mark IIc gyro sight. The lethal range of the rear turret guns due to the new sight had increased from 600 yards to 800. One of the officers giving instruction on the new turret and sight was a very pleasant and capable air gunner, Flying Officer Pogson.

Later in the day Peter and I went to DI our turrets on 'Able Two'. We noted that she was already 'bombed up' with a 4000-lb cookie and numerous incendiaries. We hoped for an early call tomorrow.

The next day the weather had clamped; there was no early call and no ops. Instead, we cleaned the guns and took them back to 'Able Two' in readiness. On 14 November we went into Lincoln for the afternoon and evening. We had a super meal at our favourite café then a couple of pints at the usual pub. We saw a good show at the Theatre Royal, finishing with a real fish and chip supper, not in newspaper but on a plate, before going back to Wickenby on the 10.30 pm bus.

On 15 November we did a 'run-up' in our Lanc. Again, we hoped for another early call, possible for the next morning. It didn't come. We got up at the normal time.

On 16 November we were detailed for briefing at 10.30 hours. The target was Düren, south-east of Cologne, in support of the US Army who were attacking the Siegfried Line.

We took off at 12.40 hours in 'Able Two', carrying a 4000-lb cookie plus 4 x 2160-lb incendiaries. In addition, we were to carry out a line overlap photograph of the bombing. This meant that in addition to the normal run up to the target, plus the time on the bomb run itself (i.e., on a perfectly steady course), we were to continue the run without evasive action for some minutes until the camera had completed its timed run. The fact that we were flying at 10,000 feet didn't help as we were within range of light flak, 20- and 40-mm, as well as the normal 88-mm.

We seemed to be on the 'bomb run' for ever and as we might have expected, we attracted quite a spell of radar-predicted flak. We were quite alone, with no escort and still on course, carrying out the photographic run. The heavier flak came as close as we had experienced; we could hear the crump and whoomph of the shells as they burst alongside and astern of our Lanc.

The bomb run seemed to go on for ever and ever, long after Fred's 'bombs gone'. Then, quite suddenly, I felt the power go out of the tail turret and operated the manual handle to bring the turret to dead astern. The predicted flak was pretty close to us now.

'What is wrong with the port outer, Stan?' asked Skipper Lane.

'It's the CSRU, Skipper. Either a flak hit or it's just gone U/S.'

'Feather the port outer.'

Stan feathered the engine.

'Rear turret U/S, Skipper,' I reported.

'OK, Frank, sorry about that, you'll be out of power.'

'OK, Skipper. Thanks.'

A few seconds later we had completed the line overlap and therefore turned 90° on to the new course and out of the target area, leaving the radar flak smartly behind, I noted with relief.

Mac gave his usual course changes on the homeward route; the Lanc was making good time on three engines. I felt that it was a good thing to be an engine short, for it almost certainly meant a quicker landing back at base. Many times in the past we would be patiently circling the drome stacked up with other aircraft, waiting to join the circuit for landing. Quite a few times we would hear someone call up the Control Tower on the R/T, giving their call sign and aircraft letter identification, followed by 'three engines, over'. This statement never failed to get an immediate instruction to join the landing circuit and 'Pancake'. It would be something to look forward to, an early landing, at least as soon as we made base. The young are always impatient and I, like most of our crew, welcomed this special opportunity to get down early.

Later I heard Mac give Skipper 'ETA Base' and then 'Base dead ahead, Skipper.'

'OK, Mac, thanks,' came the reply.

'Athurst "Able Two", three engines, over.'

Back came the reply from the WAAF in Flying Control. '"Able Two", 6000, out.'

I heard Skipper make a grunt of disbelief. Like the rest of us, he was evidently disappointed at the cool reception.

'They must be joking,' I thought. They must have heard us incorrectly. The thrill of the early landing disappeared with the gloomy prospect of circling base at 6000 feet in completely overcast conditions.

We circled and circled. There was nothing on the R/T and time passed by.

'Think they've forgotten us, Stan?' asked Skipper.

'Looks like it, Skip. Why not give them another call?'

'Sounds a good idea,' came the reply. Gone off to bloody tea, I thought.

'Athurst "Able Two", three engines 6000 over.'

'Pancake, "Able Two",' came the swift reply.

'"Able Two", Roger, wilco, out.'

About b— time too,' came Dickie's retort over the crew intercom. We joined the circuit and gave our progress as normal.

'"Able Two", downwind.'

'"Able Two", funnels, out.'

'Pancake, "Able Two",' came the WAAF's reply. Then down we were, all in one piece. A very smooth landing, one of Skipper's best.

One thing I noticed about Skipper's landing had happened before. If we had any difficulties we always landed perfectly, really greasy stuff, whereas on normal routine landings yours truly really bounced up and down in the rear turret!

'How's that then, Frank? Ha, ha, ha,' Dickie's voice came over the intercom.

My thoughts about Skipper on those occasions were anything but pure. It was quite the thing for Dickie to bounce them in and so I got ready for him and his bounces by suspending myself some six inches off the turret seat and wedging myself clear of the turret roof at the same time. More often than not the idea worked perfectly, except that a heavy landing almost shook the turret off its mountings. No wonder we needed to harmonise the guns regularly. Perhaps it had happened to Flight Lieutenant Willie Whitehouse too. This must have been why he became quite insistent about regular and frequent harmonisation.

We left the aircraft and dispersal fairly soon and after interrogation we had our flying meal, which was always worth coming home to. I am sure it meant as much to us as completing another op. The fact that we'd had problems with the port outer engine, rear turret power failure, Gee U/S and used emergency air to get the undercarriage down, seemed to daunt us none! Any such mishaps only added to the thrill of operational flying. Besides, we would have something to brag about to other crews in addition to the line overlap.

Readers will realise that a line overlap takes more time on the bomb run. The latter is often normally long enough, but the additional sixty seconds for the line overlap photograph makes one's hair stand on end, for life, seemingly. I felt that the flak at the back end was getting closer, but maybe it was just my imagination?

Later, when discussing this op with other crewmembers, it seemed we all had similar experiences. Almost certainly we all thought it rather 'hairier' than most daylight ops to date.

One of the good things about the Düren operation was that it was an Army Co-op sortie. These sorties presented a welcome change from bombing industrial areas and gave crews the added thrill of directly aiding the current daily war effort by helping the 'brown jobs' crush the resistance of the German Army. The normal heavy bomber ops were really a long-term job, because attacking industrial areas usually produced a more delayed effect on the German war effort.

CHAPTER 15

'Birds not Bullets' and a Happy Christmas 1944

The day following the Düren operation was spent fairly quietly. We reported to 'flights' and then to the Gunnery Section. There was nothing doing in the way of ops. Our aircraft had gone in for a full inspection due to our battle damage and subsequent mechanical and hydraulic failures.

On 18 November Peter and I removed the guns from the aircraft, taking them into the Gun Room for cleaning. The four Brownings from the rear turret were in a hell of a mess! The barrels were sweating badly, due to being fired at the flak defences on the Düren line overlap photo run. We managed to get all eight guns in good shape by 14.00 hours. They would remain in this condition until required on the next operation, that is, with periodical cleaning in between, as required – usually two- to four-day intervals. All Brownings were checked for perfect firing sequence, with dummy ammunition, before storage in the Gun Room.

In the late afternoon I spent just over half an hour in the new FN121 Ground Training Turret. When this was finished I returned to the billet with Bert. We changed into best uniform and took a lift into Lincoln. We had a very pleasant evening and the beer was good (so the diary says). I gather it wasn't 'Tenpenny' as offered in the Sergeant's Mess! We returned to camp at 22.45 hours on the RAF bus.

We were up early next day, managing to get breakfast at 08.25 hours. Being Sunday, the meal was extra special for wartime: egg, bacon, sausage meat and potatoes. We always tried not to miss these Sunday specials. After this, we spent most of the morning tidying the hut ready for inspection the following day. One crew from our hut was posted to PFF. We therefore made more room and borrowed the odd blanket or two, a very common practice at Wickenby during winter. In the afternoon, I spent a further hour on the FN121. I enjoyed these spells of turret manip – the first since the ground training turrets at Macdonald. The new turret was superb, especially the gyro sight, which did all the work for the gunner. We needed as much extra training as we could get. All rear gunners were expected to put in as much training time as possible. All new Lancasters arriving on the station were now equipped with the FN121.

Again, Flying Officer Pogson was in attendance for first-hand knowledge and assistance with the new sight and turret. He appeared to be the main instructor and was always available for consultation. He was a tall, well-built, good looking air gunner, very pleasant to all ranks. I took it that he was either a second tour man or he'd previously been an instructor, perhaps at a gunnery school or maybe an operational training unit (the latter if he was now second tour). He was Canadian and seemed a really great guy, like all the Commonwealth and Empire airmen. He was easy to get on with and didn't pull rank at all. NCOs often set great store on the officer, of any aircrew trade, who didn't pull rank on the rest of us. Most aircrew officers, especially those engaged on bomber operations, were first class!

Regrettably, we were to lose Flying Officer Pogson in just a few more weeks. He was to fly in a Lancaster on New Year's Eve 1944! He flew as 'spare bod' rear gunner in Flying Officer Beattie's crew on that night.

The main feature of the new turret was its completely new gyro sight. The training turret was situated outside the main flight buildings, facing the peri-track and the NW/SE (shortest) runway. We were to spend quite a few hours learning to manipulate the controls that operated the sight. Firstly, we had to set the Lanc's flying height, followed by setting the wingspan of the attacking aircraft! These settings were simple enough, for all rear gunners could hear their navigator and captain's conversations on the intercom regarding the height of the Lanc. When it came to selecting a wingspan, we were advised to set for the Me 110 or Ju 88 at 60 feet as this wingspan covered also the Do 217 and Hs 129. The Me 110 was only 50 feet and therefore 'may' need alteration if time permitted? We chose 60 feet because this was the average for enemy twin-engined night fighters. The Fw 190 and Bf 109 single-engined jobs (Hajo Herman's *Wilde Sau*) were in the 30 feet span group. The sight would need alteration to the span setting for these types. It was unlikely, unless the fighter was seen early by the gunner, that time would allow any alteration. We did not at that time have any wingspan data for the new German jet fighters like the He 280 and Me 262, both being twin-engine types. The 60 feet setting would therefore hopefully cover these aircraft as well.

Both the height and wingspan settings were set by the gunner on the black box mounted on part of the turret internal structure. It was a simple operation by knurled knob on two marked dials, giving a choice of either height band or wingspan. This part of the gyro sight was relatively easy – time and sighting permitting!

The sight itself was an entirely different proposition! The gunner had a choice of two sights. One was the normal *original* reflector sight, a luminous ring with centre dot. The other was a circular set of diamonds, also illuminated. This was the *gyro sight*.

The main feature that needed lots of practice was the operation of the gyro by means of two foot pedals situated in the bottom of the turret floor. These pedals, one for each foot, operated the circle of diamonds (i.e., opening wide or closing down the size of the illuminated circle in the sight). The idea was to position an attacking aircraft, wing tip to wing tip across the circle of diamonds, and to keep this attacker within the ring by means of the pedals for range and also turret rotation, for position. Hence the reason for plenty of practice with the foot pedals to get smooth co-ordination between gunner, sight and turret manipulation. This would be essential in any combat. It would be especially valuable during the 'corkscrew' manoeuvre. I didn't see any particular problem in the use of the gyro sight during the Lancaster 'corkscrew'. The criterion in any combat would still be *sighting* the fighter *before* it opened fire!

Almost every gunner was delighted with the new sight. A few preferred to rely on the old reflector sight and, according to them, it was selected in preference to the gyro type. As I mentioned, both sights were contained within the new design. It was left to the gunner which he chose to use. It was just a flick of a switch.

I cannot recall that the gyro sight meant any change of routine for harmonisation except that we were not allowed to do any adjustment to the sight itself. This was left to the Squadron armourers. I wondered whether this was a wise decision. How often would the armourers re-harmonise the guns and sight? Would it be as good as some of the turret maintenance? Take for instance, the *bloody awful fault* on the hydraulic firing system, at altitude. I shudder now, when I think of it; lord knows what I felt like then? The hydraulic gun firing system on the FN120 rear turrets at Wickenby (while I was there) was something like 50 per cent useless at altitude. When I complained to the aircraft maintenance crew, at our various and different aircraft dispersals, usually before take-off, all I received was 'get the skipper to rev up the engines, Chiefy, they'll fire then.' Yes they did, but later, *not* always at altitude! The malfunction of the hydraulic firing system, due to lack of pressure, usually meant air in the system. We, as gunners (yes, those who used the guns in the air, often in a fight to the death) were not allowed to bleed the air out of the system! This could have been carried out on rear turrets, especially if an experienced operational gunner and a gun turret armourer accompanied a newcomer on the first couple of 'bleed trials'.

On numerous operational sorties (at *least* five and possibly more) I had reason to report that the gun firing system on those aircraft (all operational Lancasters) was sometimes partly, sometimes wholly, unsatisfactory. Very often it was the same aircraft repeatedly (i.e., the rear turret Palmer firing system was unserviceable). To the best of my knowledge, at that time, nothing was done that *fully corrected* the fault. I made my report to the Interrogating Officer on return from the particular operational sortie. In turn, I made sure that 626 Gunnery Section and the armoury knew about these failings. In those days, if one made too much fuss about a technical matter, repeatedly, there was a high risk (unofficially) of being labelled LMF. One can imagine our relief from these problems when the Lane crew eventually received a brand-new Lancaster, especially after losing some of our former favourites to an unknown cause!

There was one occasion when the reflector gunsight in the rear turret in which the Lane crew flew once on ops was $2\frac{1}{2}$ rads *outside* the normal possible adjustment during harmonisation carried out before the sortie by 'Bone & Broome'. Next day, after the op, I reported the fault to the Squadron Armaments Section, as directed by our Gunnery Leader. To my knowledge at the time, no adjustment had been carried out to the sight. This was borne out by the fact that the next time the aircraft was due to fly on ops, the rear gunner, Flight Sergeant J Webber, after consulting the fault-finding gunner, re-harmonised the rear guns and sight with some difficulty. Webber was an above average gunner and exceptionally conscientious. It is very likely that he was able, with assistance from the armaments staff, to obtain the required harmonisation. It apparently took some patience and determination by Jack Webber, who was eventually satisfied that all was OK with the sight.

Tragically, in the weeks to come, Flying Officer Lucas and crew, of which Jack Webber was rear gunner, failed to return from a 'Gardening Sortie' – more about that in due course. Peter Bone and I knew the Lucas crew very well, especially Flight Sergeant Webber and his mid-upper gunner, Sergeant Underhill. It was an extremely sad loss to both of us.

After we'd sorted the sight and turret problems, we had tea and later in the evening Bert and I decided we'd go for a shower. One of the main reasons for this decision was that we thought we were both dirty enough to risk the late November temperatures, plus other inconveniences like the one-mile walk to the Sergeants' Mess site containing the nearest shower block. As the winter weather grew colder, the prospect of having a shower became a more daunting experience, especially when compared with modern day bathrooms and shower units!

The shower block was part of the main dispersed 626 Squadron site of the Sergeants' Mess, Officers' Mess and cinema (all separate buildings), in common with many wartime Nissen-hutted sites. The shower building itself was completely blacked out, with all the windows painted black, so that no matter what time of day you went for a shower, you needed the lights on. Generally, we went in pairs, usually one or more of our crew colleagues, depending on who was the dirtiest or perhaps the bravest! Having plucked up enough courage to go, we would go armed with a bulb, borrowed under protest, from our own billet light sockets. We'd found out much earlier, that the shower building was always bulbless, seemingly unheated, cheerless and invariably vacant and otherwise quite bloody awful! Electric bulbs were never plentiful in any of the site buildings. Billets that were not occupied would very soon become bulbless, as well as lacking other things, like blankets, pillows and even mattresses.

Once we'd managed to fix up a light bulb, we then tried the water temperature. The latter was not at all reliable, although with both patience and manipulation we usually were able to get it reasonably high enough to risk getting undressed! This meant stripping in a cold, concrete-floored, brick-built shower monstrosity. Quite often, the floor immediately outside the communal shower cubicle, would be flooded to a depth of at least 25 mm , especially if used in the last couple of days. Dressing and undressing, particularly the former, were often performed standing on one of the concrete, wooden-topped fixed benches. Once in the shower, if one was lucky with the temperature, luxury prevailed! That is, if it can, in a wartime communal unheated shower building with outside temperatures often below zero! Lord knows how long we spent under the water? The length of time generally depended on the water temperature, the amount of amiable chatter and the number of other users, if any.

Once we were in, with the water nice and hot, we took our time getting out of the shower. It took as much courage to shower in those conditions, as it did to get the idea just to go, in the first place. Maybe we'd be back in two or three weeks, with luck! Is it any wonder we never found the showers full? Seems strange now, but I don't remember anyone complaining of BO. Mind you, the billet huts smelled terrible first thing in the morning, especially on return from the local site washhouse, outside, in the fresh field air! The washhouses (ablutions, as they were called) were similar cold inhospitable places, often with frozen taps in wintertime. On these occasions we'd all opt for a wash and shave in the washroom of the Sergeants' Mess, where we could be sure of real piping hot water! That's if you could find room! The best time was *after* breakfast!

Really, the winter scene at Wickenby for the sergeants, was an experience not to be repeated, we hoped! We all wore our long-sleeved, long-legged silk and wool underwear and normal Air Force blue shirt. Nearly all of us wore two woollen jumpers underneath the battledress blouse!

Next day, 20 November, was another relatively uneventful day. We reported to 'flights' as usual and then to the Gunnery Flight and on to the Gun Room to check on our Brownings. It was always a good skive, but this day again the visit was important. I found that the rear guns were sweating badly, due to the recent firing, and therefore spent till lunchtime cleaning all four once more.

In the evening we found we'd been booked for a new duty! We were to be the guard for a Sergeant gunner who was on 'Close Arrest' for being AWOL. We spent the night, all of us, in the Picket hut, carrying out this unenviable job. The Sergeant we took care of was a cocky but amiable guy. The Station Warrant Officer (SWO) warned us to be careful, saying that our 'prisoner' was a bit of a 'Barrack Room Lawyer' and therefore knew all the ropes! The SWO was quite concerned and advised us to be really vigilant and not take any chances. Later, we were to have a bit of a set to with the Sergeant when he discovered that Stan had locked the outside door and removed the key. The guy was sharp enough to tell us that sort of thing was 'not on' – he wasn't to be locked in! He was right of course. Mac didn't seem to be with us, perhaps he'd nipped into town before we got the job! Somehow, we didn't seem to need a navigator for this particular effort.

Whether correct or not, we understood that because this prisoner had gone AWOL, his crew had flown their next op after leave, with a 'spare bod' rear gunner. All of them went *missing* on the op. (Later, we learnt from our Orderly Room that the Sergeant gunner walked scot free from the Court Martial! Our SWO had advised us well!)

Fortunately, the next day Skipper came to see us and told us that we were on ops with the Wingco that night. You can perhaps imagine our delight. To have got rid of a job we didn't want and to fly with Wingco Molesworth that night was really something to be pleased about!

21 November – Checked rear turret, cleaned Perspex, trued up servo feed of 'ABLE TWO' during the morning in preparation. Briefing was at 13.15, target ASCHAFFENBURG – 25 miles SE of FRANKFURT (Southern Germany), Bomb Load 1 x 4000 lb cookie plus 16 x 500 lb HE. Take-off 15.30. Checked all aircraft systems, loaded and cocked all four guns – 'on fire' – before take off! Easy trip to target, very cloudy. Wingco his usual morale-inspiring self. We bombed at 19.17 hrs subject to moderate flak at our height of 13,000 ft, some near us, one burst below the tail, I was momentarily lifted off the turret seat, luckily no damage to turret! Searchlights ineffective due to 9/10 cloud. We bombed red TIs through break in clouds. TIs were easily seen. Wingco and bomb aimer seemed to think target well pranged. I was too busy looking for fighters. Saw 2 single-engined fighters, over target, looked like Me 109s high above us, not in attacking position so didn't need to warn crew. Later, observed a twin-engined fighter possibly a Ju 88, below and flying across our track, again, not in an attacking position, this was as we took our return course out of target area. NB 626 Sqdn diary records: 21.11.44 'Enemy Fighters Active in target area'. Return journey was uneventful, landed at 22.45.

The interrogation was similar to before, Wingco managing to delay till his favourite WAAF officer was again available! All the Squadron and station notables were present and as usual the crew enjoyed their interrogation, the mug of cocoa, the chatter and all the smiling faces. The Briefing Room was the height of activity on these special tension-relieving occasions! The target at Aschaffenburg had been the railway marshalling yards and railway workshops. Two Lancasters from other squadrons failed to return.

Next day we slept till 11.30 hours and managed to get to the Mess for lunch at 12.30 hours. We then discovered we were on the Battle Order for a night op. The briefing was at 18.00 hours, our meal at 17.15 hours.

During the afternoon, we ran up the aircraft engines, checked all systems, guns, turret, ammo etc. At 17.00 hours the op was cancelled. We spent the evening at the camp cinema. The film was 'Sweet Rosie O'Grady' starring Betty Grable.

The following day was uneventful, with no ops at all. The main duty was pay parade, which no one missed, and then clothing parade. I managed to change a few items like three pairs of socks, battledress trousers and Canadian blue tunic. This was all before lunch, so I spent part of the afternoon sewing stripes and my half wing on my new RAF tunic. Later Fred, Bert and I got tickets for the RAF bus into Lincoln. We left after tea at 18.00 hours. The diary simply states: 'Had a few pints, plus fish and chip supper, came "home" on the 22.15 RAF bus.'

We had a complete day off on 24 November. I spent most of the day in the Mess writing letters to Edna and my family, plus friends in other armed forces. I saw a film again in the evening. It was 'The Stage Door Canteen', which was OK by Yankee film standards, but as I'd already visited the real thing earlier in New York, the film set up wasn't quite so good.

On 25 November, Peter and I were surprised, after our usual report to 'flights' and the Gunnery Section, to find that we'd been put on an 'air to sea' firing exercise in the afternoon. I think the diary entry explains it all:

25 November – Got up at usual time, breakfast and then to 'flights'. Nothing doing in the morning. Our skipper put Peter and myself on an 'air to sea' firing exercise in the afternoon with Flying Officer Fitzsimmons. We took off about 14.30, and as we went along the runway, about 200–300 seagulls suddenly arose and we flew into them at 110 mph. The view from the tail was tragically quite spectacular! The Lancaster's airscrews were chopping four whirling tunnels right through the seabird flock. Over the roar of the engines, I could hear the screams of distress and the thump of birds' bodies as they hit the runway. For the seagulls it was a scene of complete disaster and devastation. We inside the Lancaster were luckier, we managed to clear the ground and get the undercarriage up! The nose Perspex was damaged, some of the crew, up front, were covered in blood and feathers, we made one circuit of the drome and landed safely. About 50 or 60 birds were scattered over the runway all dead or nearly, some were cut to pieces, poor beggars! The damage to the aircraft wasn't too serious, the bomb aimer's Perspex nose was broken and cracked badly, one of the spinners (port inner engine) had a large dent in it, there were feathers and blood etc., even birds in the radiators. Due to the damage, the flight was cancelled (both Peter and myself were highly delighted!)

Flying Officer Fitzsimmons and crew, especially the Canadian Captain, dealt with what could have been a far more serious accident, in a superbly competent manner.

26 November – Got up for bacon and eggs. Cleaned the rear guns thoroughly. Peter cleaned his and Fred's also – lucky Fred? Spent afternoon in the Mess.

We'd been very fortunate to be able to fly the op on 21 November, as this 'let us off the hook' as regards looking after our prisoner! None of us were very keen on these odd jobs that befell all NCO crewmembers at sometime. Generally, one can safely assume that if we were not flying an op or at large in Lincoln, or perhaps even luckier – on leave – we were very 'cheesed' or 'browned off'. Training sorties like that of 25 November with Flying Officer Fitzsimmons were not really our cup of tea. By this time in our lives, as bomber crewmen we thought we were perhaps too good to do more training.

Let me make it quite clear that while we were all now fairly confident flying as a crew, we were not necessarily over-confident! The dangers of becoming too confident were very obvious, even at this time. Yet, the more ops one did and the more 'hairy' occurrences we survived, the more we began to think, especially later on, that we were perhaps too good to be caught napping by any bunch of squarehead Germans, the weather, or any equipment malfunction when airborne. We learned small lessons on survival on almost every trip. The sortie to Aschaffenburg with the Wingco gave us a ringside seat of crews not so lucky as us, perhaps with Gee or H2S malfunctions, or perhaps simply just poor navigation. These hapless bods flew slap into the Frankfurt defences *en route* to target. It was a fearsome sight to see some other heavy bomber getting yet another pasting, by what was now the all-too-familiar sight of what would befall any crew, foolish or unlucky enough, to become 'off track' and therefore fly 'solo' over one of Germany's heavily defended towns or cities. The outcome of these errors or bad luck was nearly always the same. The German heavy flak was anything but inaccurate! Later, when the op was over, there would be much laughter and joking about these luckless crews. Sometimes there was the odd suggestion as to whom it might be. This nervous jollity inevitably took place in the Mess while waiting for, or eating our return flying meal. It was mostly due to the release of tension from young men, all sergeants, mainly lads of nineteen to twenty-two years, following a bomber sortie of some six to eight hours' duration. In many respects we were very childish in our reactions at the time. We were very silly guys in some respects. We never realised, or at least if some did, it was not apparent at that time, that most of the aircraft shot down by flak or fighters were to have only one survivor at best, not five, six or seven as most of us expected! Perhaps if we hadn't been so boyish, so full of life, with so much horseplay and silly games, maybe we could not have done what we did with little apparent effect to mind and body. Any talk at the time about going LMF was always treated as a huge joke!

It was quite a treat to get off into Lincoln for the evening and more especially the afternoon and evening if we were lucky! We were luckier than most crews, as our Skipper had now become the new 'A' Flight Commander. This had its rewards and its extra binds. It meant a lot more hard work for Skipper, together with the heavy responsibility of actually being Flight Commander and looking after some twelve or more Lancasters and crews. All this became Dickie's lot in addition to being a normal aircraft captain with his own crew and its responsibilities. Our rate of operations was to fall, unfortunately for all of us. We naturally wanted to get our full quota of ops in as soon as possible. Also, Wickenby wasn't the best of RAF stations, as layouts of aerodromes went. It was the normal wartime build, very widely dispersed Nissen-hutted air force establishment! However, although our operational flying quota had now fallen to a mere four per month, i.e. two with Dickie and two with the Wingco (this was considered the monthly quota for a Flight Commander and a Squadron Commander), it meant we could have more time off than most crews. We probably spent as much time in Lincoln as any Flight Commander's crew. This was both officially and non-officially! Sometimes we would persuade Mac, who being the navigator, and still only a sergeant, was the second in command of the crew, to phone Skipper to ask permission to go out if we were not required.

Mostly Dickie gave us the OK, but sometimes according to Mac, he seemed offish about it. I suppose this could be purely because of his position of Flight Commander. Maybe he could not get out very often? Certainly, if there was an op on and we as a crew were not flying, then we might be free to go into the city. However, Skipper Lane would have his part to play in organising his Flight for the op. He'd need to attend to any last-minute mishaps or alterations to the main operational plan, postponement due to weather and/or revised take-off times, replacement of sick crewmembers and possible last-minute technical malfunctions in aircraft already bombed up and fuelled for the op. We always had a spare crew standing by, already briefed for the op, and a spare aircraft already 'bombed up' and fuelled for the trip. Sometimes these crews and aircraft would be needed, sometimes not. The Lane crew have a story to tell about the 'spare crew' on a certain night, but that will come along later!

I am sure that very few of our crew really appreciated at that time the strain that Dickie was under, as Flight Commander. We knew his promotion to Squadron Leader would be through shortly. This appointment alone tells its own tale. Anyone getting a worthwhile rank in the RAF didn't get it for nothing! The responsibilities put onto young men in wartime was quite beyond the norm of today. (Dickie was about twenty-eight and he was also a second tour man.)

The younger members of the crew, myself included, often felt slighted if we didn't get Skipper's immediate approval to our request, via Mac, and so be able to go into Lincoln! Sometimes even, we evaded the responsibility of asking! If we got turned down, which rarely happened, we really got the mopes! Fred was quite good at getting me to accompany him to the transport section to get the local RAF bus tickets. We rarely waited to get the bus out of camp, preferring to go earlier, if possible before tea, intending to use the tickets for return. We'd have the choice when Lincoln-bound, of thumbing a lift or getting the local civvie bus. The latter was quite frequent, and rarely had we gone too far before one or the other turned up. Quite often the familiar Lincolnshire buses would stop for us, absolutely anywhere. We didn't have to be near a bus stop. We were too impatient to wait at the usual stopping places, choosing instead to try our luck at getting a lift in any sort of vehicle, which often worked just as well. The big snag was getting back again and *unless* one was returning from leave, there was no certainty of getting the RAF bus from Lincoln railway station, unless one had bought a ticket! The only other way was by taxi, which cost £2.10s (£2.50) and wasn't too bad if you could find four or five other bods to share the cost!

Our main effort in Lincoln was to get to the Theatre Royal at about 4 or 5 pm and book a couple of seats for the show, probably one of Emile Littler's shows. Fred seemed to know the guy; at least he seemed quite sure of seeing a good show and was never ever wrong on a booking.

Next, we would look around at the cafes and teashops to see what we could get for about 1s 6d (7½p). Sometimes it was sausage and chips, sometimes Spam and chips (Fred was never a lover of Spam), or perhaps corned beef and chips. They all went down well with bags of bread and marg, followed by numerous cups of tea. We never ever seemed to be anything but starving! We looked forward to these simple wartime meals as a special treat! After all, it was quite easy to become fed up with the RAF fare at the Sergeants' Mess at Wickenby, which was not the best of establishments for superb cuisine. Their flying meals were great, but you'd have a job to stuff the rest. After the show, Fred and I sought a friendly pub for the odd drink and then on to another eating establishment for a further feed. The place that was our favourite was a very special classy restaurant, which was up a narrow staircase not far from the Stonebow. At the time a great speciality was rabbit casserole, served as a high tea, with silver-plated cutlery and matching tea service. It was the top-class meal of our visits to the Bomber City! We finished with a final pint, then a dash for the bus at the station. The RAF bus left at about 10.15 pm, the last being about 10.45 pm. The civvie buses finished about 9.00 pm. It took about twenty-five minutes to travel the 11 miles or so to the 626 Squadron Sergeants' Mess site. Once there, it took two or three minutes to reach our hut and into bed.

27 November – Went to the Gun Room and cleaned guns again. Afterwards I filled in the 'Leave Book'. Nothing else doing so I returned to the billets and packed some of my kit. Went to station cinema in evening and saw 'Jack London'.

While we were preparing for our leave, nineteen Squadron Lancasters took off in the afternoon to attack Freiburg after dark. All aircraft returned safely to Wickenby. One Lancaster failed to return to another unit. Flying Officer Fitzsimmons (RCAF) and his crew completed their tour of operations.

Our leave was the first we'd had since that on our arrival at Wickenby. We'd overrun the normal six weeks, which was the approximate time between leaves on bomber operations. I was never quite sure of the reason for this. Perhaps it had something to do with getting a week's leave on our arrival? Otherwise, it could have been the pressure of bomber ops at that time. We'd flown nine ops since joining 626 Squadron. We were never to do as many in such a short time in the future.

28 November – Got up *early* 07.45! Best Blue, breakfast 08.15. Took our kit down to the guardroom. Caught RAF transport to RAF Station Faldingworth and went to pay accounts and drew SLSA £3 [Special Leave and Subsistence Allowance – Lord Nuffield Scheme]. Took 14.00 hrs RAF transport back to Wickenby and collected our passes. Left Lincoln LMS Station at 17.00 with Bert, arrived home at 11.30! Goodness me, steak and chips for supper!

While we were travelling away on leave, eighteen 626 Squadron Lancasters were bombed up and fuelled for a midday take-off. Only fifteen were able to take off and attack Dortmund – all returned to Wickenby safely at dusk. The three remaining aircraft had various technical problems that prevented take-off.

On arrival at Coventry, I went to my parents' new home at Shakespeare Street, where, early in October they'd bought a grocery business. The first morning at home always started with breakfast in bed, Mum's speciality. It seemed terrific, just being able to 'lay in' peacefully to about 10 or 11 am, followed by the luxury of a private bath, in warm and comfortable surroundings! One of the pleasures of operational leave was the extra cash allowance we received through the Lord Nuffield Scheme. I'm not quite sure of the origin. It was strongly rumoured that the scheme came into being when Lord Nuffield met two aircrew NCOs on leave in London who were absolutely broke and thoroughly depressed. The good Lordship decided to alter that in future, realising that young bods on leave can get through money far too fast. This would particularly apply to overseas crews, the Aussies, Newzies and Canucks, who needed much more cash to support themselves in favourite places and cities of interest like London. We local lads were in clover, by comparison, spending our leave with our families in our own homes and might not have had the same expenses. Nevertheless, the extra cash was well appreciated, especially by the lowly paid air gunners. The Nuffield allowance was 5/- (25p) per day of leave, which doesn't seem much now, but was $^5/_8$ of a day's pay extra at that time for the lowest paid bomber crewman.

29 November to 6 December – 7 days' leave. Spent a very nice time at home. Visited the town three times and Scala once. Edna arrived Friday night and went back Monday afternoon. Saw amateur boxing match at Wyken Club with Dad on Saturday. Visited Bill Hall at his parents' home on Sunday.

It was good to see Bill Hall again. It was quite by chance that he was on leave at the same time. It was over fifteen months since I had last seen Bill. He was now a flight lieutenant and this time he was at a bomber OTU! He was already flying Wimpeys together with his own crew. He seemed very keen to find out what he could from me about the various types of bomber training unit that we had been through. (Just for once, I was ahead of him!) This was quite natural among wartime colleagues. We all gave out 'words of wisdom' to our old friends (i.e. 'Pukka Gen'). It was partly expected! No one wanted to spread any doubtful or unreliable information, and so become a dreaded 'duff gen wallah'.

I think by this time Bill had married his Canadian fiancée, Camile. I didn't see Bill again. After the war he went to live in Canada. (I suppose that by now, like Peter Bone, he'll be truly a naturalised Canadian.)

While we were away, on 3 December sixteen Lancasters from Wickenby took part in a proposed daylight attack on the Erft Dam – 30 miles SW of Cologne. The weather over the target itself was so poor that all crews were ordered not to bomb and to return to base. On 4 December sixteen 626 Squadron Lancasters took off during the afternoon to bomb Karlsruhe. One Lancaster returned early with a feathered starboard inner engine. Flight Lieutenant Blennerhassett also had to feather an engine just after take-off but continued to complete the sortie. All the aircraft returned safely by midnight.

On 6 December sixteen Lancasters were prepared to bomb the oil plant at Merseburg. Fourteen aircraft bombed successfully. One failed to take off due to a technical fault. One returned early following icing problems, due to cumulo-nimbus cloud *en route*. In spite of considerable cloud over the target area the synthetic oil plant was well pranged. Five Lancasters failed to return to other squadrons.

7 December – Back to 'Work'! Up at 07.50. Good start, brekker at 08.15. A bit of a difference from home. Cleaned guns in the morning. Nothing else doing.

8 December – Got up at 08.00. Brekker 08.25. Cleaned guns again. Nothing doing for the rest of the day.

9 December – Got up at 08.10. Brekker 08.35. Reported at 09.30 for roll call. DI turret for ops. Should be on Battle Order tomorrow. Wrote letters etc.

10 December – Ops on! Briefing 13.00. Target Merseburg, height 17,000 feet. Cookie and 6 x 500-lb HE, duration 9 hours. Cancelled just before take-off. Returned to Mess. Went to cinema in the evening.

11 December – Briefing 14.00. Target Schwerte in the Ruhr, 4000-lb cookie and 16 x 500-lb HEs. Take-off 16.00. Scrubbed as usual, bad weather. Wrote letters in Mess. Spent quiet evening.

12 December – Got up at 08.05. Breakfast 08.35. Reported at 09.30. DI turret and left guns in aircraft. Briefing at 13.45. Target Essen, 16 x 500-lb HEs, 1 x 4000-lb cookie. T/O 16.12. H Hr 19.33, 17,000 feet, 3rd and last wave. Bombed Wanganui red/green flares. Red TIs also observed. 10/10 cloud over target area. Searchlights nil. Flak slightly 'Heavy'. No night fighters seen. Intercom in rear turret U/S. Returned to base and landed at 22.15. Interrogated. Meal at 23.30. Bed 00.30.

After having two ops scrubbed in daily succession, on 10 and 11 December, we were pleased to get off on the comparatively short trip to Essen. The total flying time was 5.45 hours. We followed the then usual climb to height over the Lincolnshire coast, out to sea and then did a 180° turn back over land until we reached our operational height for the route to target. As we took off at 16.12 BST, (DBST – double BST – was in force during the summer and BST – single BST – during the winter, i.e. one hour ahead of GMT), it was still quite light. We could therefore see the other Lancasters of 1 and 5 Groups climbing to their height for the route ahead. It was quite a hectic time, all the crew keeping a good lookout for aircraft on a possible collision course. This was never very easy, certainly not to be precise! It was necessary to warn Skipper of any aircraft near enough to become a hazard. Our captain always seemed to appreciate these efforts to assist him on a safe flight, over friendly territory. Especially as, according to the Intelligence Office at Wickenby, the reports from Group re the many collisions, were all too often! It wasn't too bad setting course in comparative daylight; one had just a chance of sighting another Lancaster before it was too late. It was 'hairy' enough even then and still more surprising now to think that there were not more such accidents, especially with the comparatively simpler Air Traffic Control. We were all on 'Radio Silence', which, of course, included no R/T transmissions. After we were airborne the only signals, apart from recall, we could expect would be night fighter intruder warnings (i.e. enemy night fighter intruders over the UK and/or our home bases).

The trip to Essen wasn't too bad. We didn't realise it at the time, but it would be our last with Skipper as a mere flight lieutenant. Soon it would be squadron leader. We were all delighted and our morale shot up tremendously. We became quite 'cocky', so the other sergeants said!

All aircraft returned safely, however Flying Officer Oram (RAAF) returned early due to fire in the port outer engine on take-off. Also, Flying Officer Wilson (RAAF) landed at Carnaby (Yorks) Emergency Runway due to U/S instruments. Six Lancasters were lost by other squadrons. This was the last heavy night attack on Krupps at Essen. It was extremely accurate: German sources assumed this was due to Oboe marking (by PFF Mosquitoes).

13 December – Got up at 08.15. Breakfast at 08.30. Returned to billet and went back to bed until 11.30. Went into Lincoln at 16.15. Saw variety show at Theatre Royal. Fish and chips. Got back by 11.30.

14 December – Got up at 08.15. Brekker 08.30. Nothing doing, had a quiet day. Wrote letters etc.

On this day three 626 Squadron Lancasters took off for a mining op. All returned safely, although one aircraft failed to locate the mining area due to H2S failure.

15 December – Cleaned guns well. Day off. Went to Lincoln. Bought Christmas cards and Edna's presents – handbag £3.16s.11d (£3.85p) and powder compact 15/- (75p). [Author's note = 164 per cent of a week's pay.] Saw two good films at the Regal. Returned on 22.45 bus, in bed at 23.30.

Fifteen 626 Squadron Lancasters prepared for bombing of Ludwigshafen. Two aircraft failed to take off due to technical problems. All returned safely.

16 December – Got up at 08.15. Brekker 08.35. Cleaned guns. Battle Orders, flying with Wingco, briefing 16.30. Meal of bacon and eggs 15.45. Target Ulm, cookie and incendiaries. Operation cancelled just as briefing began.

17 December – Cleaned guns, Battle Order out, flying with the Wingco, briefing 13.00. T/O 15.00. S/C 15.50. Target Ulm, 50 miles ESE of Stuttgart. 1 x 4000-lb cookie and 1350 x 4 lb incendiaries, took 8 hours. Flew out at 2–4000 ft owing to bad weather. Bombed at 19.30, height 10,000 ft. Flak was slight, plenty of Wanganui flares and TIs. Arrived back safely at 23.00. Interrogated and meal (2 eggs, sausage meat, bacon and chips). Bed 01.10.

Nineteen aircraft were detailed from 626 Squadron. One Lancaster failed to take off due to a fuel tank leak. Seventeen Lancasters returned to Wickenby. Flying Officer Vidler and crew landed at Woodbridge due to cannon fire damage after being attacked by a night fighter in the target area. Both Flying Officer Ford and Flying Officer Winder completed their operational tour with the attack on the important rail junction at Ulm. In addition, twenty-nine industrial and fourteen *Wehrmacht* establishments were severely damaged or destroyed. Two Lancasters from other squadrons were lost.

Again, we were relieved to get off to Ulm at last. It was good to be flying with the Wingco. It was our fourth op with the CO as aircraft captain. I still felt elated flying with Wingco Molesworth! It was quite an honour and a pleasure to be able to fly with the CO. I'm also very sure that this kept us on our toes, for apart from ourselves and the Wingco, we would not let Skipper Lane down either! I have often wondered how Dick Lane felt on those occasions. How much faith did he have in his crew? Perhaps, more than we knew? What would he think if we 'failed to return'? From where would Skipper get his new crew? Would he have to go back to OTU? (Very unlikely.) Would he be lucky enough to get an odd crew minus a sick or wounded skipper? What would Skipper have thought of them? We could (not so easily) have been lost on ops with the Wingco. Perhaps we might all buried be in the same hole? (The hole we made in the ground!) At the time, we never gave it a thought, but with hindsight, it was quite a possibility. It may be of note to mention that Ulm was the burial place of Field Marshal Erwin Rommel (not that we realised it at the time).

The trip to Ulm was flown out at possibly the lowest altitude of any previous op. I am surprised now to think that we didn't do this more often from an anti-radar point of view. I know that we used this method of approach occasionally, but I'm surprised we didn't use it even more! For many of the Ruhr trips the Group had gone straight in, over Belgium and on into Germany. We'd flown to Bochum almost right over the Hague!

This time we flew home from Ulm right over fog-bound NW Germany. Surely we could have chosen safer routes via Allied-occupied France or perhaps we were still busy foxing the Hun? It was on this type of routeing that we frequently heard the comment from other crews, 'Christ, "Butch" must be mad'!

18 December – Got up at 11.30. Dinner 12.30. On H2S training flight. T/O 15.00 hrs. Cancelled; aircraft unserviceable. Went to station cinema 'The Hard Way', fairly good.

19 December – Nothing doing for us today, returned to billets. Packed parcel for Mother and Dad, barley sugars, chocolate (my surplus flying rations), cigs, chewing gum and 21/- Postal Order. Wrote letters in evening.

21 December – Reported to section at 09.30. Went to clay pigeon shooting, fired 5 rounds – no hits. Cleaned guns in the afternoon. Went to station cinema in the evening.

23 December – Got up at 08.20. Breakfast at 08.45. Reported at 09.30. Nothing doing for us, the rest of the boys went to Koblenz. 'Easy Two' turned back – one engine packed up, the Lanc overshot the aerodrome, a second engine cut at 200 feet, the aircraft dived into the deck and exploded!

I was on my way from our living site when I heard and saw a Lancaster apparently on the flying circuit. Although a cloudy night, I could easily see one engine feathered. My immediate thoughts were – 'Hm'mm, an early return, someone's in trouble, wonder who it is?' I had not long to wait, having just entered the Mess foyer. There was a terrific bang, the building shook and the floor trembled! Several of the sergeants, including myself, ran out to look. We could see quite a blaze and red sky from the bomb dump. We were all shaken by the incident. One of the sergeants ran into the anteroom to see if the new red brick chimney and fireplace was still standing (he'd helped to build it). Fortunately it was, much to the his apparent relief! Later we were to find that fourteen Lancasters had taken off to bomb Koblenz. There were no losses from enemy action. It was 'Easy Two' that pranged on the edge of the bomb dump. The aircraft was flown by Flying Officer Preece and crew – all perished. It was a sad loss to all of us, especially to one of 626 Squadron's catering staff. Her boyfriend was one of Flying Officer Preece's gunners. It was a devastatingly sad day for her and for many days to come.

Next day on our way to the 'flights', we passed the empty dispersal previously used by 'Easy Two'. There had been two 'Easys' in the dispersal quite recently. Flying Officer Preece's Lancaster had been a recent replacement for a previous 'Easy Two'; both were lost from that particular dispersal. A day or so later, our 'Able Two' was moved to this dispersal, due to the dispersal being alongside the flight offices. It would become handy for both Dickie and the Wingco. We were quite pleased too, because we would have less distance to carry all our gear. We also spent more time, Peter and I, cleaning and keeping the guns and turrets in first-class order. One day soon, the Grim Reaper was to show his fascination for the third Lancaster to occupy this dispersal.

On 24 December I was absolutely staggered to find I was on the Battle Order that night as a 'spare bod' of all things! It was Stan who noticed my name on the Battle Order, flying with Flying Officer Gilmore and crew, as rear gunner in 'X-ray Two'. I'd been quite elated earlier, as I knew that our crew would not be flying. Naturally, we all looked forward to spending a happy Christmas in the Mess together. Now I thought 'Hell of a fine Christmas present from Skipper.' I was in a foul and mystified mood, as I sought out the almost all Canadian crew that I was to fly with; we met in the Briefing Room during mid-afternoon. The mid-upper gunner, a Canadian, soon singled me out after the briefing, which was for an op to Cologne.

'What's your night vision like, Sergeant?' asked the Canadian mid-upper gunner, Flight Sergeant Pickup (RCAF).

'Fine, says I, what's yours like?'

I thought to myself 'Cheeky beggar! He should worry, I've got to fly with them! Who do they think they are?'

'How many ops you done, lad,' says this Flight Sergeant.

'Twenty,' says I, 'How many you done, Chiefy?' I hadn't done twenty, but this bunch was no better than our crew!

'Hello, there Sergeant. I see you've met some of my team?' came a cheery voice. I looked up at the tall, calm-looking newcomer. It was the crew captain, Flying Officer Gilmore.

'Well,' he drawled, 'Canuck' style, 'Meet Dick Lane's rear gunner!'

Unexpectedly, it went very quiet! I swear you could hear the German flak at Cologne loading up! Dickie had just got his promotion to Squadron Leader. There wasn't another word said! We climbed into the same truck with our parachutes, Mae Wests, nav bags, coffee flasks and flying rations and drove out to 'X-ray Two' dispersal. During the journey, I ignored the ever-present nervous jokes ('Mind the flak Jack', 'Don't pull your chute, Luke') and had time to reflect on dear Bert's farewell handshake at the entrance to the parachute store. I remembered I was wearing Bert's weatherproof green outer suit, in preference to that useless yellow 'tyre advert man' buoyancy suit. I'd made some silly comment that if I baled out I would send the suit back by parcel post. Bert just grinned and said 'forget it'. He wouldn't, I thought, he'd have to pay for it! It would be like the WAAF Sergeant at the parachute store who said 'Don't forget, Chiefy, if it doesn't work bring it back, we'll change it for you!'

'X-ray Two.' The WAAF driver's announcement woke me from my dream. Out we clambered, gear and all.

'Our Nav will give you a lift with your guns, Sergeant.' Christ, I thought, was I hearing straight? The navigator helping the rear gunner?

True enough, Flight Sergeant Mitchell (RCAF) came round to the back end and lifted the guns one by one through the clear vision panel, so that I could more easily install them in the four gun mountings. The tension over their 'spare bod' rear gunner seemed to have gone. I was even offered a whole flask of coffee to myself. They were now all very friendly and much more helpful than my own crew just before take-off on an op. I was very impressed. I'd never expect help from our own navigator or anyone else; we all managed to sort out our own job without help. Fred once commented that Peter should have mounted the guns in the front turret for him, but it was 'news to me'!

Whilst I was in the process of loading the guns, I received a very unexpected visitor. A head and shoulder popped between the guns and through the clear vision panel.

'How do you like this one, Frank?'

'Hi Skipper! What did you put me on as a "spare bod"' for ?' said I, thinking of spending Christmas Eve with the crew in the Mess.

'What's up, Frank? Want to go LMF?' Cheeky beggar, I thought. I'd fly anywhere with Dickie or Wingco Molesworth but you can stuff these 'spare bod' trips! 'Christ, Skipper! It's Christmas Eve, you could have let me off?'

'Ha, Ha, Ha, you'll be all right with Flying Officer Gilmore, he's a good steady type, one of the best.' I didn't argue.

Dickie left with 'All the best Frank.'

It was as much as I could do to muster up 'Cheerio Skipper!' I felt like saying 'Stuff you too, Squadron Leader!'

After loading up the four guns and checking the sight, I joined the rest of the crew assembled near the rear door for a smoke and the inevitable last-minute pee. The mist around the airfield was thickening. It was now quite dark and looked a really murky night.

I looked up at the dull night sky and thought 'Even He doesn't care either, goddammit!' Suddenly phutt...phutt! Two white Very lights streaked up from the Control Tower! 'Scrubbed' yelled everybody. We could hear the cheers going up from neighbouring dispersals. I knew then, that I would spend Christmas 1944 in the Sergeants' Mess and not at 20,000 feet over Cologne!

We were too far out on the aerodrome to walk back to the 'flights' and so had to wait for the transport. We soon de-kitted and found our way back to the Mess. Sometimes one could be lucky enough to get transport to the site, but sometimes we'd just miss it and so had to walk back the odd couple of miles to the Mess. If you were in 'A' Flight, there was the extra mile to the billets, whereas 'B' Flight was right on the opposite corner to the 626 Squadron Sergeants' Mess. The news of the 'scrub' spread rapidly and by the time I reached the bar and anteroom everyone in the Lane crew knew of my good fortune. There were five bright happy faces to greet me. Mac took me off to the bar for a pint, saying 'Told you, you wouldn't go didn't I? Silly bugger!' Apparently, Mac had heard on the navigator grapevine that the weather was likely to 'clamp' down. We had a pleasant and fairly quiet boozy night finishing with a lively singsong before finally retiring to await the perils of Christmas Day RAF cooking! There were no duties for the flying types. We didn't fly again until 29 December.

25 December Christmas Day – Got up at 09.15. Breakfast at 09.30. Spent the morning in the hut recuperating after last night, had a pretty thick head. Had cold buffet at 13.30. Christmas dinner at 18.30 – soup, fish, chicken, turkey, pork, ham, potatoes, sprouts and peas – Christmas pudding, Xmas cake, mince pies, nuts etc. 15.00 camp cinema, pictures – 'Passage to Marseilles'. Drinks in Mess at 19.30, port and beer, didn't have much. Bed at 22.30.

26 December Boxing Day – Fog prevented operations today. Anyway, all the boys were still under the influence, so it was all to the good. Spent afternoon in the billets. Wrote to Edna.

27 December – Nothing doing, operations cancelled. Spent afternoon in billet. Had a shower in the evening.

28 December – Got up at 08.30. Breakfast at 08.45. Reported at 09.00, cleaned guns. Posted parcel of laundry in the afternoon. Afternoon off. Tried to start a fire in the stove three times with no result. Operations on, we didn't go, no aircraft available. Wrote letters in the Mess.

CHAPTER 16

Achtung Terrorflieger

A Cat May Have Nine Lives – How Many Have *We* Left Now?

29 December – Reported at 09.30. Battle Order out, we are on. Briefing 13.15. Target – oil at Scholven, Gelsenkirchen (Ruhr), ht 20,000 ft, 4000 lb cookie and 16 x 500 lb HEs. 14.00 took guns to aircraft 'Jig 2'. Take-off 15.15, set course 15.35.

Saw Ju 88 night fighter over France. 18.35 off track over Cologne. Experienced heavy predicted flak, very accurate, slight damage to aircraft. H2S & Gee U/S. Port outer engine hit but continued to operate satisfactorily. Only luck and chance saved us! (If there had been searchlights in action we would most likely have been shot down.) Shook us all very badly. 19.00 over target – slight/heavy flak, no searchlights. Two large explosions were seen (most likely oil storage tanks blowing up) thick smoke up to 12,000 ft! The Huns were also using smoke screens. Two aircraft were hit by flak and blew up, possibly a third followed a similar fate? 'A scarecrow?' said the Intelligence Officer on return. [After the war, German sources denied the existence of 'scarecrows'.] The trip home was uneventful, we kept well in the bomber stream. Landed safely at 21.00. Interrogated at 21.30. Meal of 2 eggs, bacon and chips at 22.30. Bed at 23.30.

The 29th was like any other winter's day at Wickenby. Somebody in the crew eyed the Battle Order. We were on, flying with Skipper. We thought nothing particular of the briefing; the target was oil at Scholven near Gelsenkirchen. We took it as a normal Ruhr trip. No one was complacent, as the Ruhr always commanded respect from all crews. It would be a short trip as most Ruhr ops were. The routeing often varied just to fox the Hun radar. The trip could be five hours' plus. Everything seemed to be going well just as we crossed the French coast in the last of the daylight. It was still quite light at our altitude but quite dark on the ground. I looked north to port and observed the bomber stream turning on to a new easterly heading. I was slightly concerned that we had not yet turned, our Lancaster 'Jig Two' still flying south into France!

'Alter course Skipper, 110°' sang out Mac on the intercom.

'OK Mac, altering course now.'

'110°.'

I felt easier when we turned on to a parallel course to the rest of the stream; they were something like 5 to 6 miles to our north. 'H'mm,' I thought, 'the stream is well off track tonight,' simulating one of Mac's past comments! Very soon, the comforting feeling would vanish. The sky gradually darkened and I could see the other Lancasters to the north for a while. Then as we proceeded flying east towards the bomb line, we passed over and on to a solid mass of strato-cumulus. There were no Lancasters to port now. I had thought earlier of letting Mac know the situation when we crossed the coast, but kept my mouth shut, purely because of the earlier Laval Nickel (OTU) *faux pas* on my part. We flew on for about an hour.

'Christ what's that?' Skipper called. 'Where are we Mac?' I gathered very swiftly that we were getting some flak up front!

'Düren, Skipper!'

'Düren my foot! More like Cologne, Chum! Full power Stan. Christ almighty!'

Mac let out a couple of loud laughs over the intercom, just as if he'd won a hand at a game of cards in the Mess (his favourite pastime at Wickenby).

'Cut that out, Mac! This lot isn't funny! You're the navigator — get us out of here!'

'Alter course to 018 degrees, Skipper,' came Mac's calm, automatic and immediate reply.

'Are you windowing Fred?'

'Just about to start, Skipper.'

'Good, get it going for Christ's sake.'

I could see the window going out, shooting past and below the rear turret in great bucketfuls, far more than the five bundles per minute max. Fred was really shovelling it out! Whilst the conflab was going on up front, I saw the flak open up astern. It came up simultaneously with Skipper's opening remark about Cologne! It wasn't spasmodic or box barrage flak but the deadly radar predicted stuff. It hadn't sunk in yet. They were after us and only us! I understood that there were about 400 heavy guns (88, 105 and 125 mm) in the Cologne area. I'd never seen anything like it. The whole sky seemed to erupt. The guns in each battery were firing in salvo. We were getting very heavy accurate salvoes of shells, all aiming in a very impressive and precise pattern. The flak was coming up in massive blocks of twenty to fifty shells, exploding all together. Most were to port and about our height in several elongated boxes, probably 200 to 300 yds away. Each predicted box was sufficiently long, wide and dense enough to wipe a Lancaster to kingdom come!

Quite suddenly, the barrage shifted to directly above with some to starboard. The bang accompanying these shells was terrific, deafening, even above the roar of the four Rolls-Royce Merlins (happily still functioning). The smell of cordite was very strong and the Lancaster bucked and shuddered. Unknown to me, we were already in a dive! Fortunately for us all, Skipper had put 'Jig Two' into a dive before the overhead salvo arrived. I'd just looked up to see the bursts where our tail would have been seconds before. The German flak was always accurate, deadly stuff especially while we were without window cover from the main bomber stream (still somewhere to the north). We were also extremely fortunate for below us was still the thick carpet of strato-cumulus. Therefore there were no searchlights, which was a major favour to us. This layer of cloud was probably the biggest single saviour of us all, except for Skipper's extreme foresight in putting the nose down. (It was some time later when discussing the Cologne flak on this particular night with Peter Bone that I learnt of the Skipper's diving tactic.)

I called to Skipper 'This flak is getting close Skipper.'

'OK Frank, I know,' came the immediate reassuring reply.

Shortly afterwards there was a bit of commotion up front. Skipper asked where the smoke was coming from. Apparently, an extra large chunk of flak had entered the starboard side of the aircraft (at an angle to the fuselage), tore across the crew passageway between the WOP and the navigator and cut right through the H2S leads, before going out through the port side and embedding itself in the port inner engine. The smoke and general dust cloud had been caused when the large shell fragment passed through the H2S cables. Bert and Mac rapidly sorted out their immediate problems. The flak stopped as suddenly as it had begun! Mac and Skipper conversed about the future navigation.

'The H2S is now U/S Skipper and Gee is being jammed.'

It was agreed to continue to the target on DR (Dead Reckoning). We later discovered that our Gee had been U/S all along and had therefore caused the navigational error, i.e., causing our Lanc to be 'off track' and well to the south of the main bomber stream. This error had taken us slap over Cologne and thereby to face one of the heaviest of flak barrages to be hurled at just one Lancaster!

Skipper asked all crewmembers if they were OK and then asked Stan to make a thorough check of the aircraft and to report any damage. Fortunately, there was nothing further and we proceeded to Scholven without mishap. The target was easily identified by the PFF marking. Fred bombed TIs seen through cloud with our 4000-lb cookie and sixteen 500-pounders. The trip home was uneventful and was completed without problems.

30 December – Got up at 08.20. Breakfast at 08.40. Collected two Xmas parcels from guardroom. Very nice gifts from Edna and Mum. Collected guns and returned to Gun Room where we promptly cleaned them! Dinner at 12.30. Nothing else doing, return to billets and wrote letters. Went to station cinema to see 'The Lodger'.

31 December New Year's Eve – Nothing doing in the way of operations for our crew today – the Wingco on leave. Harmonised front, mid-upper and rear turrets of 'Jig Two'. Peter also harmonised the mid-upper turret of 'Able Two'. Thirteen 626 Lancasters went to the railway yards at Osterfeld tonight. Flying Officer Beattie missing, 3 of crew safe having baled out, others believed OK. Two 626 aircraft were shot up by night fighters and landed one at Woodbridge and one at Manston. Had a booze up in Mess, got very merry on sherry and beer.

'X-ray Two' damaged, landed at Manston after fighter attack, Rear Gunner wounded.

'X-ray Two', flown by Flying Officer White, was badly damaged by cannon fire from an enemy fighter. Sergeant Adamson (flight engineer) and Sergeant Hopkins (rear gunner) were both wounded. Flying Officer Smith and Flying Officer Driver also had combats and both claim 'strikes' on enemy fighters.

Towards the end of the year, a modification took place in the rear turret of most Lancasters, eventually to affect them all. This was to remove the padded seat including (6 mm) armour plate under the seat cushion. The modification was to accommodate the issue of a pilot-type parachute pack to the rear gunner. This replaced the crew-type harness with separate chute pack clipped in stowage to the side of the aircraft, just forward and outside of the turret doors on the port side.

This was a welcome and acceptable modification in most cases. It gave a boost to the rear gunner's morale to know that, like the skipper, he was to wear the chute all the time, when in the turret. I vaguely wondered why this alteration was taking place. Perhaps someone was really concerned about the poor old rear gunner? I didn't dwell too much on the thought that perhaps too many luckless rear gunners had been found dead in the turret. Possibly after the tail section broke off complete with gunner and turret, following hits during a fighter attack, a heavy spell of accurate flak, or simply a collision. (This was in fact the real reason. Not a word was said at the time!)

Once a seat modification had been carried out it was imperative that the aircraft's rear gunner took steps to get a seat chute issued. In the early days, while we had aircraft both of pre-mod and post-mod stages, it was essential to discover how a 'kite' stood as regards the adaptation. It would be no use turning up for an op with the wrong type of chute for the wrong seating. It was up to the gunner to find out, especially if he were suddenly required to fly in an unfamiliar aircraft. When we were due to fly the very next op, I was informed by our Gunnery Leader, Willie Whitehouse, that I would need to draw a seat chute from the main parachute section. We had our own para and Mae West stores, but they only looked after the individual's issued equipment. It was necessary for me to take an extra walk one crisp, frosty winter's eve, with dusk approaching, and find the parachute section. This was not difficult due to the tall shape of part of the building (where opened chutes were hung vertically for airing and drying prior to packing). The attractive WAAF parachute packer very quickly fitted me out with a pilot-type chute. The whole parachute section was aware that rear gunners were now to be issued with these. When fitting the familiar harness and making adjustments, I was reminded of days' past spent at 33 EFTS, Caron, Saskatchewan. Needless to say, I needed no instructions to fit the harness. The WAAF obligingly adjusting the straps where necessary.

When all this was completed, there was a cheery smile and 'Good luck, Sergeant!' I thought the remark was nice and pleasantly made, after all they must be sick of attending to blokes like me? I'm sure many aircrew felt a great lift at the 'back-up' we got from most ground staff sections, particularly from the parachute wallahs.

One of the snags to the modified rear turret was the loss of the seat armour. There was absolutely no comment from anyone in the Squadron. I know that I felt the loss in more ways than one! A bullet up the ass was not a special favour. Sometimes previously, I'd wondered how on earth a piece of quarter-inch plate was supposed to protect you. Who could hit you there? No fighter could attack from directly below? Little did we know! As most people realise, there was no undergun position on the Lancasters of No. 1 Group.

Another disadvantage that I soon discovered was that once seated in the turret, that was it! It was almost impossible to move one's body without disturbing the parachute pack. The pack sat rather uncommodiously on the wide edge of the turret structure, the same ledge that had previously held the bolted seat and cushion. The parachute was an afterthought and not a designed feature, so there were certainly going to be operating snags, which I soon found out. The extra comfort and peace of mind that came with being inseparable from the chute, was partly dispelled by not being able to perform my *stand up search* (body at 90° i.e., feet at far bottom of turret, backside hard against turret door and with head *out* of the clear vision panel) in the turret without risk of snagging the chute pack, ripcord and pins! The seat chute was never designed so that the pilot could stand up in the aircraft with it on, unless he was about to use it! Like the pilots, we put the chute in the turret first and then climbed in and sat over it while putting on the straps. It soon became second nature and was a very popular modification. However, I became quite disturbed when I realised that my standing search (to look straight down below) could not now be carried out. I tried several times, and found that the risk of opening the chute plus the encumbrance of the parachute pack when standing up in such a small space became a definite 'no go'. Later on, I was to inadvertently open the parachute pack simply by trying to retrieve a gun-cocking toggle, which had fallen to the floor of the turret. More about that later. I very soon discovered that the seat chute in the rear turret was as much of a problem, as the problem it solved. From a safety angle it was great but from a search angle, especially below the aircraft, it was a menace! It made my standing search an impossibility! It was a good job I didn't know then about the *Schrage Musik* type of attack used by German night fighters. The only alternative would be the standard Lancaster rolling search, i.e., rolling to port or starboard, until the wings were in the vertical position, enabling both gunners to look below. This manoeuvre would only be completely successful if used frequently, say every three to five minutes! It could never be 100 per cent foolproof and relied on regular as well as frequent early timing of the rolls to port and starboard. In view of the then unknown *Schrage Musik* attacks on night bombers, the rolling search was not used enough. I could still look down at 85° from horizontal, through the sliding side window panels. This wasn't too bad, but not as good as the standing search. The latter was perfection in itself, also needing regular timing.

Fishpond, the fighter warning system used by the wireless operator on the Lancaster, would have been quite useful to indicate an attack from below except for two things. First, there was the problem of the density of the bomber stream, as Fishpond didn't differentiate between friend and foe. Second, Fishpond also couldn't give an indication of the height of the aircraft blip on its radar screen (i.e. above or below the Lancaster) – only its position. Fishpond would be more useful to a bomber not in the stream (i.e., possibly 'off track'). However, when H2S was being used (which Fishpond was part of) the enemy could track the bomber, if the night fighter was fitted with Naxos (*Luftwaffe* night fighter radar designed to locate and track H2S transmissions).

We learnt on 1 January 1945 that Flying Officer Beattie had been shot down. At first, we understood that all the crew had baled out. Later, we discovered that three of the crew were missing. News came through that Sergeant Ken Austin (our WOP's mate) was dead, the two gunners Sergeant Casey and Flying Officer Pogson were missing and Flying Officer Beattie was safe but wounded. Ken Austin was found in a field in Belgium, parachute unopened, and he was thought to have hit the Lancaster tailplane as he jumped. This tragedy shook all the Lane crew, especially as we'd trained with Flying Officer Beattie and crew at OTU, Conversion unit etc. We knew all the members personally. We still thought we'd hear from the two gunners.

Pilot Officer Brown, who was Beattie's rear gunner, had been taken ill and therefore had been unable to fly. I asked Pilot Officer Brown how he felt knowing his crew had been shot down. Brown was obviously very grieved but stated he wished he'd been the rear gunner on that trip, as he may have been able to have done something. He added that Sergeant Casey wasn't a chap that couldn't look after himself and he expected to hear from him. Flying Officer Pogson was the 'spare bod' rear gunner. The bomb aimer on his return to Wickenby said that he gave the order to 'corkscrew' when he observed tracer from beneath the aircraft. (Normally, *Schrage Musik* equipped night fighters used *no tracer*.) The flight engineer,

Sergeant Harrison, later recalled that the wing tank was ablaze. They were unable to put it out; the fire was so hot that the metallic skin was melting and dripping off the wing. It now seems likely that the Lancaster had been subject to an attack from immediately below, possibly by a night fighter using upward-firing *Schrage Musik* cannon. No one at that time mentioned to me that any warning had come from either of the two gunners. Unfortunately, also at that time, nothing was known to the crews of Bomber Command about this form of attack. One further point is that in addition to the 'spare bod' rear gunner, the crew also carried a second pilot, Flying Officer Benoit, who, fortunately, was safe.

Almost all bomber crews felt that 'spare bods' and 'second dickies' (second pilot) were often a jinx, as many aircraft carrying these extra crewmembers frequently went missing. Silly as it may seem to sound now, it was unfortunately a very popular belief. Flying Officer Benoit and the other surviving crewmembers went on bravely to continue their tour with their own or other crews or squadrons. I later saw Flying Officer Beattie on crutches with his calf and foot in bandages and/or plaster. It's doubtful whether he flew on ops again. We never did hear anything further about the two gunners. (It was not until after the war, that I discovered their names were included in the No. 1 Group Roll of Honour Memorial booklet issued in 1948.) It came as a great shock to know so many of our missing comrades were dead and particularly that they had been dead for so long, without our previous knowledge.

1 January 1945 New Year's Day – Got up at 08.15. Breakfast 08.35. Reported at 09.30. Harmonised rear and front turrets of 'Able Two'. Spent afternoon in billets. Went to Mess Social and Dance at 19.45. Had one pint of beer and a feed at the buffet. Bert our WOP is 21 today, he got blind drunk and later passed out altogether. Mac, Fred and I, brought him home in a wheelbarrow and put him to bed. Not before he was sick all over the back of Mac's best tunic! Went back to the 'do' but returned and went to bed.

2 January – Got up at 08.30 just in time for breakfast. Nothing doing in the way of ops! Cleaned guns and spent afternoon in Mess.

3 January – Nothing doing again, Weather PP. Spent afternoon writing letters and reading. Went to station cinema. Flying Officer White and crew were flown back to Wickenby by Flying Officer

Gilmore from Manston. Presumably 'X-ray Two' stayed behind for repair of battle damage.

4 January – Cleaned guns. Thoroughly checked rear turret of 'Able Two', everything OK. Spent afternoon in the billet reading murder stories.

5 January – Herbert – Flying Officer Beattie's Flight Engineer – turned up. Navigator, Air Bomber and Second Pilot also returned, 'baled out' over enemy lines. Three landed in British-occupied territory and Flight Engineer in 'NO MAN'S LAND'.

Herbert later told me that he tried to obtain assistance from several farmhouses. Unfortunately, due to nearby enemy presence, they were unable to help him. He finally made it back to Allied-occupied territory on his own. After spending seven days on survivor's leave, Herbert was posted to our neighbouring 101 Squadron at Ludford Magna to complete his tour with another crew.

6 January – Briefed for attack on Neuss (Ruhr) T/O 15.30. H HR 18.30. (1 x 4000 lb, 16 x 500 lb HEs) Aircraft was U/S so we didn't go. Pretty easy trip from reports of returning crews.

7 January – Our aircraft 'Able Two' is now fit. We were briefed at 16.30 after meal of bacon and eggs. Target Munich, 17,000 ft. 1 x 4000 lb cookie and 8 SBC of incendiaries – 4 lb type (total 1170). T/O 18.00, S/C 18.40. H HR 23.30 arrived 8 minutes early. Bombed fires of previous attack by No. 5 Group. Coming out of target, an aircraft came in to us astern from the dark side of sky, starboard to port. I gave combat manoeuvre 'Corkscrew Port' and opened fire – fired 200 rounds and then identified the aircraft as a Lancaster at 800–1000 yards range. Peter our mid-upper gunner fired about 100 rounds. (NB it could have been a Do 217 twin-engined and twin-ruddered night fighter at 400 yards, this was my immediate impression and reason for ordering the 'Corkscrew' and opening fire.) Returned to base at 03.30. Interrogated, meal and bed at 05.55. Flying Officer Stroh, gunners Flight Sergeant Joslin and Flight Sergeant Rakohla missing. Flying Officer White, attacked by Me 109F. Aircraft damaged. Rear gunner wounded. Flight Sergeant Jones the mid-upper gunner claims Me 109F as destroyed.

The op to Munich on 7 January 1945 was an interesting one. We were leaving the target after bombing the fires left by No. 5 Group and we saw our cookie explode on the edge of these fires. Then quite suddenly, without warning, I saw an aircraft with twin fins and rudders flying from starboard to port, and then turning in towards us from port! I called to Skipper 'Corkscrew Port Go!' I thought it looked like a Do 217 night fighter – it had twin engines, twin fins and rudders, and was very hazy in the gloom after coming out of the glare from the target fires now reflected on the clouds. I opened fire with all four rear guns; the tracer arched towards the 'enemy' who was higher than us and now turning in from our port quarter. The aircraft then came between the fires and us, now that we were in our 'corkscrew'. I could almost see four engines.

I gave the order to 'Resume course Skipper.'

'What was it, Frank?' came Skipper's reply.

'It was only a Lanc, sorry Skipper.' I had to disappoint (or reassure) them all.

'Oh Christ,' said Skipper. 'Did you hit it?'

'No Skipper, it was out of range.'

I'd seen my tracers falling below. I'd allowed for the 60-foot wingspan of the Do 217 and not the 100 feet for the Lancaster, hence I was out of range for the latter. Peter Bone fired quite well and gave a splendid back up. He fired long steady bursts from the mid-upper's two guns, firing about 100 rounds. It was a great pity to disappoint the crew, but I felt later that most sighed only with relief! It was a long and uneventful trip home, $8^3/_4$ hours' total duration. After landing, I apologised to Skipper for opening fire on what I then believed was a Lancaster. I got the reassuring reply 'Better to fire first and ask questions afterwards', which I thought summed up my own feelings, plus I had the added backing of Skipper! It was very reassuring indeed and perhaps all the more needed when you'd unwittingly dropped a clanger! As you see by the diary entry, there were fighters about, Also we'd lost a Lancaster and crew to an unknown cause. Flying Officer Stroh's aircraft contained a crew that was with us at Peplow. We knew most of them by sight, particularly the two Canadian gunners, Flight Sergeants Joslin and Rakohla, who were from No. 3 Bombing & Gunnery School, Macdonald. We never saw or heard of them again. Like so many of our good friends and colleagues of those days, regrettably I discovered they were *all* dead. (No. 1 Group Roll of Honour 1939–45.)

8 January – Got up at 12.00. Had dinner. Attended MI9 lecture. A Flight Engineer from another Squadron gave experiences of evading capture, walking home thro' Germany and France to Spain. Went to station cinema.

Some weeks before, I'd mentioned to Bert that I'd thought of carrying my old civvy mackintosh, plus coloured tie and shoes, in case of a 'bale out' over enemy territory. Bert thought I was mad and told me I'd be shot as a spy! Maybe, but certain bomber crewmen did just that, carry civvy clothes, and got home via Spain as a result!

9 January – Cleaned guns, checked turret of 'Able Two'. Nothing doing.

10 January – As above, having a dull time.

11 January – Cleaned guns. Went to cinema again in the afternoon.

12 January – No ops on. Nothing doing for us. Very little work to be done.

13 January – Harmonised 'Able Two'. Checked R/T during the engine run up for Flight Lieutenant Nelson. REAR TURRET FIRING GEAR U/S, reported this to Gunnery Section! Ops cancelled.

I cannot remember precisely what happened about the Merseburg op. Prior to 14 January, I am fairly certain that we were on the Battle Order twice and that we were briefed for that target on both occasions (i.e., the op was cancelled). Apparently, there was some good-natured comment from Flight Lieutenant Nelson and crew, who shared our aircraft 'Able Two'. Nelson deputised as Flight Commander for Dickie when we were on ops or leave. Flight Lieutenant Nelson and crew were very keen to get off on the final op to complete their tour and it seemed that Dickie agreed. After all, we went to DI the kite ourselves on the 13th – I couldn't see why we would do it for another crew and therefore it seemed likely that it was an agreed change between Skipper Lane and Flight Lieutenant Nelson. Merseburg had been a popular target recently due to the Leuna oil plant. It was a fairly long trip and so it was a happy agreement for most of us, as we didn't fancy the long ops (though we often bragged about those we had done, *afterwards*).

14 January – Ops on. Nothing doing for us. Squadron attacked Merseburg (Central Germany). One aircraft missing. Dear old and faithful 'Able Two' had made its last trip with Flight Lieutenant Nelson who was on his 29th trip. 'Able Two' had done almost 90 ops. Now she is at the airfield in the stars, flying with champagne in her fuel tanks, and landing on silver runways lined with gold studded drim lamps.

Being as we were not on ops tonight, went to Lincoln with Fred to see 'Jane' (*The Daily Mirror* comic strip/girl) at the Theatre Royal. Very good show. Well I thought so!

The 'Able Two' dispersal, next to the flight offices, was vacant the following morning (14 January). This we noticed on our way to report to the 'flights' for the normal role call. We were quite surprised and dismayed at the empty space and wondered what had befallen our aircraft, and Flight Lieutenant Nelson and crew? Maybe the aircraft had been damaged and had to land away? We could hardly believe our eyes – the unfamiliar empty space that had been the home of 'Able Two'. Yet, we remembered that 'Easy Two' had pranged at base from that dispersal only a few weeks earlier, on 23 December (Flying Officer Preece and crew). Later when we saw Skipper, he confirmed our worst fears that Flight Lieutenant Nelson and crew were missing. We were very sad about this and it took a few days to adjust to the loss of both aircraft and crew. We knew no more for some eight or ten weeks or so, when Flight Lieutenant Nelson returned to the Squadron after being a POW for this length of time. The story about the tragedy is worth a mention, especially because there is no other report that I know.

'Able Two' had arrived over Merseburg possibly early and before the PFF markers had gone down. They were circling the target when there was a terrific bang. Flight Lieutenant Nelson came to, falling through the air attached to a piece of the Lancaster and passed out again while struggling to free himself. Next thing he knew he was suspended by his parachute, which apparently had opened! Shortly afterwards the Canadian pilot landed in a gravel pit. He buried his chute and harness, found a way out of the pit and climbed to the surface. On emerging from the earthworks he was immediately captured by *Luftwaffe* personnel from a nearby flak position. Flight Lieutenant Nelson was not able to tell us exactly what it was that destroyed 'Able Two'. The aircraft had apparently exploded while circling the target. It was feared at that time that it could have been flak, or a ground-fired rocket of some kind. There had been reports of large missile-type (ground to air) rockets homing onto bombers. Again, the fate of the rest of the crew was not known. Regrettably, like so many other comrades of those days, they too were all dead.

During his capture, Flight Lieutenant Nelson reported that he was subjected to a very thorough interrogation by *Luftwaffe* intelligence officers who seemed determined to find out as much information about Loran, as possible. It appeared that the Germans had a working model of the new navigation aid but were still in need of some information regarding its operation. I remember thinking at the time whether or not the interrogators knew he was from 626 Squadron or whether they thought Nelson was from PFF. We at 626 Squadron knew nothing of Loran – at least so I then believed. (Cliff Wheeler and crew, who had recently joined 150 Squadron, were operational in Lancasters from Hemswell. Little did I realise, that Cliff, now a navigator, was familiar with and used Loran, a form of long-range Gee. However, their aircraft did not have H2S as did the 12 and 626 Squadron Wickenby Lancasters.) Nelson also mentioned that in order to obtain information his captors withheld things considered necessary, like shaving tackle, baths etc., offering them only if he gave them information. He would have been kept in solitary confinement, a frequent method of RAF POW interrogation by the German *Luftwaffe* in World War II.

16 January – On ops. Briefing 13.30. T/O 17.30 Target Zeitz, 17000'. B/L 4000 lb cookie and 12 x 500 lb HEs. Flew with Wingco in 'Baker Two'. Visibility good over target. Searchlights very active. Frankfurt's defences in action with unfortunate aircraft off track. Slight flak over target, wizard prang, bags of explosions – Oil? Returned safely by way of long trip over enemy territory. Landed at 02.30. Interrogated and meal and bed at 04.00.

We flew a good op to Zeitz with the Wingco, on 16 January, attacking the oil targets in that area. An interesting recollection is that on the last leg (navigationally) but one, running into the target area – immediately the Wingco switched on the VHF to hear the Master Bomber's instructions – we could hear some other crew who were apparently unwittingly *transmitting* on their VHF. (Only the Master Bomber or one of his deputies would normally transmit on VHF.) The conversation coming in on the VHF receiver was almost unbelievable. It appeared to be normal crew run-up procedure in English and continued into the final leg of bombing run, right into the target. I kept thinking why don't they realise that they are transmitting? The VHF button must have got knocked on or left on. The crew who were transmitting seemed a panicky lot. There was a slight foreign accent to the conversation, which made me think that it was possibly a European Allied crew:

'Watch that Lanc ahead.'

'How much longer on this bloody "bomb run"?'

'Can't you find a nice big TI bomb aimer?'

'Any bloody TI will do.'

'Let's get out of here while we have the chance.'

'Bugger the TIs, drop them anywhere.'

'For Christ's sake hurry up, bomb aimer.'

'Let's get the hell out of here.'

'Drop 'em anywhere, let's get off home.'

'Damn the PFF, any TI will do.'

'Bugger the TIs, it's too bloody dangerous up here.'

'For Christ's sake let's go home.'

'Shit, what are we messing at, we are going home now!'

I thought to myself what a 'shower' of a crew! I couldn't really believe my own ears. I badly wanted someone to shut off their VHF. Not that it bothered me anyway, except that I found it embarrassing. Finally, as we approached on the bomb run, we could hear the Master Bomber fairly well in spite of the other transmission. The Master Bomber was much clearer, much more distinct. He spoke good English, with no accent except good Oxford English. We bombed OK and came home all right.

After landing, when the opportunity arose I asked our other NCO crewmembers what they thought of the extra VHF transmissions? They were all much embarrassed and thought as I did – a right load of twerps, that crew! Later, much later, I thought that *we* were also a bunch of twerps! But not so big a bunch as the enemy transmitters were – because it didn't work, did it? The accent had given them away; it was a German spoof transmission designed to panic any of the borderline or fringe merchants (that we were supposed to have). It had no noticeable effect as far as we could tell. The attack appeared to have been a good one from all reports – both marking and bombing appeared very good. So the German transmission was a failure! We were more amused than panicked! Another point worth mention was the negative effect of the spoof TIs displayed by the enemy. These were often observed during most attacks. The first thing that gave them away was the dull red colour, plus the fact that the enemy dummies were quite obviously away from the centre of that city's manufacturing installations. I only observed the German interpretation of our red TI. I never saw any other coloured dummy on any of our ops.

The red TI dropped by our own PFF was the *primary marker*! Hence the enemy's choice of colour.

The winter weather at home in Lincolnshire was now becoming fairly severe. We were having the odd snowfall in addition to cold frosty periods and foggy spells. The fog prevented ops on a number of occasions both day and night. Lincolnshire was an ideal county for bomber ops due to its flat terrain, but it also gave rise to a considerable risk of fog; the low-lying countryside did nothing to help the problem, if anything it increased the risk. We were always prepared for diversion to another airfield and although FIDO (Fog Intense Dispersal Of) was in use, it was not available at all aerodromes. Our nearest FIDO airfield was at nearby Ludford Magna.

The dispersed living sites were in one respect a good thing – a wartime necessity, due to the possibility of intruder bombing attacks on our airfields. Otherwise, they were a bit of a bind. It was a cold wind that blew over the airfield and living sites during the winter of 1944/5.

Setting out from 'A' Flight site to walk to the Sergeants' Mess, a good mile away, one would have to walk along a very lonely, dark and cold windy lane. Within seconds of setting out on a winter evening we'd be shivering in our socks. In order to offset the cold, we'd put our best foot forward to walk as fast as possible. The 'ITW pace' at 180–200 paces a minute was useful, in an effort to keep warm and so put an end to the feeling of virtually freezing to death!

During this time of the year, most of us continued to wear our silk and wool long underwear. For as unglamorous as they were, they certainly helped us to keep warm. Some guys wore an extra pullover in addition to the service issue; a few, like Bert, wore the jumper over their singlet but under their shirt – so perishing was the weather. We were forever getting soaked, for Lincolnshire had its share of winter rains. Often Peter and I would get a real soaking, setting out to fetch the guns from one of our Lancasters, having missed the transport. Sometimes we'd start off in the dry and perhaps be lucky enough to be on the way back with up to *four* Brownings each. Broome with the rear four and Peter with four (his and Fred's). When the downpour began, there was little or no shelter till we reached the 'flights' or the Gun Room. Then there was the walk back to the Mess of some 2 miles, including 1½ miles round the perimeter track. *Our* Lancasters seemed always the furthest away.

Getting clothes dry was always a problem; there were drying rooms, if the heat was on! During the winter the RAF like everyone else was subject to fuel rationing, so this meant the monthly coke ration for the billet was used up in two or three days. We managed for a time to rustle up a bit of 'illegal' coal or coke from the boiler house at the Sergeants' Mess, until this source disappeared entirely, probably under lock and key! Some nights Fred and I ventured on 'sorties' to the coal and coke compound, behind barbed wire, chain link fencing and locked gates to obtain extra (illicit) supplies. We found a suitable large hole in the fencing, very kindly left by some other thoughtful guy. One night we thought we'd had our chips (or coke) for we were nicely installed in the compound when we heard approaching footsteps and unfamiliar voices. Fred and I looked at each other. 'Cor blimey, who is this – the station police?' We tried to look inconspicuous inside a large space in between heaps of coke, as there was little or no cover. We could clearly hear the progress of someone coming through the hole in the fence. Then quite suddenly, they were upon us. 'Hello there, I see you've found a good big sack and a lot of coke!' Fred and I were too relieved for words; it was just a couple of sergeants from the next billet!

17 January – Got up at 12.00, Dinner. Collected guns from aircraft, returned them to gun cleaning room and cleaned them. Fixed up about leave and pay tomorrow. Went to cinema and saw a 'Tarzan' film.

18 January – Got up at 08.00, made up bed and packed kit. Roll call 09.15. Pay parade 11.30 £6.16/- [£6.80]. Passes drawn at 12.50. Returned to billet and changed into best uniform. Hitched into Lincoln and just made the 2.50 pm train to Derby. Arrived in Coventry at 20.40. Good old home sweet home.

As I arrived in the evening of 19 January, I was surprised to find Dad coming downstairs in his dressing gown to greet me. He'd been ill in bed for three weeks. Mother said he'd not been up before and that he'd had a very bad attack of bronchitis. Dad seemed very pleased to see me and never went back to bed. He'd recovered completely by the time the leave was finished. I've wondered since, if he had any particular worries due to the start of our operational tour. He'd been a World War I Regular and would have many recurring memories and thoughts about that war. Also, he could have been concerned about the bomber losses of the previous winter period 1943/4 – Berlin (seventy-two), Leipzig (seventy-eight) and Nuremberg (ninety-six) – when RAF Bomber Command went through a very tough time, especially for the crews involved. It is one thing to be young and involved in war as I was and another to be an ex-wartime bod and have a son to fight in the next! (This is something I realised, many years later, when I had a twenty-year-old son of my own, who wanted to volunteer for the Paras who were then in action in the Falklands!) Dad got considerable satisfaction and peace of mind in the fact that Skipper had previous operational experience. Just how much our current ops worried him he never let on. Mother was more carefree, choosing to believe our very fine propaganda and gladly seizing the opportunity to proudly tell of her son's exploits over the Third Reich, to the many customers of the family business!

19–26 January LEAVE – Edna came down on 19th and stayed until the 26th. Dad was ill, had a spot of Flu followed by Bronchitis but recovered before I left. I had a very good time at home with Edna, we saw various films, some of them especially good. Saw 'Babes in the Wood' at the Hippodrome. Snowed heavily several times, also foggy and cold. Stayed at home most of the time. I bought a record of 'The Two O'clock Jump' by Harry James. Quite good but not quite as good as expected. Wrote to Les Linstead and Bill Bayliss. Went to the Langans (family friends) for tea on Thursday 25th. On the 26th Edna left for Manchester at 1.51 and I left at 2.07 for Lincoln. Slow journey for both of us, trains late. Met Bert at Birmingham. Arrived in Lincoln at 8.15 pm. Had supper in YMCA. Caught 9.30 civvy bus to Claybridge. Walked the odd 2 miles to our site. Bed at 12.00.

27 January – Woke up with headache, had cold and sore throat, felt pretty rotten. Didn't do a lot, reporting sick tomorrow.

28 January – Sunday. Reported sick at 14.00. Treatment 3 times a day. Nothing doing for the rest of the day.

I came back to Wickenby with a bad chest cold plus heavy catarrh. The treatment prescribed for the latter by the MO was menthol crystals dissolved in hot water inhaled under a service blanket, at Sick Quarters.

Two things bothered me about catarrh. Firstly, I was not happy with the prospect of flying with a blocked nose and ears. I'd had considerable pain and discomfort on recent trips due to being unable to clear my ears prior to landing. I was not at all keen to operate like this, being less than normal in health. The second point was a combined thing – I didn't want the crew to fly without me and leave me to do a number of 'spare bod' trips to catch up. I thought I'd had enough of this on Christmas Eve (when any other night might have been acceptable)! Two other members of the crew, Fred and Bert, were also unwell. Both were down with heavy colds, which seemingly made our crew non-operational! Dickie didn't seem very pleased about it, which was understandable! Also, the MO seemed very concerned that three crewmembers from the same crew had gone sick. Someone, it seemed, suspected LMF. It surprised me a little, although no one really put a name to it. However, there seemed to be far too many questions asked. Perhaps we were too sensitive? I personally never knew *any* of our crew coming anywhere near to LMF! Or any other crew either! I don't think any of us were very keen to fly with other crews. Also, we preferred not to carry 'second dickies' or 'spare bods', but cheerfully accepted it at least *four* times. We were always quite happy to fly together as a crew and to fly anywhere, at anytime, to any target. Sometimes, there would be a certain amount of bitching about long trips or a renowned tough target, but never any question of *not* flying as a crew at anytime. (Just for the record: the Lane crew *never ever* failed to reach a primary enemy target, whether the aircraft was damaged, equipment or engines malfunctioning or not. Regardless of any type of enemy opposition, flak or fighters!)

Looking back, I think beyond reasonable doubt, that during the time I was at Wickenby I never knew any bomber crewmember that showed any sign of being LMF. There were possibly some people who were liable to crack up due to abnormal mental stress, but in the main it was probably imagination. It certainly did not apply to any member of the Lane crew.

One rear gunner reported the gun firing system U/S after each of a number of sorties and still flew with the same failure on further ops. The 626 Gunnery Leader was aware of these failures and did all he could at the time to eliminate the fault, through the Armament Section.

The op to Cleves on 7 February was unusual and also very disappointing. We arrived at the target area, on an Army Support sortie to immobilise *Panzer* troops opposing the Canadian Army, only to find our VHF set was unserviceable. Both Dickie and Bert tried to get the set operational with no success. We had been told very clearly at briefing that, due to the closeness of Canadian troops to the target area, we were on no account to bomb if we could not hear the Master Bomber on the VHF. We flew round for some minutes trying vainly to remedy matters. The whole area was covered in stratus (layer) cloud, alto above and cumulo below. We could see very clearly in this brightly illuminated area. The illumination being the PFF illuminator flares, it was very bright so near to the ground and reflected by the layer cloud. We stooged around for several minutes. I could see for miles – completely unrestricted visibility. I'd never seen it so bright before during a night attack! There was no chance of collision, there being no other aircraft in sight – no friendly Lancaster or enemy night fighter! I'd never had vision so good before, and it was never to come again.

We could see the attack taking place; we could see the flashes of the HE bombs and a certain amount of light flak. We didn't realise then, that the Master Bomber had called all Main Force aircraft down to 4000 feet and therefore they were carrying out their attack below cloud.

We reluctantly returned to base still carrying all the bombs. Fortunately, our loaded weight was below the danger level for the return landing. Later, we gathered from Skipper that there had been some doubt as to whether or not our sortie would count as an op. Apparently Skipper told them a thing or two, including the prominent fact that our instruction at briefing had been quite plain – 'Do *not* bomb if you cannot hear the Master Bomber!' The next day, the VHF on our Lancaster was found to be quite definitely U/S by the Ground Signals bods. We found our sortie accepted as an op – I should think so too! Just fancy all that time, a lone four-engined bomber orbiting Cleves for about twenty minutes – a sitting duck! We must have stood out like a sore thumb on German radar! A night fighter or flak gunner's dream?

8 February – Got up at 12.15. No mail. Checked up on guns. Nothing doing for us, but other crews are on ops. Spent afternoon in billet. Wrote to Edna.

14 Squadron Lancasters detailed for operations, reduced to twelve on new target and then cancelled just as the aircraft were taxying out for take-off at 19.00.

9 February – Got up in time to wash and have breakfast. Roll call at 9.15. Returned guns to gun cleaning room and cleaned them. Spent half an hour in the Intelligence Library – aircraft recognition, combat reports etc. Nothing doing in afternoon, saw 'Chip off the old block' – Donald O'Connor and Peggy Ray – at camp cinema. 16 aircraft detailed for ops – cancelled at 14.00.

10 February – Roll call 09.15. 9.30 – the Wing Commander told us of 36 ops to a tour – new ruling – 20 ops 2nd tour. 10.00 lecture by Gunnery Leader, now Flying Officer (later Flight Lieutenant) Horsfall. On German jet jobs.

[The new ruling of thirty-six ops would cost the lives of some experienced Squadron crews who would normally have finished at thirty.]

Nothing doing for the rest of the day, repaired my punctured bicycle tyre and cleaned bike, first time since joining up.

16 aircraft detailed for ops – cancelled at 16.00.

11 February – Got up at 08.10. Breakfast at 08.40, egg on toast. Reported at 09.15. Our training flight was cancelled. Had haircut. Our crew is on duty this afternoon – window party! [Delivering window parcels to all Squadron aircraft.] 16 aircraft detailed – op cancelled at 16.40. Wrote to Edna. Spent evening in billet.

12 February – Nothing doing for us today. Spent the day generally lazing around. Went to station cinema, saw pretty good film. Weather very poor today, no flying possible. Squadron given a stand-down, which meant crews could go in to town.

For four days out of five, operations were laid on and cancelled within the span of a few hours, due to bad weather over eastern England, mostly at bases. Sometimes the operation was cancelled just before or just after the briefing, but sometimes the crews were already in their aircraft.

Perhaps one can imagine the tension these changes caused to the crews involved? Once an operation is scheduled by Bomber Command, the Bomber Group(s) concerned issue orders to their Squadrons who in turn issue a notice entitled 'Orders for Flying' (known in aircrew slang as the Battle Order).

This notice appears in both the Officers' and Sergeants' Messes. Usually someone will chalk up the various major details on an adjacent notice board in the Mess foyer, e.g. Flying meal 11.00,

Transport 12.00, Briefing 12.30, Take-off 14.00! It wasn't long before most individuals were scanning the Battle Order. This was a complete list of crew names together with the aircraft identification letter i.e. W2 etc. These crews would fly that day or night. It was at this time, when crews knew that 'they' were liable to fly an operation, that the tension began! Slightly at first, the average Bomber crewman would be looking forward to his flying meal, often a super one comprising egg, bacon, sausage, chips or similar. An egg was always treated like gold in wartime! (Some of the guys who flew, might be dead before they had fully digested their 'Golden' egg.) Tension increased slightly after the meal when boarding the transport already waiting, engines running, outside the Mess.

Usually the journey was fairly quiet. The odd sergeant would make a corny joke, often greeted by nervous but agreeable laughter or dry comment. Arrival at the Briefing Room was perhaps the first high point on the ground. On entry, one could hear already the comments of the crews that by now had a view of the large map of Europe showing the red tape, zigzagging towards a German industrial city. The volume of the exclamations depended on the depth of penetration into enemy territory. This occurred when crews knew the actual target! Usually, it was inside the Third Reich. Where the target was and how deep the penetration *into enemy territory* were the most important factors. This was followed closely by the density of its defences, the time of day or night and the routeing into and out of the particular industrial area.

During the briefing certain humorous comments by the Briefing Officer, the ever-popular dark-haired Flight Lieutenant, brought howls of approval from the seated crews. These comments were perhaps designed to lift morale and relieve tension. On one occasion, I remember distinctly a warning issued by this officer, to keep a very good lookout for 'cat's-eye' night fighters. (These were known in Germany as *Wilde Zau* and were commanded by Major Hajo Hermann.) This was greeted with the loudest howls of ridicule I was ever to hear! It was a good job poor Hajo wasn't present. He'd have run home in disgust! Incidentally, Major Hajo Hermann was twice shot down by Lancaster rear gunners. (Some historians have exaggerated the value of the *Luftwaffe* 'cat's-eye' night fighter, especially as an answer to the effect of our window on the radar-controlled enemy night fighter *Zahme Sau*.) We didn't give a hoot for the 'cat's-eye' types! It was the unseen, radar-guided Me 110 and Ju 88 armed with four cannon and four machine-guns, that gave us real concern! Fortunately, bomber crewmen did not know anything about

German night fighter radar (Liechtenstein SN1 or SN2) or the *Shrage Musik* — twin upward-firing cannons – at that time. So much for the Night Bomber Fallacy – And darkness shall cover me. The radar war was turning darkness into daylight!

The Briefing Officer continued giving target details with names like BMW, IG Faben, Rhinemetall Borsig, Daimler-Benz, Siemens, MAN, Krupps etc., followed by expected enemy opposition, flak, searchlights etc. He would also detail the type of target marking by PFF crews. Morale at this time was also boosted by details of certain Bomber Command diversions performed by OTU and HCU aircraft, possibly one or two other Bomber Groups routed to different targets. Not forgetting the valuable support of 100 Group with their radio countermeasures and, if really lucky, sometimes six or more Bomber Command Mosquito night fighters, operating within the bomber stream. The latter carried Serrate or other radar in order to home onto and destroy *Luftwaffe* night fighters. Finally, we were briefed on evasion/escape routes to Spain, Switzerland or Sweden, depending on the routeing of the bomber stream, and also positions of possible bale out. Once the briefing was complete the crews often chatted among themselves about the proposed sortie. Alternatively, they were dead quiet. Crews then made their way to the crew rooms, to collect and dress into flying clothing and survival gear. A short time later, crews boarded the waiting transport, followed by a journey to the various aircraft dispersals. During the active periods described, the personal tension remained at a steady level. One didn't think too much, when busy with some minor or major pre take-off duty. There was still, however, a feeling of foreboding.

Once again the tension disappeared, temporarily, while getting settled at one's crew position in the Lancaster and checking various items of equipment. In my case my tasks included loading guns, checking the turret mechanism and gunsight, firing guns on 'safe', and plugging in intercom, oxygen and heated suit connections. Finally, I reported that all was OK to the captain.

Once the engines had been started and tested on the run up to full power at dispersal, followed by a check by the captain to all crewmembers, the Lancaster was then ready to taxi to the main runway. The take-off was a serious business for *all* bomber crewmen, especially the pilot and flight engineer. Tension was probably at the highest level at that time, prior to leaving the ground. Once the Lancaster was at 'full power', on take-off, carrying a full bomb and fuel load, there was little chance of stopping her on the main runway. It was almost a life or death situation; it was a very tense time for all the crew. The captain and flight engineer were doing all the work with five other 'idle' guys just listening to their essential and critical jargon! Midway down the main runway a fully bombed up and fuelled Lancaster could not be stopped without serious damage at least and possible death for some if not all the crew. (The all-up weight was 62,000 lb (30 tons/28,182 kg) at 110 knots.)

Once airborne, some tension was relieved until the bombers set course over base. There would be simply dozens of bombers, including those from nearby squadrons, all setting course at the same time. Once on course, the captain and his gunners would keep a lookout for other bombers on possible collision courses. The risk of collision was always high and always present for any aircraft in the bomber stream. On certain nights there would be something like an average of eight collisions, most of them with fatalities and aircraft loss. This figure of eight applies to 'maximum effort' raids that contained 600 to 1000+ four-engined heavy bombers. Main areas for collision were often at navigational turning points, i.e. setting course over base, turning points *en route*, target area, including bombs falling from other aircraft, homeward turning points and over bases on return. With seventy bases in Lincolnshire alone and most circuits overlapping, eight aircraft on a maximum effort is perhaps not too bad, especially when the number of aircraft and length of sortie are considered. Nevertheless, all perhaps were avoidable tragedies.

Normally, in many crews after take-off and setting course, tension was relieved to some degree. Also, on becoming airborne the crew settled to their varying jobs in the Lancaster. Once they reach the bomb line – a variable line between Allied ground forces and the enemy. The term speaks for itself (we wouldn't drop bombs on the Allied side). Tension combined with increased alertness continued until the target area was reached. Then, during the actual bomb run, everyone in the Lancaster was extremely tense and fully alert. This was often the worst time for most crews! Once the Lancaster had bombed, with a photo flash record of the point of impact on target, we turned away, usually in a diving turn, onto a homeward course.

The return journey often brought some relaxation to certain crewmembers. The captain and the two gunners, supported when possible by the bomb aimer, flight engineer and wireless operator (the latter, in the astrodome), would continue their 360° horizontal and vertical air search for any sort of possible threat. It was a very dangerous time, as by now the enemy, confident of the direction, would be tracking the bomber stream on their homeward route and after they left enemy territory, often well out over the North Sea.

There was still plenty of time for a night fighter to catch the unwary, especially just before they reached friendly territory. Fortunately, in 1944/5, due to the stupidity of Adolf Hitler, the *Luftwaffe* was prevented from conducting regular night fighter intruder sorties over UK bomber airfields. Dear Adolf decreed that his night fighter force should bring down RAF heavy bombers over Germany, in order 'to put on a show' for the German public. If he'd have reversed this decision so that the *Luftwaffe* concentrated on the bombers over their home bases in England, it could well have been a complete disaster for Bomber Command. If this were so, it is likely that our own Mosquito or Beaufighter-armed night fighter force would also have had a birthday party! Whether any intervention by RAF night fighters would have solved this situation, we will never know. Bomber crews always welcomed any assistance from Fighter Command, day or night!

(One day, at the Wickenby Intelligence Library, Peter and I read of a report by a Halifax rear gunner who opened fire on a twin-engined fighter while returning home over the North Sea. The Halifax was one of the latest variants, fitted with a Boulton Paul rear turret, carrying twin .50-inch (12.7-mm) calibre Brownings. That same night, an RAF Mosquito intruder/night fighter crash-landed at Manston emergency landing ground, having been seriously damaged by .50-inch (12.7-mm) calibre bullets!)

Considering crew morale when air operations were imminent, I've often wondered (in later years) what would I have done if someone had appeared at the time of boarding our Lancaster to tell me I would not be going, someone else would take my place? I've always been quite sure that if the Lane crew were flying I would *always* fly with them. I would quite definitely be unhappy about being left behind! It was bad enough when the Squadron flew without the Lane crew! There was one occasion when it was rumoured that an officer gunner was having problems while over enemy territory. His captain was continually having to 'corkscrew' on his instructions, possibly to evade a non-existent enemy fighter. It was additionally rumoured that the Wing Commander was to take this rear gunner on operations, leaving his usual sergeant gunner behind! The Commanding Officer's normal crew said 'they weren't having that!' and would refuse to fly without their own rear gunner. Fortunately the situation never arose, which was perhaps all to the good. It was pleasant to hear of such loyalty but I wouldn't have given much for the crew's choice from a military point of view. I imagine, if the incident had really come to fact, then the crew would have been expected to perform quite normally and fly the operation as expected, regardless of who the rear gunner was.

Another instance of crew loyalty, which came as quite a surprise at the time, took place in the crew billet on 'A' site. Stan raised the question to me 'Can you fly the Lancaster home, Frank, if the Skipper got hit?' I was absolutely staggered! My reply was that I could only fly the Anson (a twin-engined aircraft), whereas the Lancaster had four engines, plus a load of different instrumentation and additional control systems – like throttle and flap settings, plus engine revs, landing speed etc. Stan's immediate answer was that if I could fly an Anson I could fly a Lancaster and he would know all the instrumentation, engine revs, flight and landing speeds etc. I asked the other two crewmen present how they felt and did they know the risks they took? Both Bert and Mac replied by saying that *anything* was better than baling out and becoming a POW! They were as keen as Stan to give it a try 'to get home'. My *only* worry was, could I get up the aircraft fuselage fast enough before the Lancaster got into its final spiral dive? Stan said he would 'hold it' till I got there. I didn't give their chances much hope, but if that was what they really wanted – how could I refuse? I realised the risks, but did they? If they were willing to put their faith in me, I'd have to give it a try!

13 February – Reported sick at 09.00 saw MO – sore throat, loss of voice etc. Excluded duties for 2 days and treatment. Changed rubber boots, old ones leaked. Operations ordered, 15 aircraft detailed. Fred on 'Spare Bod' trip tonight. Spent afternoon and evening writing letters. Two aircraft collided above our aerodrome at about 5/6000 ft, both came down very quickly – one exploded on impact and the other caught fire and blew up later – bomb load went up, 'Cookies' and incendiaries. Neither aircraft was from Wickenby, no survivors!

[The target was Dresden. When our lads returned, they joked about breaking all the Dresden china!]

14 February – The boys got back by about 7 am. Fred OK. One crew from 626 missing – Flying Officer Driver and one from 12 Squadron. [Total losses for Dresden were nine Lancasters, including two that crashed in France and one in the UK.]

At 16.00 ops were on again. Target Chemnitz. Both Dresden and Chemnitz were Russian front support targets. Went to station cinema.

Total losses for Chemnitz were eight Lancasters and five Halifaxes. Cloud obscured the target area therefore Wanganui skymarkers were used throughout the two-phase attack (three hours apart). Air reconnaissance later showed poor bombing results.

15 February – The boys got back at about 5 am. Flying Officer Driver and crew turned up all OK. Landed in France, instruments useless. No ops on. Went on training flight, air to air firing, 200 rounds per gun – 1 stoppage in one gun, due to duff ammo, airborne 1.40 hours, Lancaster PD393 'Nan Two'. Owing to being diverted due to fog at base we landed at Ludford Magna the home of 101 Squadron Special duties: 'Airborne Cigar'. We returned to base later when visibility had improved.

16 February – Went into Lincoln. Had a nice meal, saw a good film at the Ritz 'Sensations of 1945', finishing for a supper of chips. Took train back to camp! [i.e. to nearby Snelland Junction. Why we did this is now quite a puzzle, especially as Snelland must have been a 2- or 3-mile walk from our site, whereas the civvy bus stop was less than $3/4$ mile). Perhaps we missed the last bus?]

17 February – Brought guns in from 'Nan Two' aircraft and returned to gun room for cleaning. They were in a poor state, rusty and dirty. We cleaned them well. Nothing else doing today.

18 February – Sunday. Got up at 08.15, breakfast of egg and toast with cornflakes and milk. Spent afternoon in billet after cleaning guns.
    626 Squadron on mining sortie, two Lancasters lost out of five, *a 40 per cent loss!* Our regular gun cleaning colleagues Flight Sergeant Webber and Sergeant Underhill of Flying Officer Lucas and crew. Sergeant Beedles, the crew wireless operator, was replaced by Flight Sergeant Jenkins for this operation to the Heligoland Bight. [Perhaps the reader will realise the sheer delight of Sergeant Beedles when he flew on the Heligoland daylight operation two months later on 18 April. He was able to watch the obliteration of the Heligoland base, which he believed was responsible for the deaths of his former crew colleagues.]

19 February – Cleaned guns again, they are sweating rather badly due to firing. Went into Lincoln, got Dad a birthday card, went and had a tea of rabbit and chips, bread and jam and cake with tea at our special restaurant near the Lincoln Stonebow. Saw film at the Regal, 'Love Story', very good indeed. We had supper at the milk bar of sausage and chips.

20 February – Got up at 07.15. Station Commander's [Group Captain Haynes] parade at 08.30. Cleaned guns again. Ops on, we are to take Flying Officer Enciso-y-Seiglie (Cuba) as 2nd pilot. Meal 17.45, briefing 18.30, take-off 21.30. Aircraft 'Tare Two', Target Dortmund. Wing Commander John Molesworth, DFC, AFC took 'Queenie Two', replacing Flight Lieutenant White who was taken ill in his Lancaster, just before take-off. Fuel load 1600 gallons, bomb load 1 x 2000 lb and 1950 x 4 lb incendiaries, including 150 x 4 lb 'X'(explosive). H-hour 01.00. Marking – Wanganui flares scattered over wide area. Bombing concentrated on markers, large fires broke out. Red and green TIs hardly visible due to 10/10 stratocumulus. Flak was slight/heavy, Searchlights ineffective, fighters active. Several Lancasters shot down over target. One aircraft shot down by American IA2 proximity fused (flak), over bomb line on return. Believed to be friendly aircraft! The Lancaster was already firing the colours of the day. Landed 04.30. 14 Lancasters failed to return. Interrogation 05.15, meal 05.45, bed 06.15.

On the run into the target at Dortmund, the last wave in which we were flying at 21,000 feet, was subject to repeated and very determined attacks by Me 110 night fighter(s). The Lancasters that were attacked were within 1000 yards of 'Tare Two'. I repeatedly reported some seven or more attacks to Skipper, who in turn requested Mac to log the losses in the positions, as reported by the rear gunner. Skipper asked Mac to stop logging the losses after seven or so. Approximately twelve Lancasters were lost from our wave. Nine of these were later credited to Major Heinz Schnaufer ('The night ghost of St Trond'), the *Luftwaffe*'s top-scoring night fighter ace. His final wartime total was 121 RAF night bombers! This Me 110 was at times *less* than 1000 yards from 'Tare Two'. During post-war interrogation by RAF officers, Major Schnaufer commented that the Lancaster 'corkscrew' manoeuvre was wholly effective and wasn't used often enough!

All the Lancasters shot down followed the same tragic unevading course. Not one of these four-engined bombers, still fully bombed up, attempted to get into the Lancaster 'corkscrew' fighter evasive manoeuvre! The reason (not known at that time) was that they were being attacked from immediately below by a night fighter equipped with twin 20-mm *Schrage Musik* upward-firing cannon. The pilot and radar operator of the Me 110 positioned their night fighter immediately below the Lancasters, as close as 100 feet, firing into the wing fuel tanks.

Each Lancaster flew steadily for some two to three minutes, wing tank ablaze, with a 100-foot plus flamer. Each was still fully under control of its captain and crew. Slowly but steadily *each* Lancaster pulled away from the bomber stream *to port*, the wing by now well ablaze. The Lancaster continued its tragic course until dead astern and downstream of the main bomber stream for a further two or three minutes. By this time I felt that all the crew had had ample time to bale out, especially as the Lancasters were all under a perfectly controlled descent, until the last death-dealing spiral dive. The end for each Lancaster came in a massive explosion, as the flaming, spiralling aircraft hit the ground. The cookie and incendiary load added to the impact in a terribly blinding white-mushroom like fireball. I kept saying to myself 'They are all out by now?' 'No one could still be in there?' Not one of these twelve bombers ever went down out of control, until a few seconds before impact! So how come there were so few survivors from Lancasters? Was this the reason that Bomber Command offered all its bomber crewmen the option of carrying a .38-inch (9.65-mm) calibre revolver? Needless to say, we bombed OK and returned to base safely. We were never ever to witness such a deadly and effective night fighter attack on *our* Lancaster Bomber Group.

Sadly, 626 Squadron lost Flying Officer Patterson and crew. A couple of months later, I was to discover that Sergeant Whitby, Flying Officer Patterson's mid-upper gunner, had returned to the Sergeants' Mess at Wickenby, having been POW for some two months' plus. He was the only survivor from 626 Squadron Lancaster LM726 'Peter Two'.

Sergeant Whitby told me that he had been wounded during an attack by a Ju 88 night fighter and didn't remember anything after seeing the fighter at 150 yards' dead astern and firing. Next thing he knew, he was suspended by his parachute rigging, his feet in a stream, the main chute caught up in a tree. He remembered the sound of voices, which came from some civilian workers peeping at him through nearby bushes! He passed out again and when he came to, he was in hospital.

Later, when interrogated by *Luftwaffe* intelligence officers, he was shown several dog tags of RAF bomber crewmen. 'Your comrade, eh! *Englander*? Your comrade, *Kaput*!' Sergeant Whitby made no reply, but recognised one of the dog tags, as his rear gunner's, Sergeant Rutt.

It was only when he returned to No. 626 Squadron at Wickenby, that he realised all the rest of his crew were dead. He had the idea that someone in the crew must have clipped on his parachute, after extricating him from the turret, then jettisoned the Lancaster rear door and thrown him out. He didn't explain how the parachute ripcord had been operated! Each Lancaster had a static line to be used for a wounded crewman on baling out. It still needs someone else to connect it up and put the wounded man out and usually through the nose escape hatch! (The mid-upper gunner normally would bale out through the rear entrance door. The nose hatch is three times further away.)

The reader may note that when Flying Officer Beattie and crew escaped from 'Queenie Two' *over the bomb line* there were *five* survivors out of a crew of eight (including 'second dickie'). In contrast, with Flight Lieutenant Nelson and crew in 'Able Two' and Flying Officer Patterson in 'Peter Two', –there was only one escapee per seven normal crew of each Lancaster. Note that the latter two Lancasters were shot down by fighters over *enemy territory*. When one considers the three to five minutes' time lapse I witnessed, between Lancaster wing tank ablaze and final ground impact – what terribly tragic misfortune overcame the rest of these crews? Most Lancaster crewmen would have each been out of their bomber in fifteen to thirty seconds, the latter if you allow for jettisoning the nose escape hatch or rear door. The bomb aimer would normally go first. He would 'get rid' of the nose hatch, and would be followed by the flight engineer, navigator and the captain. The WOP, mid-upper gunner and rear gunner would normally leave via the rear door, on the starboard side of the Lancaster (if the rear gunner was not equipped with the pilot-type parachute). If the starboard wing tank(s) were ablaze, it could become impossible to bale out through the 100–150-foot flame from the inboard main tank! This still would not prevent the other four bomber crewmen escaping from the 'office' up front, through the nose hatch. So why the horrendous loss of bomber crewmen, so far completely unexplained? Historians have often given the explanation that the Lancaster:

1. Was difficult to escape from, due to the position of the hatches.
2. Went down *immediately* out of control – after fighter attack.
3. Disintegrated in mid air.

From our experience at Dortmund (the best operational example for the Lane crew), *none* of the above points would apply!

It appears from the experience of ex-bomber POWs that the German military treated our airmen with respect and often with some admiration. In many instances the Geneva Convention was more than observed. My present-day colleague, Jack Forrest, was a sergeant flight engineer of a 619 Squadron Lancaster LL783, Squadron code PG-C for 'Charlie', which was shot down on 5 June 1944 by a Ju 88 night fighter after attacking Caen. Jack was one of two survivors (his bomb aimer also survived) from this Ju 88 night fighter attack at only 1700 feet. He refers to the statement by their immediate captors – German paratroopers. They claimed that they would be safe with them because German civilians referred to RAF bomber crews as 'gangsters' and may well have dealt with our crews accordingly. What on earth did these German civilians think Germany did to most of Europe in the 1940s? There were only two sets of 'gangsters' in World War II and everyone knows which countries acted in this way. One on 1 September 1939 with the invasion of Poland, and the other with the attack on Pearl Harbor on 7 December 1941.

Also, while Jack and his bomber crew colleague were travelling as POWs between Paris and Frankfurt, they were protected by German military personnel from insults and threatening behaviour from German civilians who called them *Luft Gangsters*.

Later on, when they were in a POW camp, Jack and his bomb aimer met another former colleague from 619 Squadron, also a flight engineer. This sergeant had been in a Lancaster crew that had attacked Aachen in April 1944 (possibly 11/12 April). He said that after bale-out and capture he saw the bodies of three of his crew hanging from lamp posts.

21 February – Got up at 13.00, had dinner. Ops on. We are not on. Our guns being used in 'Tare Two'. Spent afternoon in billet. 14 Lancasters took off at 19.45.

22 February – Last night's operations were on Duisburg. One aircraft from 626 failed to return – Flying Officer Rodgers in 'Tare Two'. Consequently *our guns* – set 22 – had made their last operation. We now have set 6. Peter and I cleaned our new guns enthusiastically. Did a spot of genning up in the intelligence library. Latest aircraft and recent combat reports.

The operation on 21 February claimed the lives of Flying Officer Rodgers and crew. Fred knew the crew navigator, Flying Officer RW Donner, very well, having trained with him on an earlier course. It was a sad day for us all. Fred was to remember the loss of his former colleague for the rest of his life. The Till family kept in touch with Mrs Donner for many years. A total of ten Lancasters were lost at Duisburg, three of these crashed behind Allied lines in Europe.

23 February – Nothing doing for us, had a very easy time. Checked up on my promotion to Flight Sergeant.

On 23 February, 626 Squadron despatched thirteen Lancasters to Pforzheim – all returned safely. We did not go. My ITW friend, Sergeant Cliff Wheeler, now a navigator with 150 Squadron, based at Hemswell, took part. Cliff later told me this sortie was the hairiest of his operational life.

The Master Bomber at Pforzheim was Captain Edwin Swales DFC of the South African Air Force (captain, in the South African Air Force, is equivalent to flight lieutenant in the RAF). During the attack Captain Swales, flying at only 8000 feet in a Lancaster, while directing the main force, was attacked twice by enemy fighters, resulting in two engines and rear turret out of action. The Master Bomber continued his directions to the main force until the end of the attack. He then ensured *all* his crew baled out, by which time it was too late for him to leave the Lancaster. He was killed when it crashed. Captain Swales received a posthumous VC.

24 February – 'Up' all afternoon, training! Flew formation 'Balbo' with Skipper. 9 Lancasters in 3 Vics of three, each Vic in line astern. Finished with Lucero landing, i.e. training for fog take-off and landing.

On 28 February fifteen Lancasters and a spare were detailed for an attack on Neuss. We were not on, *again*! Flying Officer Wilson was unable to take off due to illness, so Flying Officer Tierney (pilot of the spare crew) took his place in the crew. All aircraft took off in poor visibility only to be recalled shortly after setting course. All Lancasters had to jettison the 4000-lb cookie to reduce maximum weight for landing. Any bombs jettisoned were normally dropped 'safe' in a specially designated area in the North Sea. All bomber crews always knew where to go. (Let us hope that the *Luftwaffe* didn't!)

1 March – Operations by 626 on Mannheim in daylight. 15 Lancasters took part, all returned safely, two on three engines. Three Lancasters lost from other Squadrons. Our next leave is due on 14/3/45. Went to Lincoln for the *usual*!

2 March – Operations on Cologne, none missing from 626. 6 Lancasters and 3 Halifaxes lost from other Squadrons. Two training accidents occurred. One crew killed. Attended funeral as pall bearers. The coffins were draped in Union Jack with wreath. The transport used was an old crappie MT truck, a pretty PP show. Had a good feed and a show in Lincoln!

While 626 Squadron was busy bombing Cologne in daylight, the Lane crew had the sad duty of acting as funeral bearers to three sergeants who were part of a crew killed on a training sortie.

The 'grapevine' had it that the mid-upper gunner, on an 'air to sea' training exercise, put a burst into the wing tanks of their Lancaster. Evidently, the gunner had possibly not checked his turret properly, namely the gunfire interruptor fitted to the Frazer Nash FN50 mid-upper turret. That is, assuming it had *not* malfunctioned *after* leaving the airfield.

Sadly, all three coffins felt light. The final line in the original diary entry for 2 March is not intended to show any disrespect for our fallen colleagues. However, it does show how twenty-year-old aircrew sergeants could react to certain terrible tragedies, in those days.

3 March – Nothing doing for us. Duly cleaned our guns. Mining operations in enemy waters by 626 aircraft, none missing. Flying Officer Fisk and crew reported combat with enemy twin-engined night fighter and shot it down in mining area! Spent evening in camp cinema – 'Goodbye Mr Chips'.

4 March – Did a spot of aircraft recognition in intelligence library in the morning. Nothing doing for us, spent afternoon in billet.

5 March – Nothing doing for us today. Our aircraft went to Chemnitz, none lost. Saw 'Hotel Reserve' at station cinema, very good.

Fourteen 626 Lancasters took off at 17.05 for Chemnitz, Russian support target. Flying Officer Enciso-y-Seiglie aborted mission, landing at Woodbridge emergency landing ground on 3 engines at 18.10.

6 March – Flew on training flight, Lucero, 'Y' cross-country and high level bombing 3 hrs 20 mins with Squadron Leader Lane (Captain).

7 March – On Battle Order 'Willie Two', briefing 14.45. Target Dessau (Oil) routeing to target a feint on Berlin. Fuel load, full tanks 2154 gals. Bomb load 1 x 2000 lb HE, 12 SBC incendiaries. TO 17.00, S/C 17.30. Bombing Ht 14,000'. The trip went well until the Bomber Stream flew over the Ruhr. There were several aircraft shot down by fighters and at least one by flak. Searchlights very active further in. 10/10 thin status over target. TIs seen clearly through the cloud. Wanganuis also dropped – slight/heavy flak over target, barrage at 12,000 and 15,000 ft. Two aircraft shot down over target, probably flak. The long tiresome trip home was uneventful. Landed safely at base 02.30, total duration 9.40 hrs. Interrogation 03.30, meal 04.30, bed 05.15.

The operation to Dessau was our longest to date and was to remain so! Dessau was our longest sortie into Eastern Germany. Eighteen Lancasters were lost, 3.4 per cent of the attacking force. As the diary entry states, we in 'Willie Two' witnessed something like half of those losses. One thing that improved my morale especially on that night was rather unexpected, for as Skipper taxied out of dispersal, I accidentally dropped the gun-cocking toggle! Normally, this is stowed in a fabricated sheath attached to the turret structure. I'd missed the sheath opening and the toggle dropped to the floor of the turret. This minor error then caused a larger one. In endeavouring to recover the toggle, I bent almost double, in the cramped space available. This in turn caused tension on the parachute ripcord and its housing. The extra tension on the ripcord opened the parachute pack beneath me. There was no way I could close it, especially while sitting on it!

I called Skipper on the intercom, 'Hi Skipper, my chute has opened in the turret.'

'Christ, Frank how did you do that?' I rapidly explained.

Skipper immediately replied 'Stan will bring you the spare.'

'That's no good Skipper, I'm wearing a seat chute!'

'Oh sod it Frank, we'll go round on the peri-track to the flight crew rooms and see what can be done.'

'OK Skipper, thanks.'

The crew rooms were adjacent to 626 Parachute and Emergency Equipment Store. It took just a few minutes to get there. The Lancaster's brakes squealed as we came to a halt. I rotated the turret to full beam and opened the sliding doors of the turret. My plight was then most obvious to the small group of aircrew NCOs that had gathered to see us take-off. One of these was Sergeant Fletcher, Flight Lieutenant Eames' flight engineer, who soon jovially organised and helped supply and fit the replacement seat parachute. This meant that with the aid of four very amused but stoical NCOs, including Sergeant Fletcher, I was lifted bodily out of the turret, still with engines running. The open chute was removed safely without it opening fully in the slipstream, by means of many willing hands. Then, with the new chute and harness speedily clipped on, I was lifted bodily back into the turret in a sitting position, feet first, all in less than three minutes! Finally, with a wave and my verbal thanks, hardly heard over the roar of four Rolls-Royce Merlins, we taxied away, turning onto the main runway nearby and took off for Dessau, still in very good time! (Flight Lieutenant Eames and crew, including Sergeant Fletcher, failed to return from Lutzkendorf on 4 April.)

The diary entry doesn't mention that eighteen Lancasters (3.4 per cent) of the force were lost, mostly to night fighters *en route*.

Thirteen aircraft from 626 Squadron took part (including Flying Officer Barnes and crew in the spare) and all returned safely. Our neighbouring 12 Squadron lost Flying Officer Belot and crew, of which Sergeant Burbidge was mid-upper gunner. The crew were on their thirty-first operational sortie.

Len Burbidge (Sergeant Burbidge's brother, now in New Zealand) informed me that his brother's Lancaster hit high-tension cables and came down at Neckartenzlingen (25 km south of Stuttgart), Germany. All the crew were killed. We presumed this was on the return trip and may well have been due to losing altitude possibly through icing up. They could also have been flying low to avoid a fighter.

Later on, we were to hear through the grapevine that our former training colleagues, Flying Officer Paley and crew of 576 Squadron, were also lost at Dessau. The crew would have been near the end of their extended tour of thirty-six operational bomber sorties. It was yet another very sad loss.

8 March – Operations on again. We are not on. Sixteen 626 Lancasters took off 17.33, target Kassel. All returned safely by 01.18. Saw 'Ghost Ship' and 'Rookies in Burma' at station cinema.

9 March – Harmonised our aircraft 'Willie Two', rear turret U/S, harmonisation useless! Left hand outer, left hand inner gun and sight OK. Right hand outer, right hand inner gun and sight unserviceable. Cleaned guns, nothing doing for us today.

10 March – Nothing doing today, Battle Order out for tomorrow morning, a daylight op, flying with Squadron Commander. Spent afternoon in billet.

11 March – Called at 07.45, meal 08.15, briefing 09.15. Target Essen. Aircraft 'William Two', Wing Commander Molesworth DFC AFC. Fuel load 1650 gals. Bomb load 1 cookie (4000 lb) and 16 500 lb HEs. Bombing height 19,000'.
　Rear turret U/S on take-off. Palmer firing gear inoperative, insufficient hydraulic pressure! We took off in spite of this at 11.30. Guns and turret OK when airborne, assumed sight had been attended to. No way of checking before take-off. ETA at target 15.00 hrs. Bombed blue smoke puffs. 10/10 cloud for the whole of trip. Very slight flak, ineffective. 3 airborne explosions seen. [Three Lancasters were lost from other Squadrons.] No fighters other than our escort, which by the way got some flak for a change. 200 escort aircraft, Spitfires and Mustangs. As we left target, smoke was coming through the cloud 7/8000'. All 626 aircraft returned safely – from a total of 1079 aircraft including PFF plus Fighter Escort. Interrogated, meal and rest.

This was the last attack by the RAF on Essen. The bombing was very accurate.

12 March – Made preparations for leave. Another operation on today – Dortmund. 15 Lancasters took off at 13.13 (including spare). Flying Officer Enciso-y-Seiglie failed to take off due to electrical failure. All returned by 19.05. Nothing much doing.

13 March – Received news of my promotion to Flight Sergeant. WEF [With Effect From] 12/3/45, pay 9/- per day [Squadron records indicate an earlier date for promotion]. Another operation on tonight. 12 626 Lancasters took off for Dahlbusch Benzol Plant at Gelsenkirchen at 17.36. All returned safely by 23.56. Left camp at 12.45. Caught 1.15pm bus into Lincoln. Had a meal at the Milk Bar and caught 2.50 to Derby. Home at 10.45.

14–20 March LEAVE – Had quite a good leave. Visited all my old pals, decided not to see Edna at weekend. Wrote air mails to Les and Bill Bayliss. Saw various films, all very good. 'White Cliffs of Dover' (Robert Donat) at the Forum, 'Laura' (Gene Tierney) at the Scala and 'Count of Monte Cristo' at the Forum.

21 March – Left home after dinner, caught 2.07 train into Birmingham. There I met Bert, we caught the 3.08 to Derby. At Derby the Nottingham train was waiting for us, the same occurred at Nottingham with the Lincoln train. We arrived in Lincoln at 7 pm. We had a few drinks and caught the 9.20 bus back to camp.

22 March – Reported to 'flights' at 09.15. Put on training flight as a 'spare', together with our Flight Engineer. Practice bombing with Flight Lieutenant Grindrod and crew. We came down just before dinner – found that our crew is on the Battle Order – mining tonight!

'Run up' and practice dinghy drill at 14.30. Our Bert was really pleased about the dinghy drill – saying that 'Dickie is a cheerful beggar isn't he'. Aircraft 'Willie Two', meal 18.15, briefing 19.00, target Sands Bay –– Oslo Fjord, Norway. Fuel load 2000 gallons, mines 6 x 1800 lb (VP). Height of release 12,000 ft. T/O 21.30, air speed indicator U/S on take-off. Also navigator's and air bomber's ASIs U/S. Decided to abort, fired off reds and flashed aircraft identity letter 'WWW' on downward identity light. We considered going to Carnaby emergency landing ground.

No spare aircraft took off, so the Skipper asked if we would prefer to return to base or press on to the target. We all agreed to carry on to target. 10/10 cloud over North Sea. H2S went U/S as soon as it was turned on. Gee went U/S over Norway, carried on using only dead reckoning navigation (which really means, that if you don't get it right you're *dead*). Fortunately, the cloud broke to clear near target area; our air bomber doing the map reading, brought our Lancaster to the target. Mines released visually. I saw them go down, parachutes opened OK. Two mines I *believe* landed on land and exploded. Later, Fred assured me they would not explode on impact! The rest went into the fjord, as intended. There was no opposition at all, at least for us. I saw some light tracer and heavy flak going up some 10–20 miles astern directed at other Lancasters mining. The only other aircraft we saw were three Lancasters, which crossed our track astern of us at 2000 yards visual, just before the target was reached, Bert had alerted me already to the three Lancasters on Fishpond prior to sighting at 3000 yards range. [The Fishpond was obviously still functionable, whereas the H2S wasn't, as a navigation aid!]

We returned to base safely and after waiting *about an hour* on the circuit we were diverted to Carnaby – emergency runway 3000 yds long. Crew took up crash positions but we landed safely. After landing at Carnaby we were offered a double rum, Mac had a double double – he had mine! He'd earned it, so had Dickie! I told Mac he owed his rear gunner a double orange in the Sergeants' Mess! Our interrogation took place some time later after further delay. A meal of egg, fried bread, bacon and beans followed, and then to bed. Our Skipper 'mucked in' with us.

Twenty-one Lancasters and eight Mosquitoes took part with no losses.

An amusing incident occurred just after landing. We'd just parked our Lancaster 'Willie Two' as directed by the Control Tower, when a flying officer engineer arrived. The first thing the officer did was to check that the pitot head cover had been removed (i.e., before take-off at Wickenby)! This was a great mistake, especially when we were lucky enough to have a squadron leader as aircraft captain. Skipper had just come down the aircraft step ladder and observed the inspection of the pitot head.

He heard the officer say 'I thought you'd still have the pitot cover on!'

'I beg your pardon,' said Skipper. 'Who do you think we are, bunch of idiots? We've not been to Oslo and back without an airspeed indicator just because we've forgotten to take the b— pitot head cover off! My engineer has more sense than that. We'd already checked the goddamn thing long ago. So stop messing about and get us some transport for Christ's sake.'

The officer went crimson. He wouldn't have known what to do next, except that Skipper had already told him!

'Right away Sir, sorry Sir.'

The rest of us nearly 'piddled' ourselves (and who wouldn't after seven hours twenty-four minutes' airborne). As bystanders, six sergeants and flight sergeants could hardly conceal their mirth at the luckless officer's plight!

23 March – Got up at 11.00. Had a cup of tea, checked up on our escape aid kits etc. 12.00 went out to our aircraft (which is now serviceable). 12.55 took off, landed at Wickenby 13.30. Dinner 14.15. The boys went in daylight to Bremen. Spent the afternoon in the hut resting, went to station cinema at night.

We were to find on return to Wickenby from our mining sortie, that no spare aircraft took off in spite of our signals directly over base on the previous night. The excuse was that Flying Control *thought* we were an aircraft from another squadron!

24 March – Nothing doing for us, spent day in billet. Went to Wragby at night for a few drinks.

25 March – Nothing doing again for us, although the boys went to Bremen in daylight again. Spent day in billet, went to Wragby for usual drink at 'The Adam and Eve'.

26 March – Nothing doing again. Spent part day in billet, went to cinema tonight 'See Here Private Macquire'.

27 March – Cleaned guns. On Battle Order with Wing Commander, target Paderborn. Meal 11.00, briefing 12.00, aircraft 'Oboe Two', height 17,000'. Fuel load 1650 gallons, bomb load 4000 lb cookie and 16 x 500 lb HEs. T/O 14.30, H-hour 17.30. 10/10 cloud over target. No flak or fighters. Escort 72 Mustangs and 38 Thunderbolts. Bombed green smoke puffs. Temperature pretty grim, almost froze to death. No aircraft lost. Arrived back safely 20.00 hrs. Interrogated, bed at 9.00, early call tomorrow, we are on!

28 March – Called at 06.30, meal put back to 10.15, briefing 11.18, target Erfurt. Ops cancelled at crew room. Spent afternoon in billet. Saw 'Captain Courageous' at station cinema – very good. Early call tomorrow.

29 March – Call 07.30, meal 08.15, briefing put back to 10.30, target Bielefeld. Ops cancelled at dispersal. Attempted to harmonise 'Willie Two', both right hand gun mountings of rear turret – harmonisation useless. Reported fault.

30 March – Put on Battle Order, mining, fuel load 1850 gals (possibly Kattegat or Skagerrak). Trip cancelled due to weather. Aircraft 'Peter Two'.

31 March – Cleaned guns. No ops. 626 Squadron aircraft went to Hamburg on previous day, none missing. 8 Lancasters and 3 Halifaxes from other squadrons were lost to *Luftwaffe* day fighters. Went to Wragby for a few drinks.

1 April – Sunday, nothing doing. All Skippers were given a 'gen' talk by the Station Commander – Group Captain P Haynes DFC – 626 and 12 Squadrons. Will be maintained on a peacetime basis as semi-operational squadrons, more bullshit – 8 hr day etc!

2 April – CO's parade 08.30. Cleaned guns. On Battle Order for mining trip, fuel 1850 gals. Cancelled after briefing. Took guns out to 'Peter Two'. Went to station cinema to see 'For whom the bell tolls', very good show.

3 April – Took cleaning rods etc. to Lancaster 'Peter Two' and cleaned guns and then wrapped them in a blanket (the guns I mean) to keep out the dust. [Author's note: a most unusual practice at 626, cleaning guns at the aircraft.) Thirteen aircraft from Wickenby on ops – bombing Nordhausen. Flying Officer Driver and crew failed to return. Flight Lieutenant Gilmore and crew completed their tour. Mining crews standing by (that included us — worse luck).

Cycled to Wragby in afternoon, got a card for Mother's birthday on 5 April.

Mining crews on standby, were allowed to go to the camp cinema. If they were required, a message would be flashed on the cinema screen: 'Mining crews report to Briefing Room'.

4 April – Ops on. Standing by, flying in 'Willie Two' with our own Skipper. Meal 18.15, briefing 19.00, take-off 21.00, target an oil refinery at Lutzkendorf. Bombing height 12,000', bomb load 1 x 4000 lb cookie, 10 x 500 lb and 1 x 250 lb HEs, fuel 2095 gals. Weather cloudy at base for take-off and return, ten tenths cloud over France, but clear over target. H-hr 01.30, bombed red TIs. Flak was moderate/heavy to intense/heavy – no searchlights or fighters seen. Our bombs went down on TIs according to Fred our bomb aimer. Oil fires seen for 70 miles. Returned safely and landed at 04.11. Two aircraft missing from 626 and 1 from 12 Squadron. Ours were Flight Lieutenant Eames and crew in 'Baker Two' (great friends of ours) and Flying Officer Reid and crew in 'Yorker Two' (new lads – 3rd op). Meal and interrogation followed by bed at 07.30.

We arrived at the target early and while orbiting, a PFF Lancaster on our starboard beam took a direct hit from flak, exploding and showering the night with ignited Wanganui flares and TIs.

5 April – Mother's birthday. Got up at 16.15, tea at 17.30. Went to cinema and saw 'The Mark of Zorro' – Tyrone Power, quite good entertainment.

6 April – Commanding Officer's inspection of our site – now 5 site. 09.15 roll call. 10.15 Went up on Lucero, flying with Wingco Molesworth and Flight Lieutenant Oram DFC and Bar for an hour. Went to Mess for dinner. Sergeant Whitby – mid-upper gunner of Flying Officer Patterson's crew – has returned to the Squadron after being POW for 6 weeks – shot down by Ju 88 over Dortmund 20/2/45. He was wounded and didn't remember baling out, the rear gunner Sergeant Rutt was killed in combat.
Collected laundry and had a shower. Tea at 16.30. Went to camp cinema in the evening 'Wing and a Prayer'.

7 April – Nothing doing for us, ops were put on for bombing and mining, both scrubbed just before briefing. Cleaned guns. Went to Wragby for a drink with Bert and another WOP, 'Rusty' Hyams. They took two Yorkshire girls home – much to my disgust! (They didn't seem to like me and they thought I was joking when I told them I was *Yorkshire* born).

8 April – Sunday, egg for breakfast. Roll call 09.15, Squadron photo was taken. Nothing doing again, went to the 'Adam & Eve' at Wragby with Mac and Stan.

9 April – Got up at 07.15, Commanding Officer's parade at 08.30. Nothing doing for us. We had a day off. Went to Lincoln for usual show and feed etc. The boys went to Kiel, bombs and mines.
Four aircraft took off for mining and twelve for bombing. Flying Officer McHarg returned early with port outer feathered. Flying

Officer Fanner returned with port inner engine feathered. Flight Lieutenant Tremblay landed at Carnaby with ASI U/S.

The mines were laid in Kiel harbour while bombing of Kiel was in progress, pilots reported a good concentrated attack.

10 April – Got up at 08.00, brekker at 08.30. Went to 'flights' at 09.30, harmonised guns in 'Willie Two'. Ops on, we are not on. Afternoon off, went to pictures at camp cinema 'Make your own bed'.

Fourteen Lancasters were detailed for an attack on Plauen. Flying Officer White and crew completed their tour.

11 April – Brought our guns in for cleaning. Nothing else doing. The boys went to Plauen – near Leipzig last night, synthetic oil.

A tour is now down to 33, may bring it down to 30 yet! Went to camp cinema and saw 'Road to Frisco' – Ann Sheridan, George Raft, Humphrey Bogart and Ida Lupino, very good film. I had seen it before but I didn't realise until I got in, but it was good enough to see again. Supper at 21.15, sandwiches and coffee.

12 April – Nothing doing today in the way of ops. Went to Intelligence Library for half an hour. Then 11.15 pay parade £4-10-00 (£4.50). 14.00 reported to 'flights' for training, supply dropping practice with sand bags (for relief of POW camps) also high level bombing at 3000' – 8 smoke bombs, four Lucero approaches and one landing. Wrote letters in the evening.

13 April – Cleaned guns, nothing doing for us. Some of our lads went over to Kiel again, four Lancasters on mining op. Saw Bing Crosby in 'Going my way' at station cinema – very good film.

Wing Commander Molesworth finished 3rd tour of ops, replaced by Wing Commander Dixon as Commanding Officer of 626 Squadron.

14 April – Battle Order out for daylight, scrubbed just before briefing. Fred our bomb aimer was on as a 'spare'. Nothing doing for us again, getting a bit 'cheesed' not doing ops. Battle Order out for a night op. Squadron went to Potsdam – 18 miles from Berlin. Went to Wragby with Bert for a few drinks – nice stuff – Youngers IPA.

14 aircraft detailed, 12 took off including 3 carrying 2nd pilots, one of these was Flight Lieutenant Stan Key taking Wing

Commander Dixon as 2nd pilot. 3 Lancasters were withdrawn, those with *first* op crews, just before take-off. [The first op crews were withdrawn because Potsdam was so close to Berlin defences!] These were Flight Sergeants Chancellor and Greene and Pilot Officer Gould. (I gather the 'spare' also took off.) Flying Officer Vidler returned early due to his wireless operator being ill.

15 April – Got up at 07.45, rather early for a change. Had fried egg on toast, cornflakes and milk, marmalade, a very nice breakfast. Spent morning in the billet writing letters etc. Hope to have a shower later on. Managed to get a shower just before dinner. Nothing doing in afternoon. Spent rest of day in billet. Operations detailed for 18 Lancasters, cancelled later.

16 April – Got up at 07.10, breakfast at 07.40. Group Captain Haynes, Station Commander's parade at 08.30. Our Squadron was inspected – Peter our mid-upper gunner got a strip torn off for needing a hair cut, although he had it done only 2 days ago along with myself, he always has flowing locks and often looks like a professor!

Nothing on for the rest of the day. Spent the afternoon reading outside the hut in the nice warm sunshine. Continued reading at night in the Mess and finished the book *Under the Red Robe* – good.

Battle Order out for tomorrow, daylight, flying with Wing Commander Dixon. Call at 05.45, 21 Lancasters detailed.

17 April – No call, got up as usual, time 08.10. Breakfast and flying meal 08.30. Times were changed, briefing at 10.00, target Heligoland, 1000 aircraft with escort of 22 Squadrons of Mustangs and Spitfires. Bomb load 12 x 1000 lb HEs, 4 x 500 lb HEs, fuel load 1350 gals, bombing ht 19,000', aircraft 'Tare Two'. Brand new kite, latest type of rear turret FN 121 Mk IIc gyro sight. Equipment on top line, Palmer firing system first class! T/O 12.50, H-Hr 15.00. Times altered while at aircraft dispersal points, another hour added on. Sandwiches and coffee brought round. Operation finally scrubbed. A bit of a bind I must say, better luck next time.

Nothing doing for the rest of day. Spent afternoon in billet reading again. Nothing else to do! Early call expected tomorrow 06.00, we hope? Again 21 Lancasters on Battle Order.

18 April – Called at 06.00, meal 06.45, briefing 07.30. Target Heligoland (German Naval Base and Airfield) with Wing

Commander Dixon. Fuel 1350 gals, bomb load 12 x 1000 lb and 4 x 500 lb HEs. Bombing ht 19,000' – 1000 aircraft took part, 12 Squadrons of Mustangs and 10 Squadrons of Spitfires as escort. T/O 10.20, S/C 10.50, H-hr 12.30 + 25. Marking, red and yellow TIs. No flak of any strength (most seen was 6 puffs), no fighters, apparently the first wave of Halifaxes that were due to bomb the airfield had done a good job! Also the second wave of Halifaxes again had put the AA guns out of action. The attack was very successful, bombing very concentrated, a very small percentage went in the sea. Target was only 2000 yds x 800 yds – absolutely obliterated by bombs bursting, huge columns of smoke rising and one large explosion shook the whole island. A terrific sight, well worth seeing. I don't think I've seen such a wizard attack, doubt very much if there are any living persons on the island now. (Photos were very good as we later discovered we were within 400 yds of our aiming point [theoretical centre of stick of bombs].) Returned to base and landed at 16.00 (having had to wait about an hour just flying round the circuit waiting for our turn to land). 'Tare Two' behaved very well, first time it flew on this station – wizard kite. Going out I saw a patch of oil on the water with six yellow dots, with fluorescent dye trails, presumably an aircraft down with the crew 'baled out' and in the sea, quite distinctive Mae Wests. Two aircraft were circling the area – looked like a Fleet Air Arm Firefly and Barracuda and a white trail, probably Air Sea Rescue launch was making towards them, no dinghy seen! Interrogation and meal 17.00. Spent evening in billet – a good day's work!

During the 'run in' to the target, because of the small size of the island, the close concentration of so many Lancasters became quite hazardous. This hazard increased on the actual bomb run. One Lancaster, with a red and white chequered Polish emblem beneath the cockpit, came close to our tail, possibly 30 feet higher, no more. He was approximately 10 to 20 feet from our port tail fin. I watched in utter amazement, with eyes and mouth wide open, at the open bomb doors, displaying the load of 1000-lb HE bombs. We were now both on the bomb run. It was of little use now to advise our captain, Wing Commander Dixon, who was, with Fred, our bomb aimer, concentrating on our own bomb run. I was transfixed by the closeness of the Polish Lancaster. I heard Fred giving bomb run corrections and finally saying 'Bombs gone Skipper' to the Wing Commander. Simultaneously, the 1000-lb bombs began to drop out of the bomb bay of the Polish Lancaster! Seemingly three or four, slightly to port of our port rudder and then as the bomber moved behind and across our path, three or four bombs followed, all at regular and steady intervals, just clear of our tail turret. The remaining three or four 1000-pounders managed to clear our starboard rudder. The Polish Lancaster was no more that 20 feet astern and 30 feet up when the bomb aimer ordered their bomb doors closed! So much for daylight bombing!

There were no losses from 626 Squadron, although three Halifaxes were lost from other squadrons. Twenty aircraft from 626 Squadron bombed; one returned early due to engine failure. Two 626 Squadron Lancasters landed at Carnaby, one with battle damage from falling bombs (Warrant Officer Vallance) and one with undercarriage malfunction (Pilot Officer Gould).

19 April – On training today, aircraft 'Tare Two', Lucero approaches, air to sea firing and fighter affiliation using the Mk IIc gyro-sight. Had some good practice shooting at sea gulls (didn't hit any). Fighter affiliation was good fun for me, our attacker was a Spitfire VB. Peter was sick again, unfortunately, so I got 'double time' on the 'corkscrews'! We had a meal at 15.30. Spent the afternoon in the Mess, went to Wragby for a few drinks in the evening.

20 April – Brought our guns in for cleaning. Nothing doing for us in the afternoon. Battle Order came out at 17.30, we were supposed to be on, but cancelled later, owing to Lord Trenchard, Marshal of RAF, visiting RAF Wickenby. Call 02.45 tomorrow.

21 April – Ops cancelled just after briefing – would have been Berchtesgaden. 10.30 assembled in Briefing Room, Lord Trenchard gave us a talk on the effects of our bombing. Op put on, call 03.30 tomorrow.

22 April – No call, ops postponed until 13.00 for briefing. Spent the morning in billet, went down for dinner at 12.30. Saw the Skipper outside the Sergeants' Mess, he said I was to go to briefing as a 'spare bod'. Had dinner and went down, but I found Skipper had made a mistake, as it was a mid-upper gunner they wanted. Target Bremen. Peter on as 'spare bod' flying with Flight Lieutenant Benoit.

Peter managed to show his appreciation of flying as a 'spare' by firing a burst from his twin Brownings, just as they were taxiing out to take off. The gun firing cables had become caught behind the armour plate mounted between the guns.

Spent the afternoon in the billet, finished my book *Flowers for the Judge*.

The boys came back at 20.00, brought their bombs back owing to cloud over target and the closeness of our troops – 3000 yds away. Peter back OK. One aircraft was shot down and a member of 12 Squadron wounded. I understand from later reports that other squadrons were able to bomb later on, as the cloud had moved away. Wrote to Cliff. Went to cinema 'The Bridge of Luis Rey'!

23 April – No Group Captain's parade for a change. Nothing doing today.

24 April – Cleaned guns. Went into Lincoln with Fred, did some shopping, saw a variety show at the theatre. Had two good meals and a drink. Returned to camp on 9.30 pm bus. Battle Order for tomorrow – call at 00.30 – worse luck. (The time of call, I mean.)

25 April – Called 01.30, meal 02.00, briefing 02.30. Flying with Wing Commander Dixon, aircraft 'Tare Two'. Target Berchtesgaden, bombing height 18,000', fuel full tanks 2154 gals. Bomb load 1 x 4000 lb, 4 x 1000 lb HEs and 1 x 500 lb, 1 x 250 lb HE. T/O 05.00, SC 05.35, H-hr 09.30. Good bombing, attack late starting so we did one orbit. Flak moderate to heavy/to slight to heavy – not directly over target, some Lancasters of 5 Group took 12,000 lb Tallboy bombs. Fighter escort of 13 squadrons of USAA.F and RAF Mustangs. Very good cover, best of escorts I have seen yet. Two USAAF Mustangs very close, pilots waving. Beautiful scenery en route particularly the Bavarian Alps. Objectives – SS Barracks (our target) and 'The Eagle's Nest' (Hitler's mountain retreat), for the Tallboys. Returned safely, landed at 13.10, we were the first back from 'B' Flight. Interrogation 13.45, meal 15.00. Pretty poor, no egg, just ordinary dinner, warmed up! Played hell about it, but got nowhere. Lousy show I think. Nothing to eat for 13 hours and only an hour's sleep in 36! An operational trip of 8.15 hours and they gave us a warmed-up dinner! The very cheek of it. Some of these ground hods want to get some flying hours in and see what it's like – I doubt if they would go again. Same with the

WAAF catering staff. Just because we refused the meal at first they made nasty cracks about us not being men! And that we didn't think of them and all the extra work they would have to do if we wanted an operational meal. Also, that we were *always wanting something special*! What did they think we had been doing for the last 8 or 9 hours? I know, we go on ops just for the fun of it! They forget that some crews don't always come back! England expects! England expects too bloody much!

Went to the billet and had a couple of hours' sleep, missed my tea, went to the cinema and saw 'Up in Mabel's Room', pretty poor. Bed at 10.15.

The Wing Commander came to the Sergeants' Mess in answer to our request regarding the dinner! He simply agreed with the Catering Officer and ordered us to go and eat the ordinary midday meal. It was a poor anti-climax for us all! We, all the NCOs, felt the Wing Commander had let us down on this occassion. However, apart from one other incident to come, in June, Wing Commander Dixon often displayed a great deal of common sense.

It was the last major raid by Bomber Command: 359 Lancasters were involved. Two Lancasters failed to return. No losses were suffered by 626 Squadron, but two aircraft failed to take off on this final bombing sortie, although no reasons were given for this.

On the way home from Bertchtesgaden we'd overtaken a Lancaster flying on three engines. A stream of white vapour came from the starboard outer engine. Later, I observed four Mustangs providing a close escort. I felt relieved, as we didn't like leaving another bomber in difficulties, over enemy territory.

26 April – Nothing doing this morning. Had a talk by the Wing Commander – he wants more bull – he'll be lucky to get it, the NCOs are almost in revolt. Our Skipper gave us some gen about 626 Lancasters being used to bring back repatriated POW from camps in Germany. May be used in conjunction with supply dropping. Pay parade at 11.15, £4.12s. [£4.60]. Nothing doing in the afternoon. Mess meeting 13.30, usual promises about improvements, hope for the best. Wrote to Cliff.

27 April – Battle Order out. We are on with our Skipper. Lecture at 10.00 in main Briefing Room on POW repatriation by Lancasters. Briefing 10.30, fuel load 1800 gals, ht 1000–3000'. Land at Brussels, Belgium and return with 24 British ex-POW. Take-off 12.35, arrived

Brussels 14.10. Ex-POW not arrived as we were not expected. The op was scrubbed as we were on the circuit at Brussels. We waited around for 3 hours in a marquee, where the Church Army canteen kindly offered us tea and biscuits! Brussels airfield is a TAF drome with Mosquitos and Mitchells. Also, a few wrecks lay around mostly Ju 188, Me 110, Fw 190 and even a battered old Wimpey.

The ex-POW arrived about 16.30. We received our quota of 24, issued them with Mae Wests and 'puke' bags. They seemed very docile and pleased to get to England, most of them had been POW for 4–5 years, some of them seemed very old guys too! T/O 17.30, arrived at RAF Dunsfold and disembarked all the ex-POW. Returned to base OK. Interrogated as usual. Had a very good meal, 2 eggs, tongue, toast and beans. Bed 22.30.

28 April – Nothing doing for us. A number of Lancasters went to Brussels again for ex-POW. Spent afternoon in billet. Went to station cinema in evening 'Patrick the Great' – Donald O'Connor.

29 April – Nothing for us today. 626 Lancasters went supply dropping in Holland. Spent afternoon reading. Spent evening packing for leave, due tomorrow, I hope?

30 April – Got up early, 07.30. Made bed and prepared for leaving. Pay parade 11.00, £3.0.0. Drew our passes at 12.15. Caught the 13.15 bus into Lincoln. Had dinner at the Rainbow Milk Bar. 14.50 took Derby train from LMS Lincoln, 13/10 (69p). Arrived home at 20.45 having been able to catch the 19.40 train from Birmingham.

1 May–7 May (7 Days' Leave) – Cliff arrived on Tuesday afternoon about 5 pm. Stayed until Thursday. We had a good time together, swapping yarns about ops etc. Went dancing on Wednesday night – Savoy (Radford). I managed to scrape up enough courage to have two dances (my very first attempts). We saw two films together at the Forum – 'The Mask of Demitrius' – and at the Scala – 'The Woman in the Window' – both very good. Also we had a few drinks together. The rest of the leave went quickly, I visited Sterling Metals and the Technical College. Saw my old friends, also I met Ted Eaves, my old pal from the Humber Ltd.

Friday night I saw 'Arsenic and Old Lace' at the Empire. Also 'Madonna of the Seven Moons' at the Gaumont on Saturday, both very good indeed.

Sunday went for a walk to Dad's allotment, took Judy our dog. Monday went down town and bought a model kit of a Lancaster.

Tuesday – VE Day. Had to return to camp as usual, met Bert at Birmingham. Arrived in Lincoln at 6.45 pm. Went for a drink at 8.15 pm to the 'William IV'. Saw our friends, Mr & Mrs Baldwin of Fossbank, Lincoln. Caught 9.30 bus for camp. We didn't see much in the way of celebrations!

9 May – Nothing doing in the way of flying. Peter hasn't returned from leave. Went into Lincoln at night. Went to our usual pub. Went home to supper with our friends at Fossbank. Took a taxi back to camp at 1.00 am.

Peter returned within two days. He'd been taken ill on leave; his absence was covered by a civilian doctor's certificate.

10 May – Cleaned guns, probably for the last time as they are not being carried any more! POW and 'Spam' trips are now being counted as ops! ['Spam' trips was the slang term for Operation *Manna*, which was supply dropping to relieve the food shortages in Holland at that time.] Our score is now 27.

Went to camp cinema and saw 'Desert Song'.

It was around this time that three of the crew put in applications to be considered for a commission. One other crewmember tore up his application when he found another air gunner reading his application in the Gunnery Leaders' Office. Peter Bone was the only crewmember who was granted a commission. In a few weeks time, Peter would become Pilot Officer EP Bone. Mac and Bert didn't apply for their own personal reasons. Both of the latter, would become warrant officers in due course.

11 May – Nothing doing for our crew. The Squadron went to Brussels for POW. We went around to collect up guns and ammo from dispersals and returned them to the Armoury. Went into Lincoln again. Went for a few drinks then to the dance at the Drill Hall.

12 May – Nothing doing at all today. Going to Lincoln tonight. Cleaned tunic buttons and boots in afternoon and then had a sleep.

Took 6.15 pm bus to Lincoln, went to the 'Steam Packet' and 'William IV', had supper at Fossbank.

We really appreciated the hospitality of the Baldwins. Bert and I had often visited the 'William IV' pub in the past but we had missed quite a few visits prior to VE Day. Mrs Baldwin became concerned about our 'lost' visits and consequently thought 'We had gone under' (to use her own terminology). The people of Lincoln 'thought the world' of Bomber Command aircrews at that time!

13 May – CO's Church Parade 10.00 am. Nothing doing for rest of the day. Going to the 'Adam & Eve' at Wragby tonight.

14 May – Training flight, low level, cross country. HLB – 3000' aerial photography, Lucero blind approach and landings (last detail cancelled owing to equipment being unserviceable).

15 May – Nothing doing again, more 'Bullshit' coming into being. AOC's thanks to No. 1 Group: all aircrew (officers and NCOs) to parade twice a day for roll call – 08.45 & 14.00 march to 'flights'. Marched back at 12.00 & 16.30. Good show I must say! 'Our heartfelt thanks to Bomber Command'!

16 May – Nothing doing except attending new parades and roll call. Getting cheesed off, applied to get screened i.e. finish operations, get leave and go on instruction or other ground work.

Wing Commander Dixon made a comment to the whole Squadron that instead of being properly screened and becoming instructors in our particular trade, most would be made into 'Butchers and Bakers'. (These were the exact words used. No disrespect was shown or intended to these valuable tradesmen.) We took no notice, but later realised how true his statement was! He was referring to our possible future training for ground trades. This seemed a good 'skive' to some aircrew NCOs. If we had any sense, we should have stayed on flying duties of some sort. Perhaps Wing Commander Dixon had more sense than the rest of us. As it was, at that time, we were completely unaware what could happen once we'd left 626 Squadron.

18 May – Nothing doing. Spent evening in Lincoln at the 'Steam Packet' and 'William IV'. Saw our friends at Fossbank and later went to supper. Taxi back at 01.30.

Taxi fare to Wickenby was £2-0-0 to £2-10/- [£2 to £2.50]. We shared the cost with other airmen to make a total of four or five passengers.

19 May – Went to Lincoln at 16.30 pm, had tea at the Baldwins. Came back on 19.30 bus. Battle Order for tomorrow, early call for POW repatriation flight?

20 May – Sunday. Nothing doing, standing by for POW. Spent afternoon and evening doing some more to my model Lancaster. It is to be UMA2 in memory of our old friend 'Able Two', which took a direct hit and blew up over Merseburg.

21 May – CO's parade at 08.30, nothing doing for the rest of day.

22 May – Nothing doing but more bull. Stood by for POW. Went to 'Adam & Eve' at Wragby for a drink or two. We went to a dance afterwards.

It was here that I met Alma Wilkinson. She was a very young and attractive girl from Wragby. It wasn't long before I was invited to meet all her family, I was treated exceptionally well. They seemed to think a lot of the Wickenby RAF personnel.

23 May – Roll call 08.45, new gen out. All Dominion personnel are to be screened and sent back to their own country. Crews to be shuffled around. Spare bods to be posted to other squadrons. We won't be screened worse luck, staying on for 3 or 4 months! 09.30 our crew on POW trip, taking ground personnel to Brussels airport. Take-off 10.30, arrived 12.00. Spent an hour in village nearby, had two glasses of Belgian beer, 5 & 10 francs per glass. Stan, our flight engineer had some Belgian money so we were OK. Take-off 17.00, returned to base, landed at 18.30. Meal of egg, beef and pickled cabbage, tea and marmalade.

24 May – Nothing much doing these days. Hoping to get screened soon? Seems unlikely. Did some more work on my Lancaster model.

26–29 May – Nothing doing but odd jobs, fortunately I managed to steer clear of them. Going on 48 hr pass tomorrow.

30 May – Our 48 hr postponed until tomorrow. Decided not to go home owing to time it takes in travelling. Going to Nottingham with Bert and Mac.

31 May – Left camp at 3.00 pm, caught 3.15 bus into Lincoln. Had a meal and then took the 5 o'clock to Derby, getting off at Nottingham. Spent the evening in the 'George & Dragon'. Slept at the YMCA.

    Next morning, I found that my Winged Bullet Badge, a souvenir from No. 3 Bombing & Gunnery School Macdonald, Canada, had been stolen.

1 June – Got up at 09.00, brekker at YMCA 09.30. Had a good look around the town. Had a drink at opening time at the 'Horse & Groom' and then went for dinner. Spent afternoon at the 'Flicks'. Tea at 'Regal Café'. Met two nice girls, a redhead and a brunette. Bert and I took them to supper and then to their train. Made a date for tomorrow! Mac made a date with another very attractive redheaded girl too! (Really super she was! Mac was too quick off the mark for me!)

2 June – Saw girls at 11 am. More drinks and dinner, followed by cinema and then another drink. Caught the train back home to Wickenby at 8 pm.

3 June Sunday – Skipper informed us that we were finished at Wickenby, screened at last! Made out our leave passes for 14 days, starting tomorrow.

    Skipper Lane had fallen out with Wing Commander Dixon over not agreeing to the removal of individual aircraft insignia like 'Sisco's Scamps' (Flying Officer Enciso-y-Seiglie's crew insignia), so we *all* got posted! (The Lancaster was UMS2, i.e. 'S' for Sugar and for 'Sisco'. Skipper Lane wanted these artistic transfers to be retained as they had been a morale booster!)

4 June – Left for Nottingham again. Met a very nice girl in the 'Rutland Arms'.

4–8 June – Leave in Nottingham. We kept in touch with all the girls we'd met before, in the 'Horse and Groom'.

8 June – Afternoon arrived home.

9–18 June – Leave in Coventry.

19 June – Got up at 08.00, had breakfast. Reported to Discip Office at 09.30. On the way to 'flights', Group Captain Haynes, Station Commander, pulled us up. We were all put on a charge for not marching down and failing to be present at the 08.45 parade! However, Wing Commander Dixon let us off owing to our 'operational record' (such as *he* said), we only did two ops with him!

At the Discip Office we were told that we were posted on indefinite leave, pending posting to ACAC Catterick. Spent afternoon getting 'Cleared'.

20 June – Got our leave passes and packed our kit. Leaving tomorrow at 08.00.

21 June – Took transport to Snelland Station, made arrangement for my cycle to be returned by Goods Train to Coventry. Left at 08.30. 'Goodbye 626 Squadron.'

22–25 June – LEAVE.

CHAPTER 17

'Screened' at Last

Ground duties; the Bomber Crew Rapport Continues

26 June – Telegram, to report to Air Crew Re-allocation Centre, RAF Catterick. What a dump it was too, from the re-allocation point of view. However, we enjoyed the privilege of 'pre-war peacetime accommodation'.

27 June–3 July – Spent the week at Catterick, mainly attending interviews, tests and kit inspections.
   My choice for ground duties:

1. Airfield Controller
2. Flying Control Assistant
3. Driver, Motor Transport
4. Clerk, Special Duties

Stan and I spent most of our time visiting Darlington. We found a good pub and a nearby dance hall. Also we visited Catterick Races with Fred. One cheerful experience too, was the various types of aircrew one met at Catterick. My nearest (next) bed contained a Warrant Officer Navigator who had been regularly navigating and flying in Mosquitoes to Berlin with the Light Night Striking Force, carrying a 4000-lb cookie on most nights, weather permitting. All good stuff! He seemed to have a high regard for Heavy Bomber Crews.
   The interviews, which we attended individually, were really a re-selection board. Two aircrew officers, of minimum flight lieutenant rank, conducted the proceedings. They asked questions about our

individual operational experience, how many bomber ops and also how many other sorties we'd flown, such as our Nickel, Diversion, three Bull's-eyes and POW repatriation flights.

I was asked if I wanted to continue flying. My reply was 'Only on a second tour in the Far East against Japan.' (It sounds rubbish now, but it was sincere at that time.) I was informed that as I was tour expired I couldn't fly operationally again for approximately six months, which was the normal rest period after being 'screened'.

I was offered the opportunity of going on an Air Gunner Instructors' course or alternatively becoming a drogue operator in a Martinet or similar target-towing aircraft. Neither of these duties appealed to me at that time. My decision was understandable to some degree. I'd forgotten Wing Commander Dixon's 'Butchers and Bakers' warning. I should have stayed on flying as long as I could.

However, having flown some 200 hours as a pilot, including twin engines, I foolishly imagined that I would have a good chance of getting one of my first two choices of ground duties, i.e. airfield controller or Flying Control assistant! The re-selection board, apparently, considered only my air gunner and bomber crew experience. The board completely overlooked my pilot flying time, including my time at Carberry as duty pilot in the Airfield Caravan, performing Flying Control duties! Some time later I was to discover, to my dismay, that other tour expired bomber crewmen, without any pilot time at all, were trained for Flying Control duties.

One item that impressed most of the aircrew attending the interviews and tests was the large notice (1 m x 3 m) boldly displayed in *every* waiting room:

YOU HAVE NOTHING TO LOSE BY CHOOSING GROUND DUTIES – YOU WILL RETAIN YOUR AIRCREW RANK AND PAY

We accepted it all without any doubt and after about a week we were posted on indefinite leave.

4 July–13 August – 6 weeks' leave.

One of the high points for me in this especially long leave, the longest leave of my RAF service (except demob leave), was to arrange for Mac to spend a 48-hour leave from his new station at RAF Finningley, staying at my family home in Coventry.

We had a really splendid time, visiting several popular dance halls, the casino, Neale's Ballroom and the odd pub like the 'Town Wall Tavern' and 'The Coundon'. It was at Neale's that I met Marjorie Gilbert, a very attractive blonde State Registered Nurse. Mac, too, seemed to be quite impressed with Marjorie (however, on this occasion it was my good fortune). Sadly his 48 went all too fast and Mac had to return to his current RAF duty of Navigation Instructor. We kept in regular touch by letter for several years. A short time after our 48 I was to learn that Mac had been awarded the DFM for his courage and determination while flying on ops as navigator from 626 Squadron at Wickenby. I am sure all the crew were very pleased with the award. We were all so very lucky to have been able to fly with the 'Unflappable Mac' (Skipper Lane's description).

13 August – Reported to RAF Portreath No. 10 ADU for u/t DMT. Given odd jobs while awaiting posting to training.

I was only partly pleased with the posting to Portreath. I'd achieved only my third choice of ground duties. Stan, also, was to be trained as a Driver, Motor Transport. He'd been posted to RAF Valley in Anglesey. We were able to meet later, in something like four weeks' time, at the RAF Technical Training School situated at Weeton, near Preston.

I was the only former Wickenby airman at Portreath! Most of my colleagues were Pathfinder crewmen, all air gunners, mostly warrant officers with the DFM. They told me that their operational theatre had been the Middle East, flying Halifaxes from Italian bases. One of the Pathfinder types was Warrant Officer Ely DFM who had completed no fewer than eighty sorties, including the European theatre.

Also, another warrant officer was a Pathfinder bomber crewman who was an air gunner with the DFM and was of similar build and age to myself. In later conversation we both realised, upon exchanging service details, that we had joined the RAF at Birmingham and Lord's cricket ground on the same days. This was probably the young lad who had been accepted as an air gunner and looked upon my RAFVR lapel badge with envy, as this was only issued to prospective pilots and observers at that time.

Yet another air gunner I got on well with, was Flight Sergeant Watts, ex-9 Squadron at Bardney (not far from Wickenby, but part of No. 5 Bomber Group). He'd previously completed an Air Gunner Instructors' Course, then been made redundant and ended up with us at Portreath, also to await an MT Course. Previous to that he'd taken part in the latest attacks on the *Tirpitz* moored in Tromsø Fjord, Norway. Flight Sergeant Watts jokingly told us that it was their 'Tallboy bomb that had gone down the funnel of the German battleship'! (This was a newspaper headline at that time.)

Our time at Portreath was spent doing all sorts of odd jobs from being an MT Driver's mate to giving local farmers a helping hand with sheaving the corn. Occasionally, when off duty we visited the pubs and dance halls of Portreath, Truro and Redruth. The girls were very nice but I wasn't too thrilled with beer 'straight from the wood' (barrel).

I became friendly with one of the WAAFs, an LACW from the same station. She was a very pleasant and attractive distraction from the dull station life we led at RAF Portreath. Unfortunately, she got posted just before our aircrew mob got posted to Weeton. We wrote a few letters to each other but eventually we lost touch.

At Weeton I met both Stan and Bert. I didn't see a great deal of Bert who was being trained as a parachute packer. Bert was even less pleased with his new 'Trade' choice than I of my MT choice. He was eventually posted to RAF Aqir in Palestine. Stan and I were on the same MT course and therefore saw a great deal of each other. We passed our spare time together at the 'Captain's Table', 'The Galleon' or the 'Tower Ballroom' – all in Blackpool of course!

After passing out at the end of the course, we were all posted on Embarkation Leave and then to the RAF PDC at North Weald. We were at the PDC for about three or four weeks. The Commanding Officer was Douglas Bader; his Spitfire was parked outside the main hangars for all to see. The Spit was coded DRB, much to everyone's instant approval.

15 August – VJ Day
THE WAR IS OVER. JAPAN ACCEPTS POTSDAM TERMS.

2 September 1945 – UNCONDITIONAL SURRENDER OF JAPANESE EMPIRE.

THE WORLD IS AT PEACE, VICTORY IS OURS!

While we were on the MT course at Weeton we found that the course comprised all sorts of aircrew types from Coastal, Bomber and Fighter Commands. Among the Coastal types were several flight sergeants who had flown Sunderland four-engined flying boats. These guys had operated from bases in West Africa, mainly Freetown,

Bathurst, Waterloo, Takoradi and Accra. They were often relating tales about sharks, scorpions and the black mamba snake. Therefore, no one was more surprised than I was when most of our intake at North Weald, excluding the ex-West African types, was posted to various RAF Staging Posts in British West Africa. We left Liverpool early in December on board the *Highland Princess* bound for Freetown, Sierra Leone, British West Africa.

On board, we met a former training colleague of Stan's, Sergeant Howard, a flight engineer who had baled out of a Halifax, south of Berlin. Apparently, Sergeant Howard was eventually taken into custody by Russian forces and was treated very roughly until they were convinced he wasn't *Luftwaffe*! The Russians weren't very pleased at first, tearing up the RAF Introduction Card, which had a Union Flag on one side and 'I am English' in Russian on the other. They were also misguided by the RAF blue battledress and light blue eagle (RAF Albatross) shoulder badges. (These items indicated to the Russian soldiers that their 'prisoner' was *Luftwaffe*.)

Sergeant Howard, Stan and I became firm companions on board the troopship. Unfortunately, we lost the company of Sergeant Howard first, as he disembarked with others at Freetown, finally being sent to Port Ettiene on the edge of French Sahara. I came second, leaving the ship at Takoradi, travelling by train 150 miles inland and north to Kumasi and then back diagonally south to the coast and to Accra. Stan went on to Lagos, disembarking there and eventually being posted to Kano in Nigeria. Stan and I kept in touch the whole time we were in West Africa, by post.

The RAF Staging Post at Accra was one of the most pleasant in West Africa! We had a very easy working day, starting at 8 am and finishing at 4 pm. Also, we had four half days off per week. Free transport was laid on for all ranks, either to visit Accra itself or to the nearby superb sandy beaches.

Needless to say, most of our free time in Accra was spent sunbathing, swimming or surf board riding. The South Atlantic Ocean provided some terrific long rolling waves for surfing. We were under constant surveillance by a very efficient West African Life Guard team, equipped with observation tower, siren and lifebelts, including reeled tow line and harness.

The town also had its attractions in the form of numerous clothes and gift shops. These were owned mainly by Syrian traders. Accra, like most West African towns, also had its share of pavement traders with whom it was necessary to bargain a suitable price before a sale was realised. The YMCA was the favourite for English-type meals;

the restaurant and gift shop were run by a very efficient and friendly British manager. We rarely missed a visit to the YMCA when visiting Accra.

The RAF MT section was run by Warrant Officer Callaghan, an RAF Regular with seventeen years' service! Good old Callaghan wasn't very pleased when he received a number of aircrew Senior NCOs to replenish his depleted MT staff. It wasn't long, a matter of a day of so, before he objected to the West African Air Force personnel addressing various aircrew as 'Sergeant' or 'Flight Sergeant', especially if the West African concerned had a query about RAF Motor Transport. This resulted in Warrant Officer Callaghan ordering us to cover our rank badges while on duty in the Motor Transport Office or driving the vehicles. He was quite in order to do this, although no one else ever made this request *to my knowledge* at Accra. (There were other remustered aircrew on the base, performing various ground trades. I'm not sure now whether or not they had a similar request by their immediate service supervisor.) However, the outcome of this request was that most of the aircrew NCOs removed their rank badges altogether. A few did as I did, covering their rank only when at work in the MT Section or driving a vehicle. The arm bands issued for this purpose soon slipped down while working, so we still got addressed as 'Sergeant' or 'Flight Sergeant' by *all* personnel, including the Wing Commander (Flying)!

After about three months, at Accra, my promotion to warrant officer came through along with other NCOs as and when due, for our 'aircrew' service. It did not seem to affect Warrant Officer Callaghan very much except that he appeared much more pleasant to me when in frequent daily personal contact!

I still took off my warrant officer's 'Royal Coat of Arms' rank badge, which was now highly polished brass worn on a wrist band (in crocodile hide), while at work in the MT Section and replaced it immediately on leaving, at lunch and in the late afternoon. I'm sure it caused some amusement at the time, especially to the 'aircrew types'!

In spite of all this silly rank-covering business, it was still deemed necessary at *all* RAF Stations for aircrew NCOs to perform such duties as Orderly Sergeant or Orderly Officer, as appropriate. This was quite understandable and correct. At Accra I performed both duties, as did my aircrew colleagues at that time.

Among the local West African population, somehow I earned the very respected yet simple title of 'Piccin WO'. It was always spoken with the biggest smile! It was soon to be adopted by my RAF aircrew colleagues, who simply abbreviated it to 'Hi, Piccin'!

As MT drivers, we did all sorts of jobs like driving the daily service bus to Accra and also to the beach. Occasionally, we took various outings to visit the African Bush villages. On one of these trips into the hilly jungle, for sightseeing and photography, I took a Bedford 3-ton lorry full of RAF of all ranks to a picturesque village high in the hills. It was during their rainy season; the roads were just mud and often without drainage. In spite of the narrow roads, the running water and the steep hills, we arrived at our village destination. We then had to seek the permission of the Head Man, as a matter of politeness. I gathered they were expecting us and it didn't take long to find the 'Chief'. A splendid fellow in tribal robes greeted me in a very pleasant manner. Noticing my 'Tate & Lyle' badge (Coat of Arms – RAF nickname) now off-duty and uncovered, he said in perfect English to his tribal bystanders 'He be a very young man – but in the RAF *he be a very big man*' This comment caused some amusement and laughter among the RAF group from Accra, but by now young Broome was quite used to it all! Incidentally, a warrant officer is correctly addressed as 'Sir' by other ranks and 'Mr Broome' by officers. (As most readers will realise, a warrant officer is not saluted.)

The accommodation for NCOs at Accra was quite good. We were billeted two NCOs to a *gydda* – a smallish square hut complete with fine wire mesh windows and attendant storm shutters. Inside, there were two beds with mosquito netting, a table, two chairs and a wardrobe. If one was lucky, there was also a radio, with which we could get the BBC Forces Overseas programme. One day a request was played for 'Warrant Officer Frank Broome serving in West Africa'! The request was 'I can't get started with you'. I was quite staggered and lucky not to have been on duty. It was requested by a really lovely girl that I met at a dance in Ongar, Essex, while I was at North Weald a few days before being posted to West Africa. Her name was Enid and she wrote regularly to me. I proudly displayed her photo in a specially made West African frame in my *gydda* on a shelf next to my bed.

Originally, the Staging Posts had been prepared specially for ferrying American aircraft to the Allied Forces engaged in the North African Campaign. A series of aerodromes had been built in most of the West African colonies owned by Britain, i.e. Gambia, Gold Coast and Nigeria. This gave an air link via the Sudan to Egypt and the Libyan Desert War.

From an entertainment point of view, the facilities were quite good. We had film shows most nights of the week in a really splendid theatre, built and decorated with bamboo. We also had a weekly gramophone record session, which was also surprisingly well attended.

Several sporting activities were available too and for the more adventurous there was a weekly swimming trip. This was especially arranged for RAF personnel to visit the ultra-modern swimming pool at Achimota College just a few miles north of Accra. The MT Section was never short of volunteer drivers for these and other out of camp activities like the photographic, scenic and beach outings.

The current activity of No. 55 Staging Post was to operate an inter-service transport air service to the various other Staging Posts in West Africa. For this operation the RAF used the Douglas Dakota C47. The Wing Commander (Flying) at Accra was none other than Wing Commander Learoyd VC (a 1940 Hampden pilot who was awarded the VC for an attack on the Dortmund-Ems canal on 12/13 August, 1940). The aircrews for the Dakota twin-engined aircraft were based at Accra and therefore frequently used the Sergeants' Mess and were accommodated in *gydda*s on the nearby site, together with ex-aircrew NCOs, like myself.

One of the Dakota pilots was Warrant Officer Dawson who was well known and well liked by all at Accra. Sadly, we lost a Dakota in a very severe storm during the rainy season. It took a couple of days' air search by the remaining Dakotas to find the one wingless and wrecked aircraft in the jungle terrain. The Dakota captain was our own Warrant Officer Dawson who with his navigator, wireless operator and passengers were killed in this terrible accident.

Our 'dhobi' boy, Paul Mensah, who looked after Warrant Officer Dawson's *gydda* as well as the one I shared, came to me the day after the Dakota was found.

'Is it true, Massa Dawson killed in aeroplane?'

I replied 'Yes Paul, sadly it is true!'

'Aaah! Massa, those stupid, stupid Germans!' said Paul standing there, shaking his head from side to side!

Paul may have got the cause of the accident wrong, but his profound grief at losing one of *his* very special Massas was unmistakable!

I shared my *gydda* with Warrant Officer Bob Evans, an ex-operational Spitfire pilot, now an MT driver. Unfortunately for me, Bob left for home on an earlier draft bound for the UK. His comradeship was surely missed.

My new *gydda* colleague was a warrant officer navigator, a real flying type, who was currently navigating one of the local Dakotas between the various West African Staging Posts. He was a great guy and tolerated very well the moans and groans of the ex-aircrew lads.

A pleasant surprise one morning at the MT Office, was the arrival of a very smart flight sergeant! A happy, smiling guy was asking for Warrant Officer Broome! It was none other than Stan Thompson, paying a quick visit to Accra, *en route* to Takoradi, his new West African base. We had a pleasant time together. Time flew and so did Stan to Takoradi.

Well before Stan's arrival at Accra, I was able to organise (connive, more likely?) two trips to 'Tak'! On the first occasion we were to drive a fully loaded Chevrolet 3-ton lorry, which broke down while we were still in the bush and jungle terrain. A Flight Lieutenant Engineer Officer very helpfully tried unsuccessfully to diagnose the cause of the engine fault. I was amazed at the Flight Lieutenant's efforts to try to solve the problem. Eventually, he and his officer colleague (both had been travelling behind the Chev truck in an RAF Hillman van as a voluntary escort) had to continue to Tak alone. They made sure that the MT Office at Accra was sending a breakdown truck, which again was extremely positive and thoughtful.

By the time the breakdown vehicle arrived, the driver had the problem sorted. It was perhaps only minutes before I was on my way. It was a long, slow, tiring journey, with the Chev bouncing and rocking along the clay-based unmade roads! Rarely did the speed get to 40 mph; even some of the 'Mammy' buses were able to pass whenever the road was wide enough. I gave a lift to a West African soldier (with a chest full of medal ribbons), trying to make his way home, after demob from the Far Eastern war zone. He was very good jovial company and was more than delighted in getting a lift home.

I arrived at Tak as dusk was falling. I'd only been in the Sergeants' Mess for a few minutes, when I was called to the Mess foyer! It was the Flight Lieutenant Engineer Officer, asking whether I'd arrived OK!

Next time I drove the Chev, all was OK – she'd been thoroughly serviced by the MT mechanics at Takoradi. There were no problems. I made the return trip alone and arrived at Accra in good time.

The other run to Tak was quite different. I took an Air Vice Marshal to the 'boat' along with his PA Sergeant. We were fortunate to have a Chevrolet Saloon and we had no problems.

The return journey was made next day in the company of Warrant Officer Knowles and two other airmen – all on posting to Accra. How splendid it would have been if Stan had been at Takoradi. Unfortunately, he was still in Kano at that time!

One of our regular weekly motoring journeys was the trip to the Army base at Achimota for films for the RAF cinema at Accra. For this venture we always took the Chev Safari. This was perhaps the most liked of all the RAF vehicles at Accra. Originally, it had been a reconnaissance vehicle and very similar to the present day Range Rover, except for its more austere upholstery and military 'square'-shaped body.

On one of the journeys to Achimota I unfortunately needed to overtake an Army vehicle. It was a Dodge 3-tonner and, unknown to me, was a left-hand drive. As we drew almost level, just before I could see the driver or he see me, the Dodge decided to turn right into a very small back gateway to the Accra General Hospital. I slammed everything on, but was unable to prevent an accident. The Chev front bumper caught the Dodge amidships with quite a loud bang! The damage to both vehicles was slight. The Chev Safari received a bent bumper on the nearside. The 3-ton Dodge showed not even a bump or paint damage. No one was more surprised nor shaken than I, except perhaps the West African Army driver! We exchanged details and the West African carried on to the hospital, my LAC Cinema Operator and I to Achimota. On our return to the MT compound at Accra, I found the Army waiting for me! That is *two* staff sergeants and *two* warrant officers (a CSM and an RSM). I was somewhat amused at the representative strength of the Army! It just goes to show what good the RAF armbands were!

It all ended very amicably, especially as I was fully backed by Warrant Officer Callaghan. The Army group 'forgot' about the accident and our MT officer straightened the 'U'-type channel bumper. Warrant Officer Callaghan used one of the many nearby heavy steel lampposts and the Chev in reverse gear.

Another amusing incident could have been the biggest bang in West Africa. Every couple of weeks we needed to get supplies of petrol for use with our various vehicles. This was collected from the Army Fuel Depot just outside Accra. For this purpose we always used drop-back open-topped trucks. I was asked to take over a Dodge 3-tonner that had already been used on one trip by a West African driver. The empty drums, twelve to fifteen per truck, held about 60 gallons each and were already loaded. I started the engine and commenced to follow the other three or four lorries. When I let out the clutch, the steering wheel juddered to some minor degree, so I stopped the Dodge, reselected the gear and tried again with the same result. I switched off the engine and reported the problem to the RAF MT Driver on duty. The airman concerned was an efficient and experienced ground staff MT driver.

When I explained the problem, he just laughed and said 'It's been on two runs this morning, so there's nothing wrong with it!' I got back into the lorry and drove to the main gate where I picked up a civilian West African worker who wanted a lift to Accra. There were always plenty of civilian workers waiting at the main gate hoping to get a lift into town.

We drove about 400 yards down the main road. The steering was still vibrating and got worse the faster we travelled. I stopped and asked the civilian, with sign language, to proceed 20–30 yards ahead and watch the nearside front – which he did, making hand signals to indicate that the nearside wheel was wobbling! Regretfully, I indicated to my helper that I'd have to return to the MT Section. I made the usual three-point turn, in spite of the monsoon ditches, and drove back to the MT area. One of my aircrew colleagues, a Flight Sergeant Gunner, observing my return, came to ask about the problem. He then drove the vehicle up and down the MT yard at full throttle on his own several times and then drove to where I was waiting and watching, shaking his head.

'Can't find anything wrong, Piccin! Seems all OK to me!'

'Rubbish, Geordie,' was my reply. 'The nearside front wheel is not secure!'

Geordie checked it, saying 'Let's take it round the drome.'

'OK,' I replied and got in with him! He was driving fairly rapidly, turning as we approached the Control Tower. The nearside front wheel left the hub shaft, rolling on by itself. The truck came to a grinding halt! We sent for the breakdown truck, and I left them to it!

Another of our duties was to man the crash tender, when required by Flying Control. We'd drive up to the edge of the main runway, the only one, when the siren sounded. It was one of the duties left to the Duty Driver.

On one occasion we were called by Flying Control to attend a grass and bush fire adjacent to the far end of the main runway. When we arrived we found an American officer burning rubbish, completely unconcerned about the bush fire. In no uncertain terms, we were told to 'Bugger off' – which we did, *after* putting the fire out! Later on, a fault was discovered on the rear drive shaft and differential gear of the Crossley tender. I got the blame, due to driving over the rough ground to reach the bush fire! There was no way that the Crossley had been subjected to any rough treatment. I'd followed a perfectly smooth but undulating path to the fire. The Corporal I/C Fire Tender also vouched for the trouble-free drive, including the lower speed and lower gear approach to the fire on the final run towards the blaze itself.

One of the more colourful ex-aircrew characters on the base was Warrant Officer Bates. He'd been a wireless operator/air gunner with Coastal Command and was now the AOC's driver. His duties were to convey the Air Vice Marshal and his Flight Lieutenant Personal Assistant to any destination, as required, in the Gold Coast Colony. Bates and I got on fairly well, therefore it wasn't too surprising to be asked if I would become the AOC's driver for the Victory Parade in Accra. Quite by chance, Warrant Officer Bates would be on leave at that time. Just why I was selected, Lord knows! As it happened, all went very well on the day, much to my amazement. I had my leg pulled about it by the other ex-aircrew types who were listening to the broadcast on the local 'Radio Accra'. I noticed beforehand that none of these guys volunteered for the job!

Warrant Officer Bates suggested I take over his job when he was posted home after his fifteen-month tour. (Fifteen months in the Gold Coast was the permitted normal tour. The colony was known as the 'White Man's Grave' and therefore officially counted as a 'Double Time' overseas station.)

Gradually, the ex-aircrew MT group was being depleted by home postings. These postings were due to individual demob dates. Eventually, much to my surprise one sunny August day, I was informed by the Orderly Room that I was to be on the next draft for return to the UK.

Although I was pleased to be going home, there were quite a few sad moments. Paul Mensah was visibly upset at the news.

'You go home to England, Massa? You come back someday?'

Paul insisted on carrying all my personal and service gear on his head to the waiting truck, on the day. I gave him my old watch and also my old Brownie box camera, which he'd asked for, on seeing the new ones I'd bought in Accra! Also, I gave him a £1.00 note since his pay from the RAF was only 10/- (50p) per week.

Normally, throughout their West African service most of the NCOs on the base gave their 'dhobi' boys a 2/- (10p) weekly 'dash', plus their own free fifty-cigarette ration and other gift items like soap and talcum powder, which could only be purchased at the Sergeants' Mess.

Our kit plus loads of presents for relatives and girlfriends was soon loaded onto a Bedford truck, while we climbed aboard another.

I was fortunate to be able to accompany the Corporal driver in the cab. The rest of the airmen had to make do with the benches under the canvas upper body of the truck. I cannot remember anything about the journey at all. I do remember arriving at Takoradi in the late afternoon. It wasn't long before I met Stan Thompson again, and, much to my complete amazement, Stan told me he was going home too, on the same draft! Stan had already made sure that I got the next bed to him in the 'transit' billet. He seemed to have an idea that I would be going home at the same time. We spent most of the next few days making the most of the African sun, sunbathing and swimming pretty well every day.

We left Takoradi in the first week of August 1946 on board HMT *Cheshire*. We were given a splendid musical send off by the band of the Gold Coast Regiment. The bandsmen were all Africans, looking superb in their brightly coloured uniforms, each man's head topped by a red fez. It was a moment of sadness and of pleasure! We were going home at last but sadly, for most of us, it was the last we'd see of the Gold Coast Colony and its very fine African tribes people.

On board the troopship, life was still military, to some degree! Sadly Stan and I were separated. Stan was now a flight sergeant and was berthed on the Mess deck with other sergeants and flight sergeants. I was one of three RAF warrant officers (the other two were senior to me) who were berthed in top-class cabins along with similar Army ranks (i.e. RSM, and CSM, equal to 1st and 2nd class warrant officers respectively). Also, the warrant officers had their own separate Mess.

I kept company with Stan most of the time. I had no duties on board the *Cheshire* until we disembarked. I remember apologising to Stan for the separation of cabins and for meals. I thought he took it all very well!

On the Warrant Officers' Mess deck, two things were rather amusing, or at least I thought so! One was the way I was obviously ignored by the Army CSMs and RSMs. There was a most obvious silence when I entered the Mess. It was very rare any of the Army warrant officers spoke to me. I had a small amount of conversation with the two RAF warrant officers – both were ground staff technicians! They were nearly twice my age, as were the Army warrant officers and their equivalent ranks of CSM and RSM. It didn't bother me greatly; I found it more amusing than disturbing.

Just before we arrived at Liverpool, perhaps two or three days' before, the occupants of our Mess began to change from tropical gear into normal Army or RAF uniform, i.e. Khaki or Blue. When I arrived for breakfast the first time in my RAF Blue, every warrant officer turned and looked. There were big smiles from them all, about twenty of them. They even said 'Good morning'! I've never seen such a change in anyone, before or since! Possibly something I wore brought the complete change of attitude. I just couldn't believe it! The visible approval remained until we disembarked two days later.

On arrival at Liverpool, I was given the job of taking the RAF contingent, some 300 airmen, by train to the RAF PDC at Burtonwood. I didn't fancy this unexpected duty at all! I offered the job to the other two RAF warrant officers, out of respect for their seniority in the rank. Also, because as an ex-operational aircrew warrant officer, I had no experience of this sort of responsibility. As it happened, all went very well. The airmen of all ranks backed me up marvellously, in spite of the reluctance of the other warrant officers to take command. It was simply 'You've got the job lad, we don't want it, you do it!' – which I did!

Once at Burtonwood, I lost the company of Stan. I knew he was to be demobbed very soon and within three or four days we were all on disembarkation leave.

The two weeks' leave went very well. It was good to be home and to be with the family again. I found time to visit all my friends and even spent a few days on a farm near Ongar, Essex.

The latter visit was intended to renew and perhaps continue my friendship with Enid, who was now in the Land Army. It was all in vain, as she now had another boyfriend. It was truly disappointing at the time. The rest of the leave went quickly. On completion, I received a telegram posting me to No. 1 OADU (Overseas Air Despatch Unit) at RAF Pershore in Worcestershire. On arrival, it wasn't long before someone in the Sergeants' Mess pointed out a very recent AMO (Air Ministry Order) regarding aircrew NCOs employed on ground duties. It drew attention to the fact that as from August 1946, all flight sergeants and warrant officers so employed, were to be reduced in rank to sergeant, effective immediately! It was a very unexpected move by the Air Ministry – especially after issuing a *guarantee* to keep our rank and pay at RAF Catterick, in June 1945. (This guarantee was issued to encourage ex-operational aircrew to apply for ground duties voluntarily.)

The very next day I went to see the SWO (Station Warrant Officer) in his office. I asked for a set of sergeant's stripes and an ordinary airman's field service cap complete with badge. The latter was to replace the regulation warrant officer's cap and badge already in my possession. (A warrant officer's cap is noticeably different but very similar to a commissioned officer's field service cap and badge.) The SWO was quite embarrassed by my request and refused at first to comply. He paid compliment to my bomber aircrew service and to my recent spell in West Africa. Eventually, after my repeated reference to the recently dated AMO, he reluctantly agreed to sign an RAF stores requisition for one cap and one set of sergeant's stripes. He pointedly refused to alter my RAF identity card, which stated my rank as warrant officer.

I believe there was only one other ex-operational aircrew warrant officer on the station. He wore stripes on his battledress only and insisted on keeping his 'Tate & Lyle' badge on his best blue tunic.

The other aircrew on ground duties at Pershore were mostly air signallers. These guys had not long completed their aircrew training and therefore retained their passing out rank of sergeant!

Most of my time at Pershore was spent as driver for the crash tender, which was crewed by a full-time RAF Crash Team. They were a very pleasant and efficient team with a coloured Flight Sergeant in command. We did 24-hour shifts, all the team bedding down in the same hut. The Flight Sergeant was a very friendly type. He was good at his job and kept order and efficiency in a very practical manner.

If we did our shifts consecutively, without standing down for 24 hours, we could take an unofficial 48- or 72-hour pass per week and so go home if we wished. This suited me fine, especially as I could arrange for my 48 or 72 to hopefully coincide with an MT journey, with another driver, going through or near Coventry. Generally it worked very well, at least three times! On other occasions, I was the driver taking a Thorneycroft 3-tonner, a very large vehicle complete with load, to the RAF MU (Maintenance Unit) at Bramcote, just north of Coventry. This gave me a couple of hours at home. Sometimes I was lucky enough to arrive home in time for lunch! One day I was early enough to take my brother Gerald, then thirteen years old, back to school in the Thorneycroft! He seemed delighted at the treat.

An interesting ride one day was the journey to a POW camp, about 30 miles from Pershore. I was ordered to take a troublesome German POW back to the camp. There was an escort of three other German POW. The vehicle was a Hillman light van, with canvas top. Three POW were in the van body and one was with me in the driver's cab. All went well until we managed to get involved in a traffic jam at Evesham, on a Friday! In an effort to 'negotiate' the narrow roads, our nearside bumper got itself wedged inside the bumper of a parked vehicle. On seeing my plight, two or three POW leapt out of the van and speedily lifted the Hillman clear of the mishap. All then leapt smartly back into the van. The troublesome prisoner gave us no problem at all. He appeared to be giving his escort colleagues advice regarding freeing the car bumper! These POW had been taken prisoner by the British Eighth Army in North Africa. They were simply great guys.

Another interesting incident was the arrival by air of an Air Vice Marshal at Pershore. The MT officer took his pick of drivers available in the Drivers' Rest Room. There were probably six drivers hoping for a nice long journey. I was the guy selected and was asked if I knew the way to the RAF Records Office at *Innsworth*, Gloucester. I replied that I did and was told to collect the Wing Commander's car from outside his office. Then I was to take the Hillman saloon to meet the Air Vice Marshal on the apron outside the Control Tower. I wondered how I managed to get all these 'posh' jobs! 'Jammie Bugger Broomie,' was the usual answer from my MT colleagues

It took just a few minutes to collect the car and to inform the Wingco I was borrowing his vehicle. The Orderly Room nearby quickly found a pennant to fly from the car wing. This was to advise everyone that my passenger was of Air Rank and therefore the car and its passenger rated a salute by *all* RAF personnel. Once the Air Vice Marshal was on board I took the shortest known route to Innsworth via numerous narrow lanes. The Air Vice Marshal became a little concerned at the minor roads we were using! We arrived at RAF Innsworth in very good time. However, on entering the camp gates, some concern was shown by the Air Vice Marshal and his PA Sergeant.

'This isn't RAF Records, Sergeant,' I was told.

'This is the only RAF Innsworth I know, Sir!' I replied.

The PA Sergeant knew no better, not having visited RAF Innsworth before. Fortunately our arrival quickly attracted the attention of a passing Wing Commander who, realising our dilemma, took charge! He suggested that he could accompany us in the car and direct us to RAF Records Office at nearby *Gloucester*. We were only too pleased to accept his kind offer. It took us about ten minutes to reach our correct destination.

Once I'd delivered the Air Vice Marshal, I returned the Wing Commander to Innsworth and then took the car back to RAF Pershore, leaving the vehicle outside our own Wingco's office.

On return to the MT Section, I mentioned to the WAAF Corporal in charge the problem regarding our incorrect routeing to Innsworth instead of Gloucester. It appeared that not many people at that time realised there was any difference between the two RAF stations.

There wasn't a great deal of flying done at Pershore. There was only an occasional visiting aircraft on odd days. Our time on the crash tender was never very busily spent.

My demob was due in November 1946. A few days before my release from the RAF, I began to collect the various signatures needed for completing my clearance chit. One of the more vital occurrences was the interview with the Station Commander, the Group Captain.

I queued up with a batch of lower rank airmen, all due for demob. Most of these guys seemed to regard the Groupie as some sort of ogre! At least that was my impression from the fidgety nervous comments they were making! Fortunately, 'Warrant Officer Broome', still wearing sergeant's stripes, was the first to be called into the Group Captain's office. The Groupie surprisingly commented on my smart appearance, as I saluted. He asked me whether I'd consider 'signing on' (i.e. for the Regular Air Force). I replied 'No Sir' and when he asked why, I mentioned the AMO reducing the rank of aircrew NCOs now on ground duties, especially after completing voluntary service with Bomber Command. His reply was that this sort of thing occurred at times when the RAF was losing many airmen through demob. I thought the reply fair comment, but *our* reduction in rank was because we were now on ground duties and had nothing to do with rank reductions due to a smaller RAF! A few weeks after demob, I received a letter and a pamphlet from the RAF offering me my existing rank of warrant officer, if I was willing to return to Flying Duties for a period of four years! The offer included a bounty of £400 (a considerable amount at that time), payable at the end of the four years.

The Groupie signed my release book and acknowledged that I would leave next day for RAF Uxbridge, the main RAF demob centre. I noted later with intense regret, that after over three years' wartime aircrew service, the only comment in the release book about my job in the RAF was 'a keen and willing worker and a conscientious and careful driver'.

I left RAF Pershore next day, together with around six other airmen. We stayed overnight at the YMCA in London, taking the train to Uxbridge next morning.

The demobilisation procedure was in some ways very similar to that used when joining the RAF at Lord's in 1942, except in reverse. We gave up all our kit other than that which we wore at that time. We were expected to keep our best blue uniform in good order – just in case we were needed in the near future (presumably, to stop Joe Stalin).

The morning went quickly. The most amusing incident of the day repeated itself in every one of many queues. The first name to be called out was that of a certain warrant officer and in each case an aircrew sergeant was allowed to vacate his mid-queue position and assume that of the first person at its head

One of the last departments at Uxbridge I visited was that of the Royal Auxiliary Air Force. I took home several informative leaflets. Unfortunately, I was to discover that the Royal Auxiliary Air Force had no bomber squadron!

Like many ex-servicemen of those days, I arrived home in the mid-afternoon carrying the very conspicuous, large cardboard box containing my demob issue civilian clothes. My family was very pleased, of course. I had some seven weeks' paid leave. I managed to spend about a fortnight visiting various old friends. Most of these were ex-service or families that I'd met during wartime service. Father had already arranged that I would be needed to assist him and Mother in the family business. On completion of various visits I started work almost immediately.

During the summer of 1947 I applied to join the RAFVR. The nearest airfield was at Desford, Leicestershire. I applied to join for pilot training. This would be carried out at weekends throughout the year plus a fortnight full time during the summer. We would receive full pay during our time at the VR Centre. Our service with the VR was similar to that of the Territorial Army.

My application was not accepted. I received a letter to this effect. Unfortunately, the RAFVR at Desford didn't advise of an alternative RAFVR service that I could apply for. It was that of air gunner, possibly on Lancaster or Lincoln bomber squadrons. It wasn't until the VR had been disbanded that I accidentally discovered at a 626 Squadron reunion, in the early 1950s, that I could have applied with my aircrew rank and trade as air gunner. I was again, very disappointed!

My work in my parents' business didn't last very long. After fifteen months I left for another sales job with a national company. Three years later, quite by chance, when applying for an advertised factory vacancy, I was offered a training course as a draughtsman at GEC Telephone works in Coventry. The pay was poor, but I was well trained in draughting and design. Five years later I joined the design staff of Armstrong Whitworth Aircraft at their Whitley factory. This lasted twelve years, until redundancy in 1968, followed by fifteen years as a designer at Rolls-Royce, Ansty, until early retirement in 1983.

It was pleasurable to note, while I was at Ansty, that most of the buildings built for the RAF pilot training scheme in the late 1930s, just prior to World War II, were still in use by Rolls-Royce.

In 1989, it was necessary to return to work as a contract draughtsman. This work was a financial lifesaver after the failure of my second marriage. The contracting was a pleasant experience both for necessity and comradeship. It continued with numerous firms, mostly good ones too, until redundancy, again, in August 1996. This unwelcome opportunity gave me time to write further and so complete this story which I started in 1982.

It has been both good and sad to recall so many memories of World War II. Hopefully it has given pleasurable reading about a period of my young life that I wouldn't have missed for anything! It was indeed a priceless experience.

Epilogue to Part II

I was able to keep in touch with most of the Lane crew from time to time.

Dick Lane (Dickie or Skipper) returned to his former employment with the civil service and joined the Home Office at an equivalent rank to that of squadron leader. He retired some years ago as an Executive Officer.

Duncan McLean (Mac) returned to his previous job of gas technician and engineer. He was a keen rugger player and played for Bomber Command and later was capped for Scotland. He married a widowed lady with two children. They lived at Stockport, Cheshire. Mac died of a heart attack at thirty-eight years of age in March 1962. It was a very sad loss to all who knew him.

Fred Till became an Airfield Controller at RAF Blakehill Farm a short time after leaving Wickenby. He returned after demob to his previous occupations of master plumber and musician. In the latter occupation he played at various holiday resorts in the UK. His home was in Bognor Regis. He and his wife Ruth had four children. Fred died at seventy-one years of age, in November 1983.

Stan Thompson took up his former employment as sewing machine mechanic at Singer's, in the Leeds area. He was married with one daughter and after being made redundant moved into his own off-licence business in Airedale, Castleford, Yorkshire. His last letter was dated 1972.

Bert Bray returned to Hereford, his hometown. We wrote to each other until 1948. In his last letter he told me he was working at Bulmers, the cider firm.

Peter Bone stayed on in the RAF for a further four years after his demob date. Most of his work at that time was spent as a Recruiting Officer. Later, he completed a short period on flying duties with a Lincoln squadron. One of his final duties was that of Public Relations Officer for the Berlin airlift in 1948/9. He left the RAF in 1951 with the rank of flight lieutenant. Peter Bone's peacetime career was spent as a probation officer at Bristol and later in Vancouver, Canada. He is now retired and lives in Vancouver.

Quite recently, Peter was responsible for proofreading the original manuscript. It was completed in an exemplary manner.

Cliff Wheeler continued his service with 150 Squadron as a warrant officer navigator on Lincoln heavy bombers until his demob in 1946. He became a schoolteacher and lived with his wife Ann in Romsey, Hants, until his untimely death in 1974 at fifty-eight years of age.

Johnny Walker (ex-6 ITW and Harrogate and later 626 Squadron) retrained as a flight engineer to join the Squadron at Wickenby. His crew saw operational service towards the end of World War II. He continued service in the RAF after the war and flew Mosquito night fighters as a warrant officer pilot. He wrote in answer to my letters in the 1980s. (I obtained his address via the Wickenby Register.) He died in 1990 after a very serious illness.

Sid Oldfield (ex-USNAS Grosse Ile), a very good friend, wrote to me until his wedding in 1944 at Lincoln. I was invited to the wedding but was unable to get leave. Our crew was then at Hemswell. Unfortunately, I lost contact afterwards.

Bill Tranter (ex-6 ITW and USNAS Grosse Ile) kept in touch until after his demob from the RAF. He lived in Portsmouth at that time. Bill and I were very good friends at Grosse Ile. It was he who sent me the US Navy pilot wings from Pensacola. I wore these under my left pocket flap as a talisman when on ops in our Lancaster from Wickenby.

Bill Hall (ex-Assiniboine, Caron, and Sterling Metals) was someone I regrettably lost touch with after the end of World War II. I understood from former Sterling Metal colleagues that Bill married Camile and returned to Canada after his demobilisation.

Bill Bayliss, my long-term school friend, obtained his pilot's wings in Canada in 1945. He was then posted to an OTU in Canada to fly Mosquitoes. He survived an horrendous accident while flying a Mossie. Later he was posted home to the UK for training as a flying instructor. The course was cancelled shortly after the end of World War II. After demob Bill became a deputy headmaster at a local school until his retirement in the early 1980s. Bill has kept in regular contact in spite of a serious immobility illness.

Den Butler (ex-626 Squadron) was Flying Officer Enciso-y-Seiglie's flight engineer and a Coventry resident in 1945. We spent some happy times together, especially when on leave at the same time. The 'Rialto Casino' was our favourite for dancing. We often met in the 'Town Wall Tavern' in Bond Street before going to the dance at the 'Casino'. Den spent his ex-aircrew time in India as a motor mechanic. He is now a retired engineer and he and his wife Barbara live in Halifax. We still keep in touch and share the odd story about the Wickenby days.

My life is now spent with Edna Cartwright O'Donnell after a separation of 63 years. I still grow my Xants but we travel quite a lot between the UK and Australia, together again at last.